THE S. MARK TAPER FOUNDATION

IMPRINT IN JEWISH STUDIES

BY THIS ENDOWMENT

THE S. MARK TAPER FOUNDATION SUPPORTS

THE APPRECIATION AND UNDERSTANDING

OF THE RICHNESS AND DIVERSITY OF

JEWISH LIFE AND CULTURE

IMAGES OF INTOLERANCE

The publisher gratefully acknowledges the generous contribution to this book provided by the following organizations:

THE S. MARK TAPER FOUNDATION

and

THE LUCIUS N. LITTAUER FOUNDATION

IMAGES OF INTOLERANCE

The Representation of Jews and Judaism in the *Bible moralisée*

Sara Lipton

UNIVERSITY OF CALIFORNIA PRESS BERKELEY LOS ANGELES LONDON

University of California Press
Berkeley and Los Angeles, California

University of California Press, Ltd.
London, England

All photographs are courtesy Österreichische Nationalbibliothek, Wien.

Portions of chapter 2 appeared in *Medieval Encounters* 1 (1995) as "The Root of All Evil: Jews, Money, and Metaphor in the *Bible moralisée*"; portions of chapter 4 were published in *Word and Image* 8 (1992) as "Jews, Heretics, and the Sign of the Cat in the *Bible moralisée.*" I thank E. J. Brill and Taylor and Francis Ltd., respectively, for permission to reprint from these works.

Library of Congress Cataloging-in-Publication Data

Lipton, Sara
Images of intolerance : the representation of Jews and Judaism in the Bible moralisée / Sara Lipton.
p. cm.—(The S. Mark Taper Foundation imprint in Jewish studies)
Includes bibliographical references and index.
ISBN 0-520-21551-6 (alk. paper)
1. Judaism—Controversial literature—History and criticism. 2. Antisemitism in art. 3. Jews in art. 4. Bible moralisée. 5. Bible—Picture Bibles. I. Title. II. Series.
BM585.L48 1999
305.892'404'0902—dc21 99-11009
CIP

Printed in the United States of America
9 8 7 6 5 4 3 2 1

The paper used in this publication meets the minimum requirements of American National Standards for Information Sciences—Permanence of Paper for Printed Library Materials, ANSI Z39.48-1984.

FOR BARBARA AND MILTON

Most tolerant of people, most supportive of parents

TOLERO

to bear, sustain; to support, nourish

CONTENTS

ILLUSTRATIONS

Diagram

Figures

ACKNOWLEDGMENTS

Like many medievalists, I was first drawn to the Middle Ages because of a childhood fascination with all things ancient and exotic. That this enthusiasm has survived sustained exposure to the intolerance, irrationality, and sheer illegibility of actual medieval sources is due in a large part to the stimulating conversation and warm fellowship of numerous teachers, friends, and colleagues. For this, and to all of them, I am very grateful.

Walter Cahn, who first introduced me to the *Bible moralisée* more than ten years ago, has generously shared his knowledge and wisdom with me many times in the years since. Robert Chazan, Jack Moore, Gordon Newby, and Harvey Stahl have provided invaluable and much-appreciated advice and encouragement. Anyone working on early thirteenth-century Paris must feel privileged to benefit from John Baldwin's learning; his graciousness has made our conversations a pleasure as well. I can hardly keep track of the debt I owe Robert Stacey, who seems to have guided this project every step of the way, and whose stunning erudition is matched by unfailing common sense and quite boundless generosity. David Nirenberg, Kathryn Miller, Bruce O'Brien, Gregory Hutcheson, Mary Shepard, Sigrid Goldiner, David Cohen, and Carol Sheriff have provided constant instruction in combining intellectual rigor with humor and humanity.

In a technically daunting (and very expensive) field, institutional and financial support are indispensable. I am grateful for the help and hospitality offered by the staff of the Bibliothèque Nationale and the Österreichische Nationalbibliothek, and for research funds provided by the Lady Davis Fellowship Trust, the National Endowment for the Humanities, the Dorot Foundation/Skirball Department of Hebrew and Judaic Studies at New York University, and the College of William and Mary.

It is only when one has worked on a book for several years that one can fully appreciate the justness of the paeans to family support traditionally included in authors' acknowledgments. My daughter, Julia, has not only tolerated her mother's peculiar interests but entered into them with warmth and eagerness. She imparts joy to everything she touches, and I am very thankful she has touched this book. All partners find their own means of providing help and encouragement: my husband, Dan Monk, questions, provokes, and reads Adorno aloud to me at breakfast, and I wouldn't have it any other way. My parents, Barbara and Milton, gave me my first history book when I was ten years old and, having created my most enduring interest, never ceased fostering and sharing in it. They remain my most enthusiastic readers and advocates, as well as unflagging exemplars of engagement, curiosity, and commitment.

Finally, I must somehow try to articulate all I received over the years from my teacher and adviser, John Boswell. Those who attended his classes at Yale know how exciting and stimulating he managed to make even the most arcane aspects of medieval studies (even Perugian wax). Those whom he advised know, too, how sage and sensible his advice could be. But when I recall our conversations, and as I continue them in my own mind—alas, now one-sided—it is his sheer delight in people, ideas, art, and music that comes through most clearly. This study of words and images owes much of its shape to his influence; I hope that it would have pleased him.

INTRODUCTION

Sometime between the years 1220 and 1229, a book was made for the king of France.[1] As seems fitting for a work presented to a monarch known as "the most Christian king,"[2] the book is a Bible (or, rather, a luxuriously illustrated Bible paraphrase); as was deemed appropriate for a Bible owned by a layperson, it is accompanied by its own explication—an illustrated moralizing commentary. At about the same time another, very similar, manuscript was made for an unknown member of the royal court. The commentary illustrations in these *Bibles moralisées* (as the manuscript type has been known since the fifteenth century) are remarkable in a number of ways: they are almost unique among medieval images in depicting contemporary figures and situations, they are exceptional in their iconographic density and sophistication, and they constitute an unprecedented visual polemic against the Jews. This last theme—the attack on Jews and Judaism in the two earliest surviving *Bibles moralisées*—is the subject of this book.[3]

The Problem: Why So Many Jews?

My study is driven by two basic questions. Jews and Judaism are a central—I would even suggest in some ways the fundamental—theme of the artistic program of these manuscripts. Why should this be? After all, the *Bibles moralisées* were made by and for Christians living in an overwhelmingly Christian kingdom; Jews were neither numerically significant nor politically predominant in this society, and Jews had not figured particularly prominently in Christian art up to this point.[4] Given the importance of the thirteenth-century *Bibles moralisées,* which are acknowledged landmarks in Gothic illumination (the two earliest exemplars have been called "the first truly spectacular creations" of the largest and most productive atelier in early thirteenth-century Paris),[5] coming to terms with the sources, motivations, and effects of one of their most distinctive iconographic themes is of considerable interest in and of itself.

Moreover, the years during which these manuscripts were produced were pivotal in several respects. First, they were close to or embraced some critical moments in the history of Jews in medieval Europe, particularly in France. To cite just a few events: in 1182 King Philip II Augustus of France barred Jews from residing in his domain, in the first known expulsion of Jews from any large territory in medieval Europe (he then reversed this decision in 1198); at the end of the twelfth century, a new legal theory regarding Jewish status began to be articulated in French royal texts; in 1198 the papacy for the first time began to concern itself with Jewish usury; in 1215 Jews living in Christendom were for the first time ordered to wear distinctive clothing; and in 1223 the French crown withdrew its long-standing protection of Jewish moneylending.[6] What light can the *Bibles moralisées*—royal manuscripts permeated with innovative and unprecedented anti-Jewish imagery—shed on the permutations in Jewish life and status during these years?

The virulent anti-Jewish imagery of the *Bibles moralisées* also coincided with (perhaps even initiated) a turning point in medieval iconography.[7] Although representations of Jews did not appear as significant focuses of medieval Christian works of art for the entire first half of the Middle Ages,[8] anti-Jewish motifs began to emerge in the late twelfth century and spread rapidly in the thirteenth, as a variety of new art forms in which Jews played a central role (such as moralized bestiaries, glossed Apocalypses, and elaborate Passion narratives) were developed.[9] Much of the visual vocabulary created to represent Jews seems to appear for the first time in the earliest surviving exemplars of the *Bible moralisée.*[10]

The creation of these earliest *Bible moralisée* manuscripts similarly falls within an important but still obscure period in the development of biblical scholarship.[11] The main project of the newly formed University of Paris—at least as the theology professors understood it—was to teach and comment upon *sacre pagine* (Holy Scripture).[12] Biblical commentary was the subject and form of all lectures given in the theology faculty and the primary occupation of the theology masters.[13] This activity bore fruit toward the end of the twelfth century, when Peter the Chanter (d. 1197) and Stephen Langton (d. 1228) became renowned as the first masters of theology to lecture on all the books of the Bible.[14] And yet, no full biblical commentaries have survived from the years between Langton's departure from Paris (1206) and the establishment of the Dominican *studium* of St.-Jacques (ca. 1236). As an extensive example of university-inspired biblical exegesis from just this period, the *Bible moralisée* can provide important evidence concerning a still unwritten chapter in the history of medieval biblical interpretation.

Finally, the first decades of the thirteenth century were without question the formative years of the Capetian monarchy.[15] Among the various successful strategies employed by Philip Augustus and his heirs was the creation of a mythology of Capetian kingship that was articulated and disseminated through art and literature as well as sermons and exegesis.[16] Of course, many factors—military, economic, political, administrative—contributed to the Capetians' consolidation of power, and obviously they cannot all be illuminated by reference to the *Bible moralisée,* much less to its depiction of Jews. It has, however, been forcefully and to my mind convincingly argued that royal Jewish policy was one of the primary mechanisms by which the Capetians effected pivotal administrative innovations.[17] Jews and Judaism occupied, or rather constituted, a highly contested space between clerical and secular authorities: church councils and papal letters from the latter years of Philip Augustus's reign are filled with exhortations to princes concerning the Jews.[18] Against such a background, the relevance of an illustrated Bible commentary owned by the king, redacted by theologians, concerned with social issues, and focusing in particular on the Jews seems clear.

Any attempt to mine visual hermeneutics for historical insight entails a tricky and potentially problematic leap from polemic to policy. I must emphasize from the outset that in pointing out correspondences between the commentary of the *Bible moralisée* and contemporary events I will *not* at any point be arguing for direct or even indirect causation. The actions of humans and governments are rarely, if ever, dictated by pure ideology, much less by exegetically filtered theology; they arise, rather, out of a complex web of social, economic, political, intellectual, cultural, and personal considerations. However, the innovative nature of the *Bibles moralisées* makes them uniquely valuable sources: as systematic and comprehensive juxtapositions of authoritative texts and original images, they express seemingly familiar ideas in, or rather translate these ideas into, a new language, a visual language of sign. We have increasingly come to recognize that language structures meaning as surely as thought determines language; like all translations, the visual commentary of the *Bible moralisée* offers readings that are not necessarily constrained by those of its prototype. Jean Chatillon has remarked that one cannot fully understand a work of medieval biblical interpretation without knowing what the author—and I would add the reader—was seeing in his mind; that is, without referring to contemporary works of art.[19] Whereas the *Bible moralisée* by no means furnishes a comprehensive or "realistic" rendering of this mental imagery, it does provide a kind of window, albeit an obscure and often distorting one, into at least a small part of the mental landscape of the people and culture that created and consulted it. In providing an unusually vivid and detailed glimpse into the "mental economies" of the royal French court, the *Bible moralisée* can help reveal some of the unarticulated but influential factors underlying French Jewish policy.

Methodology: Reading Text and Image in the Bible moralisée

One of the most dangerous and misleading tendencies of any study of Jewish-Christian relations is to examine Jews and anti-Jewish polemic in isolation from their surroundings; I have endeavored throughout this book to avoid that pitfall. In any case, the *Bibles moralisées* rarely show Jews on their own: they are almost inevitably depicted in conjunction with non-Jewish figures, who themselves usually represent a diverse company. For this reason, the following pages deal with broad themes that are by no means exclusively Jewish. Rather than focusing on the narrower polemical questions typically at issue between Jews and Christians (the election of the Gentiles, messianism, Christology) or on the traditional loci of anti-Jewish imagery (such as Passion iconography), I examine the relationship posited or constructed between Jews and large social and theological issues (economic activity, biblical study, philosophical speculation, punishment, and salvation) by means of recurrent and persistent visual topoi (moneybags, scrolls, cats, idols, and flames). The representation of Jews in the *Bibles moralisées,* then, can illuminate not only theological anti-Jewish polemic or Capetian Jewish policy but also some of the values and concerns permeating thirteenth-century French Christian culture proper—or at least the segment of Christian society involved in the production of these manuscripts.

Consequently, the framework for my analysis is always the immediate and the larger contexts. As I examine each text or image, I consider not only what the figures in question might "mean" (bearing in mind that meaning can be multiform and unstable) but also how they function within the phrase or roundel in which they appear, how the phrase or roundel functions within the page on which it appears, how the page relates to the overall exegetical sequence, and in what ways the commentary texts and images of the *Bibles moralisées* draw on—or subvert—traditional iconographic or exegetical approaches.[20]

Similarly, religious polemic is never written in a social or political vacuum. The interdisciplinary nature of this study entails far more than simply searching for textual sources for the visual images. The relevant broader contexts for the anti-Jewish polemic in the *Bibles moralisées* include the changing medieval economy; Capetian theories and practice of power; and the attitudes of various streams of clerical thought toward money, morality, learning, and authority. For each significant anti-Jewish topos, or theme, that can be identified in the *Bibles moralisées,* I examine relevant contemporary developments in these and other areas to explore the range of nuances and readings the symbols might have invoked.

The *Bibles moralisées* are works of biblical interpretation assembled—rather haphazardly at times—for a lay audience; they are *not* scholarly *Summae.*[21] It is therefore not surprising that the manuscripts fail to articulate a coherent theology or doctrine regarding Jews and Judaism (or any other topic, for that matter); nor have I made any attempt to impose artificially such coherence on the manuscripts. In general, I have found that the anti-Jewish polemic in the *Bibles moralisées* falls, with a few fascinating exceptions, well within the boundaries defined by tradition—which, for medieval exegetical texts, means Scripture and patristic and earlier medieval commentaries. Nevertheless, Latin writings on Jews and Judaism allowed for considerable latitude within these boundaries; for example, although all orthodox Christian writers agreed that the Jews' denial of Jesus' divinity was wrong, some saw the Jews as innocently ignorant, others as reprehensibly blind, others still as intentionally and fiendishly recalcitrant. In my discussion I seek to identify the most consistent anti-Jewish themes and to map out where on the continuum of possible opinions and reactions regarding those themes the *Bibles moralisées* fall, as well as explore the contexts and considerations that structure those positions.

The Making of the Bibles moralisées

The Question of Date and Patronage Any attempt to address the issues outlined here must begin by asking questions that are basic to historical inquiry: What is the exact date of these sources, and for what purpose and/or patron were they made? In spite of the great importance of the *Bibles moralisées,* we still know relatively little about their creation. No thirteenth-century documentation regarding either *Bible moralisée* survives, and no comprehensive modern study of the manuscript form has yet been published, although most art historical discussions of early Gothic illumination touch on the *Bibles moralisées,* and many studies, including three recent dissertations, have focused on some aspect of the manuscripts.[22] As one might expect, given the complexity of the manuscripts and the lack of contemporary sources, many issues remain unresolved, including the precise dating of the thirteenth-century exemplars, the identity of their patrons, and the textual sources for the commentary. The earliest date proposed for the royal manuscript (Vienna ÖNB cod. 1179) has been ca. 1215; the latest, ca. 1250.[23] Since we do not have a full understanding of the chronology of Gothic illumination in early thirteenth-century Paris, the issue of the exact dating of the *Bible moralisée* manuscripts is unlikely to be resolved through stylistic analysis alone.[24] Hypotheses concerning patronage have hinged entirely upon the proposed dating; in general, scholars agree that the Latin manuscript was made for Philip Augustus (1180–1223), Louis VIII (1223–26), or Louis IX (1226–70), and that the French manuscript was made for a courtier or relative of one of these figures.[25]

Although scholars differ in their dating of the earliest manuscript by only a few years, I revisit the issue here because the years in question were (as I have already noted) crucial ones in the history of royal Jewish policy in France. By the early thirteenth century, the king of France had a peculiar relationship to French Jews.[26] During the course of the twelfth century, it had come to be accepted that secular lords had unique rights to tax and administer justice for the Jews in their territories, and as part of their larger project to improve their financial status, administrative efficiency, and political and religious prestige, the Capetians were particularly protective of these rights.[27] Throughout his reign, Philip Augustus exercised them with bewildering capriciousness. He staged a raid on synagogues in order to hold valuable liturgical objects for ransom in 1181; expelled all Jews from his domain in 1182; presided over a massacre of Jews accused of murder in the county of Champagne in 1192; and then readmitted Jews to his domain in 1198.[28] His subsequent Jewish policy was equally erratic: he sometimes protected Jews' livelihood and sometimes exploited Jews mercilessly, always, however, maintaining the symbiotic relationship between Jewish economic activities and the crown. A crucial change in this relationship was effected in the first year—in fact the first few months—of Louis VIII's reign: in November 1223 he issued a *Stabilimentum* that broke with his father's Jewish policy in two important respects.[29] First, it asserted a heretofore unexploited royal privilege over Jews in the territories of the king's vassals by forbidding all French barons to offer refuge to Jews fleeing from other lords (this is analogous to federal regulation of interstate commerce). Second, the *Stabilimentum* in essence ended the long partnership between the crown and the Jews by putting an end to the practice of authenticating Jewish loan contracts with government seals. Although the effects of the *Stabilimentum* are relatively clear, the reasons for Louis's actions remain obscure.[30] The connections between this revolution in Capetian economic policy and the presentation to the Capetian court of an illuminated manuscript harshly critical of moneylending are certainly worth exploring. Historians of this moment in royal Capetian policy have therefore missed a significant source in their neglect of the *Bible moralisée;* they have reason to be interested in the question of whether the newly codified anti-Judaism represented in these manuscripts coincided with the end of the reign of Philip Augustus or with the reigns of Louis VIII or Louis IX.

New Light on Patronage The patronage of the manuscript was not, of course, originally intended to be a mystery (then, as now, one point of philanthropy was publicity): an inscription in the margin next to the dedication portrait in Vienna ÖNB cod. 1179 identified the figure and perhaps explained the impetus for the commission and the identity of the redactor as well. This inscription has been purposely effaced and is largely illegible. Nevertheless, it is possible to decipher seven words from the third, fourth, and fifth lines of the inscription. They read, "Rex attavis natus regibus orbis honor, quem . . . " ("King born to royal ancestors, glory of the world, whom . . . ").[31] Scholars have not previously found these words particularly illuminating, pointing out that they might, after all, be presumed to refer equally well to any king of France.[32] This phrase, however, is not merely a generic assemblage of words in praise of a king; it is actually a learned classical quotation. The first four words are, with slight modifications, the opening line of Horace's Ode I, Liber 1, with which he dedicates his work to Maecenas, confidant of Augustus and noted patron of the arts.[33] The lines refer to Maecenas's alleged descent from the ancient Etruscan kings. Does the identification of this line from the dedicatory inscription bring us any closer to determining the patronage of the manuscript? I believe it does.

First, and most tellingly, the very same quotation from Horace was used in another dedicatory passage addressed to one of the kings proposed as patron: Louis VIII. In the epistle of ca. 1200 with which Rigord, monk of St.-Denis, rededicated his chronicle of the reign of Philip Augustus to the young Prince Louis, the biographer wrote, "Hinc est, o puer, atavis edite regibus, quia literas discitis et diligitis . . . " ("Here it is, O youth, sprung from royal ancestors, because you have studied and loved letters . . . ").[34]

It is naturally impossible to prove that the same line was never applied to Louis's father, Philip Augustus, but it would be far less apposite, if not downright inappropriate, in regard to Philip. As Rigord's dedication suggests, the primary effect of implicitly associating a figure with Maecenas (famous above all as a benefactor of the arts) is to attribute to that figure learning and literary patronage. This tribute, although obvious flattery, may have been justified in Louis's case: in marked contrast to his father, who was almost if not entirely illiterate (i.e., without Latin), Louis VIII was the first Capetian heir to have been provided with a scholarly education.[35] He was tutored in his youth by a member of the theology faculty of the University of Paris, and his mastery of learning was, as we have seen, extolled by Rigord. Several literary works are known to have been written for Louis, including the epic *Philippides* of Guillaume le Breton and the epic *Karolinus,* essentially a versified *Miroir des princes,* by Gilles de Paris.[36] Gerald of Wales apparently hoped to dedicate his *De principis instructione* to Louis.[37]

The ancestral resonances of the quotation may also be linked to specific developments at the Capetian court. By the first decades of the thirteenth century, pride in a glorious (specifically, Carolingian) lineage had become an important part of Capetian propaganda of legitimacy. This had not always been the case. Indeed, the Capetians, descendants of the usurper Hugh Capet, had long been acutely conscious of the fact that they did not belong to an ancient royal line, and they downplayed dynastic merit in favor of spiritual virtue as the basis of their claim to the throne of France.[38] Apologists for Philip Augustus generally stressed his praiseworthy acts and moral worth rather than his genealogy; according to John Baldwin, it was only at the very end of Philip's reign that members of the royal entourage began to mention the king's Carolingian blood.[39] At that point, royal propaganda does begin to highlight the Capetians' Carolingian ties, and a recension of a legend known as the "Reditus regni ad stirpem Karoli Magni" ("Return of the kingdom to the line of Charlemagne"), which claims that virtuous rulership would bring about the restoration of the French throne to the line of Charlemagne after seven generations of Capetians, comes to the fore.[40] Louis VIII was the seventh in line after Hugh Capet; he was also descended from Charlemagne both on his father's side (via Adèle of Champagne) and by virtue of the impeccable Carolingian ancestry of his mother, Isabelle of Hainault.[41] By the early years of Louis's reign, Carolingian dynasticism had assumed a major role in Capetian ideology. Gilles de Paris celebrated him as "heir by blood, this blood whose virtue will make you king, offspring of a holy race";[42] subsequent royal manuscripts compared Louis with Charlemagne,[43] and Louis's lily-strewn coronation robes were modeled on those of the great Carolingian.[44] Strikingly, an image in the Latin manuscript depicts a king wearing just such robes; the corresponding commentary text praises princes who "receive their crosses and promise to kill all Albigensians with all their offspring."[45] Philip Augustus was notoriously unresponsive to the papal call for a crusade against the Albigensians, but Prince Louis took the cross in 1213 (against his father's wishes) and led campaigns against the Albigensians in 1215, 1219, and, as king, in 1226.[46] He died on the way home from this last war. In sum, although nothing precludes the application of the phrase "natus attavis regibus" or flattery concerning illustrious ancestry, virtue, learning, patronage, or anti-Albigensian activity to Philip Augustus, they fit Louis VIII much more comfortably, both according to the historical facts as the early thirteenth-century court understood them and according to prevailing ideological discourse. These considerations, together with the fact that the phrase in the *Bible moralisée* dedicatory inscription was actually used in a dedication addressed to Louis, suggest to me that Louis VIII was the intended recipient of the manuscript now known as Vienna ÖNB cod. 1179.[47]

The Question of Sources Identification of the source of the commentary text has also proven elusive. The very name assigned to the manuscript form attests to the fact that the majority of commentary texts are moralistic.[48] Reiner Haussherr noted that this tendency is in accord with late twelfth-century exegetical developments, but he did not identify the direct source of the commentary more specifically.[49] Others have proposed as project overseer Hugh of St. Cher (director of the Dominican *studium* mentioned earlier) or Vincent of Beauvais.[50] More recently, in the wake of John Baldwin's magisterial study of the Parisian "biblical moral school," which has provided invaluable information regarding the intellectual milieu in Paris in the years directly preceding the redaction of the *Bible moralisée,* several scholars have assumed that a member of the circle of Peter the Chanter supervised the redaction.[51]

None of these suggestions is completely satisfactory. The passages in the *Bible moralisée* represented by Laborde as having been derived from Hugh of St. Cher's *Postillae* also appear in the *Glossa ordinaria,* the standard medieval compilation of biblical exegesis.[52] Moreover, as I argued previously, although I think it very likely that the later three-volume versions (replete, it will be recalled, with images of mendicants) benefited from Hugh of St. Cher's project, the earliest surviving exemplar most likely predates the establishment of the Dominican *studium* by at least ten years. The attribution of the *Bible moralisée* commentary to "a member" of the biblical moral school, although more convincing (I and others have been able to identify correspondences with the works of Peter the Chanter, Stephen Langton, Robert de Courson, Thomas of Chobham, Jacques de Vitry, and Odo of Cheriton, to name just a few),[53] also sidesteps some important considerations. The "school" was hardly univocal—among the students of Peter the Chanter there was considerable diversity of opinion about a range of subjects, including substantial matters of policy and doctrine.[54] Attributing the redaction of the *Bible moralisée* to "a follower of Peter the Chanter" tells us, in the end, little more than that the commentary was composed by a Parisian cleric interested in the moralistic implications of the biblical text—something the very name assigned to the manuscript form tells us already.

More important, none of the theories hazarded thus far about the redaction of the *Bible moralisée* takes into account the fact that the commentary text is far from homogeneous. Vienna ÖNB cod. 1179 includes commentaries on the biblical books of Genesis, Exodus, Leviticus, Numbers, Deuteronomy, Joshua, Judges, Ruth, I–IV Kings, I and II Esdras, Job, Daniel, Tobit, Judith, Esther, I and II Maccabees, and the Apocalypse of John, in that order.[55] There is great uniformity of style, concerns, and language in the treatment of the first fourteen of these biblical books (i.e., Genesis through II Esdras): the biblical excerpts are generally brief paraphrases of the Latin text, focusing on the most concrete or active narrative episodes, and the interpretation of each of these episodes is likewise relatively concise, self-contained, and specific.[56] Vienna ÖNB cod. 2554, which breaks off in the middle of IV Kings, is closely related to this part of the Latin manuscript in choice of both biblical and commentary texts.[57] These commentaries were most likely drawn from university lectures dating from about 1205 to 1220.[58] The language and style of the commentaries to Job, Daniel, Tobit, Judith, Esther, I and II Maccabees, and the Apocalypse (all of which are found only in the Latin manuscript) differ considerably from each other and from the first fourteen books. They tend to be considerably longer, more abstract, and less moralistic in nature. The commentary texts to Esther, Tobit, and Judith are closely dependent on but not identical to the *Glossa ordinaria* (the standard biblical commentary, compiled during the course of the twelfth century);[59] the Apocalypse commentary is a late twelfth-century northern French or English composition;[60] I have not yet identified the Maccabees and Daniel commentaries. The composite nature of the *Bible moralisée* text would seem to argue against its redaction by an active or prominent exegete; at the very least, any suggestion regarding the redactor of the *Bible moralisée* has to take its heterogeneity into account.

The Making of the Bible moralisée: *A Reconstruction* How, then, did these works come into being? Here is a hypothetical reconstruction of the redaction of the *Bibles moralisées.*[61] Sometime shortly before or immediately upon Louis VIII's assumption of the throne (i.e., ca. 1220–25), it occurred to Louis (or perhaps to his confessor, to his wife, Blanche de Castile, a noted patron of manuscripts,[62] or to one of his friends or advisers) that the new king, a scholar and pious Christian, would profit from having an authoritative illustrated commentary on the Bible. Such a project, although as far as we know without precedent, would have been in keeping with a venerable tradition of looking to the Old Testament for models of kingship, as well as with a more recent tendency in Parisian exegesis to apply the lessons of Scripture to contemporary society. Either a parallel vernacular version was commissioned at the same time, or the need or desire for one was felt very soon.

A cleric, or perhaps a committee of clerics, close to the French court was then appointed to coordinate the compilation of the texts and the creation of the images. The supervising figure was most likely *not* one of the great theologians teaching at Paris at that time—it is unlikely that an original thinker, whose profession it was to comment on the Bible, would have done such a patchwork job of selecting exegetical texts.[63] The director was most likely someone who had attended the university for some years between 1205 and 1220 but had not continued on to lecture on *sacre pagine* himself; he was probably employed in some capacity at the royal court or chapel.[64] He abridged university lecture notes (his own or from manuscripts at his disposal) for the earlier books of the Bible, and then for the remaining biblical books consulted a library that contained manuscripts of the *Glossa ordinaria* and other commentaries. Because it was close physically and institutionally to the royal court, and because it was renowned for its tradition of biblical study, the library of the Abbey of St.-Victor seems a likely location; the Royal Abbey of St.-Denis, where Rigord had been a monk, or the Augustinian Abbey of Ste.-Geneviève, where Louis VIII's godfather, Stephen of Tournai, had been abbot, are also possibilities.[65]

The fact that the commentary texts of the *Bible moralisée* were not original compositions of the redactor does not mean that the work lacks a distinct and original—although by no means unvarying—point of view. By the opening of the thirteenth century, a multiplicity of commentary texts was available for each Bible verse. The redactor was therefore obliged to carefully select which texts were to be included; evidently, specific texts were chosen and others discarded because of their content.

Once the text was compiled, or perhaps while the compilation was still ongoing, the director would have hired an artistic workshop to execute the illuminations; in this era, both secular and monastic workshops would have been available.[66] Robert Branner has pointed out that few secular workshops would have had the space or the resources for a project of this scope and has suggested that one of the great monastic scriptoria—such as the one at St.-Victor, which had an established illumination tradition—was more likely.[67] This accords well with my suggestions regarding the compilation of the text. The director would have had to consult with the artists on a regular basis: no visual models existed for many of the biblical images or for the vast majority of the commentary illustrations, and the clerical redactor(s) would have had to provide the artists with suggestions, guidelines, even detailed instructions. The sources of these illustrations are numerous and varied. Many commentary roundels adapt, manipulate, or reuse gestures from other artistic cycles, such as Theophilus windows.[68] In some cases, the commentary texts are more or less directly translated into images; in others, preaching aids such as animal fables, sermon exempla, or collections of *distinctiones* such as the *Summa Abel* of Peter the Chanter clearly provide the inspiration for the imagery.[69]

The close relationship between the commentary images and preaching aids helps illuminate the question of how these manuscripts were read and used. It seems highly unlikely that they were read straight through from beginning to end—the sheer size of the manuscripts (the Latin manuscript measures 29.5 by 43 centimeters and is very heavy) makes them far too unwieldy for concentrated examination, and the incomplete nature of the biblical text renders them useless for serious scriptural study.

Rather, I take as a model for their use the most common form in which a lay audience encountered exegesis: preaching. Most medieval sermons were, like the *Bible moralisée,* commentaries on the Bible, but they were not running chronological commentaries. The typical process for assembling a sermon was to identify a biblical theme and subtheme, and to construct hermeneutical chains around them.[70] The links could be ideas, images, even auditory connections.[71] Meaning is built up through not linear but associative logic, and the Bible text consequently becomes a vehicle for extended meditation on a range of seemingly remote topics. I imagine the readers of the *Bibles moralisées*—the king and members of his court—would similarly have engaged with the manuscripts in a thematic rather than a linear manner, perusing the pages and stopping at symbols, topics, or episodes that caught their eye. In this way an almost infinite number of "sermons" could have emerged from these remarkable manuscripts, each one speaking to the interests and outlook of the reader and requiring his (or her) active participation.

The active role I have envisioned for the reader in such a process goes a considerable way toward explaining the formal—as well as some substantive—differences between the two earliest *Bible moralisée* manuscripts. The *Bibles moralisées,* like sermons, present the Bible to the laity in a controlled and mediated form. In fact, the presence of the controlling and mediating segment of the manuscripts—the commentary—may be considered a prerequisite for the creation of the French-language *Bible moralisée.* It frequently has been noted that Vienna ÖNB cod. 2554 was made at a time when translating Scripture into the vernacular was a highly controversial endeavor.[72] The more insightful writers on the *Bibles moralisées* have justly pointed out that because the French paraphrase of the biblical text in Vienna ÖNB cod. 2554 is accompanied by its own commentary, the work cannot be considered a violation of papal decrees forbidding to the laity unmediated access to vernacular texts of the Bible.[73] But in acknowledging this truth scholars have, I believe, overlooked the still potentially problematic nature of even a commented vernacular Bible: the reader of this manuscript has a freedom not enjoyed by the audience of a sermon to survey and organize the material in his or her own way. The primary interpretive guides for the reader are the Bible illustrations, the commentary text, and, finally and above all, the commentary images. This, I believe, explains the different formats selected for the two Vienna codices (Diagram 1). The Latin manuscript was necessarily made for a "literatus" (learned) figure—in fact, for a king of quasi-sacerdotal status who had been provided with a Latin and almost clerical education; its layout accordingly allows one to read down the text columns directly and with minimal visual interruption. The images, placed to the side of their respective texts, may be referred

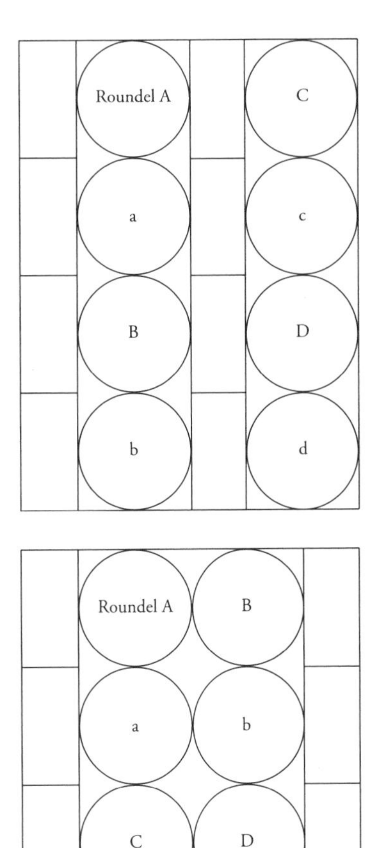

Diag. 1. Typical page layouts of Vienna ÖNB codices 1179 (*top*) and 2554.

to at will—indeed, they frequently must be consulted for the commentary text to be comprehensible—but they do not necessarily intrude themselves into the reading process. The layout of the French-language manuscript, whose readership was almost certainly unlearned in Latin and therefore without access to theological training or subtleties, exercises an additional degree of control. The eye of the reader *must* pass from the text in the left-hand column *across* the images in the center before encountering the succeeding text; it must then move back down *across* the roundels in the center before finding the third text, and so on. The images, placed so prominently in the center of each folio, necessarily interrupt and thereby control and shape the reading of the text: continuous reading of the Bible text and even of the commentary text is rendered impossible.[74] The page layouts of each manuscript are thus intimately related to their divergent natures and audiences; for this reason I consider attempts to date the manuscripts according to the "adoption" or "abandonment" of the layout unhelpful. I will argue in the following pages that the different natures of and audiences for the two manuscripts dictate subtle differences in content as well.

The *Bibles moralisées* are, in sum, relatively simple-to-read picture books that, although paid for *by* the king and court, present a unified and forceful argument *to* the king and court. To understand the nature of that argument, we must look especially to the commentary images, which most forcefully inform the reading of the manuscripts, and which, in contrast to the commentary text, display a homogeneity of style and technique. The commentary roundels serve both to unify and to manipulate the message of the text; in so doing, they often reveal the convictions embedded in its creation more faithfully than does the text itself. One thing that is made clear by these images is that the *Bible moralisée* is intended not so much to elucidate the meaning of the Bible as to utilize familiar biblical scenes to promote certain ideas, readings, and even, occasionally, specific clerical policies. What these ideas and readings were, and what considerations and processes influenced the redactor in the formulation of the artistic program, is the subject of this book.

ONE: A DISCERNIBLE DIFFERENCE

The Image of the Jew

Here God plants his orchard
with good trees and with thorns,
and plants the tree of life.

The good trees signify good men who rest in good works and are crowned with flowers in Paradise. The thorns signify those who rest in bad works and are crowned with the thorns of the world.[1]

The commentary roundel accompanying the moralization opposite encapsulates many of the themes and techniques with which this book is concerned (Fig. 1). Humanity is rigidly divided into good and bad. The representation of the "good" is characterized by order and regularity: the figures are uniform in size, dress, and gesture; serene in expression; focused in gaze; and carefully organized in their placement. They are encompassed within a circular crenelated structure, which signifies the unity, but also the exclusiveness, of the Heavenly City. The "bad" are, in representation as well as by definition, all that is opposite to the "good." They are literally "outsiders," situated outside the walls of paradise. They are inconsistent in size, dress, and gesture; their varying expressions indicate distress, regret, and indifference. They are also alien to each other: gazing up, down, to the right, and to the left, but in no case interacting. One carries a moneybag; two wear crowns of thorns; and a third, dwarfing the rest, wears a tall, pointed red cap. These three attributes especially bring us to the subject of this book, for each is in its own way (in the closed world of these manuscripts, but also beyond) a symbol relating to Jewishness. Why the crowns on the heads of the "bad" imperfectly mimic those of the good while recalling the headgear of Christ himself, why physiognomically and sartorially diverse figures are each endowed with a sign of Jewishness, and especially why the figure of a Jew looms over this gathering of the "bad" can be answered only by careful study of all the techniques for signifying "otherness" displayed in these rich and complex manuscripts.

FIG. 1. Gen. 2:8–9. The good, crowned with flowers in paradise, and the bad, crowned with "thorns of the world." Cod. 2554, fol. 1vd.

Identifying Jews: The Pointed Hat as Signifier and Sign

The keynote of the iconography of Jews and Judaism in the *Bible moralisée* is ambiguity; it is no simple matter to isolate references to Jews in either the text or the images. Many names are used for Jews, figures may bear only some of the visual attributes assigned to Jews, and the attributes may be equivocal, or even entirely absent from characters apparently intended to be read as Jews. A similar ambiguity is evident throughout the *Bible moralisée* in images dealing with almost every imaginable subject: the status of the law, the value of money, the behavior of the clergy and the laity. In this chapter and throughout this book, I argue that this ambiguity of representation is both intentional and meaningful. The ambivalence of the textual and visual commentary serves to deepen and make flexible the meaning of the Bible—a common approach in high medieval exegesis and, indeed, a necessary project for any intellectual endeavor designed to present antique Hebrew scriptures as a blueprint for all aspects of medieval Christian life.[2] At the same time, the abstruseness in the treatment of the Jews in these manuscripts bears witness to and seeks to control a range of very real social and religious ambiguities that seem to have been viewed as menacing by the clerics involved in the making of the *Bible moralisée.*

Nevertheless, a "standard" method for depicting Jews can be identified in the manuscripts and may serve as a norm by which to assess the more complex representations. In the images accompanying texts that refer explicitly to Jews, the roundels generally show bearded men wearing various forms of a conical or pointed hat (*pileum cornutum*).[3] This representation is, of course, not unique to the *Bible moralisée;* the use of the pointed hat as a Jewish attribute in medieval art dates back to the eleventh century and by the thirteenth century was widespread and conventional.[4] In the *Bible moralisée* the "Jew's hat" takes various shapes: it may be very tall and sharply pointed; it may be of the so-called oil-can type (broad-brimmed with a knob at the top); or it may be soft, low, and only slightly peaked. This last type is identical to the headgear of many Christian figures, begging the question of to what extent it is a "Jew's hat" (as opposed to the hat of a Jew) at all. The hats appear in green, blue, tan, red, or brown; no iconographic significance appears to be attached to the colors.

Although it has long been accepted that the pointed hat was the standard Christian iconographic convention for identifying Jews throughout the High Middle Ages, there is still disagreement concerning the full significance of this sign in Gothic art.[5] Some scholars have noted that Jews were depicted wearing the pointed hat in the Jews' own Hebrew manuscripts and have concluded that the depiction of the Jewish hat in art was mimetic, that is, a faithful documentation of historical reality bearing no spiritual import.[6] Others have asserted that the sign was employed primarily as a pejorative identifier and almost inevitably carried an anti-Jewish connotation.[7]

The first assertion is not convincing, as far as French Gothic iconography goes. The *pileum* may have been worn by Jews (as well as by other peoples) as early as the ninth century B.C.,[8] but it is doubtful whether by the thirteenth century Jews in northern France regularly wore the pointed hat or, indeed, covered their heads at all.[9] Although the Talmud recommends that boys cover their heads, there is no Talmudic regulation requiring Jewish men to cover their heads,[10] and contemporary Jewish texts refer to various kinds of hats, of all materials and shapes, as well as to the practice of going about bareheaded.[11] Canon 68 of the Fourth Lateran Council, which called for the imposition of distinctive clothing on Jews, began with the statement: "In some provinces a difference of dress distinguishes the Jews and Saracens from the Christians, but in others confusion has developed to such a degree that no difference is discernible."[12] It seems likely that the Jewish communities of northern France, by no means the least assimilated of European Jewries, included members who were visually indistinguishable from Christians.[13] The use of the *pileum* as an iconographic attribute of the Jews, then, was not based on actual practice but was an external and largely arbitrary sign devised by Christian iconographers in order to create certain modes of perception. Precisely because the position of Jews in late twelfth- and early thirteenth-century Europe was not exactly what the dominant stream of clerical ideology—that informing the canons of the Fourth Lateran Council—determined it should be, the Jew in works such as the *Bible moralisée* is generally, though not inevitably, made identifiable in a way that the Jew in Christian society was not. Like the provisions for distinguishing clothing imposed by the Fourth Lateran Council, the use of the *pileum* in Christian art was an attempt to visually codify a certain attitude toward Jews.

This ongoing tension between the Jews' constructed Otherness and actual visual sameness is evident in the Jews' clothing. Jews are rendered in a variety of clothing styles in the *Bible moralisée.*[14] They generally wear long cloaks, with or without hoods, over calf-length belted robes with long sleeves, but they may also be seen wearing shorter cloaks with slit sleeves, shorter robes with wide sleeves, and so forth.[15] Christians are depicted wearing similar clothes in the manuscripts, and it is impossible to identify a figure as a Jew from his clothing alone. This situation mimics the confusion that occasionally arose from the similarity of Jewish and Christian dress in real life—confusion that clearly was a source of concern to some members of the Church hierarchy. In addition to the excerpt from the decrees of the Fourth Lateran Council cited earlier, decrees from the Council of Valladolid (1228)[16] and the Council of Albi (1254)[17] declare that Jews were not to wear round or wide capes or cloaks, since these garments were too similar to the vestments of the clergy. Although it is possible that Jews were indeed occasionally mistaken for clerics, it is hard to believe that this was a serious practical problem. Rather, the primary concern of the councils in issuing this decree was to protect the dignity and honor of clerical rank.[18] The conceptual anomaly presented by diametrically opposed spiritual groups displaying similar outward appearances posed a threat to proper order and hierarchy.

However, the assumption that the pointed hat clearly and un-

FIG. 2 (TOP). Josh. 5:2–3. Joshua orders the circumcision of the Israelite children. Cod. 1179, fol. 63C. FIG. 3. Exod. 7:10–12. Good prelates devour the false words of Jews. Cod. 1179, fol. 25c.

avoidably conveyed anti-Jewish polemic is equally problematic. It does not seem that the hat was regarded as a degrading object by medieval Jews: they had themselves portrayed wearing pointed hats in their own manuscripts, and they used the pointed hats on their own seals and coats of arms.[19] Nor can the use of a particular article of clothing to identify the Jews as a group necessarily be considered an anti-Jewish practice, for many social groups were iconographically distinguished in medieval art. Kings are depicted wearing crowns and fur cloaks, prelates wearing miters, nobles wearing diadems, soldiers wearing mail, students wearing sleeved cloaks, and so forth.[20] The fact that Old Testament patriarchs and prophets as well as certain revered New Testament Hebrews such as Joseph, Joachim, or Joseph of Arimathea are depicted with Jewish hats would argue against any *automatic* negative connotation.[21] On the other hand, a self-contained sign system can, of course, construct a polemical message through the development and elaboration of a traditional iconographic motif. Just such a development is detectable in regard to the pointed hat in the *Bible moralisée* manuscripts; I will now trace its chief outlines.

The most basic function of the pointed hat in the *Bible moralisée* is simply to denote the concept "Hebrew." Thus, in Vienna ÖNB cod. 1179, fol. 63C, Joshua orders the circumcision of the Israelite children, and both he and the Israelites who perform the ritual wear pointed hats to indicate their "Hebrewness" (Fig. 2). The commentary interprets this circumcision as a figure for Christian baptism, and there is no reason to suspect any negative intent in the use of the *pileum* in the biblical illustration.

However, symbols change and take on new meanings within sophisticated systems of communication, and the *Bible moralisée* is just such a system. Thus, the *pileum cornutum,* already developed in Christian art and used in the *Bible moralisée* as a straightforward signifier for the concept of "Jew," evolves within the visual system of the *Bible moralisée* into a more abstract symbol for the various elements associated with Jewishness. We can see such transformation in the illustration of Exod. 7:10–12, in which Aaron's rod-turned-serpent devours the serpents of the Egyptian magicians (Fig. 3). Moses and Aaron are bareheaded, whereas the magicians of Pharaoh wear the pointed hat. Here, it is the non-Israelites in the scene who have been assigned the Hebrew attribute; clearly the hat is signifying not "Hebrew" or "Jewish" identity but rather "being like a Jew." What a Jew is "like" is indicated in the commentary roundel below, which explains, "[Moses and Aaron] signify good prelates who, in explaining the words of the Gospel, devour the false words of the Jews."[22] Thus, to the Christian commentator, the non-Israelites of the Old Testament represent contemporary Jews, who in turn represent deceit. The pointed hat is not strictly necessary for identifying the prelates' adversaries as Jews: in addition to the identification made by the text, the Jews carry scrolls inscribed *"infideles filii."* But the hats do distinguish them in one powerful visual stroke from the Christians; their dark head coverings seem to weigh them down and render them foreboding when contrasted with the light, tonsured heads of the prelates.

The revision of the straightforward hat-signifier into a more sophisticated sign entails the transmission of a variety of meanings. In this roundel, the concept of the "Hebrew" has a very definite connotation. The "Hebrews" are portrayed rejecting the salvific message contained in the Christian prelates' gospel preaching, rendered as a tiny human soul emerging from an open codex. The "Hebrews" stand next to a figure that, by analogy with the composition of the Bible illustration above, must be considered their "king": the devil. The hat-as-sign therefore takes on the various elements associated with the concept of "Jew": opposition to Christianity, fraud, unbelief, diabolical connections. And the presence of the pointed hats on the Egyptian magicians who give evil counsel to Pharaoh thus signifies their embodiment of the pejorative values crystallized in the sign of the hat. Within the iconographic language of the *Bible moralisée,* the original "signifier" (the hat already established in the lexicon of Christian iconography as a symbol for Judaism) becomes the "sign" for more complex polemical ideas.

This emergence of the hat as a sign for the negative attributes of Jewishness, apparent in the Exodus illustration, is fully realized in certain later scenes in the manuscripts. For example, in Vienna ÖNB cod. 1179, fol. 181a, Tobias's joyful welcome of his son and daughter-in-law is compared to the ultimate conversion of the infidels at the end of the world. The commentary roundel depicts the conversion process as a series of visually distinct stages, each of which uses the pointed hat (as well as the beard) in a different way with respect to the convert (Fig. 4). The reader consequently gauges each convert's spiritual progress according to his age, the placement of his hat, and the nature of his beard. Directly in front of the standing Christ kneels a young, bareheaded, and closely shaven figure. Slightly behind this convert is a mature, bareheaded, and dark-bearded figure shown in the act of kneeling. Next in the group is a white-bearded figure who has taken off his hat and is holding it by its strap. The fourth figure is a man with a bushy white beard reaching up to his pointed cap, about to lift it off his head. The last figure in the group is still wearing a tall pointed hat. As each figure in this sequence approaches Jesus, then, he sheds the marks of his Judaism. The concentration of iconographic interest in the hat is telling: the hat does not just identify Jews; it functions independently of its placement to signify infidelity and recalcitrant Jewishness.[23]

FIG. 4. Tob. 11:10–11. The conversion of the infidels at the end of the world. Cod. 1179, fol. 181a.

The Face of Evil: Jewish Physiognomy and Caricature

The depiction of Jews with beards similarly cannot be considered a purely mimetic device. Although the Talmud (which discourages shaving but permits the clipping of beards in certain cases)[24] probably arrived in northern Europe sometime in the ninth century,[25] bearded Jews began appearing in European art only in the eleventh century.[26] In any case, the canon from the Fourth Lateran Council, cited previously, suggests that in the early thirteenth century there was no fixed Jewish custom concerning beards that could help to clearly distinguish Jews.[27] The beard probably became a standard iconographic device associated with Jews not because all Jews wore them but because particularly pious Jews wore them; beards consequently could be associated with the Jewish religion.[28]

But the significance of the beard in medieval culture is hardly exhausted with this statement. Common attributes of kings from the very beginnings of Western civilization,[29] beards could signify maturity and masculinity, nobility and power: qualities suitable for a ruler but inappropriate for figures assigned a subordinate position, such as Jews.[30] This association with worldliness may explain why in many cultures, including Latin Christianity, priests were required to be clean-shaven.[31] Beards could also and conversely, however, be associated with asceticism and piety.[32] Christians, particularly prelates and princes (including the royal patron in the dedication roundel of the Latin manuscript), are frequently shown in the *Bible moralisée* with beards, as, of course, is Christ himself. My point is not that the beard signifies so many contrasting things as to signify nothing, but rather that it is a powerful image that can convey a range of meanings in association with different figures.[33] In one context, such as the conversion image discussed earlier, the beard signifies Jewishness and the attendant negative qualities evoked by worldly or powerful Jews; in another context (as when, for example, clean-shaven figures mock or torment a bearded Christ),[34] it signifies the opposite.

FIG. 5. Gen 39:17–18. A grotesquely scowling Jew in profile. Cod. 1179, fol. 16d.

No standard physiognomy is allotted to Jews in the *Bible moralisée.*[35] Although Jews tend to be bearded in the manuscripts, many figures identifiable as Jews are clean-shaven. Jews' beards may be long or short, dark or fair. No individual facial features specifically identify Jews, and their expressions vary considerably. One convention almost amounting to a caricature, however, does emerge: the depiction of Jews displaying venomous grimaces. This caricature is employed for evil Hebrews in the Old Testament roundels as well as for New Testament and contemporary Jews in the commentary roundels. In such images, the Jew in question (usually a single individual) is distinguished by a noticeably darker complexion and a fierce, scowling expression, with heavy brows and a gaping mouth (Fig. 5).[36] But the chief features of the early modern anti-Semitic caricature (as defined, for example, by Eric M. Zafran in his study of fifteenth- and sixteenth-century imagery)[37]—heavy hooked nose, lidded eyes, and protruding lips—do not appear.[38] The scowling expressions seem to accord with what Zafran characterized as a general trend in High Gothic art of representing Jews as evil and ugly,[39] yet they constitute the minority of anti-Jewish images in the *Bible moralisée.* The "caricature" appears infrequently in Vienna ÖNB cod. 1179; it is slightly more common in Vienna ÖNB cod. 2554.[40]

Jews are often drawn in profile in the *Bible moralisée.* This is a common medieval pictorial device that has been explained as serving to convey an impression of two-dimensionality and unreality, preventing the viewer from perceiving the figure as belonging to his world.[41] The proposed linkage of the profile convention to the anti-Semitic racial stereotype of the hooked nose is not substantiated by the *Bible moralisée* images:[42] it should not be surprising at this point that the profile view is utilized in the manuscript for many evil figures, Jewish and non-Jewish alike.

Context, Text, and Image: Jews, Infidels, and the Vocabulary of Otherness

The complexity and resulting ambiguity of the rendering of Jews in the images of the *Bible moralisée* are more than matched by an intricate and sophisticated interplay of context, text, and image. The images are far more than mere illustrations of the text, just as the text does far more than simply caption the images.[43] Neither text nor image can stand alone; they must be read together, for they serve to explain and interpret each other. Other practices contribute to the conveyance of meaning in these manuscripts as well: formal similarities between roundel pairs, visual allusions, visual metaphors. The creators of the artistic program were not just illustrators; they must be counted among the primary authors of the work, and their strategies treated as integral aspects of the "meaning" (or meanings) of the *Bible moralisée.*

In sorting out such dense and complex literary and artistic imagery, careful attention to context is naturally essential. Although it is obviously impossible to deal with the larger setting for every image examined here (for many of the images I examine the relevant context is no less than the visual and polemical world of the manuscripts as a whole), there are some commentary sequences in the manuscripts that must be treated together as they extend over several folios and function as coherent units. When these sequences take Jews as their focus, innovative and perhaps unexpected anti-Jewish themes emerge, as the commentary takes up and embroiders upon (for example) the marital and class relations in the proof texts and explores the multiple associations of such traits as "seductiveness," "fidelity," and "sterility." These themes may be largely unintended by-products of the exegetical process, but they nevertheless assume a life of their own and necessarily inform subsequent images of Jews.

An example of this process may be seen in a long and rather dense explication of the attempted seduction of Joseph by the wife of Potiphar (Gen. 39:7–20), in which Jewish law and learning are woven almost inextricably together with carnality and temptation, avarice and pride (Fig. 6).

The first biblical excerpt in this eight-medallion sequence (in the lower left quadrant of the page) reads: "Here the wife of Potiphar, perceiving the beauty of Joseph, accosts him concerning illicit love." According to the commentary text, "By that woman is designated carnal molestation, which compels even perfect men to sin, whence no one lives without stain. She who approached Jesus Christ with threats and flatteries found nothing in Him which is vicious, because He did not sin, nor in His mouth has mendacity been found."[44] The accompanying image forgoes depicting Jesus' resistance to temptation in favor of showing a man succumbing to the sins of pride (depicted via the signs of a hawk and a servant putting on his shoe), gluttony (symbolized by a double cup), avarice (embodied in fur-trimmed robes), and carnal desire (signified by a female-headed snake). Although there is no explicit association in text or image of carnal molestation with Jews or Judaism, given the frequency with which Synagoga, the female personification of Judaism, is accused in the *Bible moralisée* manuscripts of threatening Jesus,[45] the (unillustrated) reference in the commentary text to a female simultaneously threatening and flattering Christ might bear subtle anti-Jewish resonance for the informed reader.

The next commentary text and roundel (in the upper right quadrant of the page) continue to interpret this episode as a figure for sexual, monetary, and intellectual temptation while subtly playing with connotations of the flesh. The female-headed serpent again appears in the commentary image, although it no longer represents Potiphar's wife, but rather the cloak of Joseph. This second biblical excerpt reads: "Here Joseph escapes unsullied from the malice of woman, with his fallen cloak held in [her] hands." The commentary text explains, "Here [is] our just man turning away the astuteness of the worldly vanity of the serpent, and he left his cloak in the hand of his provoker, choosing to be debased in the House of the Lord rather than to dwell in the tabernacles of sinners."[46] Sin is still represented primarily as carnal desire and greed, although the references to "astuteness" and "tabernacles" and to a torn, fallen cloak cannot help but have special resonance for anyone familiar with contemporary anti-Jewish polemic, which repeatedly accuses Jews of cunning and takes the tearing of the veil of the Temple at the time of the Crucifixion as a demonstration of the end of the Old Law.

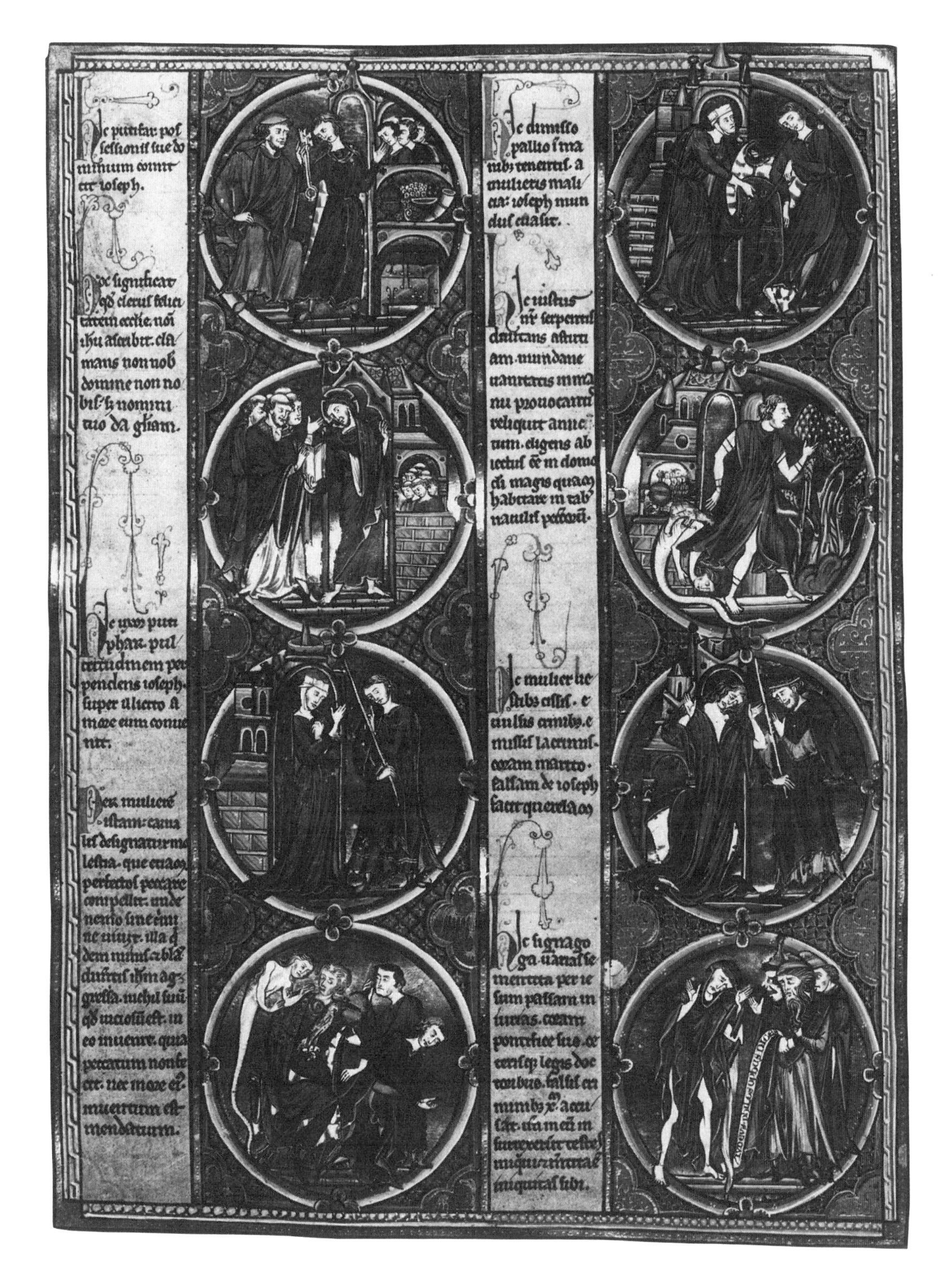

FIG. 6. Gen. 39:4–18. The attempted seduction of Joseph by the wife of Potiphar. Cod. 1179, fol. 16.

In fact, these very subtle anti-Jewish resonances seem to have been deliberate and meaningful. The next biblical text in the sequence (bottom right quadrant of the page) states: "Here the woman with ripped clothes and torn hair and spent tears makes false complaint about Joseph before her husband." According to the interpretation, "Here Synagoga, having feigned herself to have suffered various injuries by Jesus, accuses Christ of false crimes before her high-priest and other doctors of the law, whence iniquitous witnesses rose up against him, and iniquity was falsely said about him."[47] In the commentary image, a disheveled, barelegged Synagoga makes a gesture of accusation and despair. Carnal molestation has suddenly been transformed into Synagoga, and not just this last commentary but the entire sequence takes on a new layer of meaning, as Jews and Judaism, Jewish ritual and Jewish law are associated with sexual, economic, and intellectual sin.

In its larger setting, moreover, the commentary image doesn't simply depict "Jewish" iniquity but, by forging visual links with the images of "Christian" sin appearing elsewhere on the folio, locates it and actively tries to combat it among Christians. On the one hand, the temptingly seductive vision presented by the female-headed serpent in the previous roundels has been negated; in fact, it has been reversed. Whereas both the serpent's hair and breasts in the previous commentary roundels and those of Potiphar's wife in the related biblical roundel are enticingly exposed, in this latest commentary image Synagoga's hair and body are covered, thereby resolutely denying her beauty or possible attraction. This last roundel similarly establishes a sharp contrast between Synagoga and the "just" man, two medallions above, whom carnality unsuccessfully attempted to seduce. Unlike this man, Synagoga is still cloaked, still veiled in the obscuring letter of the Law, while her indecently exposed legs (he's wearing hose) identify her and the religion she represents as an embodiment of hideous and specifically female carnality. On the other hand, the Synagoga roundel exactly echoes in composition the first roundel in the series, which is situated to the immediate left, thereby creating an implicit correlation between the Christians falling into carnal sin and the group of Jews to whom Synagoga appeals. To confuse matters further, these Jews hold a scroll identifying them not as the specifically Hebraic types "Priests" or "Doctors of the Law," as the text would seem to dictate, but as much more ecumenical "Philosophers"! The overall effect of these visual and verbal allusions and juxtapositions is to imply that carnality and worldliness are at the same time peculiarly characteristic of Judaism and unavoidably attractive and dangerous to Christians. Although the initial roundels in the series would not seem to touch upon Jews at all, read as an organic whole all the images in the Joseph sequence take on deepened polemical import, and both the arsenal and the targets of anti-Jewish imagery have been considerably expanded.

There are places in the *Bible moralisée* where the relationship of word and image seems to be quite straightforward, with both text and illustration clearly referring to Jews. Thus, the commentary for folio 14b of the Latin manuscript states that Judas sold Jesus to the Jews, and the accompanying image depicts a bearded Judas in profile, wearing a pointed cap and handing Jesus over to figures displaying the same attributes as the betrayer himself (Fig. 7). Yet even here, the enigmatic temporal juxtapositions (Is Judas to be regarded as a contemporary of medieval Jews? Are medieval Jews considered the accomplices of Judas?) and group affiliations (Is Judas "one of" the medieval Jews? Does he become "like" the medieval Jews through his actions? Is he the source of their corruption?) intensify the potential ideological resonances of an already highly charged episode.

Even the instances of apparently simple correspondence between textual and visual references to Jews are nuanced: for example, groups of figures are frequently identified as Jews by means of a categorical association with a single figure who alone exhibits the signs of Jewishness. In Vienna ÖNB cod. 2554, fol. 20vb, one of the "miscreants" referred to in the text wears a tallish peaked hat and is bearded; another is beardless and wears a soft, semi-peaked cap. The rest have no distinctive iconographic features (Fig. 8). This iconographic pattern reinforces the conclusion that differences not evident in reality were perceptually and symbolically created in the *Bible moralisée,* creating the illusion that the posited spiritual distinctions were indeed constitutive of the social order. Moreover, since such distinctions were essentially ideological strategies, the signs of Jewishness could be employed as the polemical occasion required, whether or not Jews were ostensibly at issue. In fact, the most common configuration of text and image in the *Bible moralisée* is one in which the image imposes "Jewish" iconography into contexts not immediately concerned with Judaism. As a result, there are far more "Jews" in the pictures than in the written moralizations.[48]

Several practices are responsible for the preponderance of Jews in the images in relation to the text. First, the images frequently interpret or represent as Jews figures whom the text refers to using different terminology. Often the term reasonably may be taken, and seemingly was taken by the creator of the artistic program, as a synonym for "Jew." In Vienna ÖNB cod. 1179, fol. 95d, for example, the text speaks of "infidels and enemies of God" who rejoice at the death of a good prelate, and the commentary roundel clearly portrays those infidels as Jews (Fig. 9). Another roundel in which Jews hold a scroll identifying them as infidels has already been discussed (see Fig. 3), and throughout the work the term is assumed to refer to Jews. This is, of course, by no means a creative

FIG. 7 (TOP). Gen. 37:28. Judas sells Jesus to the Jews. Cod. 1179, fol. 14b.
FIG. 8. Exod. 12:43. Jesus prevents miscreants from approaching or touching "his body." Cod. 2554, fol. 20vb.

FIG. 9 (TOP). I Kings 25:1. Infidels rejoice at a good prelate's death. Cod. 1179, fol. 95d.
FIG. 10. Gen. 2:2. Judgment Day: Christ tramples his enemies in hell. Cod. 1179, fol. 3c.

interpretation on the part of the artist or iconographer; one of the most common definitions of "infidel" is "Jew."[49] The same meaning is assigned in the French manuscript to the word *mescreant.*

In other cases, however, the visual rendering involves a more subjective act of interpretation. The commentary from Vienna ÖNB cod. 2554, fol. 1vd, quoted at the opening of this chapter, compares the thorns planted in paradise to "those who live in bad works and are crowned with thorns of the world." The accompanying roundel clearly depicts at least one of those "in bad works" as a Jew (see Fig. 1). In Vienna ÖNB cod. 1179, fol. 3c, the commentary establishes a moral dichotomy that does not exist in the biblical excerpt, which states simply: "Here God rests on the seventh day after he finished the work of seven days." According to the commentary text: "That God rested on the seventh day signifies Christ who will rest on the day of judgment and embrace his friends, and will trample his enemies in hell under his feet."[50] The enemies depicted in the roundel include a tonsured cleric, a bishop, and, most prominently (because placed front and center), a Jew (Fig. 10). Other terms that are similarly accompanied by images of Jews include *pravi, iniqui,* and *peccatores,* as well as "heretics" and "philosophers."[51]

Second, and more ominously still, Jews are regularly and rather gratuitously inserted into scenes dealing with the devil and damnation. For example, on folio 87b of the Latin manuscript, the commentary text compares the destruction of Dagon (I Kings 5:3) to "Holy Church who brought down and destroyed and confounded the Devil."[52] In the image, a personification of Holy Church waves the devil down toward hell; the devil is bound together with three Jews. In this socially oriented iconographic program, the devil inevitably works through and is accompanied by his contemporary surrogates—and they are, more likely than not, Jews.

Finally, Jews may be depicted in the image when no evil personage or group of any kind is mentioned in the text. In folio 10a of the Latin manuscript, the text follows long-standing exegetical tradition in interpreting the sacrifice of Isaac as a figure for God's sacrifice of his own son "for the salvation of the faithful."[53] The image depicts Jesus Christ standing in the center of the roundel (Fig. 11). To Jesus' right is a bearded prophet holding a scroll that displays the prophetic words "sicut ovis ducet . . ."[54] To Jesus' left (that is, his "sinister" side, reserved in these manuscripts as in many medieval works of art for the morally abhorrent) stand two bearded Jews with pointed hats, one of whom puts his hand to Christ's shoulder in a shoving or spurning motion. Although only believers are mentioned in the text, in this context the Jews clearly represent the implicit antithesis to those believers: the unbelievers who perpetrated the slaughter of the Son of God.

This dichotomizing strategy—the tendency to balance the

"good" by positing or constructing the existence of the "bad"—is evident throughout the *Bible moralisée:* common in the commentary texts, it is pervasive in the images. Of course, the *Bible moralisée* is by no means unique in this respect; such symmetry is evident in many medieval artistic and literary monuments. The elect are balanced by the damned; saints trod upon the demons they conquer; God the Father overshadows Satan, who rejected him; virtues are assigned their corresponding vices—each of these examples vividly demonstrates the essential role played by the category of the "Other" in high medieval Christian works of art.[55] In the *Bible moralisée,* this process of establishing or reinforcing identity through alterity serves to heighten the manuscripts' anti-Judaism: Jews are almost inevitably chosen as visual inversions of the "good."

FIG. 11. Gen. 22:1–5. Abraham's sacrifice of Isaac signifies God's sacrifice of his own son. Jews appear as implicit antitheses to the believers mentioned in the commentary text. Cod. 1179, fol. 10a.

Several explanations for the assignment of Jews to this role come to mind. The first—and this is essentially the approach adopted by Kraus, Trachtenberg, and others—is that Jews were simply so hated and feared that they were considered *the* prototypical evildoers, clearly implicated when any vice or mischief was discussed, and the natural allies of other evildoers (such as heretics) by nature of their evil. No more specific reasons were, it is assumed, needed by medieval theologians; consequently, none are explored by these scholars. And yet, this approach sidesteps vital considerations. First, as pointed out in the introduction, Jews did not feature prominently in medieval works of art before the thirteenth century. If Jews were deeply, uniformly, and inevitably hated and feared in medieval Christendom on account of their rejection of Christ and/or the authority of the Church, why did this hatred not find visual expression during the entire first millennium of Christian art? Second, this approach is essentially circular, adopting the effects of a phenomenon (the impression given by anti-Jewish art of intense hatred of Jews) to explain that same phenomenon. Although this is clearly a subject I cannot satisfactorily address here, I must point out that it is by no means clear that Jews *were* universally and unvaryingly hated and feared—either in early thirteenth-century Paris or at almost any other point in the High Middle Ages. The plethora of ecclesiastical canons attempting to limit Jewish-Christian social interaction suggests the existence of a diversity of attitudes toward Jews within Christian society.[56] Similarly, there are very few accounts of anti-Jewish violence that do not refer to Christian neighbors, friends, or overlords who attempted to stem the violence. Although such protection was frequently motivated by self-interest, it does not logically follow that in the absence of self-interest fear and loathing would dominate. Even among clerics trained in very similar traditions, a range of attitudes toward Jews and Judaism was possible[57]—how much more likely among the still highly diverse population of medieval "France" (which, of course, scarcely existed as either a political or a cultural entity in this period). While I by no means wish to deny that significant sectors—perhaps the majority—of the medieval Christian population regarded Jews and Judaism with animosity, at the very least one must try to establish the depth and extent, not to mention the causes, of such feelings among the segments of society for or by whom works of art were made before asserting that they determined those works' artistic programs.

An alternative explanation might hold that the images were not intended to be anti-Jewish at all. Jews were chosen as signs for other reviled figures in the *Bibles moralisées* because the artists, faced with the task of depicting concepts for which no pictorial models had been devised, turned to the only "outsiders" for whom there were iconographic traditions of long standing. In this approach, the anti-Jewish imagery of these manuscripts would be considered merely an unintentional by-product of the unprecedented demands of this unique manuscript form. This suggestion is unsatisfactory for two reasons. First, it strikes me as inconceivable that theologians immersed in contemporary theories regarding the meaning and interpretation of Scripture—as the directors of the *Bible moralisée* iconographic program clearly were—would be uncritical or unself-conscious about the import of the form and content of such a massive work of biblical exegesis. Moreover, many innovative iconographic devices were, in fact, devised for a range of "outsider" groups in the images of the *Bible moralisée.*[58] Whatever else their limitations, the makers of the *Bible moralisée* cannot be accused of lacking imagination.

A third possibility is that the iconography reflected some specific grievance against the Jews that held them directly responsible for damage perceived by the supervising clerics to have been done to Christian society. This third suggestion also fails to satisfy, since it begs the questions: What could this grievance have been, and why was it not articulated or even hinted at in the textual commentary?

No Fixed Identity

A more basic reason that none of these explanations is, in my view, entirely satisfactory, is that each accepts as natural and unproblematic the opposition constructed in the manuscript imagery between Jew and Christian. Let me emphasize that I am not questioning the fact that religious affiliation determined identity (legal, social, economic, etc.) in medieval France as in Europe as a whole, and that Jews were, indeed, utterly distinct from Christians. Rather, I am urging the reexamination of (medieval) assertions about the antithetical and irreconcilable nature of those distinct identities. In spite of the insistently dichotomizing tendency of the *Bible moralisée,* what is repeatedly noticeable in the use of Jews to represent excoriated groups (infidels, enemies, heretics, and philosophers) is the permeability of religious and social boundaries. Just as Jews are regarded as potential Christians in the myriad texts and roundels imagining or forecasting their conversion, so Christians are represented as equally—or rather more—liable to evolve (or devolve) into "Jews."[59] Fluidity between Judaism and Christianity is thus simultaneously courted (in calls for conversion) and repudiated (in condemnations of "Judaizing"), acknowledged and denied. In order, then, to answer the questions posed at the outset of this book—Why so many Jews? And why so anti-Jewish?—it is also necessary to ask, What (in this particular discursive context) is a Jew? And what is a Christian? I have already emphasized the consistent ambiguity in the representation of Jews in these manuscripts; in the chapters that follow I propose that most (negative) attributes associated with Jews accompany Christian figures as well, including clerics, prelates, and kings. The image of the Jew presented in the *Bible moralisée,* then, in a very real way mirrors (in the sense of reflects, but also reverses, distorts, and distances) this corner of medieval Christendom's image of itself.

TWO: THE ROOT OF ALL EVIL

Jews, Money, and Metaphor

All Scripture is like a lyre,
and the lower string on its own does not create harmony,
but [only when combined] with all the others.[1]

The single most common iconographic attribute associated with Jews in the *Bible moralisée* is the moneybag: Jews are shown holding these purses in more than fifty roundels in each of the Vienna manuscripts. The meanings attached to this sign are driven by and play upon several long-standing anti-Jewish biases, but the commentary imagery in the *Bible moralisée* also manipulates the various connotations of the moneybag to foster new perceptions about both Jews and Christian society itself. Essentially, the manuscripts employ a general strategy in which a negative polemic against an economic activity—moneylending—is displaced through the use of increasingly more sophisticated figurations (borrowed from the disciplines of logic, rhetoric, and the natural sciences) onto the Jew, who appears as a sign for usury, avarice, and the destructive effects of money capital as a whole. Analysis of this strategy, then, helps to disentangle the intricate processes by which specific developments in the society and economy of early thirteenth-century France intersected with the representation of Jews in this period.

The Social Background: Christian Moralists and the Rise of a Money Economy

From about the year 1050, the rapid expansion and increasing sophistication of the economy of Western Christendom led many Christian writers and thinkers to direct their attention to money and its manipulation. That notice was often hostile; when the mid-eleventh-century reformer Peter Damian declared that "avarice is the root of all evil," he was reflecting a growing trend among Christian moralists to attribute most social and spiritual abuses to the love of money.[2] By the late twelfth and early thirteenth centuries, many treatises on the sin of avarice were singling out for special censure the practice of "usury," defined as the collecting of any amount above the principal.[3] However, although it is possible to trace a consistent scholastic tradition concerning usury, there are nevertheless some subtle differences in theoretical approaches to moneylending, and greater variation still in attitudes toward regulating actual economic practice, indicating the ambivalence within scholarly circles (and medieval society as a whole) regarding the expanding realm of capital.[4] Some canonists conceded that the Bible permitted the exaction of interest from "aliens" or "enemies" (that is, from infidels and heretics by Christians and/or from Christians by Jews);[5] the popes themselves apparently countenanced lending at interest by Jews;[6] and both civil legists and penitentialists carefully analyzed and dissected commercial transactions in an effort to distinguish acceptable profit from improper gain.[7] By contrast, certain conservative members of the theology faculty at the University of Paris went far beyond papal and canonical positions to proscribe a broad range of profitable business transactions, including lending at interest by or to infidels, on the grounds that any and all usury is sinful.[8] Reflecting their specialized training and mission, and perhaps, too, in an attempt to assert their spiritual authority over the issue, these conservative moralists framed the debate in terms other than purely financial, employing in their discussions of moneylending a vehemently hostile rhetoric that served to demonize its practitioners.[9]

The representation of money and moneylending in the *Bible moralisée* echoes the most censorious of the theological approaches; its complex layering similarly parallels the elaborate interpretive methods developed by the twelfth- and thirteenth-century Scholastics. A complete understanding of the imagery's formative ideas can be reached only by examining the representation one piece at a time and then reassembling it after careful analysis.

Jews as Usurers; Usurers as Jews

There is little question but that in the *Bible moralisée* the sign of the moneybag serves, in its most fundamental role, to associate the figure carrying it with professional moneylending. The moneybag became the traditional emblem associated with the occupation of moneylending (in both art and life) probably already in the eleventh century. Moneybags were suspended outside the houses of professional moneylenders to indicate their occupation,[10] and they appear in conjunction with usurers in many works of medieval art.[11] The regularity with which Jews are shown with moneybags, then, echoes and serves to perpetuate an impression that Jews and moneylending were inextricably intertwined.[12]

The juxtaposition of commentary images and texts does the same. The *Bibles moralisées* contain an inordinate number of texts concerned with moneylending; in the vast majority of these cases, textual references to usurers are accompanied by depictions of Jews. For example, on folio 47a of the Latin manuscript, the raven cursed by Moses in Lev. 11:15–19 is said to represent usurers (*feneratores*), rendered in the roundel as a Jew hiding moneybags within his hood (Fig. 12). In the commentary on chapter 21 of the same biblical book, the man afflicted with "worms" (*tineam*) is interpreted as a great usurer (*maximum feneratorem*) and is depicted as a bearded figure wearing a slightly pointed cap (that is, as either a Jew or a man dressed in Jewish fashion) with a moneybag hung around his neck, three moneybags balanced on each arm, and a bowl of coins balanced on his head (Fig. 13).

It is by no means surprising that usurers are generally identified as Jews in the *Bible moralisée,* as they are in many other twelfth- and thirteenth-century works of art.[13] Although the question of the origins, extent, and relative importance of Jewish participation in moneylending is still unresolved, it seems clear that, in contrast to the eleventh and earlier twelfth centuries, by the early thirteenth century lending at interest had indeed become an important factor in Jewish economic life.[14] Various reasons for the increased concentration on credit lending by Jews during the course of the twelfth century have been hazarded in many recent works, including the exclusion of Jews from various crafts owing to the growing religious and social nature of the guilds, the separation of Jews from the land as a result of the reliance on oaths as a building block of the feudal relationship, and the need for an easily transportable form of wealth because of the increased uncertainty of Jewish life.[15] Whatever the truth of these claims (and the fact that, in effect, these restrictions allegedly imposed on Jews anticipate the forms of "alienation" that capital would impose on European society as a whole suggests that the entire subject bears reexamination),[16] by the year 1150 the Jew had become the "stereotypical" moneylender in the eyes of most Christians, or at least in Christian writings. The term "usurer," meaning either "illicit moneylender" or simply "moneylender," was considered practically synonymous with the term "Jew."[17] Many thirteenth-century discussions of usury perpetuated these impressions: Robert de Courson, for example, stated in the section of his *Summa* dealing with usury that "Jews have nothing except what they have gained through usury."[18] This sentence is repeated verbatim in the contemporary *Summa* for confessors by the English cleric Thomas of Chobham (formerly a colleague of Courson at the University of Paris) and probably reflects widespread popular conceptions in England and on the Continent.[19] Similarly, the term "usurer" was used virtually interchangeably with "Jew" in secular texts, and regulation of usury generally figures prominently in sections of both secular[20] and ecclesiastical legislation assigned to Jewish issues. The Fourth Lateran Council's legislation concerning usury, for example, occurs in the context of the canons dealing with the Jews.[21] The employment of images of Jews to illustrate textual references to usurers in the *Bible moralisée* mirrors this tendency to equate the terms.[22]

FIG. 12 (TOP). Lev. 11:15–19. Cursed creatures: a worldly bishop; a usurer. Cod. 1179, fol. 47a. FIG. 13. Lev. 21:20. A great usurer. Cod. 1179, fol. 51b.

FIG. 14 (TOP). Gen. 1:9–22. Diverse people "hook" or "pawn" Holy Church. Cod. 2554, fol. 1c. FIG. 15. Gen. 1:9–22. Diverse people abuse power in diverse ways. Cod. 1179, fol. 3a.

However, the concept "Jew" was not only employed by Christian theologians as a synonym for "usurer"; it also frequently functioned as a synecdoche (a figure in which a less inclusive term is used for a more inclusive term), as "Jews" came to stand for the entire practice of moneylending and its negative economic effects as a whole. Bernard of Clairvaux used the term *judaizare* to mean any form of moneylending,[23] and the Council of Paris (1213) called financial institutions "synagogues for the wicked."[24] This synecdochic utilization had, of course, polemical implications. Since many of the late twelfth- and early thirteenth-century objections to moneylending described it as inflicting both concrete and spiritual harm on society, the stereotype of the usurer as Jew consequently suggests that Jews were dangerous to Christians.

One common area of concern was the effect of moneylending on poor Christians. Concern for protecting the indebted poor from predation figures prominently, for example, in an ordinance on the Jews dealing mainly with usury, issued by Philip Augustus in 1219. Loans to poorer laborers were prohibited outright, a three-year grace period was prescribed for poorer debtors, and the taking in gage of tools necessary for the earning of livelihood was forbidden.[25] Innocent IV claimed that many people were reduced to poverty by the heavy exactions of usurers (not identified as Jewish), and he warned that the abandonment of agricultural pursuits by farmers who preferred usurious moneylending to hard work would lead to famine, from which the poor suffered disproportionately.[26]

The text of the *Bible moralisée* echoes these concerns about the effect of usury on the poor. On the first folio of the French manuscript, the birds created by God at the beginning of time (Gen. 1:20–22) signify "diverse people of the world who hook Holy Church" while the "big fish" signify "great usurers who devour the little, that is, the poor people."[27] Commentary roundel *c* illustrates only the first half of this text, showing Holy Church personified seated in the midst of various figures (a white monk, a black monk, secular clerics, and a bareheaded layman—all, that is, Christians) who flail at the shrine surrounding her with hooks; the devouring of the poor people is not addressed in the illustration (Fig. 14). But, interestingly, this part of the French commentary text *is* realized in a roundel on the next folio as well as in the corresponding illustration in the Latin manuscript (Fig. 15). Although both this second French commentary text on the creation of fish and the analogous Latin commentary text remark simply, "The diverse kinds of fish signify diverse kinds of people,"[28] the respective commentary roundels, which are nearly identical, are considerably more specific. In each, four professions/ranks are presented: in one quadrant, falcon-bearing noblemen ride on a horse; in the next, female customers holding out coins gesture rather imperiously toward a butcher; in a third, paddle-wielding teachers scold two young tonsured pupils (who are nearly naked in the Latin manuscript); and in each lower-left quadrant, a moneylender or moneychanger (in the Latin manuscript he is bearded and wearing a white cap) weighs out coins on a scale while customers wait apprehensively. All of these scenes recall in some way the abuse of power hinted at in the earlier French commentary text (the last scene even plays on a French pun based on that earlier text: *accrocher,* "to hook," is also slang for "to pawn"). In the Latin moneylending quadrant the potential social tensions engendered by this method of wielding power are compounded by the ambiguities inherent in the term "usurer" and maintained in the depiction of the moneylender, who can be read as a Jew or as a Christian exhibiting "Jewishness" because of his occupation.

The *Bible moralisée* also depicts a Jewish-type figure actively engaged in perhaps the most objectionable of all possible financial activities. In the commentary on the Levitical precepts, the French manuscript interprets the hunchback, the lame, and the scurvied man (all barred from becoming priests in Lev. 21:20) as usurers.[29] The commentary roundel consequently has three representations of usurers. Two—both of whom are beardless—are portrayed statically: one is holding a chest of money on his back, another is holding a scale for weighing coins. The third—a bearded figure wearing a round red cap—is more active: he holds a baby away from a woman (Fig. 16). This seems to depict a particularly repugnant transaction: the indenturing, or perhaps the pawning, of a child. The image suggests that this woman is a mother who has lost her child (perhaps even put her child up as a gage for a loan) because of her inability to pay off a debt. Such transactions may indeed have taken place (at least in the earlier Middle Ages), and reports of them, whether or not true, would certainly have added to popular hatred of pawnbrokers.[30] It is striking that the most vigorously destructive usurer depicted is the one represented as a Jew—or in clothes similar to those of a Jew.

The exegetical setting for this image of a baby-stealing usurer provides the essential framework for its interpretation. Like so many of the anti-usury texts in the *Bible moralisée* and in the writings of contemporary theologians,[31] it appears in the commentary on Levitical laws of purity and exclusion; this context, I believe, highlights at least some of the concepts underlying the anti-usury polemic here and elsewhere. The primary function of the Levitical precepts, as Mary Douglas has compellingly argued, was to establish visible signs that would inspire meditation among the Hebrews on the purity and unity of God.[32] The equation in Scholastic Levitical commentaries of usurers with unclean ele-

FIG. 16. Lev. 21:18–20. Three usurers: one seems to take a child in pawn. Cod. 2554, fol. 30a.

ments arises out of similar needs. Under the influence of Pauline Christianity's emphasis on the "spirit" rather than the "letter" of the law, Christian polemicists typically claimed that Christianity rose above Jewish literalness in understanding purity and pollution on an entirely spiritual plane.[33] However, even the "spiritualized" notions of purity so self-consciously privileged in medieval Christian writings were accorded specific, concretized forms. Communal life requires communal demonstrations and testimony. It is not enough to condemn sin: for a community to unite behind the concept of cleanliness, pollution must be rendered recognizable. The *Glossa ordinaria* comment flanking the injunction that lepers be expelled from the Hebrews' midst (Lev. 13:1) remarks: "A clear transposition from the letter of the law, which among the Jews [is observed], as it were, in sacrifices and purgations and the like; and among Gentile communities, for instance, concerns adultery, rapine, avarice, and the like."[34] And of course, ideas of physical pollution were never completely eradicated from medieval Christianity. Peter of Poitiers, an early twelfth-century canon of St.-Victor, insisted that the Eucharist "requires not only goodness of life, but also bodily cleanliness."[35] With the official adoption of the doctrine of transubstantiation at the Fourth Lateran Council (1215), physical as well as spiritual cleanliness (of the Host, the celebrant, and the communicants) was brought into still sharper focus. So, for example, Alexander Nequam (1157–1217) preached on the responsibility of priests to wash their hands before handling the Body of Christ,[36] priests were enjoined by Innocent III to wear white when celebrating the Easter Mass,[37] and ever more elaborate measures for assuring the integrity of the consecrated wafers were adopted.[38] Such measures did not serve just to protect the purity of the Host but also to publicly signify it.

Condemnations of usurers fulfilled a similar function. Associated rhetorically and metaphorically with "filth" in a myriad of Christian texts (to the extent that "filthy lucre" is still a cliché),[39] money was repeatedly linked with actual filth in the form of excrement and the "filthy" fluid blood in those most vivid and concrete of medieval narratives, the exempla (illustrative or amusing anecdotes inserted into a sermon).[40] Money, then, was not just an agent but a tangible sign of sin and pollution, and usurers were considered not only morally tainted (in that they were sinful) but also physically tainted (by virtue of their intimacy with "filthy lucre").

Such associations, then, form the backdrop for both the child-pawning and other anti-usury images in the *Bible moralisée* Leviticus commentary as well as the two great anti-Jewish libels to which they are thematically related: the accusation of ritual child murder, which was leveled against Jews from about the middle of the twelfth century (just when Jews began to be strongly identified with moneylending), and the Host desecration accusation, which appeared early in the thirteenth century and whose villain was stereotypically a Jewish usurer.[41] Allegedly wallowing in a "filthy" and "bloodsucking" temporal occupation,[42] Jews could, when circumstances arose or polemical needs dictated, be presented as threatening to corrupt Christendom (the spiritual Body of Christ) in general, and, especially, its two most sacred precincts: the real body of Christ and the purest and most Christlike of all Christians, innocent children.[43] A very early report of attempted abuse of a Host by a Jew, conveyed in a letter written by Pope Innocent III in 1213, recounts that a certain French Jew placed a stolen Host in a box of coins; the coins were miraculously turned into wafers. This element of the story serves to associate the Jew with money; it also underscores the extent to which money was considered to be the diametric opposite of, and thus incompatible with, the Body of Christ.[44] The Host desecration and child murder tales, then, use the child's body and the Body of Christ as synecdoches for the Body Social—encouraging meditation on the purity of the latter by first identifying and then purging (the Jew and his client are usually burned) those dirty elements of society that pollute the former.[45] And always the background to such complicated layerings would have been the (perceived) reality of Jewish responsibility for the spread of indebtedness, buttressed by stories, rumors, or memories of its "bloodsucking" consequences.

A roundel in the Latin manuscript depicts a more common and much-criticized aspect of pawnbroking—the transfer to Jews of Church possessions. Folio 77d of Vienna ÖNB cod. 1179 paraphrases the moment in Judg. 16:19 when Delilah cuts off Samson's hair and thus renders him powerless. In the moralization, Delilah is held to signify the flesh, which makes the soul (Samson) "sleep from greed and gluttony and carries away from it the seven virtues and thus it relinquishes the grace of God."[46] In a very complicated pictorial translation of the commentary, the soul is depicted in the center of the roundel as a tonsured cleric drinking from a horn; this signifies gluttony. From his left shoulder a small figure representing his soul steps into a bowl of money being poured by another figure. Seven doves symbolizing the virtues fly away to the right. With his left hand the cleric hands a cloak to a standing bearded figure holding out a bag of money (Fig. 17).

FIG. 17. Judg. 16:19. Flesh makes the soul sleep in greed and gluttony. Cod. 1179, fol. 77d.

The taking of Church vestments and vessels in gage was, in fact, the single most censured aspect of credit lending; in addition to the monetary loss suffered by the Church, the critics stressed, such transactions caused "scandal" and rendered vessels and vestments unavailable for spiritual uses. Objections to this practice consequently constituted a very old refrain in canon law;[47] when Jews were the lenders the complaints found their way into royal texts as well. A prohibition against receiving Church vessels was included in Philip Augustus's 1206 charter for the Jews and reiterated in the ordinance of 1219.[48] The situation was considered so scandalous that it was brought to the notice of the pope: in 1205 Innocent III complained to Philip about Jewish appropriation of ecclesiastical goods by means of usury.[49] An additional and, I believe, crucial dimension, though, resides in the fact that indebtedness entails emotional and social as well as legal obligation. Power over the clerical debtor is conferred upon the lay creditor, and the superiority of clergy (as clerical ideology envisioned spiritual hierarchy) is consequently undermined. Moreover, if lay power over the clergy was at all times a cause for concern, when the laymen in question were infidels a disturbing religious dimension came into play. Reflecting this, in the twelfth century a virulent twist was added to the objections.[50] Peter the Venerable alleged that Jews did "horrible things" to the liturgical items that came into their possession through usury.[51] Jewish "defiling" of Church goods was cited by Rigord with outrage in his account of Philip Augustus's expulsion of Jews from the royal domain in 1182,[52] and similar expressions are repeated in many subsequent condemnations of Jewish usury. Jewish moneylending becomes not only a way to oppress and offend Christians but also a form of sacrilege.

The assumptions embedded in such texts cannot fail but to infiltrate the early thirteenth-century patron's reading of the pawnbroking and moneylending imagery in the *Bible moralisée;* in turn, the images reinforce such cultural suppositions. The peopling of familiar, or least plausible, scenes of contemporary economic distress with Jews or Jew-like figures thus plays upon and perpetuates the (widespread? or constructed?) belief that all the ill effects of usury were perpetrated by or linked to Jews. The resulting impression is that Jews bore responsibility for almost all the financial calamities that might befall a thirteenth-century Christian.

But the image of the money-clutching Jew in the *Bible moralisée* does more than merely propagate this rather crude economic scapegoating. The relationships established in the text and images of the *Bible moralisée* between Jews and usurers, and Jews and moneylending as a whole, pave the way for another kind of figuration. Images that function metonymically (representing an idea by means of an associated concept) employ Jews-as-surrogates-for-usury to designate both the sin of avarice and the entire concept of sin itself.

Signs of Avarice

The linkage of Jews and money in the illustrations of the *Bible moralisée* is clearly informed by and plays upon the well-established

Christian literary topos of Jewish greed. As early as the fourth century, John Chrysostom delivered violently anti-Jewish sermons accusing Jews of, among many other things, greed and thievery;[53] and in the twelfth-century *Disputatio* of Pseudo-Gilbert Crispin, Holy Church remarks to Synagoga, "There is no calculating the extent of your avarice."[54] Judas, who was often taken to epitomize all of the Jews, was alleged to have been motivated by avarice in his betrayal of Christ.[55] Thomas Aquinas wrote that the Israelites of the biblical period were known to be prone to avarice.[56]

There are several texts in the *Bible moralisée* that explicitly link Jewish moneylending to this stereotypical Jewish vice. For example, in the French manuscript's paraphrase of the offerings of the sons of Adam to God (Gen. 4:3–5), Cain is compared to "the Jews, who make offering of their confiscations and avarice and God refuses them."[57] (In the Latin version, "confiscations" is replaced with "usuries.")

But more commonly, it is the images that link Jews to vice; and the majority of these images do not restrict the vice in question to avarice but instead enlist signs associated with avarice to promote a conception of the overall sinfulness of the Jews. So, for example, a general reference to sinners on folio 4c of Vienna ÖNB cod. 1179 is illustrated with a depiction of a Jew with one moneybag suspended around his neck and another in his hand (Fig. 18). Similarly, on folio 104c of the same manuscript, where the bathing Bathsheba is said to signify Holy Church cleansing herself of "dirty sinners," the unspecified sinners are portrayed as Jews walking away from Holy Church, who indicates her rejection of the Jews with a downward wave. One of the Jews holds a moneybag (Fig. 19).[58]

However, the imagery of the *Bible moralisée* does considerably more than just illustrate or reinforce the topos of Jewish avarice; many roundels go beyond the rather uncomplicated accusations embedded in the synonyms that equate Jews with usurers or even the broader metonymic use of Jews as figures for avarice and sin in general. They also use metaphor—a relation of condensation rather than displacement—to establish the effect of a motivated relationship between Jews and avarice.[59] In other words, they affirm not only that Jews are avaricious and sinful (and that avarice and sin are "Jewish") but also that Judaism by its very nature is avaricious and sinful. For example, the commentary on folio 74c of the Latin manuscript links essential Jewish rites to greed by comparing Jephtah's daughter, who rejoiced in her father's military victory (Jud. 11), to Synagoga, who rejoiced in front of Christ in "worldly" things, specified as ceremonies, money, and flesh.[60] The accompanying roundel underscores the unity of the three manifestations of "worldliness" mentioned in the text by conflat-

FIG. 18 (TOP). Gen. 3:9–12. Sinners invoke astrology to excuse themselves; a Jew with a moneybag is prominent. Cod. 1179, fol. 4c.
FIG. 19. II Kings 11:2. Holy Church cleanses herself of dirty sinners. Cod. 1179, fol. 104c.

FIG. 20 (TOP). Judg. 11:34. Synagoga rejoices in ceremonies, money, and flesh. Cod. 1179, fol. 74c. FIG. 21. II Kings 11:14–15. Jews misunderstand the Old Law, given to them by Jesus Christ. Cod. 1179, fol. 105b.

ing all three within one sign: Synagoga, holding a moneybag, stands at the head of a group of Jews, one of whom holds a bowl filled with coins (Fig. 20). (I will say more later about the intricate interplay of text and image on this folio.)

The Idol and the Heart of the Avaricious Man

Within the complex iconographic system of the *Bible moralisée,* then, Jewish greed is reconfigured through a variety of visual emblems as inextricably related to Jewish infidelity.[61] Also, a series of similar metaphoric condensations (of greed and idolatry, of avarice and the Antichrist) represents the nexus of Judaism, usury, and avarice not simply as non-Christian but as actively and willfully anti-Christian.

In the Latin version of the *Bible moralisée,* the paraphrase of II Kings 11 recounts, "David wrote to Joab a letter and sent it by the hand of Uriah saying, put Uriah in the hardest part of the battle and abandon him, that he might be struck down."[62] According to the commentary text, "This signifies Jesus Christ who gave to the Jews the Old Law, which they did not understand, and for which continual incomprehension they will be fittingly damned."[63] In the accompanying image, Christ, on the left, hands the tablets of the law to two Jews. Their "lack of understanding" is represented by an idiotic expression on the face of one who is drawn in profile. On the right, the "lack of understanding" is more actively portrayed: two Jews, one of whom holds a moneybag, pray to an idol (Fig. 21).

The practice of idolatry is, in fact, regularly associated in the manuscripts with the love of money, and Jews are particularly liable to being portrayed as idolaters.[64] Such an association is not grounded in dogma: although the extensive self-criticism of the Hebrew Scriptures and a few statements in the New Testament might be thought to provide textual support for calling Jews idolaters,[65] Augustine stated positively that Judaism was not to be considered idolatrous,[66] and subsequent Christian doctrine never revised this statement. In the early thirteenth century Alexander of Hales, for example, explicitly resolved in his *Summa* that Jewish rites were not to be considered the equivalent of idolatry.[67]

However, the association of Jews with idolatry persisted. John Chrysostom, eloquent as always on the subject, insisted that Judaism was as perfidious as paganism: "Even if there is no idol [in the synagogue], still demons do inhabit the place. . . . For, tell me, is not the dwelling place of demons a place of impiety even if no god's statue stands there? Here the slayers of Christ gather together, here the cross is driven out, here God is blasphemed, here the Father is ignored, here the Son is outraged, here the grace of the Spirit is rejected. . . . So the godlessness of the Jews and the pagans is on par."[68] Most likely, rhetoric associating Jews with idolatry continued to figure in high medieval Christian texts (in spite of the fact that Christian polemicists were often put on the defensive in the face of actual Jewish revulsion for any form of image worship)[69] because economic developments accorded the metaphoric significance of idolatry renewed resonance. In Eph. 5:5 and Col. 3:5, Paul identified an idolater as one who is covetous, and idolatry came to be defined as the mistaken worship of a thing in place of God. Adopting this approach in critiques of contemporary society, Alan of Lille recommended Eph. 5:5 as the theme for a sermon against avarice;[70] Peter the Chanter (glossing the same biblical verse) remarked that "just as idolatry renders to an idol the worship and service owed to God, an avaricious man, serving money rather than God, tenders to money and wealth the veneration owed to God";[71] and Innocent III compared a miser to an idolater.[72] Such statements are echoed throughout the commentary of the *Bible moralisée.* On folio 68a of the Latin manuscript, for example, the idolatry of the Israelites in Judg. 2:13 is treated as a figure for greed: "The Sons of Israel who dismissed God and adored the devil signify those who despair of God and adore cupidity and lust and scorn God."[73] In the commentary roundel, literal and symbolical renderings of the "adoration of cupidity" overlap: a bearded man with a peaked hat kneels and prays before a table on which rest various golden objects (Fig. 22).[74] The "avaricious nature" of the Jewish people (again, as ensconced in Christian polemics) was, then, conceived or represented in certain clerical circles as inescapably tainting their religion, worship of money being incompatible with true monotheism.

It is in the area of this kind of metaphoric condensation that the complex interplay of text and image—and the overall signifying techniques—of the *Bible moralisée* becomes most evident. The texts I have cited here—both those of contemporary theologians and many in the *Bible moralisée* itself—preserve the mediating term of a logical syllogism: Jews are avaricious; avarice is idolatry; therefore Jews are idolatrous. But in many images in the manuscripts, there is a passage from syllogism to visual metaphor, as the original associative inspiration is eliminated and figures (usually Jews) are depicted simply worshiping idols without any accompanying moneybags (Fig. 23).[75] With the mediating term of the syllogism omitted, an effect of motivation is established in the signs of usury, and the audience is free (or rather induced) to read both roundel and text as actually accusing contemporary Jews of practicing idolatry.[76]

This technique, this condensation, brings into play the entire range of connotations enlisted by the metaphors in question, and it permits the *Bible moralisée* to portray Jews as engaged in worse

FIG. 22 (TOP). Judg. 2:12–13. Those who despair of God adore cupidity. Cod. 1179, fol. 68a. FIG. 23. III Kings 18:26–29. Miscreants and heretics offer to their wicked God: idolatry unmediated by signs of money. Cod. 2554, fol. 53d.

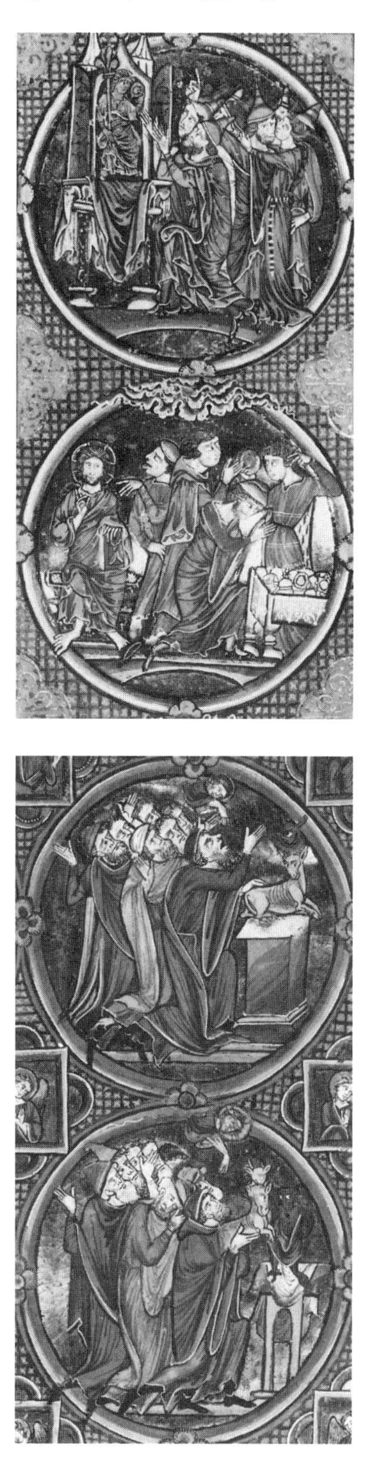

FIG. 24 (TOP). Judg. 6:28. Jews-usurers-infidels destroyed on Judgment Day. Cod. 1179, fol. 69d. FIG. 25. Judg. 9:3–4. Infidels honor Antichrist with greed and usury. Cod. 1179, fol. 71d.

offenses still than idolatry (Fig. 24). Gideon's destruction of a pagan idol (Judg. 6:28) is interpreted on folio 69d of the Latin manuscript as a figure for Jesus' triumph over the Antichrist, while the grove in which the idol was located is said to signify "Jewish usurers [or Jews and usurers] and infidels whom God will destroy on Judgment Day in eternal punishment."[77] The roundel echoes the implication conveyed by the text that Jews are accomplices of the Antichrist on account of their usury by placing a moneybag in the hand of a Jew to the right of the Antichrist. The action depicted, however, is not related to usury; rather, the Jews and the Antichrist are shown falling off to an unspecified location to the right, and the majority carry no sign related to usury. The same insinuation is apparent two folios later, again in the context of pagan idolatry (Fig. 25). Judges 9:3 records that the worst of Gideon's sons was chosen to be king by his brothers, who adorned him with gold and silver taken from the idols Baal and Berith. According to the moralization, those who chose Abimelech to be king "signify Jews and bad youths [?] who will make the Antichrist (born of the devil) their king." Those who despoiled the idols "signify bad people and infidels who will adore the Antichrist and honor him with greed and usury."[78] The commentary image, however, does not depict the practice of usury, specified in the text as the means by which infidels worship the Antichrist. Instead, it transfers emphasis from the exercise to the effects of greed: a horned, three-faced Antichrist is triumphantly enthroned beneath a crenelated trefoil arch. Three figures present the Antichrist with items associated with wealth (a coin, a moneybag, and a crown). The remaining three kneel in unmediated worship; one kisses the Antichrist's foot.

Folio 25va of Vienna ÖNB cod. 2554 contains another serious allegation concerning Jewish avarice (Fig. 26). It illustrates the episode that must be the fundamental text for any metaphoric conflation of idolatry and Jewish greed: the worship of the golden calf (Exod. 32:4). According to the commentary, the Hebrews who performed this act signify those who "form the devil and believe in a *boc* [he-goat] and adore it."[79] This time, the visual exegesis is conflating concepts articulated not in the accompanying commentary text but in moralizing texts by contemporary exegetes such as William of Auvergne, who explained that the prohibition against worshiping the golden calf was actually an injunction against avarice.[80] The roundel expands upon the commentary text by explicitly identifying both those who conjure/worship the devil and the vices through which such worship is manifested. The devil is portrayed as a horned goat upon an altar.[81] In front of the altar is a large group of worshipers. The central figure is a bearded Jew with a pointed cap, drawn in profile, holding a moneybag toward the goat.[82] Two other figures kiss the goat on its anus. Worship of the devil, then, is translated into the sin of avarice, signified by the moneybag and linked to the Jews.[83] The obscene gesture, in turn, equates these devil-worshiping Jews with contemporary heretics, accused of similar perversities.[84] In such images, the moneybag no longer signifies the specific practice of usury but instead has evolved into a sign for all the Jews' perfidies, arising from but going beyond their sinful attachment to money. However, the sign never would have entirely shed its original associations with usury, which would have enhanced the plausibility and immediacy of the scene by constituting a link with the more familiar activity of moneylending and the more traditional charge of avarice.

FIG. 26 (TOP). Exod. 32:4–6. Miscreants and heretics form the devil and adore the he-goat. Cod. 2554, fol. 25va. FIG. 27. Judg. 11:37. Synagoga seeks to linger in temporal wealth. Cod. 1179, fol. 74d.

New Signs for Old Sins: The Raven and the Frog

The extension of the sins of the Jews to encompass not only greed but also idolatry and devil worship is strengthened by means of still more inventive practices: entirely new iconographic devices are drawn from syllogistic textual relations in order to identify Jews with evil. Like the images of idolatry and devil worship, symbols of the raven and the frog (appearing, so far as I can tell, for the first time as significant emblems in medieval art) attain special meaning within the manuscripts, and not only reinforce established images regarding Jewish greed but also impose new associations and force new readings of traditional signs.

Figure 27, for example, reproduces a roundel (folio 74d of Vienna ÖNB cod. 1179) that follows the already cited reference to Synagoga's attachment to money. The daughter of Jephtah is again held to signify Synagoga, who "desired and sought that her life be prolonged, because she wished once more to linger in temporal wealth."[85] (The Latin word used for wealth, *lucrum,* is also a technical term for interest on a loan.) The commentary roundel depicts Synagoga handing a moneybag and a dark bird—a crow or raven—to two Jews. The commentary text does not explain the introduction here of this bird, but contemporary texts indicate that crows were associated with greed because of certain habits attributed to them in medieval nature lore. For example, William of Rennes included the following comment in his gloss on Raymond de Penaforte's *Decretum* (ca. 1241–50): "Cupidity is the desire for riches based not on need but on curiosity . . . just as a magpie or a crow is enticed by coins, which they discover and hide away."[86] This piece of lore about crows is also invoked metaphorically in contemporary works, such as Robert de Courson's comment that overworldly abbots "bring together ravens, that is, other usurers like themselves, that they might effect similar contracts."[87]

However, the sign of the raven, particularly when depicted in conjunction with Synagoga and Jewish figures, could hardly fail to connote something far more sinister still than usury, for the raven was linked in a general way with evil in many Christian exegetical texts. In his *Liber de Noe et Arca* Ambrose concluded that the raven who failed to return to Noah's ark after having been sent in search of land was a symbol of evil,[88] and Hilary of Poitiers compared the raven to a sinner.[89] The interpretation of the Flood in the *Glossa ordinaria* held that the raven signified the "dirtiness of earthly cupidity,"[90] and when Thomas of Chobham wanted to criticize his contemporaries he thundered, "They do not make their paschal meal in the church at the table of the Lord, but they feast with the raven on the foul cadaver."[91] According to the *Bestiary* of Guillaume le Clerc, the night raven "indicates Jews who rejected God . . . [and] are in darkness / And see not the truth,"[92] and animal fabulists employed the raven as a sign for the devil.[93] Such associations provide depth to the symbol of the raven, and would have informed the viewers' reading of the iconography and affected their attitudes toward its surface referent, usury.

One last innovation used to align Jews with usury again, like the raven, transforms a syllogistic relation in the text into visual metaphor, but in this case the textual inspiration is provided by the *Bible moralisée* itself (Fig. 28). In a text from folio 2vb of Vienna ÖNB cod. 2554 (already cited), Cain's offering of the fruits of the harvest is held to signify the offerings of the Jews "of confiscations and of cupidity" ("de fraimture et de couvoitise"). The commentary roundel depicts a Jew lifting a toad or frog toward God, who rejects it with a downward wave. This unusual image of a toad, an animal not commonly accorded symbolic function in medieval art or discussed in the moralizing bestiaries,[94] may be understood by consulting a text located on another folio of the *Bible moralisée*. According to the interpretation of the dietary restrictions imposed by Moses (Lev. 11:20–31), the toad signifies "great usurers" (*magnos feneratores*).

FIG. 28. Gen. 4:3–5. The Jews make offering to God of "confiscations and cupidity." Cod. 2554, fol. 2vb.

The same interpretation appears on folio 29b of the French manuscript, whose more elaborate commentary text reveals the logic behind the symbolism: "The frog signifies the usurer who is swollen with usury and greed."[95] Thus, the manuscript creates in one text a new verbal signifier for the concept of usury, which is then translated elsewhere into an image. But although the symbol might originally have derived from a specific attribute of frogs, the omission of the explanatory detail from the image allows it to convey implications beyond its original inspiration. For if frogs are not frequently represented in medieval art, they did begin to make their appearance in a certain literary format in the late twelfth century—the exemplum. In his *Dialogue of Miracles* Caesarius of Heisterbach repeats an exemplum about a toad that was found on the altar of Jews, who, it is implied, worshiped the creature.[96] Nor were stories associating toads with devil worship limited to fictional or instructional genres. Joshua Trachtenberg recounts that in the fourteenth century an episcopal investigation alleged that a Jew placed the devil, in the form of a toad, in a box together with a Host in order to harm the consecrated wafer.[97] In 1233 Gregory IX issued a bull authorizing a crusade against German heretics that stated: "When a novice is admitted and first enters the school of these [heretics] a sort of frog, or as many call it, a toad, appears before him. Some of them kiss it disgracefully on its posterior."[98] The appearance of the toad in the hands of a Jew rejected by Christ, then, would have been read by the medieval audience in the light of such current references, and necessarily played into circulating conceptions of Jews as heretics and devil worshipers.[99]

In the Company of Thieves: Christian Cupidity

At this point I must reiterate that Jews are by no means the only figures in the *Bible moralisée* to carry moneybags, to worship lucre, or to go against the will of God on account of greed. Christians are portrayed doing all these things, and in just as much variety and with even greater frequency than Jews.[100] There are solid reasons for this. The theological attacks on moneylending did not, of course, cleanse medieval Christendom of the practice: the rapidly developing commercial economy was predicated upon the availability of borrowed capital; indeed, many clerics as well as Christian laymen were deeply implicated in that economy.[101] Moneylending, then, is not condemned because it is exclusively or primarily a "Jewish" activity; rather, because moneylending is condemned, it becomes in the sign system of the *Bible moralisée* (as in many contemporary theological works) a "Jewish" activity. The regularity with which Jews are associated with money and greed in the images of the manuscripts serves to essentialize the Jewish (for which read: un-Christian) nature of such activities. Similarly, just as greed and usury are not the exclusive purview of Jews, so too idolatrous and devil-worshiping Jews have many partners in both the images and the texts of the *Bible moralisée.*

Clerics are often depicted as involved in Jewish moneylending. For example, the Bible text on folio 82d of the Latin manuscript discusses the "Sodomites" who fled to the rocks and mountains (Judg. 20:45).[102] According to the commentary text, the Sodomites "signify infidels who left God and are dispersed through the world and live in diverse places among Christians."[103] The "infidels" are clearly identified in the roundel as Jews: one is bearded, one is not; both wear tall, pointed caps. The Jew on the left takes a shirt from a cleric; another seated, tonsured cleric leans

FIG. 29 (TOP). Judg. 20:45. Clerics patronize and assist Jewish moneylenders. Cod. 1179, fol. 82d. FIG. 30. Job 14:17–19. A Jew and a monk exchange a moneybag; the monk rejects the Gospels. Cod. 1179, fol. 152a.

over a counting board. Two clerics stand before the Jew on the right. One hands an object to the Jew in exchange for a bowl of money; the other records the transaction on a table with a stylus (Fig. 29).[104]

Clerics were, in fact, frequently associated with Jewish moneylending. Many were regular customers. In addition to the condemnations of pawning Church goods (discussed previously), ecclesiastics are castigated for allowing Church landed property to fall into the hands of Jews.[105] In 1206, Philip Augustus forbade the pledging, without express permission, of Church lands to Jews in security for loans.[106] Among the most deeply implicated were the monasteries: in 1216 a council at Melun ordered priors to cease borrowing from Jews, and in 1219 Philip Augustus stipulated that no monk, canon regular, or cleric of any order could borrow from a Jew without a superior's permission.[107] The widespread indebtedness of monastic foundations is hinted at on folio 152a of Vienna ÖNB cod. 1179, in which a depiction of a Jew and a monk exchanging a moneybag is used to illustrate the text "the mind of the just removed from justice to guilt" (Fig. 30).[108]

One segment of Christian society, identified on folio 65c of Vienna ÖNB cod. 1179, is more liable still to be seen as supporting Jewish moneylending. The commentary to Josh. 9:3–15 states that "lying Jewish usurers [or Jews and usurers] tell princes and prelates that they are better than they are, so that thus their life [*sic*] might be preserved unharmed."[109] The depiction of the deception perpetrated by the "Jewish usurers" is very subtle (Fig. 31). On the left stand a young bishop and an equally young beardless prince carrying a fleur-de-lis scepter;[110] their youthful appearances might be designed to indicate their naïveté. Both figures lean toward the usurers and gesture sympathetically. The "deceiving usurers" (as they are labeled by a scroll) stand in a crowd on the right; their appearances vary somewhat. The one in the front has a very short beard and a rounded or slightly peaked hat; he carries a moneybag and bends humbly in the direction of the prince and the prelate. Paralleling the biblical illustration above, in which "Gabaonites" wear torn clothes and old shoes in an effort to appear poor, the clothes of this foremost usurer and that of the usurer directly behind him are tattered; both figures are barefoot. By contrast, the usurer in the back (the one carrying the scroll inscribed "feneratores decipi . . .") has a longer beard, is wearing shoes, and is well dressed in an intact robe and cloak. The image seems to imply that "pretending to be better" is understood here as "pretending to be poor" (signified by the torn clothing), as "pretending to be humble or pure" (the customary connotation of bare feet in the manuscripts), and as "hiding their Jewishness" (indicated by the shorter beard and cap of the figure in front). Since a Jew could hardly hide his religion from his prince in thirteenth-century France, this last imputed pretense must be metaphoric: the "Jewishness" that the moneylenders attempt to obscure is the sinful nature of their profits, their own moral turpitude, or perhaps both.

Two aspects of this commentary are particularly interesting. First, it highlights the ambiguous status of moneylending in thirteenth-century Christendom. In implying that usurers presented an attractive, or at any rate not automatically repugnant, front to at least some members of the higher echelons of lay and clerical society, the text acknowledges the potential benefits conferred by and the potential respect accorded to moneylenders.[111] It seems that in certain circles moneylending had a neutral value unacceptable to the more extreme anti-usury clerics. By refocusing attention on the "Jewish" nature of moneylenders (and, again, it is difficult to determine whether this applies just to Jewish moneylenders or to Christian moneylenders as well), the Joshua commentary repudiates this neutrality, enlisting the negative connotations accorded "Jewishness" in Christian polemic to label lenders and their profession as inherently perfidious and contaminated.[112] (The commentary also, tactfully, attributes princely toleration of such perfidy to misunderstanding rather than to conscious indifference to spiritual mores.)

FIG. 31. Josh. 9:3–15. Lying Jew-usurers tell princes and prelates that they are better than they are. Cod. 1179, fol. 65c.

Second, this commentary seems to assume that Jewish usurers have no inherent right to safety, suggesting that if they had not deceived princes and prelates, they would not have been preserved unharmed. Although such an assumption runs counter to all practical experience, it presumably reflects the wishes of those same Parisian theologians who formulated the uncompromising opposition to Jewish lending echoed in the *Bible moralisée,* and who vociferously objected to the princes' protection of and profiting from Jewish lending.

The close connection between Jewish moneylenders and secular princes captured in this commentary is well attested in contemporary sources. The "peculiar" relationship between the French kings and regional princes and "their" Jews mentioned in the introduction[113] was largely predicated upon the Jews' financial usefulness to their overlords. This usefulness stemmed jointly from the profitability and vulnerability of the Jews' moneylending enterprises: in exchange for recording and enforcing the Jews' contracts, the lords were able to tallage Jewish communities almost at will.[114] Through this rhythm of enforcement and exploitation, secular lords essentially became "silent partners" in the Jews' financial activities—a fact that was by no means unrecognized by contemporary observers. Peter the Chanter remarked in his *Verbum Abbreviatum* that usurers "are now the close companions [chamber servants] of princes and prelates. . . . they are both coffers and leeches of princes, because all things they shall have sucked up, they vomit into the fisc."[115] Jacques de Vitry reiterated his master's opinion, stating that kings were thieves' accomplices because they favor Jews and usurers.[116] Thomas of Chobham expressed wonder that the Church allowed princes to profit from Jewish usury.[117]

The Joshua commentary consequently may be seen as part of a broader polemical campaign against princely-Jewish cooperation, for the proponents of such views placed increasing pressure on secular authorities to suppress Jewish moneylending.[118] This pressure was received at the Capetian court with varying reactions. Philip Augustus's policy toward Jewish lending was notoriously erratic. He expelled Jews from the Île-de-France in 1182, ostensibly because of their usury, only to readmit them in 1198.[119] In 1206 and 1219 he issued two different edicts on Jewish usury that limited the amount of interest charged and attempted to minimize the damage done to Christian society.[120] Nevertheless, these edicts still amounted to governmental sanction of Jewish usury: a decree issued in this period ended with a directive instructing royal officials to enforce Jewish loans.[121] Royal involvement in Jewish moneylending was withdrawn only upon the 1223 accession of Louis VIII, who in that same year issued an ordinance that constituted a radical break from the past. The driving intention of this ordinance (known as the *Stabilimentum*) remains elusive, but one clear effect was to end all royal and princely enforcement of Jewish usury in Louis's realm.[122] The hostility of Louis IX toward Jewish usury is so well documented that there is little need to detail it here.[123]

Why were these later Capetians so much stricter concerning Jewish usury than were the popes themselves? The forceful and polemically dexterous critique of princely involvement in Jewish moneylending presented in this royal *Bible moralisée* manuscript is an important and heretofore unnoticed piece of evidence for this question. Kenneth Stow has recently argued that in addition to various political considerations, the anti-usury measures of Philip Augustus and other lay rulers were motivated by genuine concern about the purity of their realms and their own souls.[124] Such concern is certainly sanctioned by the program of the *Bible moralisée:* in addition to the overall and consistent conflation of usury with Judaism, perfidy, and allied abominations, the manuscripts pointedly and graphically illustrate the threat to the kings' claim to be virtuous rulers and to their own chances for salvation brought about by their tolerance of usury. Just to the left of the roundel containing the "lying Jewish usurers," discussed earlier, is one showing a king (holding a calf and a sheaf of wheat) and a Jew (holding a moneybag) being ordered into hell by Christ; the devil stones them on their way down. Although the text explicitly censures the characters for disparate offenses ("bad princes who retain the tithes of Holy Church and bad usurers who hide all their goods"), the proximity of the two figures to each other as well as the image's proximity to the text criticizing princes for tolerating Jewish usury cannot be overlooked. The overall effect on the reader/viewer is to subsume all the characters and practices—Jews and their usury, which was often criticized for leading to the Church's loss of tithe income; princes and their greed—into one set and to identify this set as damnable and damned.

This and other images of money-clutching kings descending into hell or being punished at the side of usurers and/or Jews[125] suggest the incorporation of a conscious political program into the *Bible moralisée.* Clearly it was assumed that kings and princes were not supporting Jewish usurers out of any deep-seated affection for them. The many illustrations of Jewish perfidy and damnation, coupled with basic Christian dogma predicating salvation on belief in Christ, would have conditioned the viewer to accept the Jews' doom as unquestioned. It must be assumed that this acceptance of the damnation of the Jews would then serve to heighten the fear and revulsion inspired at being depicted as partnered with them. The power of the *Bible moralisée* roundels showing crowned figures falling into hell with Jews lies in the fact that they alter a standard image in only one respect, but in just that respect best designed to gain the attention of a proud and pious ruler. Although no single text can possibly be held to account adequately for highly complex decisions, the "new phase" in Capetian Jewish policy inaugurated by Louis VIII and noted by so many historians[126] becomes considerably more comprehensible in light of the harsh and uniquely forcible indictment of Jewish lending conveyed by this work of art made (I believe) for that king.

FIG. 32. Ruth 1:4–16. Those who follow Holy Church (on the right) and those who reject and leave her (on the left). Cod. 1179, fol. 83a.

The Threat to Christendom

If Christians of various kinds are implicated in usury, then (according to the iconography of the *Bible moralisée*) they must necessarily be implicated in the still more evil correlates of usury—idolatry, devil worship, and worship of the Antichrist. A catalogue of all the images in the *Bible moralisée* linking Christians to such activities would be impossibly long as well as tediously repetitive. The incompatibility of Christianity and avarice is succinctly summarized in an image on folio 83a of the Latin manuscript. The text, commenting loosely on Ruth 1:4–16, divides all Christendom into two kinds of men: those who follow Holy Church and those who reject and leave her.[127] One of the figures abandoning the church is represented by a man offering a moneybag to an idol; another kisses the anus of a cat (Fig. 32).

Such images and the mental economies underlying them help explain a striking but somewhat perplexing contemporary phenomenon. The visual links forged in the *Bible moralisée* between usury and the abandonment of the Church, inspired by the internal logic of the iconography, echo an attitude that was increasingly gaining ground among thirteenth-century theologians: the tendency to associate usury with heresy.

Robert de Courson, as always the most severe against usury, called usury and heresy the two greatest evils of his age, and he opined in his *Summa* that usurers ought to be denounced like heretics.[128] The treatise *Contra Amaurianos* called those university sectarians *pecunie cupidi,* and Etienne de Bourbon asserted that because Manichaeans believed their *perfecti* could dismiss any sin, they indulged in usury with impunity.[129] During the Albigensian Crusade, a White League was formed to combat the dual sins of usury and heresy; anti-Cathar polemics regularly accused their *credentes* of usury.[130] These perceptions were eventually incorporated into legislation: the Council of Vienne decreed in 1311 that the failure to condemn usury was to be punished like heresy.[131] Most of these texts, however, do not elaborate upon the reasons that usury was suddenly associated with heresy. The images of the *Bible moralisée* make explicit the logic implicit in such an equation: if the avarice from which usury stemmed was equivalent to misdirected worship, then its practitioners had to be considered enemies of Christ. The implications of this train of thought would be especially ominous for Jews, who were inextricably associated with usury in the writings of so many thirteenth-century ecclesiastics.[132]

The Power of Visual Metaphor

The images described here, when taken together and read as part of a coherent symbolic system, construct a creative and overwhelmingly hostile representation of what were, after all, common and even ubiquitous financial practices. They forcefully align moneylending, which was practiced extensively by both Jews and Christians, with Jewry and Judaism; they intimate that it hurts Christian society not just in practical but also in spiritual ways; they suggest that Jewish usury stems from and is inextricably associated with the worst sins against Christ; and they insist that both Jews and those who support them in their endeavors are doomed. These insinuations are made by repeatedly displacing onto the Jew or condensing within the figure of the Jew those religious, moral, or economic activities and concepts considered most reprehensible by Christian theologians, and such displacements and condensation are effected by recourse (in the text and images) to a wide array of signifying practices—synonym, synecdoche, metonymy, and metaphor.

It is possible that such images represent a conscious attempt to combat vice among Christians—and more particularly among the royal and noble patrons of these manuscripts—by linking usury and greed to activities incompatible with Christian salvation in a vivid and frightening way. The very fact that the displacement of the negative effects of moneylending onto Jews had to be overdetermined through recourse to a host of unprecedented signs supports the conclusion that these relations were *not* self-evident or widespread; there may therefore have been a perceived need for a self-consciously polemical treatise. This approach would accord closely with the thesis propounded by R. I. Moore in his *Formation of a Persecuting Society.*[133] Moore argued that the increasing repression of Jews, lepers, heretics, and other "deviant" groups in high medieval Europe was not perpetrated by irrational masses but was, rather, promoted by the authorities as an essential element in the construction of a unified and cohesive high medieval culture.

However, I think that it is more likely that the demonization of usury in the *Bible moralisée* was the product of a considerably less self-conscious process, and that its extreme anti-Judaism grew out of a combination of semantic, pastoral, and social considerations. Early thirteenth-century exegesis, and especially the Parisian biblical moral school—to which the *Bible moralisée,* as its very name implies, is clearly related—had a double project. First, it endeavored to extract from the Bible teachings relevant to contemporary situations; it did so by applying sophisticated rhetorical devices to the biblical text and constructing elaborate chains of association around key terms. Second, it promoted the dissemination of the meaning thus extracted among the broader lay public through the formulation and promulgation of effective preaching techniques.[134] Among the most successful of these didactic strategies was the exemplum—the illustrative anecdote.[135] These exempla converted abstract theological concepts into concrete terms, and they employed the characters and vocabulary of the markets and streets familiar both to the lay listeners and to the urban preachers themselves. The fact that numerous visual signs in the manuscripts seem to be inspired by exempla confirms the impression that the *Bible moralisée* was created by clerics trained in and committed to popular preaching. But this process must surely have had a two-way effect: as the preachers sought out situations and figures that could adequately embody theological notions, their views of both the figures and the notions in question would have been subtly modified.

The proliferation of moneylending—a form of exchange to

which the conservative theologians were deeply opposed but in the face of which they were seemingly impotent—lent itself to just such a semantic process. In their search for means by which to understand and describe an economy that differed considerably from that portrayed in the Bible, the theologians constructed metaphors and associative chains that, although artificial, were not necessarily arbitrary—they made use of both traditional exegetical and widespread popular conceptions. In turn, these chains of association were represented as natural and motivated to the lay public through their expression in vivid and striking metaphors, just as the redactors of the *Bible moralisée* converted their explicitly syllogistic texts into vivid and striking visual signs. R. I. Moore rather despairingly called the kind of linkage of Jews, usurers, and various demonic and anti-Christian activities such as we have seen in the *Bible moralisée* a "tangled nightmare of association and assumption."[136] To attribute, as Moore does, such rich and evocative imagery primarily to fear and confusion seems unsatisfactory. If clerics trained to categorize, classify, and clarify presided over the creation of what seems to be a polemical tangle, it may well be that this "tangle" is actually the logical outcome of an emerging tendency, from the later twelfth century on, for theological concepts to be articulated in a new rhetorical form—the lay sermon. Moreover, the way the aggregate images of the *Bible moralisée* were read may well have differed from the way they were intended to have been read, and these manuscripts may thus help reveal the means by which some anti-Jewish topoi came to proliferate in the High Middle Ages. The power of the *Bible moralisée* imagery stems from the success of its metaphoric condensation; the images veil the elaborate intellectual processes that went into their development and engage the emotions of the viewer in a very direct way, taking on immediate force and commanding novel readings. The depiction of the goat worship described earlier (Fig. 26), by translating metaphoric references to the devil into literal terms, inevitably evokes other accusations against the Jews of devil worship and sorcery, and re-creates the rage and fear such accusations inspired. Depictions of Jews worshiping idols come to be read as illustrations of actual perfidious practices, independent of any allegorical significance. Images such as these could have been enlisted to justify, perhaps on occasion even facilitated, the hysterical anti-Jewish accusations that had already been used and were again to be used to attempt to drive the Jews from Christian lands. Figure 33 shows an image of a goat being consumed by flames from folio 37d of the Latin manuscript; it closely follows the commentary roundel that portrays Jews worshiping the devil in the form of a goat. Given the impossibility of reading the image of the burning goat entirely in isola-

FIG. 33. Exod. 32:20. A goat consumed by flames. Elsewhere on the same folio the goat was depicted being worshiped by Jews. Cod. 1179, fol. 37d.

tion from the previous image of his Jewish worshipers, this roundel seems an ominous reflection of actual anti-Jewish persecutions, and suggests that the resonances of the new semantic practices were not always confined to the illustrated page or to the spoken word.

THREE: THE PEOPLE OF THE BOOK

Old Law, New Rituals, and the Word of God

They hung Nicanor's head and right hand, which they [sic] had insolently extended, in front of Jerusalem.

(I MACC. 7:47)

This signifies that in a church a figure of the Crucified One is raised up in front of the choir, as a sign of His victory. And Jews are permitted to live among Christians in testimony of the faith, because of the books of the law which they bear in the captivity in which they are because of their sins.[1]

I open my discussion of the approach to the Old Law in the *Bible moralisée* with this commentary text from the Latin manuscript for two reasons. A near-verbatim citation of the traditional justification for allowing Jews to exist unharmed within Christendom, the second sentence of the commentary cogently encapsulates the double-edged attitude toward Jewish law that prevailed throughout the Middle Ages. However, in juxtaposing this traditional text with a novel one—a description and explication of an element of church architecture—this commentary also forces reconsideration of the meaning and relevance of what was already a clichéd formulation. My goal in this chapter is not to establish whether the *Bible moralisée* manuscripts under consideration are predominantly sympathetic or antipathetic toward the Old Law, or even merely to determine where on the spectrum of possible attitudes toward the Old Law they lie. Rather, I am interested in exploring the various issues with which the Old Law became intertwined and the various circumstances and forms in which it is invoked, in order to understand how the matter of the Old Law resonated in the specific context out of which the manuscripts sprung.

The Theological Background: Jewish Law in Christian Thought

From its very beginnings, Christianity was in a large part defined by its attitude toward Mosaic law and the Hebrew Scriptures.[2] Like the Jews, and in contrast to Gentile pagans, the earliest followers of Jesus and all subsequent orthodox Christians accepted the divine origins and absolute authority of the books of Moses. The historical truth of the events recorded in the Hebrew Scriptures was affirmed, and the patriarchs, judges, and prophets of the Hebrews were revered as righteous and believed to have a share in the world to come. Early Christian theologians defended the sanctity of the Hebrew Scriptures against both pagans and Manichaean and Marcionite heretics.[3]

This positive regard for the Hebrew Scriptures was balanced by a complementary aspect of Christian theology, which asserted that although given by God, the Law was no longer to be literally observed in the Christian era. Following ideas formulated in the Epistles of Paul, patristic and subsequent Christian writers held that the "Old Testament" period of a religion of works was replaced upon the incarnation of Christ by a period of righteousness through grace. According to this doctrine, the Law was given to the Chosen People to prepare them to receive the New Law of the Gospels. The ceremonies of the Mosaic law were henceforth to be interpreted spiritually: physical circumcision, for example, was replaced with "circumcision of the heart," as realized in the Church through the sacrament of baptism.[4] The oxen, calves, and goats of the Levitical sacrifices were now replaced by the Body of Christ in the form of the eucharistic Host on the Christian altar.

This double-edged (or, in Gilbert Dahan's terminology, "bipolar")[5] attitude toward the Hebrew Scriptures and Mosaic law naturally influenced, though it by no means rigidly dictated, medieval Christian approaches to Judaism and its contemporary adherents. On the one hand, the Jews' status as living testimony to the authenticity of scriptural events guaranteed them continued tolerance within Christendom.[6] In what became the most influential formulation of Christian doctrine regarding the Jews, Augustine stated that they should be allowed to live among Christians because they preserved the original text of Holy Scripture and because their very existence served as proof and living reminder of the actuality of scriptural events.[7] On the other hand, the principle that Mosaic law had been abrogated by the coming of Christ led to condemnation of postbiblical Judaism, which insisted on the ongoing validity of the letter of the law: Augustine also required that Jews be maintained in a subjugated state as testimony to the fact that they had lost spiritual legitimacy and all claim to temporal authority.[8]

At the time of the making of the *Bible moralisée,* the basic contours of this Christian approach to Judaism still prevailed. Augustine's justification for tolerance continued to define thirteenth-century discussions of issue, his terminology permeating works of law, polemic, and theology. Augustine is paraphrased, for example, in (among many other texts) a letter of Bernard of Clairvaux promoting the Second Crusade (1146),[9] the article "Iudei" in Peter the Chanter's *Summa Abel,*[10] the *Constitutio pro Judeis* of Innocent III (1199),[11] the *Contra Perfidiam Judeorum* of Peter of Blois (ca. 1200),[12] and the *Summa confessorum* of Thomas of Chobham (ca. 1216).[13] The first chapter of the Titulus *De Iudaeis et Paganis* in Alexander of Hales's *Summa* asks "whether Jews are to be tolerated"; it is concluded that Jews are to be allowed to live and to dwell among Christians because "we received the Old Law from the Jews, [and] because Christ came from that seed." [14]

However, to say that Augustine's approach to Jews and Judaism was adopted by most medieval theologians is not to say that thinking on these subjects was monolithic throughout the Middle Ages. The discussions regarding Jews and Judaism in the works of medieval Christians, even when staying within Augustine's basic framework, reveal substantial differences in emphasis.[15] Jewish insistence on maintaining the Old Law could be attributed to ignorance, to insanity, or to willful malice.[16] The rituals of the Old Law could be viewed with respect, as honorable if outdated artifacts, or with revulsion.[17] To counter claims, whether Jewish or Christian, of the continuing validity of the Old Law, some church fathers—Origen is an early example—mixed acknowledgment of the historicity of the letter with mockery of the absurdity of many of the legal precepts, pointing to impossibilities or contradictions in their literal observance.[18] In an extreme statement of the spiritual interpretation, Ralph of Flaix's commentary on Leviticus (twelfth century) denied any historical reality or social or moral value to many of the Mosaic precepts. Ralph's work became the standard commentary on Leviticus for much of the Middle Ages, and was regularly used by school and university masters to supplement the *Glossa ordinaria* on Leviticus.[19]

Antique Emblems and the Question of the New

An essential component of the Augustinian justification, historians often assert, is an enduring belief that Judaism was a static and sterile relic, unchanged and unchangeable since the coming of Christ rendered literal observance of the Old Law obsolete.[20] Art historians have echoed this approach in identifying the symbols of Judaism (when they have studied them at all) as fixed signs derived from or reflecting Judaism's ancient biblical past. The traditional use of the pointed hat to signify Jewish figures in Gothic art, for example, has been explained by that garment's (alleged) status as the ancestral headgear of medieval Jews.[21] A similar line of thought—that is, that differentiating clothing for Jews had an ancient, even biblical, origin—permeates the canon of the Fourth Lateran Council prescribing an identifying badge: "We decree that [Jews] of both sexes . . . be distinguished in public from other people by a difference of dress, since this was also enjoined on them by Moses." [22]

Likewise, the two other well-established emblems associated with Jewish law in medieval art—the scroll and the calf—have been read as symbolic of Judaism's antiquity. The scroll, which is generally depicted in the hands of prophets or other Old Testament figures, has been explained as representing prophetic words;[23] its meaning could also be extended to encompass the entire Mosaic law,[24] or to serve as an indication of venerable antiquity.[25] The symbols of a calf (or sometimes a lamb or a goat) and/or a knife, held either separately or together in a sacrificial context, have normally been taken to refer to the sacrifices of the Old Testament Hebrews.[26]

However, in the past few decades some historians have begun to assert that the medieval Christian view of Judaism changed in response to perceived Jewish changes during the course of the Middle Ages. The most notable of these is Jeremy Cohen, who in 1982 published his now famous and highly controversial thesis that influential members of the Dominican and Franciscan orders—the friars—were responsible for articulating a new theology regarding the Jews.[27] According to Cohen, the friars' study of medieval Jewish texts led them to conclude that medieval rabbinic Judaism's (perceived) privileging of the Talmud over the Old Testament was a deviation from tradition tantamount to heresy, and thus invalidated the Augustinian adage that Jews merited toleration within Christendom because they guarded the original text of the Hebrew Scriptures. Although Cohen's thesis has been subject to considerable criticism,[28] it continues to influence discussions of the question.[29]

The *Bible moralisée* can contribute to a reconsideration of the issue of high medieval Christian attitudes toward the Old Law in general, and of Cohen's thesis in particular, in two significant ways. While most texts dealing with the Law reflect traditional doctrine, others powerfully, albeit ambiguously, convey the impression that a new attitude, if not a new ideology, regarding Jewish law was being articulated in Paris in the first decades of the thirteenth century.[30] In addition, the references to the Old Law in the text and images of the *Bible moralisée* are consistently interwoven with a myriad of other motifs, and thereby help to situate the broader context in which some of the intensified anti-Jewish animus and (perhaps) novel anti-Jewish themes were being developed.

The Old Law in Text and Image

As one might expect, given the centrality of the Old Law in Christian doctrine, the issue of the Old Law permeates the texts and images of the *Bible moralisée.* The scroll of the law is, in fact, the second most common object (after the moneybag) connected with Jews in the commentary roundels, and other familiar symbols of the Old Law, such as sacrificial animals and implements, also regularly appear.

Both the positive and the negative dimensions of the traditional theological approach outlined here are reflected in the text of the *Bible moralisée.* In a clear assertion of the divine origin and continuing sacredness of the Old Law, to be expected in an exegetical work redacted by a student or master of *sacre pagine,* the commentary to Exod. 34:29 states that God's bestowal of two rays of light on Moses' head as the prophet descended Mount Sinai signifies that Jesus Christ gave the two laws to his prelates for speaking to his people.[31] In the French manuscript, Jesus is shown handing the two laws to two bishops: a codex in his right hand represents the New Law, and a long scroll already held by one of the bishops symbolizes the Old Law (Fig. 34). Although this image seems on the surface a straightforward and still affirmative rendition of the generally beneficent textual commentary, I shall argue later that the illustration subtly undermines any philo-Judaic reading that potentially might be drawn from this text.

The other and balancing component of orthodox Christian thought regarding the Law—the abrogation of the Mosaic precepts—is similarly taken for granted in the *Bible moralisée.* However, there is considerable variation in tone in articulating even this most formulaic of concepts. Occasionally the abrogated Old Law is treated with considerable respect. For example, the Latin commentary to Deut. 34:5–6 states: "Moses who died on the mountain and was buried signifies the death of the Old Law, which Christians bury with honor."[32] The rather odd juxtaposition of reverence and dismissal in this text is perpetuated in the commentary medallion: Holy Church personified presides over a group of clerics tenderly lowering the lid onto Synagoga's casket (Fig. 35).[33]

But far more often undiluted hostility dominates. In text after text, the Law's obsolescence is attributed not to its honorable expiration or to an orderly passing of the baton but to its own inherent aridity, deformity, and ugliness. The French Gen. (29:28–30) commentary states that just as Jacob left his old wife (Lea) and took a young one (Rachel), so Jesus Christ rejected the Old Law and took Holy Church, who is young and beautiful.[34] Identifying Rachel with Holy Church and Lea with Synagoga are entirely standard interpretations, obviously related to the topos of the Church as the bride of Christ.[35] However, the *Bible moralisée* heightens the anti-Jewish tenor of the commentary by altering the biblical text, since according to the Vulgate, Jacob did not desert Lea, who continued to bear him children. In the Latin *Bible moralisée* manuscript, the contrast between Church and Synagoga is made even more pointed. The biblical paraphrase dwells on the physical afflictions of Lea, who is described as "sore-eyed"; the commentary explains that Synagoga is stained in one eye by incredulity and in the other by envy.[36]

FIG. 34 (TOP). Exod. 34:29. Jesus Christ presents the two laws to his prelates. Cod. 2554, fol. 26va. FIG. 35. Deut. 34:5–6. Christians bury the Old Law with honor. Cod. 1179, fol. 62c.

FIG. 36 (TOP). Num. 13:24–25. Jews bear but do not understand the Law. Cod. 1179, fol. 56b. FIG. 37. Exod. 34:29. Jesus presents the two laws to his prelates, but only the "Christian" form of the Law is depicted. Cod. 1179, fol. 39c.

If the entire gamut of emotions toward the Old Law is reflected in the *Bible moralisée,* its attitude toward Jews' relation to that Law is unremittingly hostile. This emerges, for example, in the interpretation of the Israelite explorers who brought back a bunch of grapes from the land of Canaan (Num. 13:24). The commentary text acknowledges Jews' guardianship of Scripture while condemning their mistaken approach in quite traditional terms: "The Jews [signified by the older of the explorers] bear the commandments of Jesus Christ, but nevertheless are ignorant of their signification."[37] In the accompanying illustration, however, the "ignorance" is rendered as willful malice. Closely paralleling the biblical illustration above it, the commentary roundel portrays a bust of Jesus emerging from an open codex that hangs from a stick resting on the shoulders of two distinct groups of people. Barefoot Christians, on the right, carry the back end of the stick, from which position they have a clear view of the codex. The Jews are on the left of the roundel, leading the way; their faces, consequently, are turned away from the codex, which they cannot see. However, in contrast to the elder explorer in the biblical roundel above, their eyes are wide open, suggesting a refusal rather than an inability to perceive the truth, and their expressions are grim and menacing, compounding the insolence implied in the fact that they turn their backs toward Jesus (Fig. 36). The parallel illustration in the French manuscript follows this implication to its logical conclusion: taking its cue from the interlinear rather than the marginal gloss,[38] it depicts Jews and Christians flanking a crucified Jesus.

The People of the Law

In fact, condemnation of the Jews' error regarding the Law imparts a kind of unity and coherence to the manuscripts' apparently contradictory judgments concerning the Old Law's value. Even what I have termed the more gracious or beneficent texts share one inescapable detail: they discuss the Old Law in isolation from its latter-day adherents, ignoring or denying Jews' relation to it. The honorable burial of Synagoga as the Old Law was effected and viewed exclusively by prelates; no Jews were present. The Exod. 34:29 commentary illustration depicts Jesus giving the two laws directly to his prelates without any intermediaries, effacing even the limited historical role usually accorded the Jews. Moreover, in the parallel illustration in the Latin manuscript, the Old Law is not portrayed as an entity separate from the New. Instead, the essential unity and inseparability of the two laws are underscored by the depiction of Holy Church seated on a single open book—the form of the Law associated with Christians, not with Jews (Fig. 37).

A New Approach?

The eradication of Jews from depictions of the giving of the Law bears distinctly ominous implications and brings us back to Jeremy Cohen's thesis, since it would seem to undermine Augustine's grounds for countenancing Jews within Christian lands. Nevertheless, although the textual commentaries discussed so far are hostile enough toward Jews and the Law, they don't, in the end, present anything other than the standard doctrine that the Old Law was incapable of securing salvation for its devotees. However, several texts directly contradict the Augustinian justification for toleration (in that they call for the Jews' expulsion from Christendom),[39] and at least one indicates that this change in approach is related to the Jews' interpretation of the Law.

The very last commentary text in the entire Latin manuscript reads: "Here are excommunicated and cursed Jews who deny the truth and the true exposition of sacred scripture. And heretics who admit their falsities into it. And false decretists who induce sacred scripture so that through it they might litigate about worldly things."[40] In the image, Jews carry a scroll of the Law (Fig. 38).

Is this criticism of Jewish doctrine and exegesis merely an extreme expression of the long-standing charge that Jews were mistaken in their maintenance of the Old Law and overly literal in their approach to Scripture? Or was there, indeed, a perception that Jews had deviated from their traditional approaches to the extent that they no longer warranted toleration? The *Bible moralisée* is ambiguous in that respect. Many texts clearly censure Jews for excessive literalism only, but others indicate that a new hostility was at least partially directed toward contemporary Jewish practice and/or rabbinic literature.

The commentary text in the Latin manuscript to Esther 3:5–6 states that Haman's desire to kill Mordechai "signifies that the Jews, *iniqui per legem,* which they had received from God himself, were wishing to destroy the Gospel and those believing in Jesus."[41] The roundel illustrates in a sequential manner the "destruction" of the good Law (Fig. 39). On the left of the roundel, a Jew has just received the Law from Jesus in the traditional form of the two round-topped tablets. This Jew is still facing Jesus. To his right, a group of Jews has turned away, their backs now turned toward Jesus and the tablets of the Law. Instead of tablets, one Jew carries a long, drooping scroll and another carries a calf. Deciphering the meaning of this commentary depends both on appropriate translation of the term *iniqui per legem* (to which I will return shortly) and on an understanding of how the two main symbols of the Law—the scroll and the calf—function in the unique semantic context of the *Bible moralisée.*

FIG. 38 (TOP). Apoc. 22:18–21. Jews, heretics, and false decretists are cursed and excommunicated. Cod. 1179, fol. 246c.
FIG. 39. Esther 3:5–6. Jews wishing to destroy the Gospel. Cod. 1179, fol. 187c.

FIG. 40. Exod. 32:19. Jesus Christ destroys the Old Law. Cod. 1179, fol. 37c.

New Interpretations of Old Signs: The Scroll

It is clear that in the *Bible moralisée* the scroll can simply be used, as it often is on church facades, to signify the Hebrew Scriptures. It will be remembered that in the illustration of the French commentary on the giving of the Law at Sinai, a codex represented the New Law and a scroll symbolized the Old Law (see Fig. 34).

However, the *Bible moralisée* illustrations also often reveal a hostile treatment of the sign of the scroll that seems inappropriate for the sacred Scriptures. Figure 40 illustrates a commentary image from folio 37c of Vienna ÖNB cod. 1179. The accompanying commentary text states, "Moses who destroyed the tablets signifies Jesus Christ who destroyed the Old Law. The people who sought forgiveness, and then Moses retrieved new tablets, signifies Jesus Christ who reforms Holy Church so that She might do his will."[42] The reference to the destruction of the Old Law is presumably an expression of the doctrine that the coming of Christ obviated the need to observe Levitical precepts. However, the illustration of this text is ambiguous. It depicts Jesus throwing several scrolls to the ground in front of a group of Jews, who look distressed. On the scrolls are inscribed the words: "Here Synagoga is broken by the Son of God."[43] Do these figures represent those Jews who at the time of Jesus refused to abandon their ancient observances, or are they intended to represent medieval Jews? Do the scrolls signify an interpretation of Scripture rooted in the past, or an ongoing repetition of the original denial of Christ? Was Judaism seen as part of God's plan for salvation, or as a departure from that plan? The point is not an art historical concern so much as one that pertains to how Judaism was defined by the people who created and read these manuscripts. And, because the Jewish figures in question are depicted as the adversaries of Christ, it also touches on what opposition—alterity—means in this political, cultural, and social context.

The setting in which the scroll symbol is depicted is central to determining its referent. When, as on church facades, it is situated in the hands of Old Testament prophets or is presented by Jesus himself, the scroll clearly signifies the words of God as delivered through the prophets. But when placed in the hands of contemporary Jews (or thrown at their feet), the scroll could have recalled to the viewer a more contemporary object, for the scroll was the form of the Torah in medieval synagogues. (This would have been known to the members of the royal court, for Jews took legal oaths on their Torah scrolls, often in the presence of the king and his court.)[44] In such a context, the scroll would come to symbolize not just the venerated Old Testament handed down by God but also the Hebrew Scriptures as read by contemporary Jews.

It is difficult to know how the Torah scroll was regarded by medieval Christians. The fact that Jews were made to swear oaths on their Torah scrolls may have been no more than recognition of the importance laid on the Torah by the Jews, or it may have been an expression of respect for the Torah itself. However, in some circumstances, that respect could have been a casualty of the process in which it was enlisted. By its very nature, oath-taking foregrounds questions of integrity and honor; for this reason and also because of specific medieval legal practices, Jews' oaths feature as areas of concern in ecclesiastical discussions of Jews' status in Christendom. Because in some regions a Jewish defendant could not be held liable on Christian testimony alone, a variety of clerics, including Alexander III and Innocent III, complained that Jewish witnesses were given preference over Christian witnesses in secular courts, thereby harming and demeaning both individual Christians and Christianity itself.[45]

Later twelfth- and early thirteenth-century changes in the nature of business and juridical procedure, too, may have affected perceptions of the scrolls on which Jews took their oaths. In government, in trade, indeed in almost all administrative realms, written documents were gradually coming to replace sworn statements as the privileged form of evidence.[46] This development manifestly caused unease among sectors of the population that felt themselves disadvantaged by the privileging of the written word and the concomitant delimiting and hardening of custom. At least one authority saw this change as beneficial to Jews and detrimental to Christian honor: the full text of Innocent's complaint cited earlier reads: "[Jews] are to this day preferred in the French realm to such an extent that Christian witnesses are not believed against them, while they are admitted to testimony against Christians. So that, if someone to whom they have loaned money on usury brings Christian witnesses about the facts of the case, [the Jews] are given more credence because of the instrument which the indiscreet debtor had left with them than are [Christian] witnesses."[47] The instrument in question is of course an economic rather than a religious document, but some Christian expressions of unease with dangerous literacy seem to relate the two realms. Innocent III goes on to allege that Jews' privileged legal position encouraged them to engage in insolent religious behavior, and a northern French council (ca. 1213) complained that "usurers and wicked persons everywhere raise up synagogues for the wicked, flaunting their rebelliousness against God and the Church, and have now erected schools for their children where they teach them their doctrines which are contrary to the true fundamentals of learning, and where they instruct them so that they might write down the debts due to their parents."[48] Is it possible that in certain contexts the highly charged nature of Jews' oaths and the negative connotations accorded written

FIG. 41 (TOP). IV Kings 2:23–24. A Jew with a scroll mocks Jesus. Cod. 2554, fol. 57va. FIG. 42. II Kings 18:9–10. Jews suspended "in the world." Cod. 1179, fol.108d.

instruments in financial and judicial contexts were transferred to the Jews' religious texts?[49] In any case, regardless of what the abstract attitude of medieval Christians toward the Torah might have been, the iconography of the *Bible moralisée* can (and does) construct a particular attitude toward the Torah within its own closed world of images. And this attitude is overwhelmingly negative.

Jews are shown holding scrolls of their own law in conjunction with a variety of unusual and damning activities. In illustrations of the Passion, the depiction of the Jews mocking Christ is not unexpected.[50] Jews carrying scrolls of the Law while mocking Christ are considerably less common, but many such images appear in the *Bible moralisée.* On folio 57va of Vienna ÖNB cod. 2554, for example, a rather standard depiction of the Crucifixion is animated by the vivid renderings of the Jews who stand beneath the cross and mock Christ. One thumbs his nose at Jesus, another sticks out his tongue while holding a scroll in his hand. In such an image, the repugnance inspired by the action would have been transferred to the sign of the Law (Fig. 41). This illustration, in fact, may be considered analogous in function to legislation that began to emerge in the early thirteenth century prohibiting Jews from appearing on the streets on Good Friday lest they mock the agony of the Lord.[51] I know of no reliable accounts of Jews actually performing such actions, and it strains credulity to believe that even if some such episodes took place they could have been so frequent as to require legislative redress. Instead, it seems likely that such legislation was passed for the same reason that the image described here was painted and Holy Week violence was enacted: to affirm the continuing relevance and ongoing nature of Christ's Passion.[52]

In Vienna ÖNB cod. 1179, fol. 108d, yet another dimension is added to the sign of the scroll. The position of Absalom, hanging by his hair from a tree (II Kings 18:9), is compared to the position of the Jews who remained "in the world" after the Resurrection of Christ "as if suspended . . . neither in heaven nor in Earth."[53] The text seems to refer to the much-criticized worldliness (luxury or avarice) of the Jews,[54] but the accompanying image does not illustrate these vices. Instead, Jews are depicted hanging from nooses descending from clouds, and holding the cause of their deaths: scrolls of the Law. On one of the scrolls is printed the words: "vani, vacui" (Fig. 42). This image expresses the oft-repeated charge that the Jews' adherence to the Law is related to their preference for the "world" over heaven, but it conveys additional resonances as well. It is unlikely that a medieval Christian could look at an image of a Jew hanged "after the Resurrection" without thinking of the most familiar representation of a hanging in Christian art: the suicide of Judas. This connection would have been reinforced by the depiction of Judas's suicide on the very next folio (Fig. 43).[55] In this roundel, then, the Law of the Jews is implicated in the betrayal, deicide, and despair of Judas.

If the Jews' rejection, mockery, and Crucifixion of Christ reiterated ancient themes indeed, another scene incorporating the sign of the scroll in the *Bible moralisée* is quite unconventional. The French paraphrase of I Kings 25:1, in accord with the overall dichotomizing tendency of the manuscripts, adds to the biblical description of the Israelites' grief at the death of Samuel an extrabiblical reference to the Philistines' exultation at this same event. The exposition states that the rejoicing Philistines signify "miscreants and bad people who rejoice and are gladdened at the death of the good prelate or the good monastic."[56] The accompanying roundel is unusually detailed. A bearded prelate lies in an open tomb, his crosier laid out alongside him. Three crosses stand on an altar near his head. Behind him are three mourners, including a black (Benedictine) monk and a monk in a dark gray habit. At the foot of the tomb stand two Jews. One, drawn in profile, sticks his tongue out toward the grieving monks; the other turns away, gesticulating down toward the deceased in scorn and clutching a scroll of the Law in his left hand. This time, the scroll is situated not in opposition to a book but to an even more powerful sign: the scroll trails limply down in the lower right corner of the roundel, contrasting strikingly with the three crosses that rise straight and tall in the upper left corner (Fig. 44). Was this scene inspired by an actual event?[57] Or is it yet another attempt to construct a gulf between Christians and Jews (physical as well as emotional space separates the two peoples in the roundel)? In either case, the sign of the scroll again insistently reminds the viewer of Jewish adherence to the Law in a context where it is not immediately relevant. Or, rather, it is an assertion that the Jews' law—the essential factor that differentiates them from Christians—is relevant in *all* contexts.

The scroll (as well as the sacrificial animal) is used to implicate Jewish observance in still another less than commonplace accusation. In Vienna ÖNB cod. 2554, fol. 66c, the commentary to Judg. 20:23 compares the Israelites who are sent back into battle by God to St. Denis and all martyrs, who ask God if they might go against the miscreants, "and God tells them: Go and die for me."[58] The "miscreants" whom St. Denis combats consist of six figures on the left of the roundel; at least two are bearded and three wear pointed hats. One holds a long scroll, and another carries a small goat or gazelle. Two of the martyrs are wearing miters (Fig. 45). The roundel is clearly ahistorical (even according to medieval understanding of the events): St. Denis was killed in Paris in the third century by Gallic pagans, not by medieval Jews.[59]

FIG. 43 (TOP). II Kings 17:23. The suicide of Judas. Cod. 1179, fol. 109c.
FIG. 44. I Kings 25:1. Miscreants rejoice at the death of a good prelate. Cod. 2554, fol. 40va.

FIG. 45 (TOP). Judg. 20:23. Miscreants opposed to St. Denis hold signs of the Jewish Law. Cod. 2554, fol. 66c. FIG. 46. Exod. 4:3. Unbelievers rejected by Jesus for maintaining the Old Law. Cod. 2554, fol. 18a.

However, during the reign of Philip Augustus, St. Denis came to be presented as an active player in the life of the realm and a powerful and ever-vigilant guardian of its welfare.[60] This depiction of Jews carrying symbols of their Law and menacing the patron saint of France suggests that on account of their Law Jews menace the entire Christian realm.

Within the iconographic world of the *Bible moralisée,* then, the scroll signifies not just an outdated but still revered Old Law (mistakenly but usefully preserved in its original form by medieval Jews), but also a dangerous text possessed—brandished—by contemporary Jews.

New Interpretations of Old Signs: Jewish Sacrifice

The sign of the calf similarly has a less fixed meaning in the *Bible moralisée* than is usually assumed. The traditional meaning certainly makes its appearance. In the commentary roundel accompanying Deut. 34:5–6 (in which the death of Moses was held to prefigure the death of the Old Law), Synagoga held a knife and a calf (Fig. 35). As I mentioned previously, the knife and the animal are generally assumed to represent the sacrifices of the Old Testament period, and in this roundel they clearly serve that function.

However, sacrificial imagery is often used in the *Bible moralisée* in contexts far removed from the period of the transition from the Old Law to the New. On folio 18a of Vienna ÖNB cod. 2554, the commentary interprets Moses' staff-turned-serpent in this way: "That Moses threw down the staff and it became a serpent signifies that Jesus Christ threw down and replaced the Old Law with the New. The serpent, which is venomous and stinging, signifies Jews and unbelievers who maintain the Old Law, and they are stung and poisoned by the serpent."[61] In the roundel, Jesus holds an open codex and gestures rejection as he walks away from a group of Jews bending away from heaven in a contorted fashion (Fig. 46). One Jew holds an animal over a table covered with a white cloth. Although the image could conceivably illustrate an Old Testament sacrifice, the text leaves no doubt that it is the contemporary maintenance of the Law by Jews that is under indictment. It emphasizes, moreover, that the Jews' continuing observance of the Law has caused their rejection by Christ (and, implicitly, their subjection to the devil—the serpent).

To my knowledge, the only attempt by any scholar to tie these sacrificial symbols to contemporary issues was made by Bernhard Blumenkranz in one of his seminal studies of Jews in medieval art.[62] Blumenkranz speculated that because the knife and the animal appear more frequently in German than in French art, the symbols may have had an implicit political significance: sacrifices in Roman Judaea required the approval of the emperor, and the sacrificial animal therefore could have been used to signify imperial authority. But Blumenkranz did not explore the other associations the image may have triggered. The Old Testament sacrifices, even those performed in biblical times before the coming of Christ abrogated the Old Law, were not contemplated with equanimity by medieval Christians. In addition to the exegetes' denial of moral worth to the performance of sacrifices, their very nature was clearly considered distasteful. Augustine invited a negative interpretation of the sacrifices of Aaron by comparing them unfavorably to the "clean" offering of Melchisadek.[63] Displaying a similar bias, Peter the Venerable wrote with palpable disgust of the "blood-soaked altars of the Jews," as contrasted with the clean altars on which Christians offered the Lamb of God.[64]

This contrast between the cleanliness of the Christian sacraments and the unclean nature of the rites they replaced is exploited to striking visual effect in several images in the *Bible moralisée.* In Vienna ÖNB cod. 1179, fol. 227c, for example, the text contrasts the Old Testament, which teaches obscurely through figures, to the Gospels, which teach manifestly. The Old Testament is represented by three Jews placed to the left of Jesus (Fig. 47). Two of the Jews place a calf on an altar; the third bends over to slit the throat of the animal. The face of the slaughtering Jew is shown in a dark and rather threatening profile. To the right of Jesus, the Gospel is represented by a priest raising a Host high above an altar on which a chalice is placed. The action of the priest is one of openness and expansion, as contrasted with the hunched posture of the Jew. Perhaps to underline the cleanliness of the Christian sacrament (in the process drawing attention to Christian anxieties concerning contamination), a figure holds above the raised Host a flabellum, a liturgical fan designed to keep flies away from the Eucharist.

On Vienna ÖNB cod. 1179, fol. 194a, a very dense commentary text–image pair links the Jews' offensive sacrificial rites to their wrongheaded biblical interpretation. The Bible text narrates the defeat of Appolonius by Judah Maccabee, who consequently despoiled the enemy nations (I Macc. 3:10–12). The commentary text interprets this as a figure for the appropriation of the Jews' great treasure by the Christians: "This signifies that the Lord spiritually expounded the Law of Moses, which led no one to perfection, and thus [spiritually] it ought to be fulfilled. Paul taught, saying, all things would come to pass in figures . . . and daily he would refute the Jews with their own law."[65] The commentary

FIG. 47. Apoc. 5:1. The "obscurity" of the Old Testament contrasted with the "clarity" of the Gospels, via imagery of blood and cleanliness. Cod. 1179, fol. 227c.

FIG. 48 (TOP). I Macc. 3:10–12. The letter contrasted with the "figure" of the Law. Cod. 1179, fol. 194a. FIG. 49. Esther 1:9–12. Jews scorn preaching. Cod. 1179, fol. 186a.

roundel realizes this text in a very complicated manner. A bust of Jesus emerges from clouds at the top of the roundel to present two tablets of the Law to Paul, who stands in the center (Fig. 48). Paul holds the Law with which he confounded the Jews: it is not the tablets, which no longer belong to the Jews, but a scroll inscribed with pseudo-Hebrew letters. Paul points with his right index finger to the right, where a Christian priest is raising a Host above an altar on which a chalice rests. This ceremony is the correct "figure" of the Law. To the left of Paul is illustrated the incorrect, nonspiritual interpretation of the Law: two Jews raise a calf toward the sky, while another hunches over to slit the throat of an animal. The devil again makes his appearance: a demon seated on the shoulder of the butchering Jew instructs him. The "letter" of the Law, then, which the Jews prefer to the Apostle's spiritual message, consists of the Jews' bloody counterpoint to the eucharistic sacrament; it is, moreover, directed by a demon.

A nearly identical image is used to illustrate a text alleging that the Law was responsible for the Jews' rejection of the Gospels. In Vienna ÖNB cod. 1179, fol. 186a, Vashti, the disobedient wife of Ahasuerus (Esther 1:9), is compared to Synagoga, "[who], invited to the faith, contemned the preaching of the faith because of *legalia sua sacramenta.*"[66] The accompanying roundel depicts two temporal stages in the Jewish-Christian encounter (Fig. 49). In the center we see the archetypal confrontation: two apostles with halos raise their hands and preach to Synagoga personified, who holds a long scroll inscribed with the words "spernit legem" (spurns the law). Flanking these figures are the medieval adherents of the opposing faiths. To the left of the apostles, a priest stands before an altar and elevates the Host. To the right of Synagoga are two bearded Jews with pointed hats. One, echoing the position of the priest, raises up a calf as if offering it to heaven; the other bends over to slit the throat of a calf with a knife. Jewish ritual is in this way set up as both a direct rival to the holiest of Christian ceremonies and the cause of the Jews' stubbornness. As in the other images contrasting the rituals, the Christian sacrament appears elevated, open, and clean, whereas the Jewish ritual appears hunched, closed, and bloody.

But there is still more to these roundels. Like the scroll, the knife and animal could well have conveyed to the medieval reader associations more immediately familiar than Old Testament sacrifices: the portrayal of the Jew in the act of slitting the throat of an animal is, in fact, a very accurate illustration of *shechita,* or ritual kosher slaughtering. A variety of medieval Jewish manuscripts illustrate this slaughter with almost identical gestures and tools.[67] (By contrast, Christian depictions of slaughtering inevitably depict the butcher standing upright with an ax in his hand.)[68] This conflation of antique Jewish sacrifices and contemporary Jewish practices subtly modifies the contours of the polemic, since medieval Jewish practices were embedded in a web of social and economic relations, and the emotions and ideas that accompanied them must infiltrate the viewer's reading of the images.

We have no direct evidence concerning how the kosher slaughtering practices of the Jews were viewed by their Christian neighbors. Ecclesiastical attempts to prohibit Christians from buying the leftover meat of the Jews indicate that some Christians, at least, had no distaste for kosher meat.[69] On the other hand, these prohibitions also bear witness to the potential for resentment and conflict inherent in such practices. The sale of meat by Jews constituted competition for Christian butchers, and, like any form of commercial exchange, these transactions could entail misunderstandings and fraudulent dealings; in an interreligious context such allegations could well be invested with ideological overtones. Such trade also brought into sharp relief the more stringent dietary and cleanliness requirements of Jewish law, implicitly, in the eyes of at least some Christians, posing a challenge to Christian prestige.[70]

Let us now return to the illustration of the commentary on Esther analyzed earlier. We have seen that it employs symbols traditionally associated with ancient Hebrew practices that are frequently reformulated in the *Bible moralisée* to signify later (i.e., medieval) texts and rites. The implication seems to be that the contemporary practices represented by the scroll and the animal have removed the Jews from their ancestors' God-given Law. But this reading, nevertheless, still begs the question that was posed by Robert Chazan and others as a challenge to Cohen's thesis: Are the practices of medieval Jews considered something radically new, or were they essentially seen as a continuation of the same basic error to which Jews have been subject since their original rejection of Christ? Answering that question hinges upon translation of the term *iniqui per legem.* If it means "iniquitous on account of their law," then the text and roundel can be understood to mean simply that the Jews' clinging to the Law has always been, and remains, the source of their perfidy. But it seems somewhat distracting to emphasize the fact that the Jews received the law from God himself ("ab ipso domino susceperant") in a text intended to censure the Jews' faithfulness to that law. An equally tenable (in grammatical terms) translation of *iniqui per legem* is: "inadequate as far as regards the law." This interpretation, which has the advantage of explaining the text's insistence on the divine origin of the law, clearly has very different implications and may indicate that Jews were seen to be failing even in their mistaken concept of their own duty to cling to the law.

FIG. 50 (TOP). IV Kings 1:2. Jews and bad philosophers consult their master. Cod. 1179, fol. 125b. FIG. 51. Exod. 7:22. Bad men who alter the word of the Lord. Cod. 1179, fol. 26a.

Ambiguous Texts: The Old Law and New Knowledge

Similarly, another roundel suggests that medieval Judaism was considered worse than atrophied or misguided. In IV Kings 1:2, the evil king Ochozias sends his servants to consult with the god Nabal, or Belzebuc. The commentary text explains, "This signifies Jews and bad philosophers who are wavering in their faith and weak in their law, and they consult the greatest of their masters . . . who is called by them by the name Bitzebuch."[71] On the left of the commentary roundel stands the devil (Fig. 50). In the center we see a group of Jews making various gestures indicative of their confusion. To their right is represented the Law: a calf seated upon an altar. This text, too, is tantalizingly ambiguous. Are Jews weak only because they cling stubbornly to the law, or does the counsel of a devilish master account for their wavering faith? Are they weakened *by* their law or weak *in* their law? What, precisely, is the nature of this weakness or wavering? What have (non-Jewish?) philosophers to do with Jews and/or Jewish law? Is the phrase "great master" used of the devil (who is given a bizarre pseudo-Hebrew version of the name Beelzebub, or Ba'al-Zvuv) in an intentional echo of the title "rabbi"? If so, are Jewish rabbis—or perhaps philosophy masters—to be compared to the devil?

The threat posed by the devil to Scripture once more figures prominently in one of the most forbidding of all depictions of Jews in the *Bible moralisée,* which also seems to touch directly upon contemporary controversies about proper exegetical hermeneutics (Fig. 51). In the commentary roundel accompanying the Bible episode in which the magicians of Pharaoh attempt to reproduce Moses' miracles (Exod. 7:22), two Jews are shown hunched over their desks, writing intently in codices. In a parody of the dove often shown whispering into the ear of St. Gregory or the evangelists as they write, a demon crouches on the shoulder of one of the Jews, while the devil sits to the left and grins. The accompanying text identifies these Jews as "bad men who try to wholly alter the word of the Lord and avert it as much as they can from its true sense."[72] Given that the Jews are writing in codices rather than the more common scrolls of the Old Law, it seems likely that the "alteration of the word of God" and the Jewish misinterpretations referred to in these texts are postbiblical works of Jewish exegesis—perhaps the Talmud itself or the literalist interpretations of such commentators as the late eleventh-century exegete Rashi (Rabbi Solomon ben Itzhak of Troyes) and his school.[73] The image of the devil dictating the Jews' writings, then, would reflect negatively upon medieval Jewish religious literature. Yet the phrase "wholly alter the word of God" has an especially ominous ring, particularly since the devil is dictating the text, and seems to go well beyond condemnation of Jews' slavish adherence to the *sensus literalis.* Rather, the accusation that Jews not only misinterpret but actually tamper with the word of God implies that Jews' guardianship of the letter of the law is being questioned, and may indicate that well before the "trial" of the Talmud in 1240, a counterargument to the Augustinian rationale for continued toleration was being articulated, at least in the works of some clerics close to the Capetian court.[74]

In the absence of more definitive evidence, it is impossible to conclude that medieval Judaism is being represented in the *Bible moralisée* as something essentially new. Too many texts preserving traditional formulations exist alongside those more hostile concerning Jews' guardianship of Scripture to provide any sense that the traditional theological approach to Jewish law has been discarded or replaced. Those innovations that can be identified are of tone and rhetoric rather than of theology, but a change in tone is nonetheless a change worth noting. For one feature of the commentary is certain: that Jewish law, whether seen as traditional or innovative, is associated with the devil and is represented as threatening not just to the Jews' own chances for salvation but to Christian society as well.

The *Bible moralisée* roundels I have described so far do not indicate *why* the Jewish approach to Scripture is considered menacing, although they do contain suggestive features. The depictions of Jewish ritual in the *Bible moralisée,* like the depictions of the Jews' financial practices analyzed in the previous chapter, adopt an archetypal Old Testament notion and construct the contrast between Christianity and Judaism in terms of cleanliness and pollution. In neither case are the Jews arbitrary targets of pollution anxiety; rather, symbols long associated with corruption occupy a necessary mediating role. The association of the exegetical "carnality" of the Jews with their alleged "cupidity" is facilitated by the "filthy" connotations of money and specie. However, although the rhetoric of "filthy lucre" can be traced in Christian texts from the Gospels onward, it only comes to the fore and infiltrates and shapes polemic when local and specific circumstances (such as the intensive anti-usury campaign mounted in Paris in the second and third decades of the thirteenth century) endow it with newly powerful resonance. Similarly, both indictments of Jewish interpretation according to the "flesh" and the powerful symbolism of blood and contamination have long prehistories, but the two strands are merged (as well as combined with the actual dynamics of social interaction) in unique ways in the illustrations of Jewish ritual in the *Bible moralisée.* To what conditions were such images responding, and

FIG. 52 (TOP). Exod. 15:23–24. Christians who cannot drink the bitter Old Law. Cod. 2554, fol. 22a. FIG. 53. Exod. 15:23–24. Students saturated with secular knowledge. Cod. 1179, fol. 32a.

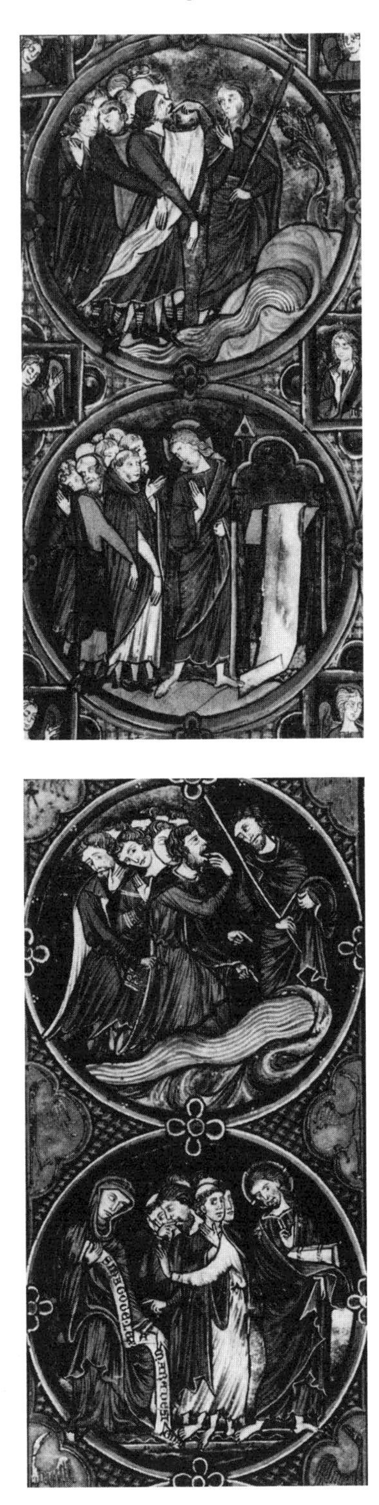

with what new resonances would they consequently have been endowed?

My attempt to answer these questions moves in two directions. First, some images provide further indications of the social and cultural context for the polemic against Jewish texts in the *Bible moralisée,* suggesting that it became absorbed into anxieties about recent developments within Christian intellectual culture—in particular, at the University of Paris. Second, analyzing the representation of the Law in the *Bible moralisée* in the light of the rhetorical strategies distinguished in the previous chapter helps explain how certain early thirteenth-century pastoral and literary developments intersected with age-old doctrinal issues.

Bitter Doctrine: Jewish Learning and the Schools

A handful of images suggest that the rhetoric of a "lethal" and "killing" Jewish literature gained renewed vigor in part because Jewish texts, or at least their techniques, were infiltrating the very bastions of Christian orthodox exegesis.

Folio 22a of the French manuscript contains the narration of the episode in Exodus concerning the bitter waters of Marach. The commentary compares the Israelites who complained to Moses that they couldn't drink the waters to "clerics and prelates and good Christians who came before Jesus Christ and complained and said that they can [not] drink the bitter water which was the doctrine of the Old Law" (Fig. 52).[75] The roundel depicts Jesus standing outside a structure in which a scroll of the Law is draped on a large desk or table. There is no indication of what kind of building the structure is meant to be or why the Christians should have been expected to partake of the Old Law. The commentary could be taken to be merely a general warning against the Old Law, and the structure to be the Temple. However, slightly different wording in the Latin text makes the reference much more specific. Here the Israelites who did not want to drink the bitter water are said to signify "scholar-clerics saturated with secular knowledge, upon whom spiritual knowledge presses [?] bitter."[76] The roundel links the secular knowledge mentioned in the Latin text to the Old Law of the French text by placing the scholars directly in front of Synagoga personified, who holds a scroll of the Law bearing the words "Synagoge lex amara designa . . . " (Fig. 53). The setting is a place of study; the bitter potion is the Old Law in the form of secular science, which embitters study of spiritual science; and the figures who are endangered are students. The image thus not only identifies Jewish knowledge as "secular" and dangerous but also attempts to counter the attraction that such Jewish "sciences" may have had for Christian students.

Jewish exegesis did indeed have a growing attraction for and influence on Christian biblical scholars during the twelfth and the thirteenth centuries.[77] Whereas in the early medieval period knowledge of Hebrew had been restricted to a small handful of scholars, in the twelfth century there was a great renewal of interest in the study of the Hebrew language among Christian scholars. An early manifestation of this trend is the work of Stephen Harding of Cîteaux, who enlisted the aid of a Jewish master in his project of compiling what he called the *Hebraica Veritas*—a corrected text of the Bible.[78] Many subsequent biblical scholars realized the value of consulting the original text and undertook the study of Hebrew themselves. For example, during the 1140s Nicholas Manjacoria, a monk of Trois-Fontaines, learned Hebrew in order to correct the text of the Psalter, and Herbert of Bosham, a follower of Becket, is said to have become completely fluent in Hebrew.[79]

Eventually certain intellectuals began to take an interest not just in the original Hebrew rendition of Scripture but also in subsequent Jewish interpretation. Spurred by their growing interest in the philological and historical explanation of Scripture, members of the school of the Abbey of St. Victor in Paris, in particular, sought out contemporary Jews to learn about their exegetical tradition. Beryl Smalley has demonstrated that Hugh of St. Victor, who explicitly stated that he had contacts with Jewish scholars, consulted the works of Rashi and his students, as well as Joseph Karo and Samuel ben Meir (Rashbam).[80] Hugh's student, Andrew of St. Victor, made even more extensive use of Jewish interpretation, and probably personally consulted Joseph Bekhor Shor, a pupil of Rashbam.[81] Michael Signer has argued recently that not just the content but also the techniques of Jewish exegesis found their way into Victorine commentary.[82] The Victorine method was eventually spread far beyond Parisian circles by their student Peter Comestor, who incorporated many of the results of their discussions with Jews into his vastly popular *Historia Scholastica.*[83]

Such contacts with Jews and Jewish learning did not meet with unanimous approval. Well before the appearance of the friars in the second decade of the thirteenth century, we find Christians expressing shock at the fact that the Old Testament was not the only basic text of contemporary Judaism. Instead it was discovered that the Jews relied heavily on the interpretations of post-biblical authorities; interpretations that were not the expected literal expositions but fanciful, "bizarre," and occasionally "blasphemous."[84] Although Richard of St. Victor himself consulted Jewish scholars, he attacked his fellow Victorine Andrew for uncritically accepting the Jewish interpretation of Isa. 7:14 and the

Jewish concept of an "Oral Law" in general, accusing Andrew of "Judaizing."[85] The decretist Rufinus (fl. ca. 1160) went even further in his opposition to "Judaizing," asserting that there was no point in studying Hebrew because the Hebrew text of the Bible had been hopelessly corrupted since Jerome's time, leaving the Vulgate the best scriptural text.[86] Influenced by the hostility of Bernard of Clairvaux to philological investigations and concerned about the possible influence of Jews on the Christian faithful, the Cistercian General Chapter prohibited the study of Hebrew with Jews in 1198.[87]

The clock could not be turned back, however. While Parisian theologians ("masters of the sacred page") such as Stephen Langton and Robert de Courson echoed their predecessors in criticizing those who understood the Bible "according to the letter,"[88] they nevertheless produced literal as well as allegorical commentaries on the Bible, and the establishment and exposition of the "plain sense" of the text remained the foundation of Scholastic exegesis.[89] This heightened attention to the letter of the Bible has, in fact, been called the "real judaizing of the thirteenth century,"[90] as Christian scholars seeking to realize a systematic and meaningful program of biblical study emulated the very people whose influence they most feared and disparaged. Anxiety over this "narcissism of minor difference,"[91] I believe, in part explains the adoption of an ever more emphatic and hostile rhetoric against Jewish interpretation.

It was not, however, Jewish literal exegesis but a Jewish philosophical approach that was to have the greater influence within the University of Paris. The 1220s saw the reception in the arts faculty of the works of Maimonides, the Jewish philosopher who died in 1204. In his attempt to harmonize the Jewish faith with Aristotelian philosophy, Maimonides proposed a rationalistic explanation of the Old Law ceremonies. They were, Maimonides said, designed to improve morals and draw the Jews away from the practices of their pagan neighbors.[92] The implication of this reasoning, as Jewish critics of Maimonides pointed out, was that with the eradication of paganism the usefulness of the ceremonies was exhausted. Maimonides' explanation was adopted (without attribution) by William of Auvergne in his work *De legibus* (ca. 1230);[93] and his synthesis of monotheism and Aristotelianism was to exert a continuing influence on medieval Christian philosophy. Not without protest, however: Maimonides was (ironically) bitterly criticized in Jewish circles for his overly allegorical interpretation, and Maimonides' own work and/or Maimonidean-style Aristotelianism continued to provoke objections and controversy in both the Jewish and the Christian communities.[94]

These developments, then, form one significant backdrop for the linkage of Jewish law and secular studies—and the consequent identification of Jewish law as a dangerous contaminant—in the *Bible moralisée.* Once again, the site of danger is not where Judaism is most specifically Jewish but where it intersects with and spills over into Christianity. Jewish literalistic interpretation and Maimonidean rationalist explication threaten, the images of the *Bible moralisée* suggest, not because they constitute deviations from age-old or internal Jewish traditions (as Jeremy Cohen posited) but because they parallel and on occasion overlap with current Christian preoccupations and controversial developments.

However, the issue of Jewish control over, access to, and interpretation of the Law is much more central to prevailing Christian concerns than the preceding discussion of the intellectual activities of a rather narrow circle of clerics would suggest. The debate over the word of God was by no means confined to university lecture halls or monastic scriptoria. The larger context for this debate is suggested by the image accompanying the text with which I opened this chapter.

On folio 202b of the Latin manuscript the commentary to I Macc. 7:47 (in which the head and hand of the defeated Syrian king Nicanor are hung from the gates of Jerusalem) states, "This signifies that in a church a figure of the Crucified One is raised up in front of the choir, as a sign of His victory. And Jews are permitted to live among Christians in testimony of the faith, because of the books of the law that they bear in the captivity in which they are because of their sins."[95] As I noted previously, the second part of this commentary text is a near-verbatim quotation of the Augustinian justification, although the tone is perhaps unusually antipathetic: the Jews' situation is not just subordination but captivity, and the captivity results not merely from ignorance or blindness but from sin. The rendering of the Jew in the commentary image similarly echoes a highly traditional iconographic motif (Fig. 54). A bearded Jew with a book of the Law on his lap sits beside, but turned away from, a church structure. A pillar passes directly behind him, creating the illusion that the Jew is supporting the portal. This Jew, in fact, appears to be a two-dimensional version of the Old Testament jamb figures carved on the west facade of so many Gothic churches and cathedrals. They, too, support the portal but gaze away from it, and have been interpreted as a sculptural expression of the idea that the Church was built upon the foundation of the prophets.[96] In the *Bible moralisée* roundel, the open codex faces away from the Jew: although he preserves the physical text, he is presented as unwilling or unable to see or benefit from the knowledge contained within, just as he is unable or unwilling to see or benefit from the Body of Christ displayed in the church structure behind him. It is interesting, moreover, that the book of the Law is represented as a codex (usually reserved for the New Law) rather than the

FIG. 54. I Macc. 7:47. A Jew seated beside but turned away from a Gothic choir screen: a visual expression of the Augustinian proposition that Jews must be allowed to live among Christians because they are witnesses to and keepers of the Law. Cod. 1179, fol. 202b.

more common scroll form, indicating that it is the Jews' preservation of the Law for the use of the Christians, not for their own use, that justifies their continued existence.

But the Jew is, in fact, neither the sole nor the central figure in this roundel, just as the polemic against Jews' interpretation of the law is not, I believe, the sole or central concern of the commentary. Dominating the image is a schematic representation of the interior of a church. In the center a crucifix and adjacent statues of Mary and John surmount a low masonry wall pierced by a central doorway. Two figures—a young student and a layman—stand to one side and raise their hands in prayer toward the crucifix. This structure is presumably the west wall of the "choir" mentioned in the commentary text. Such walls were built around the choirs of congregational churches from about the eleventh century to prevent the laity from intruding upon the canons.[97] Concern for separating the clergy and the laity continued to mount, and starting in the thirteenth century increasingly elaborate barriers came to be erected between the choir and the nave.[98] These barriers fulfilled symbolic as well as practical and liturgical functions: they served to separate, to render holy, the space (likened to the ancient biblical "Holy of Holies") in which the services were sung and the Eucharist was performed.[99] Choir screens similarly highlighted the unique role and condition of the clergy: Prévostin of Cremona, chancellor at Paris from 1206 to 1210, noted that "there ought to be three types of veils. . . . one is between the clerics and the people in front of the choir enclosure. . . . [This] is . . . a sign of the continence of the clergy, and it was made higher than the choir enclosure so that the clergy could not see the populace nor the populace the clergy."[100] The commanding visual presence of the choir barrier in this commentary roundel brings the question of controlling lay access to the sacred mysteries to the fore, and in doing so constructs a strange equation between Jew and Christian layman. Although the Christians gaze adoringly upon the Body of Christ and the Jew turns away, both Jew and Christian laymen are situated outside the sanctuary, and both are denied visions of the sanctuary *and* of Scripture—for the text of the Jew's codex is equally concealed from the Christian lay figures.

In fact, throughout the *Bible moralisée* Christian laymen are presented as having almost as problematic a relationship to Scripture as Jews. The commentary texts and roundels discussing the presentation of the law to Moses make this clear: this episode was held to signify that Jesus Christ handed his law to his *prelates,* not to the Christian people as a whole. Both manuscripts interpret the Israelites' subsequent inability to look upon the shining face of Moses as a figure for the inability of "the people" to understand the "subtlety of Jesus Christ." The commentary goes on to instruct the theologian to speak "grossly" to the people and strive to keep the subtlety of Scripture for the proper time and place.[101] This advice echoes that offered in numerous contemporary manuals of preaching, which stressed not only the need to engage and entertain the people but also the dangers inherent in exposing them to complex doctrinal discussions.[102] The same concern underlies the misgivings about, and opposition to, vernacular translations of Scripture expressed by various clerical authorities around the turn of the thirteenth century.[103] Although it has been persuasively argued that Innocent III never intended to issue a blanket condemnation of all vernacular translations,[104] it is clear that the ecclesiastical hierarchy was troubled by the prospect of unmediated lay access to Scripture, and that its primary concern hinged upon the potential of such access to breed heresy.[105] This overlap of concerns helps explain the adjacency of Jew and Christian laymen in the Maccabees commentary roundel: both groups constitute a threat when they try to pierce the "veil" of God's mystery by peering too closely and without guidance at God's words.

The centrality of such concerns to the very project of the *Bible moralisée* is obvious. These manuscripts and contemporary preachers faced the same task: to mediate between sacred texts and secular audiences, to reveal the essence of God's word while protecting its full force and glory. And as in sacred space itself, in the *Bible moralisée* manuscripts several layers of screening are inserted between the reader and the sacred text: the paraphrasing rather than replication of the Bible, the biblical illustrations that isolate or reconfigure select episodes, the commentary text that controls understanding, the commentary images that further channel interpretation—all inhibit the reader's access to the "naked" word of Scripture. Perhaps, too, the unique aspects of the representation of Jews in the vernacular version of the *Bible moralisée* may be traced to the particular nature of its audience: *illiterati* and entirely lay. The more intense demonization and more marked physical ugliness of Jews in the French manuscript serve as yet another interpretive guide for the unlettered viewer, perceived to need greater protection from "Jewish" transgressions and surer safeguards against "Jewish" allurements.[106]

"The Letter Killeth"

In the *Bible moralisée,* then, polemic against Jewish literalist interpretation becomes intertwined with current debates concerning access to and interpretation of the text of Scripture. But this debate, in turn, is folded into more general anxiety over the infiltration of the "world" into the realm of the sacred, for if im-

FIG. 55 (TOP). Exod. 14:9–10. Bad people and worldliness. Cod. 2554, fol. 21d.
FIG. 56. IV Kings 2:8–9. Jews leave their error and infidelity. Cod. 1179, fol. 127b.

pressionable Christians are intrigued by new forms of knowledge, they tend to be even more liable (in moralists' admonitions) to be drawn to other forms of worldliness, including greed, ambition, and lust. All of these vices, it turns out, are linked in the *Bible moralisée* to "carnal" interpretation and/or the Old Law, through the sort of rhetorical adjustments and metaphoric condensations previously described in relation to money.

For example, an image on folio 21d of Vienna ÖNB cod. 2554 uses a myriad of iconographic motifs to associate Jewish law (already identified with worldliness in the roundel condemning "secular studies" discussed earlier) with both Jewish and non-Jewish "worldliness." In the Bible text, the Jews flee Pharaoh but are caught between two mountains and the Red Sea. The commentary explains, "Like the sons of Israel, the apostles were caught between two mountains. One of the mountains signifies the devil and the other signifies the bad people. And the Sea is the world."[107] The commentary roundel depicts the apostles, led by Jesus Christ, standing before three types of figures (Fig. 55). On the left, the "world" is depicted as a globe filled with various luxury objects: a pile of coins, a piece of red- and green-colored cloth, a double-cup, and a horn. Above the "world" stands a red-faced, beardless devil with horns. These objects may represent luxury items in general or, more specifically, items pledged in pawn. To the right of the devil stand the "bad people": two Jews, one of whom carries both a moneybag and a scroll of the Law. In this striking image, the Jews seem to be allied with the devil and "worldliness" by virtue of their adherence both to money and to the Old Law.

I have already discussed the establishment of the idol as a metaphor for avarice.[108] On folio 127b of the Latin manuscript, through association with the scroll, connotations of idolatry adhere to Jewish observance of the Law as well. The commentary text, comparing Elisha to the preaching apostles, calls for a picture of Jews converting to Christianity. The accompanying roundel depicts four figures turning to the left to kneel before Christ (Fig. 56). Two have already raised their hands in prayer toward him; another is removing a pointed hat from his head and is waving his right hand to signal his rejection of two objects falling to the right: a pagan idol enshrined upon a pedestal and a scroll of the Law.

The linkage of Jewish ritual with idolatry is also expressed through the use of the sign of the sacrificial animal. In Vienna ÖNB cod. 1179, fol. 91a, the demonically possessed Saul is held to signify "Jews who act against the will of God and because of this are possessed; and the devil enters their hearts, by which they are destroyed body and soul."[109] In the medallion two actions "against the will of God" are depicted (Fig. 57). On the right, two Jews kneel and place the head of an animal on an altar. Small demons dive into their mouths. This imagery is complicated and densely layered. The altar and animal head are reminiscent of the Old Testament sacrifices, but the kneeling of the Jews seems to indicate that they are worshiping rather than sacrificing the animal. This linkage of Jewish observance to idolatry is made explicit on the left side of the medallion, where a kneeling bearded figure wearing a rounded cap prays to a naked statue within a small shrine as a demon leaps into his mouth.

In Vienna ÖNB cod. 1179, fol. 180c, the conflation of Jewish observance and idolatry is conveyed in a slightly different manner. The grief of Tobias's parents at his departure (Tob. 10:3) is compared in the commentary text to the grief of the apostles and "antique Jews" at the permanent infidelity of their nation. In the accompanying roundel, the apostles are depicted grieving at the actions of two Jews. One Jew leans over to slit the throat of a sheep with a knife; the other worships the statue of a calf enclosed within a small shrine (Fig. 58). This image merges the two concepts of Jewish ritual and idolatry within the single figure of the calf-idol.

Examples of this technique—the merging of standard anti-"letter" polemic with other manifestations of "carnality" (money, sex, the secularization of higher education, the proliferation of heresy)—are exceedingly numerous. In their variety and frequency they convey far more powerfully than just scattered textual references to misleading Jewish exegesis possibly can the idea that Jewish law is seductive, infectious, and dangerous. Moreover, the excommunication text cited earlier, which links the Jews' flawed doctrine and misreading of Scripture with Christian misuse of Scripture and with greed and "worldly things," suggests that the impact of this new way of framing the contrasts between Christianity and Judaism might, at least theoretically, inspire novel responses.

FIG. 57 (TOP). I Kings 16:23. Jews are possessed by the devil. Cod. 1179, fol. 91a.
FIG. 58. Tob. 10:1–3. The apostles grieve at their people's infidelity. Cod. 1179, fol. 180c.

The imagery of the *Bible moralisée* reflects a myriad of different issues raised by the question of the Law. The vast choice of possible texts and the eclectic nature of the sources utilized prevent the commentary text from presenting a monolithic point of view. In general, the selection seems designed to satisfy the different and often conflicting needs of the project: to warn against both antinomian heresy and Judaizing, to instruct the readers in the complex and delicate middle road that orthodoxy must march. But the imagery goes much further than did contemporary theological and exegetical debates. Old Testament observances are intricately associated with a wide range of Jewish crimes. They are portrayed as being related to, perhaps even inspiring, the murder of Jesus Christ and worship of the devil, which in turn is linked to idolatry, avarice, and heresy. Through the vehicle of the imagery devised for the Old Testament, the Jewish position regarding the Law is injected into a variety of novel contexts, forcing a reassessment of that position and of those contexts.

It is clear, then, that many of the newly hostile formulations toward Jews that eventually permeated the sermons and writings of friars were present in at least some circles in Paris well before the period of the mendicants' major activity. I must hasten to add that I am not suggesting that precedence is tantamount to causation, nor that this Parisian context is the *real* or only source of the anti-Jewish rhetoric of the friars and other later medieval polemicists. Rather, I think the lesson to be drawn is that each specific historical context provides its own impetus for reformulating ideas. The reformulations—in this case, the anti-Jewish motifs—end up looking similar because they draw on similar traditions, have some circumstances in common, and, most important, utilize similar rhetorical methods.

I believe, therefore, that although the *Bible moralisée* provides no convincing evidence (in spite of some tantalizing signs) that a fundamental reassessment of Jews' faithfulness to their own Law, and thereby of their status within Christendom, was taking place (as Jeremy Cohen has argued), there is more than enough evidence to talk about a new rhetorical strategy regarding the Jews. This observation addresses the question posed at the end of Cohen's book (a question that, I believe, was not fully resolved): Why the friars? Although Cohen's sources demonstrate admirably that the friars shared the concerns and prejudices of their age, Cohen did not adequately explain why members of the mendicant orders should have created a unique and novel ideology regarding the Jews. But they did, of course, embrace a new kind of lifestyle, one that both grew out of and heralded significant changes in residential and devotional patterns. These changes exhilaratingly but also frighteningly blurred the barriers and distinctions between clerical and lay, sacred and profane. The friars, following techniques pioneered by Parisian moralists, also employed a unique and still innovative medium and strategy: popular preaching. And the form and requirements of popular preaching—the need to simplify, concretize, and make immediately relevant an abstract message for the benefit of a lay audience—parallel the form and requirements of the *Bible moralisée* to a remarkable degree. Perhaps one explanation for the fact that the mendicants came to be seen by some medieval Jews, as well as by some modern scholars, as the archenemies of the Jews is that in the process of reformulating traditional theology to fit new rhetorical models and respond to a host of local and specific conditions, they absorbed, rationalized, and systematized long-standing negative attitudes and signs that carried the most resonance with the general population. In the next chapter I examine the context in which the Parisian moralists, the friars, and other thirteenth-century writers and preachers frequently—and for the Jews most ominously—employed these themes: in the fight against heresy.

FOUR: THE SIGN OF THE CAT

Jews and Heretics in the Bible moralisée

Populus qui intravit fluvium
Iordanis cuius altera pars ascendit
in modo muri significat iudeos et
publicanos qui simul sunt et contra
evangelium ad modo lapidis
remanent indurati.

The people who entered the river
Jordan, whose other part rose up like
a wall, signify Jews and heretics who
are together and remain hardened
like a stone against the gospel.[1]

This commentary text to Josh. 3:17 from Vienna ÖNB cod. 1179 embodies a practice (already encountered in previous chapters) that is reiterated throughout the *Bible moralisée:* the linkage of Jews and heretics.[2] Understanding why and to what effect Jews and heretics are associated in the *Bible moralisée* is as complex a task as interpreting the commentary text above. Just as *simul* may be translated as "at the same time," "in a similar way," "in a single group," "in cooperation," or simply "both," so the coupling of Jews and heretics may be seen as a random pairing of extra-Catholic groups, an assertion that Jews and heretics are similar in a particular way, or an accusation of complicity between Jews and heretics. This linkage consequently raises questions (What gave rise to such allegations? What attributes were Jews and heretics alleged to share? What were the effects of such perceptions?) whose resolution is central to deciphering the full force of the representation of Jews in the *Bible moralisée.*

The pairing of Jews and heretics is by no means unprecedented in Christian religious works: the practice is found across patristic texts,[3] and by the beginning of the thirteenth century it had become commonplace. Jews and heretics are frequently censured together in sermons of the period. To cite only a few examples, Stephen Langton favorably compared good Christians to "Jews, heretics, and false Christians" in a sermon on the birth of Christ,[4] and in an early thirteenth-century homily on the Gospels, Jean Halgrin d'Abbeville remarks that "[Infidelitas] est in iudeis et hereticis."[5] The famous preacher Eudes de Chateauroux declaimed in a sermon delivered at the University of Paris in 1231 that "through craftiness the world conquers heretics, Jews, and Gentiles," and in another sermon of the same year he likened heretics, Jews, Gentiles, and the lustful to the animals excluded from Noah's ark.[6] Many heresiological treatises, such as the *De Fide Catholica* of Alan of Lille, incorporate anti-Jewish tracts;[7] and the canons of church councils dealing with Jews are generally found adjacent to those dealing with heretics, such as the anti-Jewish legislation of the Third Lateran Council of 1179.[8] Secular legislation also tended to deal with Jews and heretics in the same passages,[9] as did secular chronicles. In his enumeration of what he considers some of Philip Augustus's most notable achievements, Guillaume le Breton includes the following lines:

Sic omnes regni fines purgavit ubique
Omnibus hereticis, Judeorumque nefanda
Perfidia, quorum sordescit fenore mundus.[10]

(Thus he cleansed the borders of the realm everywhere
of all heretics, and the abominable perfidy of the Jews,
from whose filth the world is soiled.)

Nevertheless, linkage of Jews and heretics in the *Bible moralisée* tends to be far more consistent, emphatic, and elaborate than such unembellished adjacent textual references. In addition, the *Bible moralisée* for the first time gives to this propensity a remarkably extensive visual expression, providing in consort with the texts a uniquely systematized and subtly nuanced catalogue of polemics.

FIG. 59. III Kings 3:23–27. Holy Church welcomes the living children given her by Jesus Christ; Synagoga grieves for her "dead" children: Jews, miscreants, heretics, and all wicked people. Cod. 2554, fol. 50a.

Simul Sunt: *"They Are Together"*

The most straightforward method employed in the manuscripts to associate Jews with heretics is similar to that of the written sources just cited: the apparently random mention of Jews and heretics together in the text, generally in the context of enmity toward or exclusion from the Church. For example, folio 50a of the French manuscript contains the story of the judgment of Solomon (III Kings 3:16–28). In this case, two women and two children (one living and one dead) were brought before the king. Each woman denied that the dead child was her own and claimed to be the mother of the living child. Solomon ordered the living child to be cut into two pieces—one for each woman—and was thus able to identify the true mother, who gave up her claim to the child rather than see it killed. The commentary explains, "That Solomon knew the true mother from the pity he saw in her and returned the infant to her signifies Jesus Christ who by his great wisdom and by the great pity he saw in her knew Holy Church as the true mother, and he gave her the living child—that is, good Christians, who live in good works. And the dead remained with Synagoga—these were Jews and infidels and heretics and all bad people."[11] The accompanying roundel does not elaborate upon this imputed shared parentage, depicting on the left Holy Church welcoming two children given her by Christ, and on the right a sorrowful Synagoga (Fig. 59). Many more examples of texts referring jointly to Jews and heretics may be cited, especially if the words "infidels" or "miscreants" are understood as referring to Jews.[12] The consistency of such pairing gives as strong an impression as any explicit accusation could of an alliance or correspondence between Jews and heretics.

The manuscripts also link Jews and heretics through exclusively visual means. Folio 204a of Vienna ÖNB cod. 1179 contains a scene from the First Book of Maccabees (I Macc. 9:16–18). The Bible excerpt runs: "Those in the left flank of the Syrian army saw the trouble of the right flank, and came upon Judah Maccabee from behind. And there was a fierce battle, and many fell, including Judah Maccabee." According to the commentary text, "This signifies that after the persecutions by the martyricides, the heretics rose up in the church and attacked the faith of Jesus Christ, attracting to their fellowship whomever they could."[13] The text seems to be alluding to an early Church heresy, but the image provides a more contemporary reference (Fig. 60). The heretics, shown attacking Jesus and a group of clerics with swords, are led by a bearded man, drawn in profile, and wearing a tall, pointed hat. The heretics behind this man wear shorter, rounded caps; one signifies his rejection of the sacraments by throwing a chalice to the ground. This illustration of "heretics," then, expands upon the textual assertion concerning the contaminous potential of heresy by depicting the transformation or assimilation of Christian dissidents into one of the least ambiguously Jewish figures in the entire manuscript.

FIG. 60. I Macc. 9:16. Heretics attack the faith of Jesus Christ: the heretics are portrayed as Jews. Cod. 1179, fol. 204a.

Just as the juxtaposition of textual references to Jews and heretics is not unique to the *Bible moralisée,* so, too, the use of Jewish figures to represent heretics is not without precedent. Although heresy was commonly depicted in high medieval art as an allegorical figure,[14] from the mid–twelfth century both heretics and pagans appeared in art, usually as otherwise unidentifiable individuals wearing pointed caps.[15] Heresy is likewise visually linked to Judaism in the *Hortus Deliciarum* of Herradis of Landsberg: the illustration of the vision of Zechariah includes a depiction of Haeresis, personified as a veiled and winged woman, handing a small figure in a bowl (i.e., a human soul) to Synagoga.[16]

The convention of assigning Jewish attributes to heretics in the *Bible moralisée* accordingly may be considered part of a larger development that, in spite of some sensitive studies of individual themes,[17] has not yet been adequately explained. Indeed, many scholars seem not to recognize the need for an explanation, assuming that because both groups were despised and feared, iconographic conflation of Jews and heretics was natural and self-evident. Henry Kraus, for example, accounted for one instance of such conflation by remarking that "many ecclesiastics regarded Jews as original heretics; heretics *par excellence,*" but did not elaborate upon this statement.[18] Blumenkranz noted the tendency of the *Bible moralisée* to turn any opposition to the Church into Jewish opposition, but likewise he did not seek to analyze the practice more closely.[19]

And yet further analysis is surely called for. Although from the orthodox point of view both Jews and heretics had always stood outside the Church, they were not, in fact, iconographically equated for the entire first half of the Middle Ages. Moreover, such conflation flies in the face of ecclesiastical policy and doctrine, which clearly differentiated the two groups. Alexander of Hales dedicated separate, albeit adjacent, titles to "Jews and Pagans" (Inq. III Tract. VIII. Sect. I. Quaest. I. Tit. II.) and to "Heresy, Apostasy, and Schism" (Inq. III Tract. VIII. Sect. I. Quaest. I. Tit. III.), defining heresy as "a departure from the faith of the Church which one formerly held"—a definition that manifestly excludes Jews.[20] That the Church always insisted that Jews had to be tolerated while heresy (and sometimes the persons of the heretics) had to be eradicated is ample testimony to the fact that the two groups were regarded differently. It should also be remembered that Gothic iconography in general—and certainly that of the *Bible moralisée*—was created or at least supervised by educated clerics, and that the central components of the Scholastic approach were description, differentiation, and categorization;[21] it seems unlikely that such figures would have demonstrated taxonomic fuzziness in such a critical area. If traditional religious categorizations began to be ignored or subverted in the art of the twelfth and thirteenth centuries, such a radical departure needs to be noted as such and accounted for.

Alternative Iconography: A Heretical Physiognomy

An alternative explanation for the use of Jews to portray heretics is that such iconographic overlapping was never intended to subsume Jews and heretics into a single conception but was entailed by the constraints of illustration. That is, when it became necessary to choose a method by which to depict heretics—a class of person not generally visually recognizable—a logical choice presented itself in the one extra-Catholic group for whom iconographic attributes had long been established: the Jews. Because both Jews and heretics, although theologically distinct entities, were regarded as outside the Church, the Jew could easily be adopted as a visual token for heretics.[22]

But this hypothesis, too, fails to address all the issues raised by the text and images of the *Bible moralisée.* For, in fact, another method *was* available—and utilized—for depicting heretics. This method may be seen in a commentary roundel on folio 120a of Vienna ÖNB cod. 1179, in which Jesus challenges "infidels and publicans" to attempt to work miracles equal to his own. The infidels are represented by Jews endowed with their standard attributes, but another figure appears who evidently is intended to represent a heretic. He is a barefoot, bearded man with a distinctly wild and hairy aspect, wearing a short, ragged, torn tunic (Fig. 61). Similar figures appear in six more roundels in the Latin *Bible moralisée.*[23]

How are these wild and hairy figures to be explained? Their appearance, which conveys both madness and extreme asceticism, is, in fact, remarkably close to high medieval descriptions of various ascetic heretical groups. The early twelfth-century heresiarch Henry of Lausanne, for example, was said to have had a distinctly "tattered appearance: long-haired and wild-eyed."[24] According to Walter Map, the Waldensians who were excommunicated and expelled from Lyons in 1182 went about "two-by-two, barefoot, clad only in simple woolen garments, owning nothing . . . naked following a naked Christ,"[25] and of course many heretical sects embraced poverty and spurned earthly considerations. The depictions of ragged heretics in Vienna ÖNB cod. 1179 seem to have been based upon such descriptions of ascetic sects, and they reveal both the inventiveness and the polemical skill of the redactor/iconographer. In the twelfth and thirteenth centuries, the ascetic preachers evoked a variety of reactions—from revulsion to passive admiration and even emulation. But the audience for the *Bible moralisée* was much more circumscribed than was the audience for the itinerant preachers, and it encountered their likenesses in a more controlled framework. In a set of manuscripts that by their very nature as well as through implicit and explicit content rank measure and order above all things, the portrayal of heretical figures as wild and disheveled would serve to emphasize the threat they posed to orderly society. The likely effect on the royal and aristocratic viewer would be to invoke distaste for and suspicion of heretics and heresy.

FIG. 61. III Kings 18:21–25. Jesus Christ challenges infidels and heretics to work miracles equal to his own. Cod. 1179, fol. 120a.

Moreover, although these ascetic figures would seem to have little to do with Jews (they embody and are castigated for values directly opposite to those imputed to "materialistic" Jews), both iconographic strategies employed in the *Bible moralisée* for representing heresy actually reflect a unified and coherent theological/moral point of view. Just as Jews' allegedly excessive love of lucre is represented as dangerous to Christendom, so, too, the ragged heretics' utter rejection of material goods appears to threaten the proper balance of society. These seemingly contradictory indictments, then, both bring the issue of the burgeoning economy into sharp focus and condemn all immoderate responses to it.

In view, therefore, of the elastic iconographic repertoire at the disposal of medieval artists, and the hermeneutic subtlety of the *Bible moralisée* (and so many other works of medieval art and exegesis), it does not seem satisfactory simply to state that Jews were conflated with heretics merely as a convenience, or even because both groups were generally despised and feared. In the following analysis, I will resist the temptation to succumb to the reductionist and rather simplistic stance of seeing the "Jew" as a generic surrogate "Other," and will read the iconography contrived to represent heresy in the light of the complex program as a whole, assuming that it has more, rather than less, to say than it seems.

Innovative Iconography: The Sign of the Cat

The most innovative aspect of the linkage of Jews and heretics in the *Bible moralisée* is the adoption of a specific iconographic symbol for heresy: the cat.[26] This animal, unlike many other domesticated animals, was not a common symbol in Gothic art. It is not mentioned in the most extensive (and highly anti-Jewish) of medieval beast allegories: the early thirteenth-century bestiary of Guillaume le Clerc.[27] The bestiaries that do include a cat refer only to its ability to see at night and to its skill at catching mice.[28] Few modern handbooks of medieval iconography mention any symbolic attributes accorded cats.[29] It seems that the adoption of this animal to represent heresy must be considered one of the important and influential innovations of the redactors of the *Bible moralisée.*[30] The inspiration for and manipulations of this sign therefore help elucidate the mechanisms through which the program of the *Bible moralisée* was formulated, and the polemical avenues to which it lent itself.

Although medieval bestiaries provide no clues concerning the meanings attached to the sign of the cat, several images in the Latin *Bible moralisée* are so unusual and so graphic as to leave its inspiration indisputable. The first appearance of this type of image occurs on folio 83a of Vienna ÖNB cod. 1179. The commentary text describes "two kinds of men whom the Church has: those who follow her, and those who reject and leave her."[31] The men who follow the Church are depicted as two clerics, one praying to Holy Church personified and the other reading an open book. Two other men are depicted deserting Holy Church: a bearded man offering a moneybag to an idol seated within a shrine, and another bearded man in profile, kneeling on one knee and holding a striped domestic cat that is pointed away from him. The cat's tail is lifted up, and the man seems to be kissing the area below (see Fig. 32).

A similar image appears on folio 171d of the same manuscript as part of a quadripartite commentary roundel. The accompanying text refers to four kinds of sin (signified by the four horns of the he-goat of Dan. 8:8). "Infidelitas judeorum" is rendered in the upper left-hand corner of the roundel as Jews slitting the throat of an animal and bearing a scroll inscribed with the word *Infidelitas.* "Crudelitas tyrannorum" is illustrated with the depiction of a king ordering his agent to decapitate a man with his sword. In the lower right-hand corner, an image of a monk seated before both a crippled beggar and a woman admiring herself in a mirror illustrates the sin "ypocresis falsorum fratrum." Thus, by elimination, the scene in the lower left-hand corner must illustrate the fourth sin: "herror hereticorum."[32] The scene consists of a man wearing a hood, who is kneeling before a domestic cat that stands on a raised pedestal and kissing the cat's anus (Fig. 62).

Yet a third depiction of the same action occurs in the Maccabees commentary, which compares the Maccabeans who flee from the battle against the Syrians to Christians who flee from the battle against the Albigensian heretics.[33] The illustration of the great army of the Syrians is paralleled in the commentary roundel by the depiction of a ragged figure kneeling before a cat on an altar and kissing it below the tail (Fig. 63).

These three unusual images correspond closely to and are indubitably inspired by antiheretical slanders, such as the following, included by Walter Map in *De Nugis Curialis* around 1185: "There is, too, another old heresy which recently has increased beyond all measure. . . . They are called Publicans or Patarenes . . . about the first watch of the night each group of these, closing all gates and doors and windows, sitteth in expectant silence in their synagogues. Then cometh down by a rope a black cat of marvellous size. [The heretics] approach, feeling their way, to the spot where they have seen their lord, and . . . they kiss him . . . some his feet, many under the tail, and very many his private parts."[34]

This and similar calumnies were evidently widespread in the late twelfth and early thirteenth centuries. Alan of Lille cited the accusation, without necessarily giving complete credence to it, in his explanation of the etymological origin of the name *Cathar:* "Cathars are called after the cat, because they kiss the posterior of a cat in whose shape, it is said, Lucifer appears to them."[35] The same practice was mentioned by Gregory IX in a bull of 1233 instructing the archbishop of Mainz to preach a crusade against German heretical sects.[36] Stephen of Bourbon referred to underground rites in which heretics conjured Lucifer in the shape of a cat and related that St. Dominic expelled the devil in the form of a black cat from female heretics in Fanjeaux.[37]

The trajectory I have already traced for the signs related to money and to the Law, then, again holds true for the sign of the cat. Specific narrative scenes, unquestionably derived from "textual" sources (especially exempla, which are, of course, primarily oral texts), establish its immediate "meaning." The sign, however, is also employed in contexts removed from the original narrative inspiration and in association with other emblems; it consequently takes on additional and metaphoric connotations until, finally, the cat can stand alone (as it does in the majority of its manifestations) as a symbol signifying a broad range of ideas.

An image on folio 52b of Vienna ÖNB cod. 2554 constitutes the intermediate stage in the evolution of the cat emblem,

FIG. 62 (TOP). Dan. 8:8. Four types of sin. Cod. 1179, fol. 171d. FIG. 63. I Macc. 9:5–6. Christians abandon the fight against Albigensian heretics to pursue secular delights. Cod. 1179, fol. 203b.

FIG. 64. III Kings 13:14–19. False miscreants deceive good students and lure them into sin. Cod. 2554, fol. 52b.

demonstrating how the narrative depiction of the heretics' cat-worshiping rites is transformed into static representations with more wide-ranging applicability. The roundel elucidates an episode from the Third Book of Kings (13:14–19), in which a false prophet of the evil Israelite king Jeroboam deceives a "man of God."[38] The commentary text compares this false prophet to the false miscreant who "deceives with false praise and false promises."[39] As is so often the case in the manuscript, the commentary image considerably amplifies the implications of the text. The miscreants seem to be identified by their beards and hats as Jews; the cat is now depicted in a new position: it sits, still and upright, on a table lined with gold coins. The cat is thus accorded a dual role: it may be seen as both a living animal perched on the equipment of its (moneylending?) confederates *and* as its metaphoric equivalent: an idol on an altar (Fig. 64).

This image reflects a complex process of syllogistic progression and metaphoric correlation. If the cat was worshiped by heretics, then it corresponded to the definition of a false god. As such, it could be associated with that other great false god of thirteenth-century moralistic treatises (and of the *Bible moralisée* in particular): lucre. The foul nature of the heretics' rites, in which they apply their mouths (site of the ingestion of the immaculate Host by good Catholics) to filthy animal orifices, moreover, provides another link to money, regarded by the moralist theologians as filthy and contaminated.[40] And, via dirt and lucre, we have come full circle to the Jews. This pattern of reasoning, in which related concepts are strung together to construct a newly significant whole, accounts for the most common context in which the sign of the cat appears: in the arms of a miscreant or a Jew, accompanying texts that do not specifically mention heresy or heretics. Such otherwise inexplicable images constitute the final permutation of the cat-sign into a completely abstract symbol, to which the images of cat-worshiping heretics inevitably form the cognitive backdrop. In this way, the iconography of the *Bible moralisée* builds upon a common calumny to create a new method for artistically representing heresy, while considerably extending the malignant implications of the slander.

What, then, is the cumulative thrust of the conflation of Jews and heretics in the *Bible moralisée*? In a pattern echoing that already described in relation to texts dealing with the Law, the relevant commentary excerpts lead us in two very different directions. First, a group of highly specific texts and images suggests that concern about Jewish and heretical influence was prevailing in precisely the same narrow and specialized context as that concerned with Jewish exegesis. Second, a host of other texts and images lead us outward from these confines, illuminating the manifold ways in which, in a broader framework, the resonance of such conflations of Jews and heretics could proliferate and deepen.

Seducing the Simple: Jews, Students, and the Theophilus Legend

The specialized context in which concern about Jews and heretics seems to have coalesced is once again suggested by the sign of the cat. For in addition to being depicted with Jews and heretics, the cat appears in the *Bible moralisée* in conjunction with two other groups: university students and philosophers.

A roundel on folio 50vd of the French manuscript depicts the students' vulnerability to heterodoxy with densely layered iconography. In the Bible illustration above, the aged Solomon is shown being lured by his young foreign wives into worshiping idols. The commentary caption states: "That Solomon was deceived by woman and denied God and adored idols signifies the bad student whom the devil tricks and deceives. And he denies his creator and becomes a man of the devil and God is angry at him."[41] A reading of the accompanying image is facilitated by its formal parallels with the roundel above. The devil, who corresponds in placement and function to the seductive young wives of Solomon, is shown as a female-headed serpent twisting sinuously around a student's body and whispering into his ear (Fig. 65). The student denies his Creator—a distraught Jesus opening a book on a desk—by throwing downward and behind him a small red object. Although the object is too small and schematically rendered to identify simply on the basis of its appearance, the student's gesture suggests that it is intended to represent straw. This is, to my knowledge, the only existing illustration of the feudal ceremony of *exfestucatio*—a ritual breaking of the ties of homage, symbolized by the casting of a handful of straw to the ground.[42] In the position parallel to the idol above appears a Jew holding up a cat, between whose paws the student places his hand. This action constitutes the formation of a feudal relationship—as the text states, the student becomes the "man" (in the technical sense of vassal) of the devil, symbolized by the cat.[43] But, in light of the other roundels in the manuscripts containing cats, it becomes clear that the cat represents the devil in his specific role as the object of heretical veneration. The Jew holding the cat can be considered the "supporter" of heresy, analogous to the altar in the roundel above.

FIG. 65. III Kings 11:1–9. A bad student becomes the "man" of the devil: a cat supported by Jews. Cod. 2554, fol. 50vd.

Two separate iconographic traditions inform this image and help explicate its themes. The figure of the snake wrapped around the student's body visually relates the student's seduction to the temptation of Adam and Eve, for in many thirteenth-century representations of the Fall, including those in the *Bible moralisée,*[44] the devil was rendered as a female-headed serpent wrapped around the trunk of the tree of knowledge. Peter Comestor explained that the female-headed serpent was chosen to deceive Eve because "like attracts like."[45] In echoing the Fall of Man, then, the commentary image illuminates the nature of the trap set for the student. Just as Eve was tempted by an enticer in her own image and, together with Adam, was driven from paradise for eating of the tree of knowledge against God's express decree, so the student, himself a repository of knowledge, is enticed into forsaking the sacred domain (explicitly connected to learning through the book opened by Jesus) by the lure of illicit knowledge, embodied in the bivalent image of the Jew/heretic.

Second, the depiction of the student paying homage to the devil closely links the scene to illustrations of the legend of Theophilus—the tale of the cleric who, embittered by resentment and frustrated ambition, sold his soul to the devil through the mediation of a Jewish sorcerer.[46] This legend, which reached its apogee of popularity in the decades around the creation of the *Bible moralisée,*[47] constitutes another conceptual window through which the *Bible moralisée* image would have been viewed. Because of this, a brief analysis of the main themes and techniques of the Theophilus legend is in order. The title assigned the tale in the Gautier de Coincy manuscripts was "Comment Theophilus vint a penitance"; in early thirteenth-century Paris, then, penitence was considered the tale's primary theme. To effectively evoke penitence, the legend must locate Theophilus's transgression within a familiar realm: the reader/listener/viewer must feel himself at home in Theophilus's world and at least potentially susceptible to the sins committed by Theophilus. The tale's most obvious and frequently noted precept is its warning concerning the dangers of clerical pride and ambition. This would certainly have rung a familiar note in university circles: there evidently was serious concern about students' inclinations in this direction. Moralists' writings and university sermons constantly inveighed against the lure of ambition—for ecclesiastical preferment, for royal employment.[48] Worldly success, in turn, could lead to excessive pride, but success was by no means the only source of this vice. Thirteenth-century Parisian masters warned students repeatedly that the primary danger of education was that it engendered pride and intellectual independence.[49] Jacques de Vitry asserted that excessive questioning would lead to heresy.[50] Caesarius of Heisterbach recorded that, when young, the abbot of Morimund had "done homage to the devil" in exchange for augmented intelligence and memory,[51] and Stephen of Bourbon reported that heretics considered themselves "wise men."[52] Even the great scholar and unquestionably orthodox Hugh of St. Victor was criticized for intellectual pride: according to an exemplum reported by Stephen of Bourbon, he was afflicted after his death because of his *zenodoxiam* (vainglory).[53]

This association between knowledge and prideful error, then, helps to explain the character of the Jewish magus in the Theophilus legend. This character has received far less attention than has the protagonist, perhaps because the "Jewish magician" is such a venerable literary stereotype and/or because the sorcerer seems an incidental figure whose primary function is to advance the narrative.[54] However, the character was not arbitrarily chosen; nor does it lack social resonance. Jews, like heretics, were frequently accused of abandoning Scripture on account of curiosity and misguided faith in their own opinions.[55] Jews, in fact, seem to have become a kind of byword for intellectual pride: a university preacher in 1230 thundered against masters who study not to be useful but in order "to appear learned and to be called rabbi,"[56] and Raoul Ardent compared overly curious masters of Scripture to Jewish scribes and Pharisees.[57] Similarly, the straying scholar in the *Bible moralisée* roundel is moving physically, intellectually, and spiritually away from sacred study and toward the Jew/heretic: "like attracts like."

But another motif is implicit in the Theophilus legend as well. In his days of struggle, before his "fall," Theophilus is severely impoverished: "Now I am reduced to dying of hunger / if I don't pawn my cloak to have bread."[58] Significant, too, is the fact that Theophilus's pact with the devil is in the form of a written and sealed document, called a *chartre,* drawn up with the help of the Jew.[59] Through such language and imagery, Theophilus's predicament is situated against a shadowy backdrop of financial struggle, of indebtedness and moneylenders, and consequently (so far as thirteenth-century French texts are concerned) of Jews. This, too, like the realms of pride and curiosity, was a universe with which Parisian students would have been acquainted; similar worries have perennially occupied the interstices of students' lives. Like Theophilus, many students at the University of Paris in the early thirteenth century experienced financial distress;[60] some of them (again like Theophilus) had recourse to moneylenders, among whom were most likely included some Jews.[61] Nor is this the only context in which students would have had exposure to and transactions with Jews. One of the Jewish quarters in Paris was on the Île-de-la-Cité between the Pont-au-Change and the Petit-Pont: a main commercial and pilgrimage thoroughfare.[62] Alexander Nequam indicated that it was common for Parisian university students to rent rooms in houses owned by Jews.[63] The Theophilus story, then, had a familiar and suggestive economic subtext, readily evoking in its audience the myriad sensations accompanying indebtedness. To the literary figure of Salatin the Jew would have adhered the various contradictory feelings with which people regard their creditors, their landlords, and any familiar yet socially aloof figures with whom they have commercial transactions entailing vulnerability and/or subordination. Although the Jew in the Solomon roundel was contemplated by a privileged and elite audience (to which, however, frustration at indebtedness was by no means alien), it would have been embedded with the cultural assumptions of the overall milieu out of which it sprang.

This economic subtext—admittedly buried very deep, if present at all, in the Solomon roundel—comes to the fore in a commentary text and roundel appearing two folios later. The full III Kings commentary text concerning the prophet "Gad" that I translated partially earlier runs, "That the false prophet deceived Gad through his false prophecy and Gad believed him signifies the false miscreant who through lies and false promises deceives the good student and attracts him to himself, and turns him to his part and makes him sin and go against the commandments of Jesus."[64] As mentioned earlier, the tempters in the accompanying roundel are, as in the Solomon roundel, portrayed as Jews with beards and pointed hats. Similarly, the sin to which the students are drawn is represented by the sign for heresy: a striped cat sits on its haunches upon an altar. Beneath the cat, however, is an additional element: a pile of coins, explicitly locating the miscreants' lies and false promises within the economic realm—identifying the students' trespasses with moneylending and consequently with greed and idolatry (see Fig. 64).[65]

In such ways, the social background, the invocation of traditional literary topoi, and the manifold meanings attached to the Jew throughout the *Bible moralisée* combine to lend depth and complexity to the charge that Jews lead students astray. But even when the social and economic factors are recognized, the implications of the antiheretical polemic in these manuscripts are still far from exhausted. Students are accused not just of sinning but, specifically, of pursuing illicit knowledge. To understand yet another possible reason for associating Jews with this activity, we must turn our attention to a third group depicted with the sign of the cat and regularly associated with both Jews and heretics in the manuscripts: philosophers.

Philosophers of Synagoga

Folio 35va of the French manuscript illustrates an episode from the First Book of Kings (2:22), in which Hebrew women are raped in the temple by depraved priests. This is compared in the commentary text to "simple [or unlearned] people who come before bad philosophers, who are miscreants and they poison [?] them and deceive them with their bad doctrine."[66] Two philosophers are depicted in the commentary roundel. One is bearded, wears a low, round, green cap and a hooded cloak, and is drawn in a rather dark and fierce profile. He clutches the wrists of a young man standing before him as a young woman looks on. The second philosopher is seated on the right of the roundel before a woman and a young man listening at his feet. This philosopher is bearded, is drawn in profile, and wears a hood and a blue cloak.

In his arms he cradles a cat, suggesting that the "bad doctrine" of the philosophers is some form of heterodoxy (Fig. 66).

However, the language of this French commentary text, which refers to "unbelievers" and to "bad doctrine," could be applied to Jews as easily as to heretics. Although the Latin version does not employ equivalent terms, the suggestion of a Jewish connection is incorporated in the accompanying image. The Latin commentary reads: "The women who went offering to the Temple and were deceived signify certain simple people who came before bad philosophers. And these philosophers deceive them through their perverse proofs."[67] The evil philosophers are represented by two figures: a beardless man with a round cap pointing to an idol—which may represent the "bad doctrine" mentioned in the text of the French commentary—and a bearded man with a pointed hat (i.e., a figure readily interpreted as a Jew) kissing a cat (Fig. 67).

A commentary text accompanying the next biblical book makes explicit what is implied in the iconography just described. In II Kings 15:2, Absalom attempts to attract the people of Jerusalem to his rebellion against his father at the urging of "a certain man who is in his counsel." According to the Latin commentary, "This signifies Jews and publicans and bad philosophers who deceive the people and through their words drag besieged peoples to their faith at the suggestion of the devil."[68] Two seated figures on the left represent the villains: a Jew in a tall, pointed hat and a beardless man in a round cap holding a striped cat (Fig. 68). Beside these figures is a tall shrine containing an idol. One hatless man kneels before the figure holding the cat and puts his hands between its front paws in a gesture of homage; behind him a crowd of beardless, hatless men (whose youth may identify them as students, although they are not visibly tonsured) worship the idol. In this text the use of the singular *suam fidem* subsumes the disparate deceiving groups within one perfidious concept; calling their victims *gentes,* one half of the traditional dichotomy Jewish/Gentile, suggests that this perfidious unity is a Jewish one. Through the use of language and symbol, heretic, philosopher, and Jew are implicated in a common malignant activity, which threatens students and laypeople alike.

This basic message is reinforced through repeated assertions that philosophers are followers of Synagoga and purveyors of intellectual error.[69] The French manuscript explains in its commentary on Gen. 39:16: "[The wife of Potiphar] who called out to her husband and complained about Joseph signifies Synagoga, who called out to the philosophers and complained about Jesus Christ and pointed to him with her finger."[70] Four figures appear in the commentary roundel (Fig. 69). On the right, Jesus walks away from the others. In the center stands Synagoga, displaying the traditional iconographic signs of her defeat: eyes closed and crown falling off her head, she points her left forefinger at Jesus.

FIG. 66 (TOP). I Kings 2:22. Simple people deceived by the bad doctrine of miscreant philosophers. Cod. 2554, fol. 35va.
FIG. 67. I Kings 2:22. Simple people deceived by the perverse proofs of bad philosophers. Cod. 1179, fol. 86a.

FIG. 68 (TOP). II Kings 15:2. Jews, heretics, and bad philosophers deceive people. Cod. 1179, fol. 108a. FIG. 69. Gen. 39:16–17. Synagoga accuses Jesus before her philosophers. Cod. 2554, fol. 10a.

To the left of Synagoga are two figures representing the "philosophers." One is a Jew drawn in profile, wearing a tall, pointed cap. He raises both hands with his palms toward Synagoga in a gesture of respect or worship. Beside him a man with a round, green cap raises one forefinger, as if to teach or to reinforce a rhetorical point. There is no way to determine the temporal context of this commentary text. The Latin version of this commentary refers to Synagoga's "priests and doctors of the Law," and it seems likely that the intended referent is an episode from the New Testament in which the Jews accuse Jesus. However, the commentary roundel offers an interpretation of its own: the two philosophers are a contemporary Jew and a figure gesturing in the manner of a teacher or logician. Synagoga's ancient betrayal of Jesus is consequently associated with contemporary problems in the schools.[71]

The suggestion that philosophy was allied with heresy, like so many opinions reflected in the *Bible moralisée,* is hardly original: it appears in a range of contemporary texts. The twelfth-century commentary *In Exodum,* written by Richard, abbot of Préaux, contains many strongly worded condemnations of both heretics and pagan philosophy.[72] Joachim da Fiore wrote in his commentary to the *Apocalypse* that a new kind of heretic adhered to the errors of philosophers,[73] and Alan of Lille said in his *Contra Hereticos* that heretics used Gentile philosophers as authorities.[74] Nor were students of theology considered immune. Peter the Chanter used his commentary on the Book of Ruth to praise students who remained faithful to God and his doctrine and rejected the teachings of the philosophers,[75] and Alan of Lille, Stephen of Tournai, and Absolom of St. Victor all had harsh words for those who abandoned theology for "inane philosophy."[76]

Several events affecting the University of Paris in the second and third decades of the thirteenth century rendered this heresy-philosophy link particularly germane. Earlier in the century, the arts master Amaury de Bène (or de Chartres) had been forced to recant many of his writings as heretical. Although Amaury did so before dying in 1206, his ideas, or ideas ascribed to him, persisted. A hunt was carried out for his "followers" in 1209, and in December 1210 several students identified as such were burned as heretics.[77] At the same time, the works of Amaury, David de Dinant, and a certain Maurice of Spain were banned. This episode, the first serious allegation of internal heresy with which the university had to grapple, was clearly felt to be related to the newly arrived philosophical works. Amaury and David were both students of dialectics, and David is believed to have been strongly influenced by Aristotle.[78] Guillaume le Breton explicitly stated that the heresy had been caused by Aristotle's *Metaphysics.*[79] The banning of the public reading of the works of Aristotle or his commentators in Robert de Courson's statutes of 1215 was very likely related to the episode.[80]

Interest in the Amauricians remained strong at the time of the creation of the *Bible moralisée,* which followed the condemnations by about ten years. The story was mentioned by both Guillaume le Breton (ca. 1220) and Caesarius of Heisterbach (ca. 1222). The banning of the works of John Scotus Eriugena by Pope Honorius in 1225, with his assertion that anyone who read them was to be considered a heretic, was probably provoked by the Amaurician affair, since Scotus was a major influence on Amaury's thought.[81]

The increasing hostility of the university's theology faculty to intellectual innovations has been linked to the Amaurician heresy.[82] University preachers of the 1220s and early 1230s become ever more vehement in their denunciations of philosophy and profane learning, and more specific in their allegations that philosophy spawned heresy, in spite of the fact (or more likely because of the fact) that a new generation of Paris masters were incorporating Aristotelian ideas into their own works.[83] Gerald of Wales asserted that some scholars had already been turned into heretics by the works of Aristotle.[84] Jacques de Vitry told an exemplum against "presumptuous people who too subtly seek into divine things and thus enter heresy."[85] Robert Pullen said that dialecticians and philosophers were responsible for religious skepticism.[86] Condemnations of philosophy and dialectic are featured prominently in sermons delivered to students in the thirteenth century.[87] Even William of Auvergne, one of the first Parisian masters to make extensive use of Aristotelian philosophy, was highly critical of the overvaluation of philosophy at the expense of theology.[88]

Controversies surrounding the status of philosophy at the University of Paris might find echoes in a biblical commentary made for the royal court for a number of reasons. By virtue of his residence in Paris, the king of France was intimately involved in the life of the university. Philip Augustus and later Blanche of Castile (as regent for Louis IX) several times intervened in matters of discipline, and, given the economic and intellectual centrality of the university, all French sovereigns took a lively interest in defending its status and health.[89] Louis VIII had a personal connection to the intellectual life of the university; he had been tutored in his youth by Amaury de Bène when the latter was a member of the arts faculty.[90] Although there is no record of whether Louis remembered his old tutor with any affection, he must have taken some interest in his fate.[91] The redactors of the *Bible moralisée* may have felt that it was particularly important to incorporate instructions concerning the proper views regarding philosophers if Louis were the recipient or a potential reader of one of the manuscripts.

But how and why would Jews or Judaism have been perceived as connected to this internal Christian problem? Here, too, some specific circumstances might account for such an attitude. Most of the Aristotelian works that had been flooding into the University of Paris since the late twelfth century had been translated from Arabic into Latin in Toledo. Jews were active participants in these translations—a fact that probably would have been familiar to most educated Parisian theologians.[92] Moreover, by the 1220s the works of several Jewish philosophers and commentators on Aristotle, most notably Maimonides, were being studied by Parisian theologians. William of Auvergne cited a variety of Muslim and Jewish thinkers in his works, including Maimonides and Avicebron (Ibn Sina), but also expressed mistrust of them.[93] Alexander of Hales also utilized Latin translations of Maimonides and Avicebron in his *Summa universae theologiae.*[94] It seems likely that some of the commentaries on Aristotle banned in 1215 were Arabo-Jewish philosophical works.

The writings of William of Auvergne point to another reason theologians might have suspected that philosophical heresies had been influenced by or were sympathetic to Jewish thought. In *De legibus,* he severely criticizes those who maintain that members of any faith could be saved if they sincerely believed that their law came from God. Beryl Smalley was unable to find any record of any Christians who held such opinions.[95] However, the author of the treatise *Contra Amaurianos* recorded that those sectarians held a not dissimilar conviction: "If a Jew has knowledge of the truth, which we have, it is not necessary that he be baptized."[96] Ironically, the antinomianism of the Amauricians led to opinions that could be labeled (at least by hostile Catholics) philo-Judaic.

There are, in addition, more general grounds for linking Jews with philosophy. We have seen how suspicions of the Jews' exegetical techniques grew as interest in and familiarity with the Hebrew text of the Bible became more common.[97] Such suspicions were sometimes explicitly linked to philosophical method. Historical / literal exegesis, which since the heyday of the rationalistic school of Rashi and certainly by the early thirteenth century was associated primarily with the Jews in polemical discourse, was generally condemned as "philosophical."[98] Peter the Chanter warned Christians not to dispute the meaning of the Scriptures with Jews because the latter were well versed in "sophistry";[99] a late twelfth-century anti-Jewish treatise asserted that Jews had recourse to a sophistry founded on lies;[100] and a university sermon delivered in 1230 used Jewish rabbis as paradigms for those who obscure the meaning of the Scriptures through involuted "sentences."[101] William of Auvergne asserted that many Jews living among the Saracens had taken up the errors of Gentile philosophy.[102] Such comments may reflect awareness of many Jews' very real interest in philosophy.[103]

However, although these specific circumstances might have encouraged the belief that Jews (or Jewish thought) posed a threat to students, it would be overly simplistic to claim that they alone inspired or explain the antiphilosophical polemic embedded in the *Bible moralisée* and so many contemporary texts. Rather, the polemic is part of an overall process in which a Christian philosophy was constructed by adopting sympathetic aspects of the ancient intellectual heritage and excluding inimical ones as "foreign" and "un-Christian."[104] So, for example, Garnier de Rochefort (d. 1225) preached that the Seven Liberal Arts were useful to theology but that Philosophy was a "prostitute, strange woman, concubine" in whom the senses reigned.[105] In its "foreignness," then, but also in its association with the flesh and with matter—in contradistinction to the spirituality of Christian theology—philosophy is constructed in such polemics as akin to Judaism. On the other hand, the very call for such polemics, of course, testifies to the existence of many general and growing similarities between the interests, influences, and techniques of high medieval Christian intellectual culture and those of "pagan/foreign/Jewish" intellectual cultures. A host of texts and images in the *Bible moralisée* confirm that such correspondences were noted and disapproved by the redactors.

The Controversy over the Secular Sciences

One of the ways in which Christian and Jewish intellectual endeavors overlapped is mentioned in a text in the Latin manuscript that details the means by which "bad philosophers" achieve their deceptions. The commentary to the Tower of Babel story (Gen. 11:1–9) remarks, "That pagans built a tower against God toward heaven signifies that astrologers and dialecticians and other philosophers teaching false proofs are blinded and confused."[106] Three clerics are depicted in the accompanying roundel being struck by pointed objects falling from the sky (Fig. 70). One cleric points into his own palm as if counting or reckoning; another lifts a round instrument that seems to be an astrolabe; and a third sits in deep thought with his chin upon his palm. Although the figures in question are clearly Christian, the references to blindness, confusion, and false proofs tie this text linguistically and conceptually to other anti-Jewish commentaries (it will be remembered that the "perverse proofs" of "bad philosophers" were also singled out as the means by which simple people were deceived in the text commenting on the rape of the Hebrew women by the evil presbyters).[107]

FIG. 70. Gen. 11:9. The university arts faculty as a medieval Babel: astrologers, dialecticians, and other philosophers blinded and confused. Cod. 1179, fol. 7d.

The motives alleged for students' infatuation with astrology and dialectic expand the resonance of the theme beyond the confines of the university and provide another conceptual link to the Jews. In the Latin manuscript, the commentary to Num. 11:1–2 explains, "The sons of Israel who vomited the manna and sought flesh [to eat] signify bad scholars who vomit theology and study secular sciences that they might become rich."[108] The biblical text, which does not specify that the Israelites vomited the manna,

FIG. 71 (TOP). Num. 11:1–2. Bad scholars vomit theology and study lucrative sciences. Cod. 1179, fol. 53d. FIG. 72. II Esd. 13:24. Law students cannot understand the gospel. Cod. 1179, fol. 143c.

seems to have been manipulated to make use of the special nuances conveyed by imagery of vomiting, which suggests not merely surfeit but bile and contamination.[109] The illustration to this text depicts three tonsured clerics (Fig. 71). One ejects volumes representing theological works from his mouth, another drops a volume with his hands, and a third throws down a book with one hand while reaching for a small building suspended in the sky—representing a prebend, the wealth for which theology was abandoned. Jesus, seated on the left of the roundel, looks on with an expression that might indicate disapproval, sadness, or anger, and seems to envelop a sacred book in his robes to protect it from defilement. In the constructed universe of the *Bible moralisée,* any greed, even—or especially—that of clerics, constitutes a link to infidelity and hence to Jews.

This theme is reiterated in texts and roundels that refer to yet another discipline much criticized by theologians: the study of the law. The last commentary text accompanying the Second Book of Esdras remarks, "That the Jews took pagan wives . . . signifies that clerics who do not have a good and holy beginning in the Church do not understand the holy gospel because of the worldly law in which they were skilled, and have no understanding except of temporal things."[110] The image contrasts holy and temporal understanding by playing off two signs against each other. On the left, one good cleric is seated before an open book (representing the Gospels and all holiness) and makes a sign of blessing with his left hand (Fig. 72). On the right are portrayed two bad clerics. One ignores the open book propped upon his lap and instead grasps a small church building representing the form of wealth most readily available to those in holy orders: a prebend. He waves rejection toward the good cleric with his left hand.

All of the disciplines mentioned here—astrology (or astronomy, as it is called in the French text), dialectics, the law, and philosophy—were known as "secular sciences" to Parisian theologians. The common denominator of these subjects—and the crux of the problem to the theologians—is that they constituted a source of knowledge about the universe that existed entirely outside of Scripture. They were consequently held to be (at best) ancillary to the primary endeavor of any medieval theologian—the study and interpretation of Holy Writ. When the "secular sciences" were put in the service of theology they were tolerated, but when they detracted from the study of Scripture they were roundly condemned.[111] The vehemence and absoluteness of the condemnations varied according to the personality and intellectual orientation of the given exegete; the *Bible moralisée* clearly reflects the more extreme, or conservative, point of view, consistently presenting astrology and dialectic as detracting from the pursuit of theology. In each of the "astrology" images discussed earlier, what is missing from the clerics' hands is as noteworthy as what is present: none of these scholarly figures holds or consults a book. The significance of this omission is clear when it is contrasted with the central role accorded books in a pair of images dealing with the "secular" discipline of legal studies. The interpretation of I Kings 13:20 states: "The Israelites who brought iron to the pagans that they might make them arms . . . signify bad scholars who leave the gospel and theology and go to Bologna that they might be able to study laws and decrees by which they are confused."[112] The commentary roundel depicts two groups of clerics debating each other (Fig. 73). One of the good students carries an open book, and another makes a gesture of blessing, while one bad student raises his forefinger as if making a rhetorical point, and another reckons on his palm. The French text of this commentary is even more vehement about the evils resulting from study of the law: the students are not merely confounded but destroyed.[113] The accompanying roundel is somewhat different from that in the Latin manuscript (Fig. 74). On the left, the abandoned study of divinity is represented by an open book propped upon a high desk; no good cleric is in evidence. In the center of the roundel, tonsured students hold small, closed books and bags of money and walk away from the book of divinity. On the right of the roundel, their destination is depicted. Several bearded and tonsured clerics with brutal expressions, and a hunched and hooded scribe writing in a codex represent the Bolognese teachers of the Law. Their overall appearance is quite sinister, as is the implication that the law masters are creating their own, novel text to rival the divinely authored writ of Theology—an anti-Bible, as it were. In appearance as well as activity, the Bolognese masters display a striking resemblance to the Jewish scribes condemned elsewhere (see Fig. 51).

FIG. 73 (TOP). I Kings 13:19–20. Bad scholars abandon theology to study laws in Bologna. Cod. 1179, fol. 89b. FIG. 74. I Kings 13:19–20. The same bad scholars are confounded and destroyed. Cod. 2554, fol. 37b.

"They Cut the Sacrament to Pieces"

One of the most prominent areas in which Jews and heretics are collectively, and damningly, implicated is the debate over the sacraments. In fact, rejection of sacraments is the most common accusation voiced in the *Bible moralisée* against heretics, whose beliefs otherwise seem to be almost entirely irrelevant.[114] The heretics' contempt for the sacraments is criticized explicitly in several texts, but it is censured even more frequently in the images, constituting one of the most common visual topoi. For example, Nabal's refusal to acknowledge David as his king (I Kings 25:10) is compared to "infidels and publicans who tell Christ's prelates that they do not know Jesus and do not want him to be their Lord, but even blaspheme him."[115] This general and rather timeless text is updated and made more specific in the commentary roundel. One of the "infidels and publicans" portrayed in the roundel is wearing a Jewish cap, one is hooded, and one car-

FIG. 75 (TOP). I Kings 25:10–11. Infidels and heretics reject the body of Christ. Cod. 1179, fol. 96b. FIG. 76. Lev. 24:10–14. Miscreants and heretics mock God and his sacraments. Cod. 2554, fol. 30d.

ries a striped cat (Fig. 75). However, the image goes beyond the text in depicting the infidels and heretics as shunning not Jesus himself but two prelates. One of the prelates holds up a chalice and a Host; the other holds an open book, extending the heretics' rejection to include the teachings and the sacraments of the Catholic Church.

The refusal to venerate the Catholic sacraments is, of course, one area of Christian dissident thought that clearly *was* shared by Jews, and the illustrations in the *Bible moralisée* consistently underscore this fact. First, all depictions of heretics rejecting the sacraments echo in composition and detail the numerous images of Jews doing the same.[116] Second, illustrations of heretical activity tend to include Jews, as in the roundel just discussed. Another example of this approach appears in the French manuscript's Leviticus commentary. Here the Israelite who mocked God (Lev. 24:14) is interpreted as signifying "*mescreanz* and *populicanz* who mock God and His sacraments and say that they are nothing."[117] Once again, the illustration concentrates the polemic by focusing on the heretics' attitudes toward the sacraments rather than toward God. On the left of the roundel, a priest raises a wafer above an altar with a chalice resting on it. To the right of the priest stands the group of four "unbelievers and heretics." As in the previous example, the roundel consciously draws a parallel between Jewish and heretical rejection of the sacraments, and does so much more explicitly than the text. The two foremost figures are drawn in profile, have dark beards, and wear low, rounded caps. One holds a lamb—a symbol of Jewish rites (Fig. 76).

Finally, this theme is treated in the longest and most elaborate commentary sequence in the *Bible moralisée,* which glosses an ugly and disturbing episode in the nineteenth chapter of Judges.[118] In the manuscripts' biblical paraphrase, a deacon comes to Bethlehem with his wife, his servants, and his ass. They find no room at the inn but are eventually given hospitality by "a certain good man." The "Sodomite" residents of the city then come to the house, wishing to seize the deacon and "satisfy their will of him libidinously." The host refuses to surrender his guest to the Sodomites, who take the deacon's wife instead. They rape and kill her, then throw her body out onto the street. The deacon finds her in the morning, is struck with grief and anger, and puts her body on his ass to take back to his home. Once there, he cuts his wife's corpse into twelve parts and sends a part to each of the twelve Hebrew tribes in order to incite them to wreak revenge.[119]

Both manuscripts explicate this episode in more or less the same way. The deacon who sought shelter signifies good philosophers (or, according to the French manuscript, Philosophy personified) who were separated from or stripped of faith by the "world."[120] The good man who gave them shelter signifies Jesus

Christ, who gave Philosophy a place within his Church.[121] The Sodomites are *infideles* and *publicani* (in French, *mescreanz* and *popelicanz*), who come (note present tense) to Holy Church to destroy her and her sacraments.[122] These infidels and heretics then took or take (both perfect and present are employed) pagan philosophy from Jerome and Augustine (with whom the "good philosophers" are now identified) and attack and abuse it.[123] After mistreating Philosophy, the heretics and infidels cast out pagan philosophy and doctrine, and Jerome and Augustine, receiving them, grieved (perfect tense).[124] The great doctors then separated philosophy from pagan doctrine, divided her into twelve volumes, and handed her over to the twelve patriarchs.[125]

Seven roundels illustrate this interpretation in the Latin manuscript. The first (in the upper left quadrant) shows two "good philosophers"—a Benedictine monk representing Jerome and an Augustinian canon representing Augustine—handing an open book to Jesus, who is standing beneath a trefoil arch signifying a church (Fig. 77, page 104).[126] In the next roundel (in the lower left quadrant) three heretics reach out in an attempt to attack a priest standing before an altar and drinking from a chalice. Jesus stands before the priest and blocks the heretics. Two of the heretics wear short peaked hats; one is bareheaded. One heretic carries a sword, and another heretic carries a striped cat. Subsequent roundels, however, portray the heretics in the ascetic fashion: barefoot, with wild hair and beards. In the third (upper right quadrant) they are pulling Philosophy (personified as a woman with a chalice) away from Jerome and Augustine; in the last roundel on the folio they beat her with staffs while one kisses the anus of a cat.

The illustrations of this episode in the French manuscript are slightly different. Jerome and Augustine are barefoot clerics and are not wearing identifiable habits. The depictions of the heretics, too, diverge from those in the Latin manuscript. In the second roundel in the series, the unbelievers and heretics are all represented (in some of the most virulent images in the manuscript) as Jews (Fig. 78). On the left of the roundel stand two Jews, both dark and fiercely grimacing. One carries an ax and sticks out his tongue in a gesture of scorn. The other is drawn in profile with an exaggeratedly long nose; he carries a sword, around which a serpentlike tail is entwined, and a demon emerges from his breast. The object of their scowls is a church building, in front of which Jesus stands as if to protect it from the Jews. Inside the building are two priests: one drinks from a chalice, and the other eats the eucharistic bread. Subsequent roundels also stress the darkness, anger, grotesqueness, and devilish possession of the "heretics"—who thus look very much like Jews.

FIG. 78. Judg. 19:22–23. Heretics and miscreants threaten the sacraments of the Holy Church. Cod. 2554, fol. 65a.

The thrust of this commentary sequence may be summarized as follows. It maintains that the discipline of Philosophy is not evil in and of itself as long as it remains firmly within the sphere

FIG. 77. Judg. 17:7–19:25. Philosophy taken from Augustine and Jerome, and abused by infidels and heretics. Cod. 1179, fol. 79.

of Catholic authority—as it does in the works of Jerome and Augustine. However, anyone who attempts to divorce Philosophy from its Christian context does harm to both the discipline of Christian philosophy and the Church itself. In order to repair this harm, sanctioned Church authorities—monks and canons? or biblical scholars in the tradition of Jerome and Augustine?—must reclaim Philosophy and locate her firmly within the framework of Scripture and tradition. Finally, the iconography and vocabulary of these and so many other texts and roundels invite the conclusion that anyone who so abuses Philosophy is both a Jew and a heretic.[127] This sequence consequently realizes visually the very point suggested by the text—that moral and spiritual truths (the perfidious equivalence of Jews and heretics) transcend categorical truths (that in canon law and theological analyses Jews and heretics are distinct).

This commentary is clearly informed on one level by Scholastic developments—the eucharistic debate of the eleventh and twelfth centuries was sparked by the application of dialectical methodologies to sacramental theology.[128] But there is a less purely intellectual element in this sequence as well: the world of this commentary set does not end at the school door. The "Philosophy of the Church" is identified with its priesthood and its sacraments—particularly the Eucharist, represented by priests drinking wine and eating a Host, but also by the Body of Christ himself, who physically prevents the infidels and publicans from entering the Church. The attack on Christian Philosophy is consequently rendered as an attack on the Eucharist *and* on the priesthood through which the eucharistic miracle is realized. Thus, the images bring the issue to the local parish church, where the Mass is celebrated, and to the streets outside, where the community of believers (symbolized by the Body of Christ) and the "infidel" attackers stage their violent physical confrontations. Such movement parallels the progression from the acerbic but largely abstract Scholastic debates over the Eucharist of the twelfth century to the rabid, and often tragic (for the targets), Host desecration accusations of the late thirteenth, of which these images may be early presages.[129]

A striking aspect of this sequence is the stark contrast drawn between the attackers and the officiating priests. In the Latin manuscript the person and posture of the tonsured priest in the lower left roundel (lips touching the rim of a chalice) embody purity, while the hairy and disheveled aspect of the heretic in the lower right roundel (lips touching a cat's anus) embodies all that is filthy and contaminated. In the French manuscript the priests' tonsures contrast with the Jews' dark and bearded complexions; the priest's raised chalice parallels an ax in the hand of one Jew, while the Host on the clean, white altar is opposed to a serpent wrapped around a sword in the hand of the other Jew. It is interesting to note that, as ever, the illustrations in the French manuscript are by far the more violent and anti-Jewish—just as Host desecration and other anti-Jewish tales in the vernacular were considerably more virulent in tone than those in Latin.[130] This very different accent adopted by the French manuscript must surely be associated with the fact that the manuscript was destined for a more purely lay audience, but whether the hostile imagery was generated by polemical considerations or was unconsciously reflective of cultural influences (or both) is impossible to say.

"Carnal Stench": Heretics and Scripture

By means of such symbols as the book and the Eucharist, the narrow topic of the dangers of secular studies repeatedly merges with much broader social themes. Just as the *Bible moralisée* bears witness to the subtle infestation of "temporal" (i.e., economic) interests both within the schools and throughout Christian, or at least urban French, society, it also dwells on the threat to the integrity of Scripture, and consequently to religious orthodoxy—that is, the threat of heresy—in the schools and in larger society. In both cases, Jews constitute connecting or intermediate elements, for, like the secularizing students, Jews and heretics are collectively as well as independently accused in the *Bible moralisée* of rejecting Scripture. At the opening of this chapter I cited a text characterizing both Jews and heretics as "hardened" against the Gospels. The image accompanying this text does not help explain the juxtaposition of the two groups: it shows only a band of Jews turning away from Jesus, led by a Jew slitting the throat of an animal; this presumably refers to the fact that Jews preferred their literal maintenance of the Old Law to the spiritual covenant offered in the Gospels (Fig. 79). The image provides no explanation for the inclusion of the reference to *publicani* or for the assertion that they and the Jews "simul sunt et contra evangelium," but several possibilities suggest themselves.

FIG. 79. Josh. 3:14–17. Jews and heretics hardened against the gospel. Cod. 1179, fol. 63d.

Throughout Christian history there appeared some heterodox sects that, like the Jews, were alleged to promote a literal interpretation of the Bible; one such group, the Passagini, was the object of a polemic written around the end of the twelfth century.[131] But this was a tiny sect that did not at any point dominate Catholic concerns; Judaizing heretics never, in fact, constituted a serious problem in the High Middle Ages. The heretics that attracted the greatest attention and inspired the most intense opposition in later twelfth- and thirteenth-century France—and in the *Bible moralisée*—were the Albigensians (Cathars), who, far from literally interpreting the Old Testament, either completely allegorized it or rejected its authority absolutely, ascribing its composition to the evil creative being.[132] Likewise, the attitude of most heretics toward the Gospels was very different from that of the

Jews; the majority of high medieval dissident religious groups not only accepted the Gospels but venerated them intensely, claiming to adhere to the apostolic life.[133] Of course, the Cathar interpretation of the New Testament differed substantially from orthodox interpretation, and this alone may account for the reference to heretics in the Joshua commentary.[134] However, in chapter 3 I suggested that the texts and images accusing Jews of attacking Scripture were employing traditional criticism of the Jews' own relationship to Scripture to express concern about the putative influence among Christians—especially the laity—of literalistic, suspiciously innovative, or simply unauthorized exegesis (all of which are subsumed under the rubric "Jewish"). The texts and images condemning heretics' relation to Scripture fit well within this framework.

In fact, in the *Bible moralisée* the heretics' rejection of Scripture is presented primarily as a challenge to the Church hierarchy's monopoly over scriptural exposition: it is not the heretics' defiance of God directly that draws attention but their defiance of his representatives on earth. A text in the French manuscript voices this accusation against the heretics: "That the people of Israel [came] before Bethlehem to take vengeance for the misdeed, and the Bethlehemites esteemed them very little, signifies the apostles who gathered together, and the power of their words spread through all the world and the *populicans* valued them and their words very little."[135] The commentary roundel ties together past and present, internal and external adversaries. It depicts the apostles standing outside a walled city, carrying open books and raising their hands as if to teach—an image that recalls not only the mission of the original apostles of Jesus, who, according to Christian histories, were ignored not by the Gentiles but by the Jews, but also the preaching of thirteenth-century prelates who aspired to emulate those apostles (Fig. 80). Likewise, the city could represent the walled city of Jerusalem or the strongholds of Languedoc, which northern prelates helped besiege throughout the Albigensian Crusade. Inside the walled city are the *populicans* who spurn the words of the apostles. These figures display signs of Jewishness: all are bearded, one is drawn in profile, one wears a tall, pointed yellow hat, and another wears a low, round white cap.

The Latin commentary to this text is identical, but it more broadly identifies those who *vilipendunt* the words of the apostles as "publicans, infidels, and all bad people." They are depicted in the roundel as a crowd standing directly before the apostles. Three are clearly Jews: they wear tall, pointed hats, and one, who gestures in rejection toward the apostles, carries a scroll. Two are barefoot heretics; one carries a striped cat (Fig. 81).

A common denominator shared by heretics, Jews, *and* students, then, is resistance to the word of God, specifically as it is embodied in the form of ecclesiastical authority. There is, of

FIG. 80 (TOP). Judg. 20:11–14. Heretics in a walled city spurn the apostles' words. Cod. 2554, fol. 65vd. FIG. 81. Judg. 20:11–14. Heretics, infidels, and bad people revile the apostles' words. Cod. 1179, fol. 81a.

course, nothing radical in the leveling of such accusations against heretics: the basic definition of a heresy is persistence in erroneous opinions, doctrines, or practices after correction by the ecclesiastical establishment.[136] Heresy was thus more a matter of trespasses against authority than ideology,[137] and even those heretical sects that had no substantial doctrinal objections to the Catholic sacraments (such as the Waldensians) were considered rebels against the Church. But how do "infidels" figure in this equation? The definition of heresy given earlier might seem to emphasize the gulf between heretics and Jews, since Jews were never theoretically subject to the authority of the Church. But because the *Bible moralisée,* a work of biblical interpretation, regularly identifies Church authority with authority over Scripture, the heretics' rejection of the Church becomes, in fact, a close link to Jews, who similarly embodied a challenge to the ecclesiastical monopoly over interpretation. However, the strongest bond forged between Jews and heretics lies in the consistent representation of the heretics' contumacy concerning Scripture as both driven by and eventuating in those "perfidious" attributes most regularly associated with Jews.

Examples of such exegetically related perversities are presented on folio 225a of the Latin manuscript. The commentary to Apoc. 2:18 runs, "Jezebel . . . signifies masters of heretics who live in carnal voluptuousness and teach against the gospel. And Christians ought not to sustain them among themselves. . . ."[138] The accompanying roundel construes the carnality of the heretics as a superabundance of vices. An older man in a fur hood is seated at a feast table while embracing a woman (Fig. 82). Before him kneels a squire offering a hawk and a bag of money. Behind this "master of the heretics" a bearded figure worships an idol. This image is a fascinating and complicated amalgamation of metaphor and imagery, drawing upon a range of antiheretical polemics and enriched with details from contemporary experience.[139] The heretic's hypocritically luxurious lifestyle is marked by his fur hood and the rich double cup resting on the table. His lust and greed are illustrated with straightforward signs—the moneybag and the woman. However, other accusations are more subtle. The figure of the squire would have recalled the attendants in the court of any great noble (secular or ecclesiastical), but it is clearly intended to be inappropriate in the company of someone aspiring to asceticism and purity (and of someone not noble by birth). The figure of the attendant may also have recalled other, similar figures commonly shown waiting upon the corrupted cleric in Theophilus cycles.[140] In this case, the added implication that heretics' masters were not merely corrupt in the fleshly sense but specifically corrupted by the devil would have been inherent in the image. The idol worshiper in the background similarly conveys a variety of meanings in this context: not merely the idola-

FIG. 82. Apoc. 2:18–28. Heretical masters living in carnal voluptuousness and teaching against the gospel. Cod. 1179, fol. 225a.

trous rites of heretics but also their lust, their greed, and their affinity with pagans and Jews.[141]

Another roundel in the same manuscript reiterates the connection between heretics' reading and teaching of the Gospels and their supposed sexual perversions. This roundel explicates the feast thrown by Balthasar in which he utilized utensils stolen from the Holy Temple of Jerusalem (Dan. 5:1–2). According to the commentary, "This signifies that heretics pervert Holy Scripture and interpret it according to their pleasure [*libitum;* etymologically linked to *libido,* lust] . . . and also those who expend the goods of Holy Church in evil and bad things."[142] The commentary image focuses on the perversions that result from false exegesis. Seated at a long table are four figures: a woman looking in a mirror represents vanity, a man embracing her represents lust, a young man with a bowl signifies gluttony or drunkenness, and an older man who embraces him exemplifies sodomy (Fig. 83).

The interrelationship of heretical exegesis, heretical vice, and the devil is asserted more explicitly still in another Apocalypse roundel. The commentary to Apoc. 16:4 explains, "This signifies the damnation of those who corrupt the scriptures and change the sweetness of scripture into the stench of carnal sensuality so that they make cursed heretics."[143] Two separate figures represent the chief heretics. On the right, a hooded, bearded man holds a moneybag and a cat, which he kisses on the mouth (Fig. 84). On the left, a cleric holds up an open book and raises his finger in exposition while a demon whispers into his ear. In the center of the roundel appear the figures whom the heretical masters are addressing: a man and a woman sit and listen while embracing each other. Again, we are presented with a triad of lust, greed, and false worship. In this image, however, a new idea appears: clerics who appear to be orthodox may actually create heresy and corrupt their congregation through false (carnal, meaning rational or literal?) interpretation of Scripture.

As we have seen so often before in the *Bible moralisée,* such images are concrete visualizations of themes expressed metaphorically in contemporary texts. Manifold polemical works from the late twelfth and early thirteenth centuries adopted the vocabulary of sexual perversion when discussing the heretics' subversion of Scripture. Bernard of Fontcaude (d. 1193) reported in his treatise *Contra Valdenses et Contra Arianos* that when, in 1190, the archbishop of Narbonne accused the "Poor of Lyons" (Waldensians) of falsifying Scripture, he called them "depravatores . . . et corruptores mentium."[144] In a letter of 1198, Innocent III accused the Albigensians of "sacrarum scripturarum intelligentiam pervertentes."[145] In his commentary on the Apocalypse, written about 1200, Joachim da Fiore said of heretics, "nevertheless, they use, or rather abuse, the authorities of Scripture, because they are incapable of demonstrating through reason what they say. . . .

FIG. 83 (TOP). Dan. 5:1–2. Heretics interpret Scripture according to their pleasure. Cod. 1179, fol. 165c. FIG. 84. Apoc. 16:4. Heretics turn sweet Scripture into carnal stench. Cod. 1179, fol. 236d.

adulterating [Scripture] through bad understanding of the letter, they are able to drag it into their perfidy."[146] This comment is echoed by Stephen of Bourbon, who says of heretics that by "perverting" the Holy Words they extract their errors from Scripture.[147] In fact, allegations that heretics were literally as well as metaphorically perverted and seductive permeate antiheretical polemics. The two types of allegations are, I believe, closely related. Just as orthodox spiritual interpretation was to be expressed in "spiritual" behavior—that is, physical needs were to be fulfilled according to ecclesiastical guidelines—so the heretics' understanding was labeled "carnal" and the countless allegations of heretics' sexual immorality assume that their behavior followed suit.[148] But in visually realizing such tropes, the *Bible moralisée* is not merely reiterating such textual antiheretical polemic in a different medium; it becomes, through its very nature, a forceful exemplar of orthodox hermeneutic. In his *Liber contra Haereticos* Evrard de Béthune exclaims, "Do you believe that one sees a letter like a picture? One sees the letter completely different from the picture. The picture is naked and open; the letter, clothed, enveloped in the cloth of carnal symbols; our understanding only attains the marrow after rejecting the veil."[149] The "naked and open" pictures of the *Bible moralisée* thus illustrate but also "uncover," that is, expose, contrast with, and in the process triumph over the heretics' carnality.

Publicans and Sinners

The key point of this chapter is that the myriad antiheretical allegations contained in the text and images of the *Bible moralisée* grow out of the same nexus of social and intellectual concerns that inform the anti-Jewish polemic. Heretics, like and with Jews, are censured for rejecting the authority of the Church, repudiating its sacraments, and challenging its intellectual hegemony, particularly in the exclusive interpretation of Scripture—especially in the form of preaching. All of these activities would seem to grow out of and magnify the distance between Jews/heretics on the one hand and faithful Christians on the other. Yet the commentary texts and images undermine this impression even while promoting it. Heretics' rejection of church teachings and authority is represented as stemming out of and/or further leading to the sins of greed, lust, and intellectual pride—sins to which orthodox clerics and laymen were all too susceptible, as the *Bible moralisée* itself eloquently laments.

This tension between difference and likeness, distance and overlap, is, in fact, inherent in the very term employed for heretics in the *Bible moralisée*. Although there is considerable confusion surrounding the origins of the word,[150] it is generally assumed that "publican" was considered a fitting term for heretics because publicans are among the most reviled figures in the New Testament—they are, for example, consistently paired with "sinners." But the connotations of "publican" have never been thoroughly explored. As tax collectors, they represented, above all, greed: imposing the term on heretics thereby serves to link them to Jews while firmly placing them on the evil, "worldly" side of the matter/spirit dichotomy that stands at the center of heretics' own ontology. However, the publicans were not just greedy tax collectors: in the eyes of the Judaean population they were locals gone over to the "enemy"—Jews working for the Roman government; this equivocal identity/allegiance was a primary source of the hatred directed at them.

And yet—is this all that is conveyed by the term? To the authors of the Gospels, the Judaean population was hardly "us," and the Roman government was by no means the principal foe: that role is occupied by (depending on the gospel) hypocrites, Pharisees, or, simply, "the Jews."[151] Moreover, while it is true that the Gospels bear ample witness to the near-universal hatred with which publicans were regarded by the inhabitants of first-century Palestine,[152] in the vast majority of New Testament references, publicans are actually depicted favorably: they dine with and listen to Jesus (Matt. 9:10–11; 11:19; Luke 15:1); they are called Jesus' friends (Luke 7:35—the accusation is voiced by Jesus' critics, but he does not gainsay them); they believe in John the Baptist's message (Matt. 21:32); the apostle Matthew (called Levi in Mark and Luke) is a repentant publican (Matt. 9:9; Mark 2:14; Luke 5:27). If unrepentant publicans are Jewish collaborators with Rome, those who became followers of Jesus were Jewish *and* Roman *and* Christian: in either case, publicans are liminal figures blurring cultural and religious boundaries. In the thirteenth-century context, then, to call a heretic a "publican" is to link contemporary dissident movements to New Testament villains and to their assumed physical and spiritual heirs—contemporary Jews—but also to implicitly acknowledge their ambiguous nature and status, and perhaps to hold out hope for their redemption as well. Through vocabulary as well as through exegesis and art, the *Bible moralisée* conflates past and present; Jews, Christian renegades, *and* the Christian faithful; and in the process forces a reexamination of Christian society, of the nature of sin, and of the criteria for salvation.

FIVE: IN AN ETERNAL FIRE

Polemic, Policy, and the Fate of the Jews

The one who is to come after me
is more powerful than I. . . . he
will baptise you in the Holy Spirit
and in fire. His winnowing-fan
is in his hand; he will clear the
threshing-floor and gather his wheat
into his barn; but the chaff he will
burn in an eternal fire.

(MATT. 3:11–12)

Throughout this book we have encountered a dizzying array of anti-Jewish themes, accusations, and images that seem to undermine theologians' careful Jewish-Christian categorical distinctions even while insisting on them. This apparent contradiction need not surprise: as the verse from the Gospel of Matthew quoted here suggests, an assumption of moral confusion—the coexistence and intermingling of "wheat" and "chaff"—was built into the Christian view of the world, and the very value laid on order in medieval writings and art (including, of course, the *Bible moralisée* manuscripts) points to the overwhelming prevalence of disorder in contemporary society. As the same verse also indicates, however, a terminus was foreseen for this confusion: the end of days is inextricably linked in Christian tradition with division, separation, and classification. In fact, more than one scholar has linked later medieval anti-Judaism to eschatological expectation, suggesting that either fear of the impending Judgment or a desire to hasten it inspired anti-Jewish violence and/or theological strictures.[1] It seems fitting, then, to conclude this study by following the representation of the Jews in the *Bible moralisée* to their—the Jews'—very end. In this final chapter, I examine how the *Bible moralisée* depicts the Jews' destiny, both in the near future and at the end of days; inquire to what extent these depictions are related to broader eschatological themes; and explore the political and social resonances with which the various projected fates of the Jews are endowed.

There is little question but that most medieval Christians assumed that Judaism was a path only to damnation—but when one has said this, one has hardly exhausted the subject. Many questions remain: How could certainty of Jews' damnation be squared with anticipation of their final conversion at the end of days? Which generation of Jews (and what proportion thereof) was expected to convert? What fate could be expected for the progenitors of potential converts—that is, since the end of time was assumed to be in the future, both long-deceased and still living Jews? And, most important, how did conceptions of the Jews' ultimate fate interact in specific contexts with a range of immediate and local concerns? In addressing these questions, I shall start by surveying images of Jews at the Last Judgment and the end of time, and then foreshorten my focus to examine representations of—and recommendations concerning—the Jews' more immediate fate.

Sleeping in the Land of Dust: Jews at the End of Days

There is no consensus in the Christian tradition concerning the timing and nature of the end of the world, much less concerning Jews' part in that event. Scripture itself offers very incomplete guidance. A general picture of the end of the world is supplied in chapters 24 and 25 of the Gospel of Matthew: a series of disasters, including war, famine, earthquakes, and lawlessness, will proclaim the beginning of the end. Signs of the coming of the "Son of Man" will then appear in the skies, and angels will gather the elect. Finally, the "Son of Man" will arrive in glory and will award eternal life to the virtuous and eternal punishment to all who fall short of righteousness.

In his Second Epistle to the Thessalonians, Paul allotted an additional dimension to this drama, asserting that the Second Coming of Christ would be preceded by the advent of a "man of sin, son of perdition," who would work counterfeit miracles, signs, and wonders. This figure, identified in subsequent Christian tradition with the Antichrist (the term first appears in I John 2:18, 22), would eventually be defeated by the Lord, and all those who by that point refused to accept the Gospel of Christ would be condemned at the Last Judgment to eternal damnation. Neither Paul nor the author of Matthew discusses precisely which segment or what proportion of humanity would persist in rejecting Christ.[2]

The Apocalypse of John considerably elaborates upon this basic scenario, graphically detailing the invasions, war, famine, and plagues that will announce the imminence of the day of liberation.[3] Following the destruction of the Beast (that is, Satan, who is Rome) and his cohort, the Church will enjoy an era of prosperity. This, in turn, will end in a new attack by Satan, leading Gog and Magog; eventually, these enemies will be definitively destroyed. Following the Resurrection of the dead and their Last Judgment, the Heavenly Jerusalem will finally be established. This violent and cataclysmic drama naturally lent itself to polemical (often antiheretical and/or anti-Jewish) allegory,[4] but its symbolism is far too difficult and obscure to constitute information concerning the Jews' or any other group's future.

As one might expect, it was Augustine's articulation of the Jews' role in the events at the end of time that contoured subsequent Catholic approaches.[5] In a sermon explicating the parable of the prodigal son (Luke 15), Augustine predicted that at the end of time the Jews, signified by the resentful older son, would return to the house of God (the Church) and reunite in Christ with the Gentiles.[6] Augustine does not specify what percentage of the Jews could be expected to return to God in this way, but he implies that it would be the greater part.[7] The same ambiguity exists in Augustine's discussion of the end of days in *De Civitate Dei.* Here (20.30) he writes, "Certainly, in the day of judgment, the Jews, including those who are to receive the spirit of grace and mercy, will grieve for the insults heaped upon Christ in His passion. They will repent when they see Him coming in His majesty. . . . And those very fathers, who were directly responsible for the great outrage, will see Him when they rise from the dead in a resurrection that will be, not for the sake of purification, but of punishment. It is not, therefore, to such 'fathers' that the words of the text . . . refer, but, rather, to those of their descendants who are destined to believe." And he concludes, "In connection with the last judgment, therefore, we who believe can be sure of the following truths: Elias the Thesbite will return; the Jews will believe; the Antichrist will persecute the Church; Christ will be the judge; the dead will rise; the good will be separated from the wicked; the world will suffer from fire, but will be renewed."[8]

Biblical and patristic vagueness on this question allowed for considerable variation in emphasis in subsequent eschatological writings: some medieval theologians focused their attention on that "remnant" of Jews who eventually would accept the Word of God, whereas others preferred to dwell on the masses of recalcitrant Jews condemned to everlasting damnation.[9] Augustine's serene confidence in the Jews' conversion is echoed, for example, in the treatise on the sacraments of Hugh of St. Victor,[10] as well as in the commentaries of Stephen Langton: "And in the end of time the Jews will come to him, that is, Jews to Christ,"[11] and of Peter the Chanter: "By Job is allegorically understood Christ or Ecclesia, to which at the end of time all Jews will come."[12] Similarly, the first chapter of the Titulus *De Iudaeis et Paganis* in Alexander of Hales's *Summa* concluded that Jews were to be allowed to remain in Christendom because "their salvation is promised, since 'he will have entered with the plenitude of the nations.'"[13] The culmination of the admittedly eccentric historical schema of Joachim of Fiore was the ushering in of a "sabbath Age of the Spirit" through the peaceful conversion of the infidels.[14]

On the other hand, many medieval commentators tended to be considerably more hostile in tone and pessimistic in their assessment of the Jews' chances for salvation than was Augustine. Peter of Blois, for example, while accepting Augustine's basic framework, argues that only a very small relic of Jews would be saved; he seems to regard the vast majority of the "reprobate Jews" as doomed.[15] Peter the Venerable considered the authors and presumably the devotees of the Talmud justly condemned "to eternal fire,"[16] Walter of Chatillon (d. ca. 1185) writes that at the end of time the Jews will be permanently blinded by the devil,[17] and in general in high medieval apocalyptic treatises it is the Jews' alliance with the Antichrist rather than their eventual conversion that draws the most attention and inspires the most comment.[18]

The Jews and the End of Time in the Bible moralisée

The commentary of the *Bible moralisée* reverberates with this essential tension. References to the Jews' fate appear unsystematically throughout the commentary program: some texts reflect the more affirmative view of the Jews' destiny, others the negative, and still others highlight the rupture that is to take place among the Jewish people at the Last Judgment. This is to be expected: such an eclectic collection of texts is unlikely to display either unwonted coherence or doctrinal originality in association with such a momentous yet obscure topic. However, although these, too, are scattered throughout the manuscripts rather than concentrated within a unified cycle,[19] illustrations of the Jews' end display a somewhat more consistent approach. In keeping with the strong pastoral thrust of the visual commentary program, a great many of the images accompanying eschatological texts situate the events ostensibly occurring at the end of time in a contemporary setting. The final drama, then, does not appear as a notable preoccupation in and of itself; rather, it is enlisted primarily as a metaphor for current struggles, and the question of the Jews' eventual damnation or salvation is subordinated to a concern for ordering their role in the present.

FIG. 85. Tob. 11:13–16. The end of the world: the malice of the devil removed from the midst of the Jews, who will be illuminated by the faith of Christ. Cod. 1179, fol. 181b.

Salvation

A handful of commentary excerpts explicitly proclaim that "the Jews" will ultimately convert to the Christian faith. The most positive articulation of this perspective appears in the Latin commentary to Tobias, which relies heavily on Bede's commentary and is therefore probably among the oldest of the exegetical works incorporated into the *Bible moralisée.*[20] The text interpreting the elder Tobias's cure from blindness (Tob. 11:13–16) confidently predicts the collective conversion of the Jews: "The gall of the fish [applied to Tobias's eyes] signifies the malice of the devil, which first the Judaic people will have perceived working within the Antichrist; then when the Lord will have taken it [or: him] away from their midst at the end of the world, all will be illuminated by the faith of Christ."[21] The text is rather benevolent toward the Jews in its intimation that they are somewhat passive victims of the Antichrist, and that they will eventually be collectively saved. The image retains the positive tone, depicting bearded and hatted Jews praying to God, who emerges from the heavens and blesses them. One Jew pointedly rejects the Antichrist, who falls off to the right, pierced by barbs from heaven (Fig. 85).[22]

However, texts and images emphasizing the redemption of the Jews form a distinct minority in the *Bible moralisée.* Generally, even those eschatological texts that might be considered optimistic concerning Jews' chances for salvation use predictions of the Jews' eventual conversion primarily to express antagonism toward contemporary Judaism. For example, in marked contrast to the Tobias commentary, a text dealing with the end of days from the university-influenced Kings commentary discusses the presumably desired event of the Jews' future conversion in decidedly censorious tones, according the Jews' trespasses as much emphasis as their final salvation. Elijah's prophecy to the wicked King Ahab that no rain would fall until the prophet should order it (III Kings 17:1) is said to signify that "Jesus Christ appeared before Jews and infidels and said to them that the Holy Spirit will not descend on them until he should order—that is, on Judgment Day, when those totally repenting of their sins and fulfilling the mandates of the Lord will be received into the Christian faith."[23] In the roundel, the Jews' past and continuing delinquency eclipses their future redemption. Jesus is shown lecturing rather sternly to three Jews, who listen passively; one holds a sacrificial animal, indicative of the nature of the sins for which the Jews must repent (Fig. 86). The corresponding French text is more belligerent still: here, Jesus Christ comes before Jews "and all those sent by devils" and tells them that on Judgment Day "you will repent and abandon your mad belief."[24] The accompanying image, like that in the Latin manuscript, forgoes illustrating the Jews' eventual repentance, instead focusing exclusively on their ongoing perfidy: Jesus gesticulates emphatically in the direction of a huge devil, who hovers over and partially embraces two small, cowering Jews, one of whom clutches a scroll of the Old Law (Fig. 87).

A similar approach—overshadowing references to the Jews' conversion with condemnations of their character and/or religion—is evident in the French commentary to III Kings 1:1–4. The biblical excerpt relates that when the aging King David couldn't keep warm, his servants brought a beautiful young girl to his bed to provide bodily heat; David slept with the girl but didn't know her carnally. The commentary explains, "That David could not warm himself with the coverlet signifies Jesus Christ who could not warm himself with the love of Jews. That David warmed himself with a maiden without engendering anything of her signifies Jesus Christ who on Judgment Day, will warm himself with Synagoga without engendering anything of her."[25] The commentary image portrays Synagoga as a modestly veiled young woman, to whom Jesus Christ reaches out a welcoming hand (Fig. 88). Synagoga signals her acceptance of his advances, and at the same time the unsuitability of the Jewish religion, by dropping a scroll of the Law. To cement the point, Jesus waves rejec-

FIG. 86 (TOP). III Kings 17:1. Jesus tells the Jews they must repent. Cod. 1179, fol. 118c.
FIG. 87. III Kings 17:1–5. Jesus tells the Jews and all those of the devil that they must repent. Cod. 2554, fol. 52va.

FIG. 88 (TOP). III Kings 1:1–4. Jesus "warms himself" with Synagoga, but they have no offspring. Cod. 2554, fol. 48vb. FIG. 89. III Kings 1:1–4. Jesus cannot warm himself in the Jews' death. Cod. 1179, fol. 111a.

tion toward a group of Jews on the left; one of the Jews holds a scroll. The attitude toward Judaism here is perhaps best described as ambivalent; however, in representing the redeemed segment of Jewry as an abstract personification and the rejecting and rejected portion of Jewry as human figures, the roundel seems to deny living and practicing Jews any hope of amendment or share in the goodwill that might be afforded by traditional conversionary expectations.

The Latin manuscript is more starkly pessimistic still. The corresponding commentary text differs slightly but significantly from the French: "This signifies Jesus Christ, who couldn't keep warm in the death of the Jews. That the girl warmed him and he didn't know her carnally signifies that on Judgment Day Jesus Christ will begin to warm himself with Synagoga without begetting anything from Synagoga."[26] The word *morte* (death) may be simply a misreading of *amore* (love), with which it is orthographically similar, and which both accords better with the biblical text and corresponds to the parallel French commentary (*l'amor*). On the other hand, the alteration may have been intentional: the Latin text as it stands falls well within the Christian exegetical traditional of associating Judaism with death.[27] The commentary image, moreover, clearly picks up on the word "death." It does not depict the sterility of Jesus' union with Synagoga but rather features Synagoga's nefarious offspring from another unmentioned but implied union—that is, Jews, in the process drawing attention to the unspoken question of their male parentage.[28] Jesus is seated in the middle of the roundel (Fig. 89). He extends a welcoming arm toward three Jews on the right; all are bearded and wear tall pointed hats. However, unlike the figure of Synagoga in the French roundel, these Jews stand passively and do not visibly respond to Jesus' advances; in fact, Jesus simultaneously gestures rejection toward what looks like the same three Jews (albeit older) on the left. One of these Jews slaughters a goat, while another holds an animal head. The image thus equates the reference to "death" in the text with the Jews' exegesis, laws, and rites. No repentant Synagoga appears. In sum, the roundel can be considered a portrayal of an abortive attempt at converting Jews on the part of Jesus himself.

The Damnation of the Jews

In fact, the antithetical position to confidence in the ultimate salvation of the Jews is far more frequently voiced: many texts and even more images take for granted the damnation of "the Jews" as a collective entity. This is, of course, far from unusual for the period, but the nature of the depictions of the Jews' damnation in the *Bible moralisée* is instructive. Two aspects of such images stand out. First, iconographic emblems repeatedly link the Jews' perdition to activities above and beyond their adherence to the Old Law. Second, Jews are rarely alone in hell. The effect of these two features is to consistently link events set in the distant future to issues dominating the contemporary context, and infidels outside the Church to sinners within it. Such shifting of eschatological events and conflation of sins and sinners reflect and underscore the pragmatic and reformist orientation of the manuscripts; they also significantly affect how "the saved" and "the damned" are perceived and defined.

An example of the first strategy may be seen on folio 6d of the French manuscript. The commentary to Gen. 27:30–35 reads: "That Esau came afterwards to ask for his [father's] blessing, and his father said that Jacob carried it away, signifies Jews and miscreants who will come before Jesus Christ on Judgment Day for his blessing, and He will tell them 'You are too late, the Christians carried it away.'"[29] This time, the commentary roundel does not identify the Jews' sins with religious obstinacy via the emblem of a scroll or a sacrificial animal but with their economic activities: Jesus gestures rejection toward several Jews holding bowls filled with coins; another falls to the right, expressing despair or entreaty with his right hand while clutching a moneybag in the left (Fig. 90).[30] In its inversion of traditional Last Judgment imagery, this roundel "judaicizes" damnation: whereas scenes such as those on the tympana of Bourges, Reims, Laon, Amiens, and Chartres present Jews as only a few among many figures doomed to hell,[31] here many diverse sinners are implicitly absorbed within the figures of Jews. If one effect of this image is to underscore that the Jews' greed will lead to their damnation (even, apparently, for those who seek out Christ), another is to suggest—against the thrust of the text—that all who share the "Jewish" attribute of cupidity, and not only those who observe Jewish rites, will be excluded from Christian salvation.[32]

Many other images echo the medallion discussed previously in concentrating all the damned within the figures of Jews, but in others the inverse process occurs: texts mentioning only Jews/infidels are illustrated with images showing a variety of figures accompanying Jews on their journey to hell. Sometimes both approaches accompany the same interpretation: on folio 29d of the Latin manuscript, for example, "infidels who are damned" are portrayed as two bishops, a monk, a Jew, and three unidentifiable characters,[33] while in the French manuscript all the "miscreants" and "publicans" (i.e., Christian heretics) mentioned in the parallel commentary text are rendered as Jews (Figs. 91 and 92).[34]

A similar contrast between an inclusive (or rather broadly exclusionary) Latin commentary medallion and a more concentratedly anti-Jewish French commentary medallion appears in

FIG. 90 (TOP). Gen. 27:30–35. Jews and miscreants damned on Judgment Day. Cod. 2554, fol. 6d. FIG. 91. Exod. 12:23–29. Infidels damned and led to hell by devils. Cod. 1179, fol. 29d.

FIG. 92 (TOP). Exod. 12:23–29. Miscreants and heretics thrust into hell. Cod. 2554, fol. 20vd. FIG. 93. IV Kings 1:11–12. Infidels and heretics devoured by the fire of hell for their pride. Cod. 1179, fol. 126a.

conjunction with the commentary on IV Kings 1:11–12. The Latin gloss reads: "[The fifty messengers of Ochozias devoured by fire] signify infidels and publicans in their pride questioning Jesus Christ about their wicked faith, whom, at the will of Jesus Christ, the fire of Gehenna devoured body and soul."[35] Although the text sounds very much like a description of a New Testament event (the boy Jesus before the doctors, or Jesus before the Sanhedrin), the accompanying image depicts Jesus' opponents in specifically medieval guise: foremost among the figures descending to hell are a bearded usurer with a low round cap and a bag of money suspended around his neck, and a heretic holding a cat (Fig. 93). Although the parallel French text also mentions both infidels and heretics,[36] the corresponding image depicts only Jews (i.e., bearded figures with pointed hats) consumed by the fire (Fig. 94). Yet again, I think what the French illustration is doing is not absolving Christians of sin and perdition but essentializing all sinful and damned figures as Jewish. A similar impression is elicited by the commentary text directly below, in which the "miscreants and heretics" are now described as "bad philosophers and grand masters of the law"—terms particularly associated in these manuscripts with Jewishness.[37] The themes are the same as those touched on in the Latin manuscript, but the implications are more forcefully presented.

There are, then, innumerable depictions of damnation in the *Bible moralisée;* although these display considerable variation, most share a consistent approach: the mixing, juxtaposing, and overlapping of Jewish and Christian identities.[38] Perhaps this is not so very remarkable in images of damnation; Christian theology never, after all, posited the salvation of all nominal Christians. But the most telling of all manifestations of this approach is encountered, in fact, in an illustration of redemption. The commentary to Tob. 11:10, 16–17 compares Tobias's joyful welcoming of his son and daughter-in-law to "the faithful at the end of the world who with great joy will run to the faith of Jesus Christ."[39] In the roundel, which we have already seen,[40] these "fideles" start, in fact, as infidels: by means of the signs of the beard and hat they are marked as Jews; each gradually sheds the marks of his Jewishness as he approaches Jesus (see Fig. 4). "Faithfulness" is constructed, then, not as an absolute but as part of a continuum: the viewer would be as hard-pressed to label the far-off yet Christ-facing figures in this image "unbelievers" as to determine at what point the figures become unadulteratedly Christian, suggesting that an unavoidable offshoot of commendable conversion is a certain degree of (anxiety-provoking?) confusion.

The aggregate effect of the various types of eschatological commentary roundel in the *Bible moralisée,* then, is (as we have seen so often before) to underscore the ambiguity and ambivalence of "Jewishness," and hence of Christian identity as well. On the road to perdition as on the road to salvation, Christians transform into Jews and Jews mingle among Christians, and the difference so carefully articulated in their appearances is effaced in their mutual destiny. In heaven and in hell, there is neither Jew nor Christian, only the saved, only sinners. Far from strengthening existing distinctions, the Last Judgment seems to be constructing new ones, in the process drawing lines that cut right across accepted groupings.

FIG. 94 (TOP). IV Kings 1:11–12. Miscreants and heretics are destroyed by fire. Cod. 2554, fol. 56va. FIG. 95. II Kings 2:8–9. Jews, heretics, and all bad people take Antichrist to be their lord. Cod. 2554, fol. 43va.

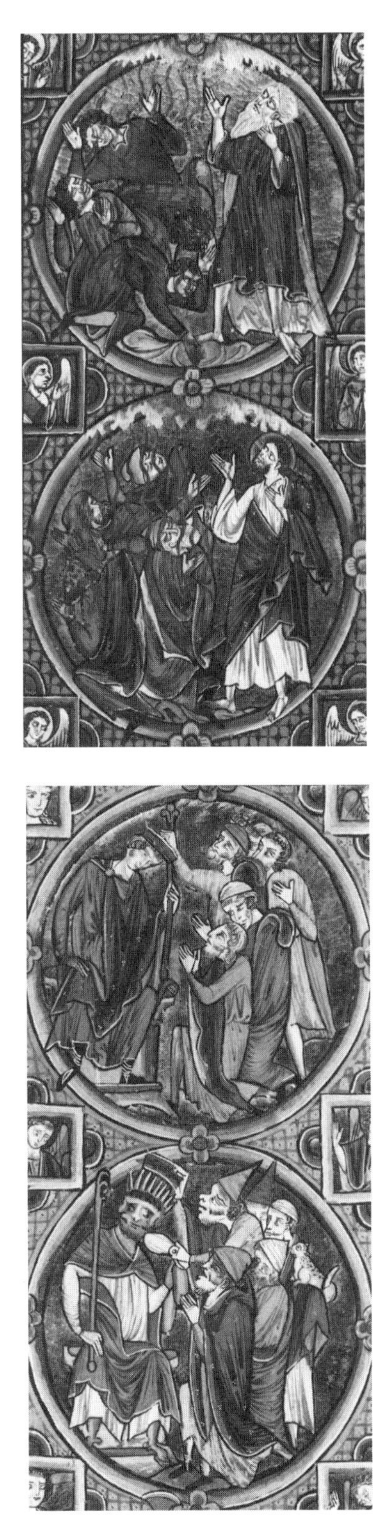

Apocalypse Now

Temporal boundaries as well as social ones are blurred in representations of the various events associated with the end of time. For example, the image of the Jews rejecting the Antichrist (see Fig. 85) is countered by others that portray those who will welcome the Antichrist. A text on folio 43v of Vienna ÖNB cod. 2554 recounts the episode from II Kings 2:8–9, in which some Israelites took Saul's son Hysbozet as their king instead of David. The commentary explains, "That the others bound themselves to Hysbozet [Ishbosheth] and took him for their lord signifies the Jews and the publicans and all the bad people who will bind themselves to the Antichrist and take him for their lord and will say that they will have no other king."[41] This text clearly echoes the language of the Gospel (John 19:15: "We have no king but Caesar"), tying the Jews' monumental historical crime to as yet uncommitted future crimes, while also connecting them to heretics and other transgressors, both Christian and non-Christian. The image does the same, associating figures explicitly rendered as Jewish with emblems not exclusively Jewish. The Antichrist, seated on the left, accepts the homage of five Jews, who wear various types of hats and are all bearded and drawn in profile (Fig. 95). One places a crown on the head of the Antichrist and offers him a moneybag. This detail implies not just that the Jews will worship the Antichrist in the future but that they—and many other people as well—already do so, in the form of greed and usury and bribery.[42] Another Jew kneels before the Antichrist and prays to him (in a Christian rather than a Jewish prayer stance), while a third figure in a rounded cap signifies the affiliation with the internal Christian offense of heresy by carrying a cat.

The corresponding Latin commentary text appears on folio 101b of Vienna ÖNB cod. 1179. Here, Jews and publicans and "all malignant ones will elect the Antichrist king and have him for their Lord and adore him as a god."[43] The commentary roundel once again conflates the past, present, and projected crimes of the three groups mentioned. Four figures—two in pointed caps and two in rounded caps—are grouped around a centrally placed Antichrist (Fig. 96). The two uppermost worshipers place a crown on his head, and the two lower worshipers offer their

FIG. 96. II Kings 2:8–9. Jews, heretics, and all malignant ones elect Antichrist king and adore him as a god. Cod. 1179, fol. 101b.

gifts: a moneybag and two domestic cats. The Antichrist crosses his arms to receive the gifts. This mock reversal of Jesus' position on the cross expresses graphically (in both senses of the term) that the figure of the Antichrist brings about the intersection and merging of Jew and Gentile, infidel and heretic—just as the moment of salvation (Christ's sacrifice) effected their distinction.[44]

Jews within the Church

Of course, associating the Antichrist with heresy and greed—that is, employing him as a metaphor for the sins with which the ecclesiastical hierarchy was most concerned at this period—was a widespread, even downright clichéd, practice.[45] But the nature of metaphor is to invite further elaboration;[46] we must ask how this trope played out in the contemporary reforming context. Describing the Antichrist as already present in this world in the form of sin and unbelief suggests that his opponent—Christ himself—can also be conjured (albeit figuratively) in the contemporary world, and that the final drama can be considered in some sense already under way. This is, in fact, implied in the *Bible moralisée.* A commentary sequence that very clearly puts an eschatological text in the service of pastoral concerns adjusts the temporal progression in a most significant way. In the Latin manuscript the commentary to Num. 12:15 runs, "Maria who cried and was repentant [for her speech against Moses] signifies Jews and all sinners who repent of their sins. Moses and Aaron praying for her signify Saints Peter and Paul who pray for sinners, whom God receives."[47] When and why the Jews repent is left unspecified—although the use of the present tense is interesting. There is also an arresting modification in the French manuscript. Here, the commentary states that "Jews and miscreants and all other sinners . . . will repent of their transgressions *before* the Day of Judgment and Saints Peter and Paul will pray to God for them."[48] Moreover, in the Vulgate text Miriam expresses no regret; the biblical text was apparently modified in the *Bible moralisée* or its source to pave the way for the endorsement in the commentary text of repentance, a principal preoccupation of the Parisian biblical moral school and other reformers.[49] The images underscore this pastoral, as opposed to eschatological, framework: neither commentary roundel employs the standard iconography associated with Judgment Day. Instead, the roundel in the Latin manuscript preserves the temporal ambiguity of the Jews' repentance, showing (in the lower left roundel) a priest baptizing a group of iconographically indistinguishable figures seated in a large baptismal font (Fig. 97). The French roundel depicts two Jews with mild (repentant?) expressions seated within an architec-

FIG. 97. Num. 12:10–13:4. Miriam's expulsion and repentance are likened to the excommunication and subsequent penitence and reconciliation of Jews and sinners. Cod. 1179, fol. 55.

tural enclosure; Peter and Paul pray beside this structure (Fig. 98). Both medallions thus highlight the centrality of genuine contrition—a major tenet in reformist thought—while emphasizing the importance of the Church as an institution. They also seem to identify the Day of Judgment and the Jews' conversion with celebration of the Catholic sacraments—implying that through these the kingdom of God could and must be prepared for, or rather, could even be in some way realized, on earth in this very age. But perhaps the most striking aspect of these two images is how inclusive they are of Jews—in the one, Jews (or rather former Jews) are cradled within a liturgical vessel; in the other, their usual situation is reversed: rather than isolated outside the Church, they are encompassed within. These depictions of Jews situated within Catholic vessels and structures seem to envision the return of Jews to the fold not at the end of time but already in the thirteenth century. Such a conception, although counter to prevailing opinion,[50] certainly accords with the conflation of eschatology and reform apparent in these manuscripts: if the reformers justified their program by identifying the Second Coming of Christ with the implementation of their reformist policies, then it follows that the Jews' reintegration into the Church, a necessary precursor to the Second Coming, would also have to be effected in contemporary society and not just at the end of days.

FIG. 98. Num. 12:10–13. Saints Peter and Paul pray for the repentance of Jews, miscreants, and all other sinners before the Day of Judgment. Cod. 2554, fol. 31vc.

Images such as these, then, suggest that a figurative eschatology harnessed to ecclesiastical reform, rather than any heightening of "real" apocalyptic fears or desires, provided or at least justified renewed impetus for addressing the problem of "Judaism"—actual and/or constructed—within some sectors of Christendom. Such an approach is, of course, simply a metaphoric version of the kind of reasoning that Jeremy Cohen and others have suggested formed the basis for various anti-Jewish manifestations in the later Middle Ages.[51] But moving the nature of apocalypticism from the realm of the actual to the metaphoric has significant implications, for metaphor is subject to manipulation and interpretation in a way that doctrine is not. The "apocalyptic" explanations for anti-Judaism offered to date have two serious weaknesses. They posit a change in doctrine for which we have no convincing textual evidence. Moreover, such a doctrinal change would seem to preclude the diversity apparent in later medieval Jewish policy, which veered in the thirteenth century alone from murderous attacks to forced preaching campaigns to expulsions to continued protection and even privileging. Attributing such disparate political and social developments to one overarching (and unproved) intellectual causation is problematic at best.

The images in the *Bible moralisée* that contain prescriptions concerning Jewish policy are as disparate as these actions, but they *are* ultimately bound together. They are unified not in con-

FIG. 99. Commentary to Exod. 32:26–28. A pope orders prelates to excommunicate usurers, heretics, and miscreants; on the right, candle-wielding prelates fulfill these orders with considerable ferocity. Cod. 2554, fol. 26c and d.

tent or conclusion but by a single, powerful visual image drawn from biblical descriptions of the final drama: the "eternal fire." And whereas on a physical level fire is notoriously difficult to control, on a metaphoric level the figure of "the eternal fire" is as subject to manipulation and flexible interpretation as are all other biblical images. The flexibility of the image is fully exploited, for example, in Hugh of St. Victor's discussion of the end of days: "For just as under the one fire gold glows [and] chaff smokes . . . so one and the same crushing force [i.e., the eternal fire] tests, purges, and clarifies the good; damns, lays waste, and exterminates the evil."[52] The flexibility of this figure was likewise fully exploited by the creators of the *Bible moralisée:* it appears in different guises in a multitude of images touching upon the Jews' fate.

"By Their Authority They Are Expelled"

A very strange set of images employs fire in a multiple role as illuminator, cleanser, and destroyer. Folio 26c and d of Vienna ÖNB cod. 2554 contains two biblical roundels illustrating, respectively, the condemnation and the execution of the Israelites who had worshiped the golden calf (Exod. 32:26–28). In both cases, the Israelites are said in the commentary to signify "usurers, publicans, and miscreants" who are to be "excommunicated" and "pushed outside of Holy Church."[53] The first commentary roundel (on the left) depicts a pope giving instruction to clerics carrying books and candles (Fig. 99). The next commentary roundel depicts the imposition of the sentence with considerable ferocity. The clerics, led by a tonsured prelate in white, grimacing fiercely, hold their books and candles up high and drive off their victims with vigorous gestures. The victims display a variety of reactions and aspects. In the center, two figures holding a cat cower, kneeling on the ground in abject fear. To their left, a cleric covers the mouth of a kneeling, bearded man in a short round cap. And on the right, the ambiguous terminology of the text is stabilized: three bearded Jews in peaked hats scuttle away while looking apprehensively backward.

The Latin version of this text explicitly includes Jews among the excommunicates, explaining that "popes order prelates to excommunicate all usurers, heretics, and Jews; and they are expelled from the Church by their authority."[54] In the subsequent commentary roundel (in the upper right quadrant), which ostensibly illustrates the expulsion and excommunication of "wicked usurers,"[55] all the excommunicates seem to be represented as Jews. One carries a moneybag, and their humiliation is emphasized: one of the excommunicating prelates sticks his tongue out at the figures, who flee him in distress (Fig. 100).[56] Another prelate dashes a candle to the ground—this is a well-documented part of the excommunication rite, signifying at the same time the extinguishing of the excommunicate's soul and the fiery punishment awaiting him should he not repent. These texts are not isolated examples; the two manuscripts contain at least eight more references to the "expulsion from the Church" of Jews and/or infidels.[57]

These references to "excommunicating" or "expelling" Jews and/or infidels pose an arresting conundrum. The closest and best-known parallel is canon 71 of the Fourth Lateran Council. This canon, after complaining that the financial strength of Christians was being sapped by Jewish usurers, orders: "that Jews be compelled by the secular power to remit interest; and, until they shall have remitted [such interest], fellowship shall be altogether denied to them by the whole body of Christian faithful, through the sentence of excommunication."[58] There is some disagreement concerning what precisely this canon means. Solomon Grayzel took it to be tantamount to a boycott of Jewish usurers, assuming that the sentence of excommunication was to be imposed upon Christians violating the boycott.[59] However, Joseph Shatzmiller speculated that it may have marked the initiation of a particular punishment, equivalent to excommunication, devised by the Church for Jewish usurers. He published several references to excommunicating Jews dating from the second half of the thirteenth century and later, but he was unable to determine when the practice started.[60] In a 1986 article, William C. Jordan identified a still earlier reference to excommunicating Jews in the *Constitutiones* of Stephen Langton, dating to 1222.[61] Jordan speculated that Langton may have deliberately misread the bull *Post miserabilem* in order to assert his control over English Jews, as well as to enforce his negative attitude toward usury. The appearance of the concept of excommunicating Jews in these Parisian manuscripts, exactly contemporary to Langton's *Constitutiones,* furnishes important evidence regarding the emergence of this novel

FIG. 100. Exod. 32:26–28. The condemnation and execution of the Israelites who had worshiped the golden calf signify the cleansing of the Church. Cod. 1179, fol. 38.

idea. They suggest that while Langton may indeed have willfully misread the papal bull for his own purposes, the impetus for and contours of this misreading were prompted by exegetical practices and theoretical ideas current among the theology faculty at Paris during his years there.

Three features of the "excommunicating" or "expelling" texts in the *Bible moralisée* command attention. The first is that, in calling for the excommunication of Jews, the manuscripts complete the identification of Jews with Christian renegades. By the thirteenth century, excommunication was the accepted method for dealing with persistent heretics: the sentence had been imposed at least from the eleventh century and was decreed the fit penalty for heresy by numerous local and ecumenical councils.[62] The consistency with which the *Bible moralisée* excommunicating texts refer concurrently to usury, to Jews, and to heretics suggests that the conventional association of Jews with the money trade was a significant factor in the articulation of an identical punitive approach toward Jews and heretics. The increasingly stringent ecclesiastical approach toward heresy gradually came to encompass themes with which heretics were rhetorically linked; one of the most constant of these themes was the heretics' hypocritical love of money. The antiheretical treatise *Contra Amaurianos* called the university pantheistic sectarians known as the "Amauricians" avaricious, and Stephen of Bourbon asserted that Manichaeans indulged in usury with impunity.[63] Such pronouncements may be related to the fact that by the thirteenth century many clerics agreed that incorrigible and immoderate (Christian) usurers should be excommunicated.[64] Moreover, by the opening of the thirteenth century some conservative members of the theology faculty in Paris had begun not just to relate heretics and usurers but also to equate usury with heresy. Robert de Courson called usury and heresy the two greatest evils of his age and urged in council that usurers be denounced like heretics.[65] During the Crusade against the Albigensian heretics of southern France in the second decade of the thirteenth century, a White League was formed to combat the dual and presumably linked sins of usury and heresy.[66] The literally dozens of images in the *Bible moralisée* referring to heretics' love of money and practice of idolatry clearly echo and endorse such ideas. The *Bible moralisée* excommunication texts may indicate that the idea of excommunicating Jews was facilitated by such chains of association connecting Jews, usurers, and heretics.

This regular association of Jews with other, Christian (albeit renegade) groups leads us to the second striking aspect of these excommunicating texts: the obvious fact that a prerequisite for the expulsion of Jews from the Church or the Christian community is the presumption that they are in some way part of the Church or the Christian community. We have seen this assumption before: I have already remarked that the images accompanying the texts comparing Miriam's (projected) contrition to the Jews' "final" repentance seemed to be unusually inclusive of Jews. In the Latin manuscript, it will be recalled, the "Jews and all repentant sinners" of the text appeared as converts within a baptismal font. Now, exactly the same visual composition appears on an earlier folio—on the same folio, in fact, as the Latin excommunicating texts discussed previously. For these two excommunicating texts are bracketed by two other texts that, although not explicitly relating to Jews, reveal much about the underlying mental economy informing attitudes toward Jews. They suggest, in short, that in their ambitious project for cleansing Christendom the reformers embarked on a path that, if followed to its terminus, would entail a redefinition of Christendom itself—to include all souls (Jewish or Christian) potentially amenable to purification and to exclude all those (Christian sinner, Christian renegade, or Jew) threatening to impede it.[67]

The first commentary text on the folio in question expounds upon Moses' instructions regarding the disposal of the dust of the golden calf. Because the wording of both the biblical text and the commentary text is crucial, I shall reproduce each in its entirety. The Bible text runs, "Moses ordered that they take the powder of the [Golden] Calf and throw it in water. And he said, 'drink your God and it will exit through the anus.'"[68] The commentary asserts, "This signifies good Christians who drink the water of baptism that through it the devil might be expelled from man."[69] The commentary image shows a priest baptizing naked men (tonsured and lay) in a large baptismal font as a tiny demon exits the font and flies off to the right (Fig. 101).

FIG. 101. Exod. 32:20. Good Christians cleansed of the devil through baptism. Cod. 1179, fol. 38a.

As the Vulgate text was yet again changed here to facilitate the desired moralization (in the Vulgate Moses makes no prediction concerning the powder's ultimate course[70]), the moralization and its illustration are presumably all the more significant. And there are, in fact, several striking aspects of this commentary. In the image all of the baptized figures are adults, and some are tonsured—that is, already members of clerical orders. The rite illustrated, then, is neither the most common form of baptism in medieval Christendom (i.e., infant baptism[71]) nor the initiation of new converts into Christian life. It is instead, as both the textual and the visual references to demons indicate, more reminiscent in form and intent of the prebaptism ceremony of exorcism, and in general invokes the spiritual cleansing rather than the initiatory aspects of baptism.[72]

The excommunicating texts that follow this, then, realize on a communal level what the exorcism / baptism ritual enacts on a personal level. This point is underscored by the compositional parallels of the adjacent commentary roundels: the gesture of the officiating priest on the left is more forcefully echoed in that of the excommunicating prelates on the right; the expelled Jews and their sacks of money are societal manifestations of the demon fleeing the font on the left (see Fig. 100). Just as the baptismal water douses the heat of the demon, the prelates' extinguishing of the candle publicly proclaims the social death of the excommunicates.[73]

The last commentary on the page—the other bracket for the excommunicating texts—confirms the institutional and reformist orientation of the entire sequence.[74] Moses' reception of the good Hebrews is compared to "the Lord Pope," who "receives good prelates with joy and restores to them grace from his bounty [i.e., awards benefices] and gives to them his blessing" (see Fig. 100).[75]

This folio, then, constitutes a blueprint for the cleansing of the Body Christian in microcosm and in macrocosm. In the first image, spiritual "converts" initiate the first stage of the purification process by turning to a priest to cleanse them of sin. The next two roundels—the excommunication roundels—portray the eviction of contaminants: all those who refuse to submit themselves in the way of the "converts" or who engage in activities that might threaten the converts' resolve. The final roundel—the pope blessing good prelates—tenders an image of a purified and perfected Church. These ideas in themselves are as unremarkable as they are unexceptionable (in the thirteenth-century context): the *Bible moralisée* adds no new theological twists or depth to contemporary reformist thought. It is not the originality of the ideas that is noteworthy, but the unusual nature of their presentation, which allows glimpses into the underlying associative patterns (and occasionally proceeds logically to conclusions) not allowed into other more systematic formats. Taken as a whole, the folio indicates that when metaphorically transferred to the social plane, the more internalized and spiritualized conception of purity promoted by the reformers could paradoxically (and when political and social circumstances aligned) inspire more concrete and communal understandings—and repressions—of corruption.

Finally, the third striking aspect of the excommunicating texts and roundels in the *Bible moralisée* is how they envision the purpose of excommunication. Although historians tend to focus on the punitive aspects of excommunication, to thirteenth-century theologians the sentence was primarily *medicinal:* it was designed first and foremost to encourage penitence and facilitate reintegration of the sinner into the community of believers. This concept is implicit in the corresponding French excommunication roundel (see Fig. 99). Here, the prelates do not throw candles to the ground but instead raise them high in vigorous gestures, wielding the candles both as illuminants and as weapons. Those excommunicates who choose to look at the open books flourished by the prelates benefit from the candles' light; the others (rendered more clearly as Jews) seem only to fear their scorching flame. Keeping in mind the multiple symbolic functions of fire, then, puts the "inclusive" images of Jews on the same folios in perspective: the depictions of Jews on these pages implicitly acknowledge the mixing of moral identities in thirteenth-century urban society and simultaneously attempt to correct that confusion by invoking the discriminating power of the flame. Remember Hugh: one and the same crushing force tests, purges, and clarifies the good; damns, lays waste, and exterminates the evil.

"The Eternal Fire"

The full range of qualities ascribed to fire (i.e., illuminative, purgative, and destructive) is summoned to similar effect in all four commentary roundels on a single folio in the Latin manuscript containing the commentary to II Macc. 12:5–43. In the first biblical excerpt Judah Maccabee, upon learning of the Joppites' treachery, burns the port and boats of Joppa under cover of night. According to the commentary, "This signifies what must be privately deplored: that those infidel heretics [or: infidels and heretics, or heretical infidels!] who pervert others must be recalled to the faith through preaching."[76] This looks distinctly like a conversionary text, perhaps a call for forced preaching. The image, however, combines the gestures and implements of preaching with another sign. On the left a group of secular clerics flourish open books, while the foremost one raises his forefinger in vigorous instruction (Fig. 102). A second cleric, however, raises high something else: a lit candle. Does this represent the illumination of the Word? Or, given the role of the candle in excommunication ceremonies and in other roundels in this manuscript, the punishment threatened those who refuse to accept the Word? Most likely, both at the same time, for the "infidel heretics" are spiritually distinguished by their disparate reactions to this candle as well as by their appearances. On the right of the roundel two listeners incline inward toward the candle and raise their hands as if to savor its light and warmth; they are young and bareheaded. A third figure seated in front of the group of heretics leans pointedly away and raises a hand as if to ward off the candle's heat or glare. He is old and bearded, is drawn in profile, and wears a soft peaked hat; that is, he is, apparently, a Jew, and he is holding a book out of which a demon springs.

FIG. 102. II Macc. 12:5–9. Infidel heretics must be recalled to the faith through preaching. Cod. 1179, fol. 221a.

All three aspects of fire are picked up by turn in the succeeding text/image pairs. The very next exegetical text confirms the excommunicatory role of the candle in the previous image, in addressing the question of what is to be done with those sinners who refuse the call to repentance. The commentary explains that just as those Joppites who escaped from the fire were killed by the

FIG. 103. II Macc. 12:17–29. Unrepentant excommunicates must be handed over to the lay power to be consumed by fire. Cod. 1179, fol. 221b.

sword (II Macc. 12:6), "those excommunicates who are truly perverse must be handed over to the lay power and consumed by fire."[77] In a complex conceptual chiasmus that constructs a connection between the reformers' cleansing rhetoric and the burning of heretics, the *fire* of the Bible episode is a figure for the spiritual purgative of excommunication, whereas the *sword* of Judah Maccabee signifies the physical and secular punishment of burning. The commentary roundel does not, however, depict execution by fire; instead it shows a bareheaded man caught between a group of clerics flourishing a closed book on one side and a king brandishing a sword on the other (Fig. 103). The effect of this omission is to focus attention on the spiritual state of the excommunicate rather than on the physical fate of his body, a focus underscored by the next two commentary images, which return to those who presumably received illumination and repented, illustrating respectively the sacraments of penance (confession and absolution) and the Eucharist (specifically, communion).[78] The privileging of spirit over body is, moreover, reinforced by the next commentary excerpt: "[That Judah found idolatrous tokens under the tunics of the slain Jews (II Macc. 12:39–40)] signifies that good prelates diligently investigate the sins of their subjects and frequently will have found in confessions that a wicked intention hid under an exterior of beautiful works."[79]

If only a few slender and isolated historical correspondences can be found for the *Bible moralisée* references to excommunicating Jews, a plethora exists for references to burning heretics. Although the burning of heretics was not universally condoned (Peter the Chanter and Thomas Gallus both wrote in opposition to killing heretics),[80] the majority of clerics upheld the legitimacy of the sentence,[81] and by the turn of the thirteenth century the consignment of heretics to the secular authorities to be burned at the stake was accepted practice in the north of France. Numerous executions by fire took place during the reign of Philip Augustus, including the burning of a group of *popelicans* in Troyes in 1198[82] and that of the Amauricians in Paris in 1210.[83] The Albigensian Crusade, launched in 1209, significantly expanded the territory in which (and boosted the frequency with which) the penalty was imposed. Although Cathars in the Midi had been pursued from the late twelfth century, Catholic authorities had generally restricted their punishments to exile and confiscation of their goods.[84] It was the northern French crusaders who brought to Languedoc the custom of burning heretics: 140 heretics were burned in Minerve in 1210,[85] about 300 heretics were burned at Lavaur in 1211,[86] and more than 50 *perfecti* were burned at Cassés, probably in 1212.[87] In spite of this frequency, however, for many years there was no written law or positive custom in France regarding the burning of heretics. The first French law that explicitly prescribed that heresy be punished by fire was issued by

Louis VIII in 1226.[88] Louis's biographer suggests that the king took this action because excommunication had ceased to be an effective deterrent; this would adequately explain recourse to execution in general, but it does not address the issue of why burning became the preferred method for dealing with heresy.[89] The images in the *Bible moralisée* suggest that the burning of heretics was an option that could be exercised in response to clerical calls for reform: it was yet another way to harness the discriminating, purgative, and destructive power of the eternal fire.[90]

A different text in the Latin *Bible moralisée* manuscript, however, adds another group to the list of those who should be burned. The order to stone a blasphemer in Lev. 24:23 ". . . signifies that God orders kings and counts to kill all infidels and populicans."[91] In the accompanying roundel the means by which they are to be killed is specified: a seated young, beardless king has several figures (two of whom are bearded) burned (Fig. 104). This text echoes the intense and ever increasing pressure exerted upon secular authorities—particularly in France—to participate in the battle against heresy, which culminated in the launching of the Albigensian Crusade in 1209.[92] The mention of "kings and counts," in particular, may be a direct reference to the baronial, and later royal, leaders of the Crusade.[93] However, the reference to infidels in this text broadens its import beyond the specific context of the Albigensian Crusade and begs the following question: Is the punishment prescribed for heretics being extended, consciously or unconsciously, to Jews?

The preceding commentary, which introduces and identifies the blasphemer whose killing is enjoined upon kings and counts, provides visual support for such an extension. The commentary runs: "He who laughed at the Lord signifies infidels and publicans who do not want nor ever have wanted to understand the word of the Lord."[94] In the adjacent image the "infidels and publicans" are unambiguously rendered as Jews: bearded and hatted, they stick their tongues out at a priest reading from a Bible on a lectern as they walk away (Fig. 105).

The parallel commentary text/roundel pair in the French manuscript likewise associates the "miscreants and populicans" who must be burned with Jews. The French commentary text translates, "That he mocked God and made a face and spoke evil of Him signifies miscreants and populicans who mock God and his sacraments and say that they are nothing, and God commands that they be burned and destroyed and they are."[95] The roundel neglects to depict the punishers and the punishments, focusing instead on the nature of the "miscreants and populicans" and contrasting them with the sacraments they mock. Within an architectural framework on the left, a priest raises a Host above an altar with a chalice. On the right, the infidels and miscreants walk away, craning their necks to cast hostile looks on the priest. Two

FIG. 104 (TOP). Lev. 24:23. Kings and counts kill infidels and heretics. Cod. 1179, fol. 52c. FIG. 105. Lev. 24:10–11. Infidels and heretics reject the word of the Lord. Cod. 1179, fol. 52b.

of them are bearded and wear low caps, and one carries a sacrificial lamb. The Catholic sacrament, then, is contrasted not with heretical practices but with Jewish ones, whose adherents, like heretics, are condemned to the flame (see Fig. 76).

In light of this iconography, of the fact that in these manuscripts "miscreants" and "infidels" almost inevitably refer to Jews, and of the fact that several other images show kings killing Jews,[96] it is difficult to avoid the conclusion that these texts do at least intermittently endorse the burning—the judicial assignment to the punishing eternal fire—of Jews as well as of heretics. Such a command would be counter to all established ecclesiastical and secular legislation and custom: the tradition of tolerating Jews goes back to the earliest Christian writings and was never formally disavowed by the medieval Church. Jews were considered part of regalian rights, and any secular authority claiming dominion must be fiercely protective of those rights, and therefore of Jews. Likewise, Church authorities repeatedly directed that as long as Jews did not commit any crimes, they were not to be killed simply because of their faith. Between the years 1120 and 1250, practically every reigning pope reissued the *Constitutio pro Judeis* forbidding violence against the Jews.[97] The massacres of the Jews during the First and Second Crusades were not approved of by secular or clerical authorities: Albert of Aix considered the murderers of the Rhineland Jews in 1096 to be motivated by "some error of mind";[98] in his letters promoting the Second Crusade, Bernard of Clairvaux reminded his correspondents that Jews were not to be molested;[99] and Peter the Chanter reiterated the established reasons for this ruling in the article *Iudei* in his *Summa Abel.*[100] There is no evidence of any serious attempts in the twelfth or thirteenth centuries to change church policy concerning the Jews' right to exist.[101]

It is consequently impossible to conceive of the *Bible moralisée* as a reflection of, much less the locus for, a rethinking of doctrine concerning Jews. Rather, because the roundels in the *Bible moralisée* visually realize ideas expressed metaphorically, much like the sermon exempla that inspired so much of the imagery, the manuscripts' commentary illustrations repeatedly forge connections and seem to draw conclusions that were not asserted in other theological genres. Moreover, as the commanding feature of the *Bible moralisée* the images dominate in an unexpected way, and from time to time the varying pictorial meditations on the ways in which the eternal fire might be realized in the here and now do seem to infiltrate the text. Thus the conclusion *not* explicitly drawn in the writings of the Parisian reformers (i.e., that there is no longer room for Jews qua Jews in Christendom) does, in fact, come to be drawn in excommunication and burning texts of the *Bible moralisée.*

This pattern exhibits itself beyond the pages of the *Bible moralisée* as well: from time to time, and clearly depending on context, the same conclusion was drawn (or the same rhetoric was summoned) to justify similar assertions in contemporary France and beyond. It was not necessary for a new theology to be articulated: traditional theology, when expressed in times of crisis in conjunction with polemical themes, can resonate in such a way as to provoke nontraditional or unprecedented forms of restriction and violence. There was, for example, a literal enactment of the *Bible moralisée*'s Lev. 24:23 commentary text not far in time from the creation of the *Bible moralisée* manuscripts: in March 1192 many Jews of "Brie" were burned by Philip Augustus. Although the Jews were ostensibly killed not on account of their religion but for obstructing justice, the violence was endowed with sectarian significance by Philip's monastic biographer, who labeled it an expression of "compassion" for the Christian faith.[102] I am not suggesting that metaphoric exegesis either provoked this attack or was cynically invoked to hardheadedly justify self-interested actions, any more than that Stephen Langton was either a captive servant or a hypocritical manipulator of his theological training. Instead, the interplay of text, image, and historical application evident in the treatment of Jews in the *Bible moralisée* points to a dialectical relationship between policy and polemic: a course of action suggested by political, economic, judicial, or personal considerations may be understood, interpreted, or justified in light of current theological, exegetical, or polemical discourse. This discourse in turn serves to shape, direct, or redirect policy.

The images of the Jews' fate in the *Bible moralisée,* then, suggest in the aggregate the following conclusions, all as unstartling as they are important to underscore. First, that eschatological imagery was forcefully and creatively invoked in the thirteenth century to justify and promote a reformist agenda. However, far from logically dictating any single course, eschatological schemas supplied a broad range of tropes relevant to Jewish policy, from which polemicists, rulers, and theologians could pick and choose; and specific, localized, and even personal considerations would consequently weigh at least as much in deciding those choices as would "pure" theology. Finally, since apocalypticism served more to reflect than to shape contemporary ideology, to understand Jewish-Christian relations in the thirteenth century, we must look not to theoretical imaginings of the end of days but to the concrete forms assigned these and other themes in the immediate historical framework. In concluding with this emphasis on the interplay between the general and the particular, the message and the audience, the rhetorical and the political, we end where the royal *Bible moralisée* manuscript ends: with the words and images of a timeless text held in the hands of a very time-bound king (Fig. 106).

FIG. 106. Dedication roundels: the royal recipient and the scribe of the Latin *Bible moralisée.* Cod. 1179, fol. 246d.

CONCLUSION

Hic sunt excommunicati et maledicti
iudei qui negant veritatem et veram
expositionem sacre scripture.
Et heretici qui in ea suas falsitates
admittent. Et falsi decretiste qui
sacram scripturam inducunt ut
per eam litigent de terrenis.

Here are excommunicated and cursed
Jews who deny the truth and the true
exposition of sacred Scripture. And
heretics who admit falsities into it.
And false decretists who induce sacred
Scripture so that through it they might
litigate about worldly things.[1]

The *Bible moralisée* concludes with this commentary on the closing verses of Apocalypse, in which the author warns that God's punishment will be brought down upon anyone who alters the words of the book he has just completed. The commentary text may be read on two levels. On the surface, it explains that the apostle John was foretelling the fate of those figures who were destined in the future to misuse his own and other sacred writings. But the text also has a second meaning: it succinctly summarizes the goals, function, and achievement of the *Bible moralisée* as a whole; for, indeed, here in the *Bible moralisée* manuscript that this text closes are condemned Jews, heretics, and those who have misapplied the study of sacred Scripture.

The practice of castigating Jews is as old as Christianity itself. Throughout this book I have hastened to acknowledge that most of the content of the commentary of the *Bible moralisée,* including the anti-Jewish polemic, draws on and echoes exegetical and theological works of the twelfth century and earlier. The Jews' nefarious role in the Crucifixion of Christ, their rejection of the message of the Gospels, and their carnality and excessive love of money were all traditional themes in Christian literature. Even the less standard topoi—the portrayal of Jews engaging in demonic, magical, and obscene activities—have significant, albeit generally less graphic, parallels in twelfth- and thirteenth-century texts. However, in spite of the conventionality and apparent randomness of much of the commentary, it is possible to detect certain patterns, consistent ways of thinking, underlying and structuring the program of the *Bible moralisée.* The selection of certain themes from among the enormous mass of material at the disposal of the redactors and, even more, the creative way in which this material was realized or adapted in the illustrations construct a coherent point of view, providing insight into the mental structures, if not the social realities, of the society by and for which the manuscripts were created.

The picture is, like a sermon, formed by a rather loose weaving together of many strands. Through the layering of language and symbol, the Jews' literalness becomes both source and example of their general carnality, which manifests itself in greed, pride, lust, and bloodthirstiness and these interior sins' concomitant social crimes. In this way Jews and the Jewish religion are associated in turn with secular knowledge, dangerous philosophy, heresy, idolatry, and usury. Jews are portrayed as threatening the purity of the Body of Christ; the integrity of the text of Scripture; the faith, mores, and study habits of students; and the spiritual health of Christendom itself.

However, the association of each of these themes with the Jews does *not* establish that they are uniquely Jewish; on the contrary, the texts and images of the *Bible moralisée* repeatedly testify to the contagious nature of "Jewish" perfidy. Jews are sometimes depicted in isolation, but they are more frequently linked to heretics and philosophers, bad kings and bad students; and their financial, intellectual, exegetical, and philosophical activities come under as much criticism as do their religious observances. If Jews "worship idols," so do many Christians; if Jews are avaricious, so are many Christians; if Jews are proud, overly curious, carnal in their interpretive approach, and so forth, Christians—especially scholars and clerics—are acknowledged to be susceptible to these failings too. Neither the anti-Jewish topoi nor the moralistic self-criticism in the *Bible moralisée* is unique, but their consistent juxtaposition and conflation are unusual, arising out of the innovative form and requirements of the manuscripts. The unique nature of the *Bible moralisée* thus allows us—forces us—to view familiar texts and tropes from a new angle.

The type of conduct censured here grows out of prosperity (greed, usury, lust) and intellectual opportunity and confidence (philosophical speculation and exegetical innovation). These are vices of a highly successful society grappling with that success: they are the product of excess, superabundance, and immoderation. This makes perfect sense: the urban northern French society out of which the *Bible moralisée* sprung underwent rapid and unprecedented economic and demographic expansion and political consolidation in the later twelfth and early thirteenth centuries, and it was experiencing the resultant growing pains as well as pleasures. Although there may have been actual instances of Jewish-heretical cooperation, Jewish influence over students, or Jewish enjoyment of royal favor, and there certainly were abundant instances of Jewish-Christian intellectual and commercial exchanges, it seems unlikely that these alone inspired the intense anti-Judaism of the *Bible moralisée* and the texts and sermons it echoes. Many other and more central and pressing circumstances contributed to its growth and elaboration. In early thirteenth-century France heterodoxy was proliferating, new non-Christian works were infiltrating the university curriculum, and the economy was becoming increasingly money-oriented. Moneylending was practiced with impunity by Christians as well as by Jews, and kings and princes were profiting from it. If these developments came to be associated with Jews, it was not just because Jews were traditional scapegoats for Christianity but because the specific ways in which society was changing (becoming more wealthy, urbanized, secular, literate, and curious) entailed the spread of qualities long labeled "Jewish."

To what extent was the strong anti-Jewish thrust of the *Bible moralisée* calculated and intentional? It is, of course, impossible to know, but I suspect that much of it was unplanned. Certainly the directors of the project strongly and consciously disapproved of Jewish moneylending and religious recalcitrance, but it seems unlikely that these attitudes translated into a self-conscious obsession with Jews' perfidies. No individual roundel or text conveys a radical change in ideology or doctrine; rather, it is the cumulative effect of the piling on, broadening, and deepening of the anti-Jewish themes and their use as signs for new and diverse activities that create the impression of a powerful and innovative anti-Jewish program. This effect arises from the particular nature of the manuscript form. Like popular preaching, with which the commentary is so concerned and whose mission was the expression of doctrine in terms familiar to the "people," the *Bible moralisée* entailed the translation of Scholastic exegetical analysis into a secular language of images. In the process of constructing this new language, of situating vague and abstract moralizations within a familiar and contemporary context, the most arresting and vivid imagery available was enlisted. Eventually these virulent (often demonic) narratives and themes came to dominate the illustrations, to infiltrate the text, and perhaps even, when a host of other conditions combined to facilitate this, to influence or at least justify policy.

Such virulent demonic imagery, whose presence most distinguishes the *Bible moralisée* from purely textual contemporary exegesis, is usually associated with "popular" anti-Semitism.[2] But these manuscripts can by no stretch of the imagination be considered "popular"; they were created by a clerical elite for a lay elite. This suggests that the typical elite/popular; clerical/lay dichotomies posited by many medievalists—particularly in conjunction with Jewish-Christian relations—are inadequate categories of historical analysis. One of the central developments of the later twelfth century was the drawing together of the "elite" and the "people"—the rise of the cities created an urban middle class to fill the space between noble and peasant; the spread of schools and universities gave people from a variety of backgrounds the opportunity to achieve literacy; and the creation of governmental bureaucracies staffed by clerics and university graduates brought people of less-than-elite background to positions of authority. Similar patterns hold for relations between the clergy and the laity. Although doctrinal developments such as the official promulgation of transubstantiation, liturgical developments such as elaborations in the rituals of priesthood, and architectural developments such as the erection and expansion of choir screens deepened the theoretical and conceptual gulf between laity and clergy, the spread of preaching, the Fourth Lateran Council's insistence on at least yearly communion, the beginnings of a lay literary culture, and the rise of first the urban secular clergy and then the mendicant orders narrowed intellectual, cultural, and physical gaps between the clergy and the people.[3]

One effect of this trend toward laicization was to extend the meanings assigned to the "Body of Christ." Traditional applications of the term to the eucharistic Host and to the priesthood and the institutional Church continued to prevail, but, in a kind of outward concentric expansion, the phrase also came to be used with increasing frequency to designate the entire body of believers, including the laity. The iconographic and polemical differences between the Latin and the vernacular *Bible moralisée* manuscripts, subtle as they are, point to possible implications of this conceptual expansion of the Body of Christ. First, including the laity within a newly reconfigured idea of religious community necessarily bears gendered implications, as the observations of Tracy Chapman concerning female imagery in the French-language manuscript and my own work on the representation of Synagoga in both manuscripts affirm.[4] The implications of this development for anti-Jewish imagery are also significant. When the Body of Christ is understood in primarily hieratic terms, as seems to be the case in the Latin manuscript, an assertion of the distance between Jews and this Body implicitly conflates Jews and the laity (as in Fig. 54); this conflation in turn inspires and spurs further clerical critique of the "material" and "fleshly" aspects of the world. Yet when the "Body of Christ" from which Jews must be excluded is understood as the entire community of Christians, a different task is faced. The enlarged circle against which Jews now must be defined requires a more pointed and less traditional critical rhetoric—explaining perhaps the more virulently hostile anti-Jewish tone and images occasionally noted in the French *Bible moralisée.* These two contemporary, similar, but not identical manuscripts seem to embody the fascinating and complex interaction between two elite cultures.

I agree, then, with R. I. Moore that it is developments in the majority rather than minority society that underlie much later medieval anti-Judaism. However, I see it not so much as a conscious technique on the part of clerical or governmental elites for securing hegemony as an epistemological development: an unconscious or semiconscious result of changes in how information was processed and disseminated. Intolerance was not the result of a spontaneous welling up of mass hatred, but neither was prejudice imposed on the masses from above. Nor was intolerance inevitable; the rhetorical rather than theological underpinning of much later medieval anti-Judaism allowed for its manipulation in a multitude of ways, some highly destructive and some much less so, as well as for its disregard: a truly comprehensive survey of medieval Jewish-Christian relations would have more than a few uneventful chapters.

This rhetorical model helps explain the apparent longevity of many of the anti-Jewish topoi elaborated in the pages of the *Bible moralisée.* The lay sermon became one of the dominant modes of Christian discourse, remaining the primary point of contact between the clergy and the "people" until, and well beyond, the onset of the Reformation and the invention of printing. Moreover, even when preaching declined as a form of public and mass entertainment and of information dissemination, its basic techniques and much of its most haunting imagery lived on. Many of the exempla that enlivened thirteenth-century sermons (and woke up their audience) and were so closely echoed in the commentary illustrations of the *Bible moralisée* appeared in popular and "high" literature (*The Decameron* and *The Canterbury Tales* and their imitators), in theater (*The Jew of Malta* and *The Merchant of Venice*), and in folk ballads (*The Jew's Daughter*). As the conditions that gave rise to such tales were forgotten, their resonances, interpretations, referents, and applications would inevitably alter. Many of the images and motifs encountered in this book reappear, for example, in visual representations of and literature dealing with witchcraft in the later Middle Ages and the early modern period. If it is impossible not to recall Nazi anti-Jewish visual propaganda at this point, let us also remember that it was created in conditions very different from those in the Middle Ages, and that its makers and viewers drew conclusions and formulated policies quite alien to thirteenth-century France. Similarity of form by no means entails identity in meaning.[5] If the power of a metaphor lies in its flexibility and transferability, then the anti-Jewish imagery of the *Bible moralisée* is powerful indeed.

FIG. 107. Exod. 7:10–12. The Gospels, the preaching of prelates, or the *Bible moralisée* itself, consuming the devilish words of the Jews. Cod. 2554, fol. 18vc.

I would like to close with two final images (Figs. 3 and 107). It will be remembered that in the commentary to Exod. 7:12, the staff of the Egyptian magicians was held to signify perfidious Jewish exegesis.[6] In both the Latin and the French texts, the enemies of this Jewish exegesis are identified as preachers: "That Moses and Aaron threw down the staff and it turned into a serpent and devoured those of the magicians signifies good prelates who, in explaining the word of the Gospel, devour the false words of the Jews."[7] The illustrations exploit the contrasting meanings assigned to the two forms of the Law in the manuscripts' iconography; they also emphasize vividly the role that preachers will come to have in the attack on the Jews. In the Latin manuscript, a soul rising out of a codex compels the Jews and their naked, bestial, and black-complexioned demonic ally to throw down their law; in the French, red flames spring out of a codex to attack two scrolls of the Law. The codices held by the clerics may be interpreted as the Gospel, as the text of a sermon, or as the *Bible moralisée* itself, attacking through its spiritual exegesis and its visual polemic the "devilish" words and works of the Jews.

ABBREVIATIONS

AASS	*Acta sanctorum quotquot toto orbe coluntur.* Edited by J. Bolland et al. Antwerp and elsewhere, 1643–.
AHDLMA	*Archives d'histoire doctrinale et littéraire du moyen âge.* Paris, 1926–.
AHR	*The American Historical Review.* Washington, D.C., 1895–.
AJS Review	*AJS Review: The Journal of the Association for Jewish Studies.* Cambridge, Mass., 1975–.
Annales ESC	*Annales: économies, sociétés, civilisations.* Paris, 1946–.
Annales HSS	*Annales: histoire, sciences sociales.* Paris, 1945–.
CCCM	*Corpus christianorum. Continuatio mediaevalis.* Turnhout, Belgium. 1966–.
CSEL	*Corpus scriptorum ecclesiasticorum latinorum.* Vienna, 1866–.
Du Cange	*Glossorium ad scriptores mediae et infimae Latinitatis.* 6 vols. Edited by Charles Dufresne Du Cange. Basel, 1762.
Mansi	*Sacrorum Conciliorum Nova et Amplissima Collectio.* Edited by Johannes Dominicus Mansi. 54 vols. Graz, 1960–61.
MGH Script.	*Monumenta Germaniae Historica: Scriptores.* Berlin, 1826–.
PL	*Patrologiae cursus completus, series Latina.* Edited by J.-P. Migne. 221 vols. Paris, 1844–1903.
REJ	*Revue des études juives.* Paris, 1880–.
RHGF	*Recueil des historiens des Gaules et de la France.* Edited by M. Bouquet et al. 24 vols. Paris, 1738–1904.
RTAM	*Recherches de théologie ancienne et médiévale.* Louvain, 1929–96.

NOTES

Introduction

1. Vienna, Österreichische Nationalbibliothek cod. 1179 (hereafter Vienna ÖNB cod. 1179). It is widely agreed that this manuscript was a royal commission: the last two roundels in the manuscript depict, respectively, a king holding an open codex with three roundels on each folio, and a scribe writing in a similar codex; these are analogous to the dedication/presentation "portraits" in many contemporary manuscripts. Beside these roundels there is a largely effaced dedicatory inscription, which I discuss later.

2. On the epithet "rex christianissimus," which was applied to all thirteenth-century French kings, see Joseph R. Strayer, "France: The Holy Land, the Chosen People, and the Most Christian King," in *Action and Conviction in Early Modern Europe,* ed. Theodore Rabb and J. Siegel (Princeton, N.J., 1969); and John W. Baldwin, "*Persona et Gesta:* The Image and Deeds of the Thirteenth-Century Capetians. The Case of Philip Augustus," *Viator* 19 (1988): 195–207.

3. The second is a roughly contemporary and closely related French-language manuscript (not, however, in any sense a "translation"): Vienna ÖNB cod. 2554. In addition to Vienna ÖNB codices 1179 and 2554, there are twelve more *Bible moralisée* manuscripts. Two three-volume versions date to the mid–thirteenth century: one is in the treasury of the Toledo Cathedral; its last folios are in the Pierpont Morgan Library in New York (MS 240). The volumes of the other have been separated and are now housed in Oxford (Bodleian MS 270b), Paris (BN lat. 11560), and London (BM Harley 1526–1527). For a complete listing of fourteenth- and fifteenth-century manuscripts, see *Bible moralisée, Faksimile-Ausgabe im Originalformat des Codex Vindobonensis 2554 der Österreichischen Nationalbibliothek,* ed. Reiner Haussherr (Graz and Paris, 1973), 5. In this book I am concerned with the manuscripts as artifacts of a particular social and cultural context; I therefore limit my examination to the two nearly contemporaneous Vienna manuscripts. The slightly later thirteenth-century exemplars differ substantially from the earlier pair in their visual and exegetical programs; I hope to address these differences in a future study.

4. See chapter 1 for a statistical summary of the preponderance of Jews in the manuscripts. Although assessing populations is one of the most vexing of all tasks faced by medieval historians, by any count Jews were a tiny minority in thirteenth-century France, and the proportion of Jews to other figures in the *Bibles moralisées* is wildly out of proportion to Jews' numerical importance in or beyond the royal domain. For population

estimates, which range between .05 and 5 percent of the population, see William Chester Jordan, *The French Monarchy and the Jews: From Philip Augustus to the Last Capetians* (Philadelphia, 1989), 5–10.

5. Robert Branner, *Manuscript Painting in Paris during the Reign of St. Louis* (Berkeley and Los Angeles, 1977), 32. In fact, they are so central to the history of Parisian manuscript illumination that the style in which they are painted is referred to as either the *muldenfaltenstil* or the "Moralized Bible style." Branner, *Manuscript Painting,* 22.

6. On these events, see especially Jordan, *The French Monarchy and the Jews,* chaps. 1–8; my reliance on and debt to Jordan's indispensable scholarship will be evident throughout this book. See also Kenneth R. Stow, "Papal and Royal Attitudes toward Jewish Lending in the Thirteenth Century," *AJS Review* 6 (1981): 161–184; and Gavin Langmuir, "*Tamquam servi:* The Change in Jewish Status in French Law about 1200," in *Les juifs dans l'histoire de France,* ed. M. Yardeni (Leiden, 1980), 24–54. Philip's reasons for readmitting Jews to his domain are unknown. The most convincing suggestion is that he felt the loss of tax revenues; other suggestions include Philip's pique at the church or a certain mellowing in his personality (Jordan, *The French Monarchy and the Jews,* 37).

7. The striking preponderance of anti-Jewish polemic in the work, evident from even a cursory examination of the manuscripts, has been remarked upon and briefly examined. Reiner Haussherr noted the mordant anti-Jewish polemic in an article examining the depiction of contemporary reality in the *Bible moralisée:* "Zur Darstellung Zeitgenössischer Wirklichkeit und Geschichte in der *Bible moralisée* und in illustrationen von Geschichtsschreibung im 13. Jahrhundert," in *Il Medio Oriente e l'Occidente nell'arte de XIII secolo,* ed. Hans Belting (Bologna, 1982), 211–220, here 212–213. Bernhard Blumenkranz focused on the *Bibles moralisées* in several studies of anti-Jewish art. His works were groundbreaking but rather limited in scope, concentrating on identifying the major anti-Jewish iconographic elements rather than elucidating the methods or the goals of the polemic. See *Le juif médiéval au miroir de l'art chrétien* (Paris, 1966), esp. 41–56; "La polémique antijuive dans l'art chrétien du moyen âge," *Bulletino d'Instituto storico italiano per il medio evo* 77 (1965): 21–43; and "La représentation de Synagoga dans les Bibles moralisées françaises du XIIIe au XVe siècle," *Proceedings of the Israel Academy of Science and Humanities* 5 (1971–76): 70–91. Michael Camille applied sophisticated art historical analysis to some specific anti-Jewish images from the *Bibles moralisées* in a valuable study of the depiction of the idol in Gothic art (*The Gothic Idol: Ideology and Image-Making in Medieval Art* [Cambridge, 1989], chap. 4), but his primary focus was not the anti-Jewish polemic of the *Bible moralisée.* In addition, Camille's discussion of anti-Jewish art is weakened by several factual errors about Jewish history. No one, as yet, has satisfactorily explained why the commentary text and images of the *Bible moralisée* were so preoccupied with the Jews or has attempted to identify the nature of and bases for the concerns.

8. On medieval anti-Jewish iconography, see Blumenkranz, *Le juif médiéval;* Henry Kraus, *The Living Theatre of Medieval Art* (Bloomington and London, 1967), chap. 7; Suzanne Lewis, "*Tractatus Adversus Judaeos* in the Gulbenkian Apocalypse," *Art Bulletin* 68 (1986): 543–566; and the works of Ruth Mellinkoff: *The Horned Moses in Medieval Art and*

Thought (Berkeley and Los Angeles, 1970); "Cain and the Jews," *Journal of Jewish Art* 6 (1979): 16–38; *The Mark of Cain* (Berkeley and Los Angeles, 1981); and *Outcasts: Signs of Otherness in Northern European Art of the Later Middle Ages,* 2 vols. (Berkeley and Los Angeles, 1993).

9. On later anti-Jewish imagery, see Eric Zafran, "The Iconography of Antisemitism: A Study of the Representation of the Jews in the Visual Arts of Europe 1400–1600" (Ph.D. diss., New York University Institute of Fine Arts, 1973); and Mellinkoff, *Outcasts.*

10. Suzanne Lewis ("*Tractatus Adversus Judaeos,*" 544) went so far as to suggest that the *Bibles moralisées* were the source for this later imagery; extensive investigation into chains of transmission would, of course, be needed to verify this suggestion. I must stress here that in identifying the *Bibles moralisées* as the earliest surviving locus for much subsequent anti-Jewish iconography, I am by no means claiming that they define the "real" meaning or context for such later imagery. On the contrary, I shall argue throughout this book that the meaning of signs in any given work of art is determined by a complicated dialogic process in which traditional motifs interact with, inform, but are also transformed by local and specific social, political, and cultural circumstances.

11. Jean Chatillon, "Le mouvement théologique dans la France de Philippe Auguste," in *La France de Philippe Auguste: Le temps des mutations* (Actes du Colloque International organisé par le CNRS, Paris, 1980), ed. Robert-Henri Bautier (Paris, 1982), 881: "The space between the first Scholastics and the great synthesizers is little known."

12. C. Spicq, *Esquisse d'une histoire de l'exégèse latine au moyen âge,* Bibliothèque Thomiste 26 (Paris, 1944), 142–143.

13. Scholarship on the teaching of *sacre pagine* in the schools is extensive and rapidly expanding. See especially Beryl Smalley, "The Bible in the Medieval Schools," in *The Cambridge History of the Bible,* vol. 2, *The West from the Fathers to the Reformation,* ed. G. W. H. Lampe (Cambridge, 1969), 197–220, and her *Study of the Bible in the Middle Ages,* 3d ed. (Oxford, 1983); L.-J. Bataillon, "De la *lectio* à la *praedicatio:* Commentaires bibliques et sermons au XIIIe siècle," *Revue des sciences philosophiques et théologiques* 70 (1986): 559–575; Jean Chatillon, "La Bible dans les écoles du XIIe siècle," in *Le Moyen Âge et la Bible,* ed. Guy Lobrichon and Pierre Riché (Paris, 1984), 163–197; J. Verger, "L'exégèse de l'université," in Lobrichon and Riché, *Le Moyen Âge et la Bible,* 199–232.

14. Spicq, *Esquisse d'une histoire de l'exégèse latine,* 290.

15. For a forceful statement of the significance of the reign of Philip Augustus (1180–1223), see Robert-Henri Bautier, "La place du règne de Philippe-Auguste dans l'histoire de la France médiévale," in *La France de Philippe Auguste: Le temps des mutations,* ed. Robert-Henri Bautier (Paris, 1982), 11–27. The best study of Philip's reign is John W. Baldwin, *The Government of Philip Augustus: Foundations of French Royal Power in the Middle Ages* (Berkeley, 1986). On the reign of Louis VIII (1223–26), see Charles Petit-Dutaillis, *Étude sur la vie et le règne de Louis VIII (1187–1226)* (Paris, 1894); and Jacques Choffel, *Louis VIII le Lion* (Paris, 1983). More general works include Robert Fawtier, *The Capetian Kings of France: Monarchy and Nation (987–1328),* trans. Lionel Butler and R. J. Adam (New York, 1960); and Elizabeth M. Hallam, *Capetian France, 987–1328* (London and New York, 1980).

16. Recent works on the creation and dissemination of Capetian mythology include Colette Beaune, *The Birth of an Ideology: Myths and Symbols of Nation in Late Medieval France,* trans. Susan Ross Huston, ed. Fredric L. Cheyette (Berkeley, Los Angeles, and Oxford, 1991); Baldwin, *The Government of Philip Augustus,* 362–393; Strayer, "France: The Holy Land"; Jacques le Goff, "Royauté biblique et idéal monarchique médiéval: Saint Louis et Josias," in *Les juifs au regard de l'histoire: Mélanges en l'honneur de Bernhard Blumenkranz,* ed. Gilbert Dahan (Paris, 1985), 157–167.

17. Gavin Langmuir, "'Judei nostri' and Capetian Legislation," *Traditio* 16 (1960): 203–239.

18. See, for example, the letters of Innocent III to Philip dated 1205 (PL 215:502), 1208 (PL 215:1470), and 1214 (PL 217:229); and the decree of the Council of Paris from 1213 (Mansi 22:850). These documents are partially reproduced and translated in Solomon Grayzel, ed., *The Church and the Jews in the XIIIth Century* (Philadelphia, 1933), 105–109, 133, 139–141, 306–307.

19. Jean Chatillon, "Introduction," in Richard of St. Victor, *Liber Exceptionum,* ed. Jean Chatillon (Paris, 1958), 10. See, too, the comments of Philippe Buc in "Pouvoir royal et commentaires de la Bible (1150–1350)," *Annales ESC* 44 (1989): 692: "The metaphors chosen by the exegete . . . reveal the structures according to which the exegete conceptualizes power and betray political preoccupations." Buc conceives of the task of the scholar of exegesis as "re-translating non-literal terms into the language of the letter"; I would add nontextual terms as well.

20. I do not address in any systematic manner the question of the biblical text itself, which is a highly technical issue beyond the scope of this study. No edition of the "Paris Bible," a corrected version of the Vulgate compiled at the same time as the *Bible moralisée,* has yet been established. For purposes of convenience, when I compare the Bible text of the *Bible moralisée* to "the Vulgate," I am referring to the Bible text accompanying the 1480/81 edition of the *Glossa ordinaria,* which, according to the editors of the modern facsimile, is quite close to the Paris Bible.

21. And a limited audience at that: it most likely consisted of the king and members of the royal family and court. I will discuss the question of audience later; at this point I will say that for a variety of reasons, including the prominence of certain exegetical themes, the primacy of the images, and the fact that at least parts of the text are watered-down and abridged versions of their sources, I do not subscribe to Michael Camille's suggestion of a clerical readership, offered in "Visual Signs of the Sacred Page: Books in the *Bible moralisée,*" *Word and Image* 5 (1989): 111–130.

22. This situation should soon be rectified: a study entitled *The Making of the Bibles moralisées* by John Lowden of the Courtauld Institute of Art is forthcoming with The Penn State Press. In addition to the works cited in notes 7 and 21, see the bibliography accompanying the recent facsimile of the French-language manuscript: *Bible moralisée. Codex Vindobonensis 2554 Vienna, Österreichische Nationalbibliothek,* commentary and translation of biblical texts by Gerald B. Guest (London, 1995). The dissertations are James Michael Heinlen, "The Ideology of Reform in the French Moralized Bible" (Ph.D. diss., Northwest-

ern University, 1991); a thesis by Hans-Walter Stork now published as *Die Wiener französische Bible moralisée Codex 2554 der Österreichischen Nationalbibliothek* (St. Ingbert, 1992); and my own dissertation, "Jews in the Commentary Texts and Illustrations of the Early Thirteenth-Century *Bibles moralisées*" (Ph.D. diss., Yale University, 1991). I became aware of the unpublished doctoral dissertation of Philippe Büttner, "Bilder zum Betreten der Zeit: Bible moralisée und Kapetingisches Königtum" (Ph.D. diss., Basel University, 1996), too late for consultation.

23. Alexandre de Laborde, in his *Étude sur la Bible moralisée illustrée,* placed them all in the middle of the thirteenth century. Hermann, in *Die Westeuropäischen Handschriften,* also dated the two Vienna manuscripts to ca. 1250; Haseloff ("La miniature en France") and Vitzthum (*Die Pariser miniatur malerei*) opted for the slightly earlier dating of 1230–50. Branner (*Manuscript Painting*) and Haussherr (*Faksimile*) agreed that Vienna ÖNB cod. 1179 was the oldest of the surviving exemplars, Branner proposing the date of 1215–25 and Haussherr of 1220–30. Most attempts to settle the question of which of the two Vienna manuscripts came first focus on the changes in page layout—some scholars accord temporal priority to cod. 1179 because they see the more symmetrical layout of cod. 2554 as a "clear improvement"; others conclude that cod. 2554 was the earlier manuscript on the basis of the fact that its layout was "abandoned" and that the "new" one adopted for cod. 1179 was retained in the two later thirteenth-century manuscripts. I believe such attempts are misguided; I argue later that the differences in layout are inextricably associated with the different languages of the two manuscripts and tell us little or nothing about the sequence of the manuscripts' creation. See Stork, *Die Wiener französische Bible moralisée,* 36–43; *Bible moralisée,* ed. Guest, 12–17; and Lipton, "Jews in the Commentary Texts and Illustrations," 2–3, for references to the positions sketched earlier and fuller surveys of the literature on the *Bible moralisée.*

24. For an excellent recent study of early thirteenth-century French illumination, see Alison Ann Merrill, "A Study of the Ingeborg Psalter Atelier" (Ph.D. diss., Columbia University, 1994).

25. Branner, *Manuscript Painting,* 48, tentatively identified the patron of Vienna ÖNB cod. 1179 as Philip Augustus, whereas Haussherr, favoring a slightly later date, hesitantly suggested that the king depicted on the last folio represented Louis VIII (*Faksimile,* 33). The dedication page of the Toledo manuscript (now, together with the rest of the last quire, Pierpont Morgan Library MS 240) shows two seated royal figures: a king and a queen. Depending again on the proposed dating, these figures have been identified either as Louis VIII and his wife, Blanche of Castile, or as Louis IX and his mother, the same Blanche (Branner, *Manuscript Painting,* 48; *Faksimile,* ed. Haussherr, 29). Laborde, relying on a linguistic study that identified the dialect as eastern, probably Champenois (Conrad Flam, "Lautlehre des französischen Textes in Codex Vindobonensis 2554" [Ph.D. diss., Halle, 1909]), proposed as a patron of Vienna ÖNB cod. 2554 Thibaut V of Champagne, later King of Navarre, who married one of the daughters of Louis IX. Haussherr (*Faksimile,* 7–9), skeptical of the linguistic study and favoring an earlier date than Laborde, expressed doubt about the identification of Thibaut but did not offer an alternative suggestion. Tracy Ann Chapman, "The Female Au-

dience for the Bible moralisée: Blanche of Castille and the Example of Vienna 2554" (master's thesis, University of Texas at Austin, 1995), argues that the French manuscript was made for Blanche. This is a perfectly plausible suggestion, but it is still largely speculative. The observations about women in the commentary images of the French manuscript with which Chapman supports this argument are interesting indeed, but as a vernacular glossed Bible is by its very nature an outgrowth of and more available to a gendered society than a Latin glossed Bible, the existence of this gendered imagery does not necessarily shed light on patronage.

26. Again, the authoritative work on this subject is Jordan, *The French Monarchy and the Jews.* For lords' rights over Jews, see pages 29 and 96.

27. Langmuir, "Judei nostri."

28. Jordan, *The French Monarchy and the Jews,* 30–37. On the massacre, see also Robert Chazan, "The Bray Incident of 1192: *Realpolitik* and Folk Slander," *Proceedings of the American Academy for Jewish Research* 37 (1969): 1–18; Chazan has since accepted Jordan's suggestions concerning the location of the incident: "Ephraim ben Jacob's Compilation of Twelfth-Century Persecutions," *Jewish Quarterly Review* 84 (1994): 397–416, here 402 n. 22. For further discussion of these events, see chapter 5.

29. Texts of the ordinance appear in *Veterum scriptorum et monumentorum historicum, dogmaticorum, moralium: Amplissima collectio,* 9 vols., ed. Edmund Martène and Ursinus Durand (Paris, 1724–33), 1:1182–1183; and *Layettes du Trésor des chartes,* 5 vols., ed. A. Teulet et al. (Paris, 1863–1909), vol. 2, no. 1610. The nature of these two texts is discussed in Jordan, *The French Monarchy and the Jews,* 285 nn. 5 and 6. For a discussion of the content, see Jordan, *The French Monarchy and the Jews,* 94–98.

30. Jordan remarks (*The French Monarchy and the Jews,* 93), "I do not know why Louis chose to act the way he did at that time." He goes on, however, to offer some very compelling suggestions.

31. The reading is my own, but it accords with that of Franz Mairinger, "Physikalische methoden zur sichtbarmachung verblasster oder getilgter Tinter," *Restoration of Book Paintings and Ink: Restaurator* 5 (1981/82): 45–56. The dedicatory inscription is also published partially in *La Bible moralisée illustrée conservée à Oxford, Paris, et Londres,* 4 vols., ed. A. de Laborde (Paris, 1911–27), 5:89.

32. See, for example, Stork, *Die Wiener französische Bible moralisée,* 36.

33. Horace, *Carmina* 1.1.1–2: "Maecenas atavis edite regibus, o et praesidium et dulce decus meum . . ." ("Maecenas, sprung from royal ancestors, O my protection and sweet glory . . .") The translation is from Matthew Santirocco, *Unity and Design in Horace's Odes* (Chapel Hill, N.C., and London, 1986), 15–16.

34. Rigord, *De Gestis Philippi Augusti, Francorum Regis,* in *Recueil des historiens des Gaules et de la France,* vol. 17, ed. M. J. J. Brial (Paris, 1878), 2c. This letter is not reproduced in Delaborde's edition of Rigord. In the same year Horace's phrase was associated with exemplary Old Testament kings, once again by a figure close to Prince Louis. In a sermon preached in chapter, Bishop Stephen of Tournai, formerly abbot of Ste. Geneviève and godfather to Prince Louis, exhorted: "Si ad natalium gloriam recurras originem duxit a rege salem . . . ab aaron . . . ab eleazaro . . . In summa

ab illo magno sacerdote qui in diebus eius placuit deo et inventus est iustus qui assistens pontifex futurorum bonorum introiuit semel in sancta aeterna redemptione inventa vere nobilis orta parentibus vere atavis edita regibus" (PL 211:568). In *De musica* Augustine used the phrase as an example of rhythm, but here the meaning of the words is irrelevant.

35. In his epic poem dedicated to Louis VIII (then Prince Louis), Gilles de Paris remarks that "your father wisely wants you to be able to read": "The *Karolinus* of Egidius Parisiensis," ed. M. L. Colker, *Traditio* 29 (1973): 199–325, Book 5. Petit-Dutaillis (*Étude sur la vie et le règne de Louis VIII,* 4) notes that Philip took care that Louis receive an education because he regretted his own lack of learning; it is the opinion of John Baldwin (*The Government of Philip Augustus,* 359) that Philip was illiterate in Latin.

36. "The *Karolinus,*" 202–204; see, too, Baldwin, *The Government of Philip Augustus,* 362–364.

37. Robert Bartlett, *Gerald of Wales, 1146–1223* (Oxford, 1982), 98.

38. This is the import of the Valerian prophecy, according to which St. Valéry promised kingship to Hugh Capet and his family for seven generations for rescuing Valéry's relics. The Valerian prophecy is cited in monastic chronicles in the twelfth century; Baldwin, however (*The Government of Philip Augustus,* 370), does not find it an important motif at Philip's court until the end of the reign.

39. Baldwin, *The Government of Philip Augustus,* 371. Philip's claim to Carolingian ancestry came via his mother, Adèle of Champagne.

40. It matters little that historians are now convinced that Philip did, indeed, have a good claim to Carolingian descent; what is relevant is that contemporary texts tended not to stress this claim. On Capetian dynasticism, see especially Karl Ferdinand Werner, "Die legitimät der Kapetinger und die Entstehung des 'Reditus regni Francorum ad stirpem Karoli,'" *Welt als Geschichte* 3 (1952): 203–225; Gabrielle M. Spiegel, "The *Reditus Regni ad Stirpem Karoli Magni:* A New Look," *French Historical Studies* 7 (1971): 145–174; Elizabeth A. R. Brown, "La notion de la légitimité et la prophétie à la cour de Philippe Auguste," in *La France de Philippe Auguste: le temps des mutations* (Actes du Colloque International organisé par le CNRS, Paris, 1980), ed. Robert-Henri Bautier (Paris, 1982), 77–110; Andrew W. Lewis, *Royal Succession in Capetian France: Studies on Familial Order and the State* (Cambridge, 1981); Beaune, *The Birth of an Ideology;* and Anne D. Hedeman, *The Royal Image: Illustrations of the 'Grandes Chroniques de France,' 1274–1422* (Berkeley and Los Angeles, 1991). Hedeman's discussion of the role of the *reditus* legend in later royalist propaganda is questioned by William Chester Jordan in a review in *Art Bulletin* 75 (1993): 723–724.

41. According to Vincent of Beauvais (*Speculum historiale,* Book 31, c. 126; cited in Werner, "Die legitimät," 204), the "reditus" to the line of Charlemagne was effected through Philip Augustus's marriage to Isabelle. One copy of the *Grandes Chroniques de France* asserted that the primary motivation for Philip's marriage to Isabelle was the accomplishment of that return: Hedeman, *The Royal Image,* 22.

42. RHGF 17:289–290.

43. Hedeman, *The Royal Image,* 158.

44. Beaune, *The Birth of an Ideology,* 202–203.

45. Vienna ÖNB cod. 1179, fol. 96c: "Nuncii redientes ad David et dixerunt ei stultum responsum Nabal et David iuravit quod eum interficeret significat nuncios iesu christi qui redeunt de terra albigensi et dicunt principibus et prelatis et bonis christianis quod deum ignorant in terra albigensi et boni principes suas cruces accipientes promittunt quod interficient omnes cum tota sua posteritate albigenses."

46. The literature on the Albigensian Crusade is vast. The most informative medieval narratives are Pierre des Vaux-de-Cernay, *Historia Albigensium,* and Guillaume de Puylaurens, *Historia Albigensium,* both in RHGF 19. An excellent modern edition with French translation of Guillaume's work is *Chronica Magistri Guillelmi de Podio Laurentii,* ed. Jean Duvernoy (Paris, 1976); for an edition and translation of Pierre's work, see *Histoire Albigeoise,* trans. Pascal Guébin and Henri Maisonneuve (Paris, 1951). The most comprehensive modern treatment of the Crusade is Michel Roquebert, *L'Épopée Cathare,* 4 vols. (Toulouse, 1970–89). For a clear narrative in English, see Joseph R. Strayer, *The Albigensian Crusades* (New York, 1971).

47. The substitution of the word "rex" for Rigord's "puer" in the Latin *Bible moralisée* inscription indicates that the manuscript was completed around the time of or shortly after Louis's accession to the throne. It will be remembered that one of Louis's first acts upon assumption of the throne was to issue the *Stabilimentum* on Jewish lending; I discuss this topic in greater depth in chapter 3. Louis seems to have been regarded, perhaps justifiably, perhaps optimistically, as more receptive to clerical guidance than was his father (it is, in fact, hard to imagine a ruler less susceptible to moral persuasion than Philip Augustus); it is certainly noteworthy that many of the commentary roundels in both *Bible moralisée* manuscripts detail the responsibilities and vices of kings. (The dissertation of James Heinlen examined this theme in the Vienna ÖNB cod. 2554: Heinlen argued that the *Bible moralisée* was essentially a *Miroir des princes;* I made a similar suggestion in my dissertation.) Although royal ancestry, vaunted learning, and notable piety are as characteristic of Louis IX as of his father, I do not think it likely that Louis IX was the patron of the earlier royal manuscript. Images of friars feature prominently in the illustrations of the two later thirteenth-century manuscripts, but there are no figures that can be identified as mendicants in the two earlier *Bible moralisée* exemplars. (On folios 79 and 80 of Vienna ÖNB cod. 1179, the figure of Augustine is depicted wearing a black cloak over a white robe. This is certainly identical to the Dominican habit, but it was chosen by the Dominican order because it was already the habit worn by Augustinian canons, whose rule the Dominicans adapted. St. Augustine is most likely attired in an Augustinian habit both for the obvious reason and because the commentary text illustrated is drawn from the exegetical tradition of the Augustinian Abbey of St.-Victor.) Although it is possible that a change in the intellectual orientation of the manuscripts accounts for this difference, I think that it is more likely related to the dates of the manuscripts: the mendicants were excluded from the earlier pair and included in the later pair because only in the intervening years had mendicants become influential in Paris and/or at the French court. The years during which this happened were early in the reign of Louis IX. Of course, it is always dangerous to argue from silence, but it is impossible for me to imagine

Dominicans participating in this project without having that participation reflected in the illustrations. For an account of the arrival of the mendicants to Paris, see M.-M. Dufeil, *Guillaume de St.-Amour et la Polémique Universitaire Parisienne, 1250–59* (Paris, 1972), 12–25. Vienna ÖNB cod. 1179 could not have been made at the very beginning of Louis IX's reign: he was a child upon accession, and the king in the dedication roundel is clearly portrayed as bearded and fully mature. Although dedication "portraits" are obviously schematicizations at this period rather than true portraiture, it would have been unusual to portray a young child as a bearded adult; see, for example, the presentation portrait of a young Prince Louis in Gilles de Paris's *Karolinus* (Paris BN lat. 6191). Moreover, the dedication portrait of a young king and a more mature queen in the Toledo manuscript (the first of the two later versions) almost certainly depicts Louis IX and his mother, Blanche of Castile; it seems likely that such an image dates to the period of the latter's greatest influence (1226–ca. 1244). It would be hard to imagine why, if Vienna ÖNB cod. 1179 had been completed only after 1226, a new version would have been required by the same patron so soon. On the other hand, if Vienna ÖNB cod. 1179 had been completed by 1225, at the latest, for Louis VIII, it is not hard to imagine that the learned and devout Blanche and Louis might want their own fuller copy, which could express their reverence for the mendicants and incorporate into its text the full biblical commentary being produced by the Dominican studium of St.-Jacques (compiled ca. 1236–39). In fact, it seems likely that the establishment of the studium of St.-Jacques provided the impetus for the commissioning of the Toledo manuscript. It is otherwise hard to explain why the royal court would spend so much money to create a larger version of what it already had. If the work of the Dominicans had made commentaries for many more books of the Bible suddenly available, it is not surprising that the court would have wanted a manuscript incorporating these exegetical advances. It is certainly interesting that in 1239 the royal treasury paid 100 solidi (part of a larger debt) to a "Master Nicholas the Illuminator" of the Rue St.-Jacques—the same street as the Dominican *studium* (RHFG 22:607, cited in Branner, *Manuscript Painting,* 6). On the studium, see Robert E. Lerner, "Poverty, Preaching, and Eschatology in the Revelation Commentaries of 'Hugh of St. Cher,'" in *The Bible in the Medieval World: Essays in Memory of Beryl Smalley,* ed. Katherine Walsh and Diane Wood (Oxford, 1985), 157–189.

48. The traditional description of the fourfold senses of Scripture defines tropology as internal and individualistic morality ("tropologia quid facies . . ."); the *Bible moralisée* commentary, on the other hand, is more concerned with social morality.

49. See Haussherr's commentary in his *Faksimile,* as well as two of his articles dealing with the texts of the various *Bibles moralisées:* "Petrus Cantor, Stephan Langton, Hugo von St. Cher und der Isaias-Prolog der *Bible moralisée,*" in *Verbum et Signum. Festschrift Friedrich Ohly,* ed. H. Fromm, W. Harms, and V. Ruberg (Munich, 1975), 347–364; and "Uber die Auswahl des Bibeltextes in der *Bible moralisée,*" *Zeitschrift für Kunstgeschichte* 51 (1988): 126–146.

50. In 1927 Laborde outlined many passages in which the Latin *Bibles moralisées* correspond word for word with the *Postillae* of Hugh of

St. Cher (which are now, however, believed to have been the joint effort of a committee of scholars rather than the work of one man) and concluded that the *Bible moralisée* was created in the house of St.-Jacques and was neither more nor less than an abridgment of the *Postillae.* Vincent of Beauvais was suggested by Franz Unterkircher in his *Abendländische Buchmalerei* (Vienna, 1952), no. 168.

51. John W. Baldwin, *Masters, Princes, and Merchants: The Social Views of Peter the Chanter and His Circle* (Princeton, N.J., 1970). Both Heinlen (who identified many correspondences between *Bible moralisée* passages and the commentaries of Stephen Langton) and Stork attributed the creation of Vienna ÖNB cod. 2554 to "the circle of Peter the Chanter." This was also the conclusion I forwarded in my own dissertation, which I will now somewhat modify here.

52. *Faksimile,* ed. Haussherr, 39. As Haussherr noted (*Faksimile,* 5 n. 8), the attribution of the commentary texts to Vincent of Beauvais is even less convincing.

53. See especially my dissertation, passim, and the theses of Heinlen and Stork.

54. Baldwin (*Masters, Princes, and Merchants*) provides ample evidence of this, now supplemented by the studies of Philippe Buc (especially *L'Ambiguïté du Livre* and "*Vox Clamantis in Deserto?* Pierre le Chantre et la prédication laïque," *Revue Mabillon,* n.s., 65 [1993]: 5–47), who is careful to stress the heterogeneity of the medieval clergy, even within the theology faculty of the University of Paris. Buc points out (*L'Ambiguïté du Livre,* 102 n. 80) that the *Bible moralisée* displays independence from the Parisian biblical-moral school on the issue of social egalitarianism, although note that the commentary text from the three-volume version that inspired this observation does not appear in either Vienna ÖNB cod. 1179 or cod. 2554.

55. The order of the various biblical books was not standardized until the creation of the so-called Parisian Bible in the second quarter of the thirteenth century; see Raphael Loewe, "The Medieval History of the Latin Vulgate," in *The Cambridge History of the Bible,* vol. 2, *The West from the Fathers to the Reformation,* ed. G. W. H. Lampe (Cambridge, 1969), 101–154, here 145–148. The *Bible moralisée* diverges from the Paris Bible in its omission of I and II Chronicles, III and IV Esdras, the Psalter and all Wisdom literature, and all the prophets except Daniel; the insertion of Job and Daniel before Tobit, Judith, and Esther; and, of course, the omission of the entire New Testament except the Apocalypse.

56. For a discussion of the choice of Bible text, see Haussherr, "Uber die Auswahl des Bibeltextes."

57. In finished form the French exemplar would have been larger than the Latin exemplar, dedicating more roundels to each biblical book. Another distinctive factor of these biblical books is the vocabulary employed for heretics: they are called *publicani* (in French, *popelicani*) through I Esdras, whereas in the commentaries to Job, Daniel, I and II Maccabees, and Apocalypse they are called *heretici.* On the term *publicanus,* see chap. 4, note 2.

58. For a description of the typical university lecture on Scripture, see Marie-Madeleine Davy, *Les sermons universitaires parisiennes de 1230–31* (Paris, 1931), 43. Although commentary texts from these books are gen-

erally similar in tone and length, and thus show fairly careful editing, every so often the sermon or lecture that inspired them breaks through. For example, commentary text 19d from Vienna ÖNB cod. 1179 retains not only the cadences of a sermon but also the second-person plural imperative with which the preacher addressed his audience: "Ecce mundani in afflictione carnis ad cor redeuntes a iesu qui est pastor et pascua et panis vivus papulum vite sine precioso indigni potulant. Sed non aufert qui differt. In quid veritas primum *querite* regnum celorum . . ." (my emphasis).

59. On the *Glossa ordinaria,* see *Biblia Latina cum Glossa Ordinaria: Facsimile Reprint of the Editio Princeps Adolph Rusch of Strassburg 1480/81,* 4 vols., introduction by Karlfried Froehlich and Margaret T. Gibson (Turnhout, Belgium, 1992), v–xi.

60. Günter Breder, *Die Lateinische Vorlage des Altfranzösischen Apokalypsenkommentars des 13. Jahrhunderts (Paris, B.N., MS. fr. 403)* (Münster, 1960).

61. John Lowden's forthcoming study promises to shed much light on this process.

62. Branner, *Manuscript Painting,* 3–4.

63. In spite of the undoubted influence of his work, it was most probably *not* Stephen Langton, who was already deeply embroiled in English politics and who had reportedly written an original gloss on the entire Bible while he was a professor in Paris. My survey of Langton's exegesis revealed many more divergences than similarities with the commentary text of the *Bible moralisée.*

64. On the employment of university-educated clerics at the royal court, see John W. Baldwin, "Studium et Regnum: The Penetration of University Personnel into French and English Administration at the Turn of the Twelfth and Thirteenth Centuries," *Revue des études Islamiques* 44 (1976): 199–215.

65. On the close connections between the Capetians (especially, it will be noted, Louis VIII) and the Victorines, see Fourier Bonnard, *L'Histoire de l'Abbaye royale et de l'Ordre des chanoines réguliers de St.-Victor de Paris,* vol. 1, *Première période (1113–1500)* (Paris, 1904), 291–303. On the library and scriptorium at St.-Victor, see Claude de Grandrue, *Le Catalogue de la bibliothèque de l'abbaye de Saint-Victor de Paris de Claude de Grandrue (1514)* (Paris, 1983); and Jean Longère, ed., *L'Abbaye Parisienne de Saint-Victor au moyen âge* (Paris and Turnhout, Belgium, 1991), 125–133. The criticism of Benedictine monks in a commentary text in Vienna ÖNB cod. 2554, fol. 54v, makes the Royal Abbey of St.-Denis a less likely choice, although of course internal criticism of monastic abuses was by no means unheard of (on the library of St.-Denis, see Donatella Nebbai-Dalla Guarda, *La Bibliothèque de l'Abbaye de Saint-Denis en France du IXe au XVIIIe siècle* [Paris, 1985]). In spite of praise of Cistercians in the same text, it seems unlikely that a Cistercian was involved in such a lavish undertaking; it may be worth noting that many Augustinian canons expressed admiration of the Cistercians—Stephen of Tournai called them the most redoubtable of God's warriors. Note, too, that the dedication roundel in Vienna ÖNB cod. 1179 shows the scribe in secular garb, but that the surrounding architecture looks like a monastic cloister.

66. On bookmaking in Paris at this time, see Christopher de Hamel, *Glossed Books of the Bible and the Origins of the Paris Booktrade* (Totowa, N.J., 1984); and Branner, *Manuscript Painting;* another highly informative work is Jonathan J. G. Alexander, *Medieval Illuminators and Their Methods of Work* (New Haven, Conn., 1992).

67. Branner, *Manuscript Painting,* 37.

68. See chapter 4.

69. For example, the use of horns in the *Bible moralisée* to symbolize pride may be traced to a fable used as an exemplum about a stag who was overly proud of his horns. See Claude Bremond, Jacques le Goff, and J.-C. Schmitt, *L'Exemplum,* Typologie des sources du moyen âge occidental 40 (Turnhout, Belgium, 1982), 157. Many of the commentary images are clearly the product of a long evolutionary process. For example, the *Bible moralisée* commentary to Judg. 9:8–15 compares Jotham's parable of the trees choosing a king to "bad princes who are like the raven and the ape, who come to scholars . . . and offer them the miter that they might be in charge of others . . ." (Vienna ÖNB cod. 1179, fol. 72c and d; Vienna ÖNB cod. 2554, fol. 60va and b; in the French manuscript, it is canons rather than princes who offer the bishopric to the students). The accompanying commentary roundels in the Latin manuscript illustrate the moralization in a rather straightforward fashion: scholars are depicted refusing a miter and staff in one; a newly consecrated bishop is shown spewing venom at the cleric who is putting the miter on his head in the next. The French commentary roundels are similar, but they include the (unexplained) references to animals from the commentary texts: an ape, a crow, and an eagle stand in front of the canons offering the miter, while the corrupted and stinging bishop sits astride a porcupine or a hedgehog. Several stages of allegorical exposition have been collapsed into this text/image sequence. Richard of St. Victor interpreted this parable as referring to a congregation seeking a wise and sweet prelate. Similarly, in his commentary on this biblical passage, Stephen Langton read the olive, vine, and fig tree as representing religious refusing a bishopric (Paris, Bibliothèque nationale MS lat. 385, fol. 150c). Beryl Smalley points out in "Exempla in the Commentaries of Stephen Langton," *Bulletin of the John Rylands Library* 17 (1933): 121–129, that the moralization also appears in the *Allegoriae in Vetus Testamentum* (her citation of Migne is wrong; it should read PL 175:679). Jacques de Vitry wrote in his treatise on preaching that fables such as this parable from Judges should be used in sermons (Paris, BN MS lat. 17509, fol. 2vb). Following this advice, Odo of Cheriton (ca. 1185–ca. 1247) included the same biblical parable and moralization in his collection of animal fables assembled for the benefit of preachers (Léopold Hervieux, *Les Fabulistes latins,* vol. 4, *Eudes de Chériton et ses dérivés* [Paris, 1896], 140, 177); see also Odo of Cheriton, *The Fables of Odo of Cheriton,* ed. and trans. John C. Jacobs (Syracuse, N.Y., 1985), 68–70. The comparison of the bad trees to apes and ravens in the commentary texts and illustrations of the *Bible moralisée* suggests that the redactor encountered the parable and its moralization in just such a fable collection. On other kinds of preaching aids, see Richard H. Rouse and Mary A. Rouse, *Preachers, Florilegia, and Sermons: Studies on the Manipulus Florum of Thomas of Ireland* (Toronto, 1979), 7–11; and idem, "Biblical Distinctions in the Thirteenth Century," AHDLMA 41 (1974): 27–37.

70. From the enormous literature on thirteenth-century preaching, I have found most useful D. L. d'Avray, *The Preaching of the Friars: Sermons Diffused from Paris before 1300* (Oxford, 1985); Jean Longère, *La prédication médiévale* (Paris, 1983); Louis-Jacques Bataillon, *La prédication au XIIIe siècle en France et Italie* (London, 1993); and, still, A. Lecoy de la Marche, *La chaire française au moyen âge,* 2d ed. (Paris, 1886). Also relevant to the concerns of the *Bible moralisée* are Davy, *Les sermons universitaires;* Bataillon, "De la *lectio* à la *praedicatio*"; J. B. Schneyer, *Die Sittenkritik in den Predigten Philipps des Kanzlers* (Münster, 1963); Ch.-V. Langlois, "Sermons parisiens de la première moitié du XIIIe siècle," *Journal des savants,* n.s., 14 (1916): 488–494, 548–559; and Charles H. Haskins, "The University of Paris in the Sermons of the Thirteenth Century," AHR 10 (1904): 1–27.

71. For a wonderfully evocative reconstruction of the making and reception of a sermon, see Peter Brown, *Augustine of Hippo* (Berkeley and Los Angeles, 1969), 252–255.

72. The central text cited for this controversy is the correspondence dating to 1199 between Pope Innocent III and the bishop of Metz, who was concerned about alleged Waldenians in his diocese preaching, studying, and translating the Bible without authorization: PL 214:695–699; 793–794. For an analysis of this correspondence, see Leonard E. Boyle, "Innocent III and Vernacular Versions of Scripture," in *The Bible in the Medieval World: Essays in Memory of Beryl Smalley,* ed. Katherine Walsh and Diane Wood (Oxford, 1985), 97–107. On vernacular scriptures in general, see C. A. Robson, "Vernacular Scriptures in France," in *The Cambridge History of the Bible,* vol. 2, *The West from the Fathers to the Reformation,* ed. G. W. H. Lampe (Cambridge, 1969), 436–452; Samuel Berger, *La Bible française au moyen âge* (Paris, 1884); Emmanuel Pétavel, *La Bible en France ou les traductions françaises des saintes écritures* (Paris, 1864); and Margaret Deanesly, *The Lollard Bible and Other Medieval Biblical Versions* (Cambridge, 1920). Also of interest is Philippe Buc, "*Vox Clamantis in Deserto?* Pierre le Chantre et la prédication laïque," *Revue Mabillon,* n.s., 65 (1993): 5–47.

73. See, for example, *Bible moralisée,* ed. Guest, 25.

74. The importance of page layout and visual experience in contouring the reading of biblical glosses is increasingly recognized by scholars of exegesis. Particularly compelling are the discussions of Buc, *L'Ambiguïté du livre,* and Michael Signer, "Reading as Subversion: Anti-Jewish Themes in the Interlinear Gloss" (paper presented at the Twenty-ninth International Congress on Medieval Studies, Kalamazoo, Michigan, May 7, 1994).

Chapter 1. A Discernible Difference

1. Vienna ÖNB cod. 2554, fol. 1vD and d (Gen. 2:8–9): "Ici plante dex son vergier de boens arbres et d'espines et planta arbres de vie." "Li boen arbre senefient les boens homes qui meinent en bones oeures et sunt coronei de flors en paradis. Les espines senefient cels qi mainent en mauveses oeures et sunt coronei des espines del munde."

2. For a stimulating and intelligent discussion of the role of ambiguity

in biblical exegesis, see Philippe Buc, *L'Ambiguïté du livre: Prince, pouvoir, et peuple dans les commentaires de la Bible au moyen âge* (Paris, 1994).

3. There are no female figures in the manuscripts that can be identified as Jewesses—a highly interesting aspect of the program that I address in a forthcoming project.

4. For a survey of the literature on the Jewish hat in medieval Christian art, see Ruth Mellinkoff, "The Round, Cap-Shaped Hats Depicted on Jews in BM Cotton Claudius B.iv," *Anglo-Saxon England* 2 (1973): 155–158. Pre- and postmedieval manifestations and sexual/psychological connotations of the "Phrygian" cap are discussed in Neil Hertz, "Medusa's Head: Male Hysteria under Political Pressure," in *The End of the Line: Essays on Psychoanalysis and the Sublime* (New York, 1985), 161–191 (esp. 179–189).

5. The most complete discussion of the issue is now Ruth Mellinkoff, *Outcasts: Signs of Otherness in Northern European Art of the Later Middle Ages,* California Studies in the History of Art 32, 2 vols. (Berkeley, Los Angeles, and Oxford, 1993), chap. 3.

6. For example, Guido Kisch, "The Yellow Badge in History," *Historia Judaica* 19 (1957): 98; Henry Kraus, *The Living Theatre of Medieval Art* (Bloomington, Ind., and London, 1967), 149; and Eric Zafran, "The Iconography of Antisemitism: A Study of the Representation of the Jews in the Visual Arts of Europe, 1400–1600" (Ph.D. diss., New York University Institute of Fine Arts, 1973), 11.

7. Ruth Mellinkoff, *Outcasts,* 93 ("Jews' hats of various kinds . . . usually, if not always, had unpleasant connotations"), and idem, *The Horned Moses in Medieval Art and Thought* (Berkeley and Los Angeles, 1970), 128–131; Michael Camille, *The Gothic Idol: Ideology and Image-Making in Medieval Art* (Cambridge, 1989), 171; and Thérèse Metzger and Mendel Metzger, *Jewish Life in the Middle Ages: Illuminated Hebrew Manuscripts of the Thirteenth to Sixteenth Centuries* (Fribourg, 1982), 145–146.

8. Alfred Rubens, *A History of Jewish Costume* (London, 1967), 3, 166. See, too, the discussion in Hertz, "Medusa's Head."

9. Kisch, "Yellow Badge," 96; Rubens, *History of Jewish Costume,* 166.

10. See *Kiddushin* 8a, 29b–30a, 31a, 33a.

11. Louis Rabinowitz, *The Social Life of the Jews of Northern France as Reflected in the Rabbinic Literature of the Period (12th to 14th centuries)* (London, 1938), 66. For a discussion of the medieval controversy surrounding the issue of the halakhic basis for the custom of covering the head, see Mellinkoff, "The Round, Cap-Shaped Hats," 159.

12. The most recent edition of the canons of the Fourth Lateran Council is *Constitutiones Concilii quarti Lateranensis una cum commentariis glossatorum,* ed. Antonio Garcia y Garcia (Vatican City, 1981); see also Solomon Grayzel, ed., *The Church and the Jews in the XIIIth Century* (Philadelphia, 1933), 308–309 for the Latin text and an English translation of this canon. I can find no support for the statement by Michael Camille (*The Gothic Idol,* 166) that the pointed hat was the form of dress imposed after the Fourth Lateran Council (at least in France; later German legislation did specify the pointed hat—see Kisch, "Yellow Badge," 89ff.). This canon was subsequently observed in some regions through the imposition of a Jewish badge. Although the badge is *not* a compo-

nent of the "standard" Jewish costume in the *Bible moralisée,* two roundels in Vienna ÖNB cod. 2554 may contain depictions of Jewish badges. Folio 2vb in this manuscript shows a Jew making an offering of greed and usury to God; there is a small yellow circle on his cloak just below the shoulder. Folio 39ra depicts Pilate, Caiaphas, and Herod instructing the Jews to bring forth Jesus. The figure of Caiaphas, the high priest, wears a tall, pointed yellow hat with a circle drawn on it. The circle, or *roue,* was indeed the shape most commonly employed in France in later periods for the Jewish badge, and it is reported to have been worn on the hat as well as (more commonly) the chest or shoulder; there is some evidence (Grayzel, *The Church and the Jews,* 65 n. 112) that round badges were worn briefly by Parisian Jews around 1217. It is difficult to explain why a badge would occur only in these two places in this one manuscript, but if that is indeed what the circles represent, these must be considered the earliest known depictions of the Jewish badge. Since there is still considerable question regarding when the Jewish badge edicts were first enforced in France, the appearance of such a badge in the *Bible moralisée,* although by no means evidence for historical reality, would constitute interesting evidence for the discussion of the whole topic. On the Jewish badge, see, in addition to Grayzel, Kisch, "Yellow Badge," and Ulysse Robert, *Les signes d'infamie au moyen âge* (Paris, 1891). For the badge in art, see Mellinkoff, *Outcasts,* 43–47. Diane Hughes, "Distinguishing Signs: Ear-rings, Jews, and Franciscan Rhetoric in the Italian Renaissance City," *Past and Present* 112 (1986): 3–59, is a stimulating and insightful discussion of distinguishing marks and pollution anxiety as evidenced in fifteenth-century Italian art and preaching. For a reference to the badge worn on the hat, see Allan Cutler, "Innocent III and the Distinctive Clothing of Jews and Muslims," *Studies in Medieval Culture* 3 (1970): 92–116.

13. Grayzel, *The Church and the Jews,* 65, argues that French Jews were distinct in appearance from Christians, but he adds on the next page (still note 112) that this may not have been true for younger and more prosperous Jews.

14. Jews are always shown wearing shoes in the *Bible moralisée.* Footwear, too, is subject to shifting significance: bare feet are used in the manuscripts to signify asceticism—a positive trait in the case of Jesus and the apostles, but an example of prideful extremism in the case of certain heretics. On the symbols associated with heresy, see chapter 4.

15. There is one context in which Jews are consistently shown with a very different type of clothing: in scenes of the Flagellation and Crucifixion of Christ. Here they are regularly depicted wearing short Roman-type tunics, and they often are bareheaded. In the *Bible moralisée* this form of clothing, as well as the composition and other iconographic details of the illustrations of Christ's Passion, is derived from common pictorial models. By the thirteenth century it was established convention in Christian literature and art to identify the Romans involved in the Passion with the Jews, and therefore a combination of Roman-type tunics, Jewish hats, and scowling caricatures characterize the figures of the tormentors of Christ. For a discussion of this phenomenon in Christian art, see Blumenkranz, *Le juif médiéval,* 37; and William Chester Jordan, "The Last Tormenter of Christ: An Image of the Jew in Ancient and Medieval Exegesis, Art, and Drama," *Jewish Quarterly Review* 78 (1987):

21–47. Scenes of the Flagellation and the Crucifixion constitute far and away the most common context for negative depictions of Jews in the manuscripts, and yet, because they generally recapitulate established artistic conventions, they reveal little about the distinctive function or orientation of the *Bible moralisée.* For a comprehensive discussion of Passion iconography, see Gertrude Schiller, *Iconography of Christian Art,* vol. 2, *The Passion of Jesus Christ,* trans. Janet Seligman (Greenwich, Conn., 1972); James H. Marrow, *Passion Iconography in Northern European Art of the Late Middle Ages and Early Renaissance* (Kortrijk, Belgium, 1979).

16. Charles Joseph Hefele, *Histoire des Conciles* (Paris, 1907–31), vol. 5, pt. 2, 1502; see, too, Grayzel, *The Church and the Jews,* 318–321.

17. The complete decrees of this council are found in Mansi 23:851: "Et quoniam ex capis rotundis, quas Judaei portant communiter, honor vehementer confunditur clericorum . . ."; the canon is discussed in Rubens, *History of Jewish Costume,* 102; excerpts also appear in Grayzel, *The Church and the Jews,* 334–337. Jewish religious authorities, too, seemed concerned lest some Jews look like clerics (Grayzel, *The Church and the Jews,* 66 n. 112).

18. As is made clear in the letter of Innocent IV to Eudes of Chateauroux (1248) in Augustus Potthast, *Regesta pontificum romanorum,* 2 vols. (Berlin, 1874–75), no. 12976; excerpted in Grayzel, *The Church and the Jews,* 280–281.

19. Zafran, "Iconography of Antisemitism," 11. Mellinkoff (*Outcasts,* 91) points out that such use of the hat by Jews was not necessarily indicative of pride in the sign. This is quite true, but it seems to me unlikely that the still self-confident Jewish communities of the thirteenth century would employ a sign that carried exclusively humiliating connotations. Her suggestion that they did so out of custom is unconvincing for the thirteenth century at least, since Jews' adoption of the sign seems to have been relatively new at that point.

20. By the same analogy, we can exclude the suggestion that the depiction of Jews in pointed hats was evidence for their general use, any more than royal iconography is evidence that medieval kings wore their crowns every day.

21. I would argue against Mellinkoff's suggestion that the use of the Jewish hat to identify Joseph necessarily conveyed mocking overtones; whatever the practice of medieval theatre, no such mockery may be detected in the *Bible moralisée* treatment of the husband of Mary, who is invariably portrayed in a dignified manner. It is also interesting to note that the popes' headgear in the *Bible moralisée* is very similar to that of the Jews: in fact, one depiction of a pope was actually mistaken for that of a Jew by an art historian.

22. Vienna ÖNB cod. 1179, fol. 25c: "Hoc significat bonos prelatos qui exponendo verba evangelii falsa verba devorant iudeorum."

23. The complex denotative and connotative roles of text and image in the *Bible moralisée* correspond to the first-order and second-order (metalinguistic) systems of signification developed in the semiology of Roland Barthes, especially as articulated in *Mythologies,* trans. Annette Lavers (New York, 1972). Barthes's observations on the purpose of metalanguage within society accord with and have helped inform my own analysis of

the ideological function of the *Bible moralisée,* although I have generally tried to avoid the more arcane semiological terminology. For a comparison of medieval and modern semiological approaches, see Gerhart B. Ladner, "Medieval and Modern Understanding of Symbolism: A Comparison," in *Images and Ideas in the Middle Ages* (Rome, 1983), 239–282.

24. *Kiddushin* 35b.

25. Kenneth Stow, *Alienated Minority: The Jews of Medieval Latin Europe* (Cambridge, Mass., and London, 1992), 138.

26. Blumenkranz, *Le juif médiéval,* 20.

27. A Rhenish rabbinic ordinance of between 1208 and 1215 ordering Jews not to shave with razors or wear their hair in Christian fashion helps confirm this suspicion. See Louis Finkelstein, *Jewish Self-Government in the Middle Ages* (New York, 1924), 59; Grayzel, *The Church and the Jews,* 66 n. 112; and Kisch, "Yellow Badge," 93. There is little evidence concerning earlier periods. According to the *Annals of the Cloister of St. Bertin,* when the Carolingian deacon Bodo converted to Judaism in 839, he "let his hair and beard grow and adopted—or rather usurped—the name Eleazar. He assumed a warrior's gear . . ." *Annals of St.-Bertin.* Ninth-Century Histories, vol. 1, trans. Janet L. Nelson (Manchester and New York, 1991), 42. At first glance, this might seem to indicate that beards (or at least long ones) were considered typically Jewish. However, it seems to me that the overall context (i.e., combined with long hair and warrior's gear) indicates that Bodo, as is often the case with converts, was above all asserting his total rejection of his previous identity—clerics were tonsured, forbidden to bear arms, and, at least through the eleventh century, required to shave (see the letter of Gregory VII: ". . . your archbishop should observe the practice of the whole Western Church from the very beginning and should shave his beard." *The Correspondence of Pope Gregory VII,* trans. Ephraim Emerton [New York and London, 1960], 164). Neither long hair nor swords can be considered peculiarly Jewish attributes; it seems unwarranted to conclude from this passage that beards were. It is also possible that upon his conversion Bodo assumed the identity of a Nazirite (Num. 6:5).

28. See Metzger and Metzger, *Jewish Life in the Middle Ages,* 147. Oddly, Mellinkoff does not discuss beards (except red beards) in any depth in her otherwise exhaustive study *Outcasts.*

29. I am thinking of Sumerian, Assyrian, and Persian art; note, too, that when Queen Hatshepsut usurped the Egyptian throne she ruled as a king and had herself portrayed as a male Pharaoh, complete with beard.

30. Jacques de Vitry tells an exemplum of a knight who lost his beard (and was consequently humiliated) when an actor whom he had refused to pay used a depilatory on him (*Die exempla aus den Sermones feriales et communes des Jakob von Vitry,* ed. Joseph Greven [Heidelberg, 1914], 46). On the other hand, another exemplum (*Die exempla,* 45–46) describing how a French nobleman was able to extract money from his Armenian father-in-law by threatening to pawn his beard seems to poke fun at "Orientals'" exaggerated regard for beards.

31. I am indebted to Daniel Fleming of New York University for this suggestion and for a truly stimulating discussion on the subject of beards.

32. For example, the Roman emperors Marcus Aurelius and Julian the Apostate grew beards to signify their affiliation with Stoic philosophy.

33. For further discussion of hair and beards as social markers, see Robert Bartlett, "Symbolic Meanings of Hair in the Middle Ages," *Transactions of the Royal Historical Society,* 6th ser., 4 (1994): 43–60.

34. See, for example, Vienna ÖNB cod. 1179, fol. 10c.

35. This emphasis on the artificial, rather than physiological, signs of Jewishness is in accord with the general tendency of thirteenth-century Christendom to focus on religion, status, or culture—not biology (i.e., "race")—as the defining features of a social group. Work on this question is still lacking; see chaps. 8 and 9 of Robert Bartlett, *The Making of Europe: Conquest, Colonization and Cultural Change, 950–1350* (Princeton, N.J., 1993); and the brief but interesting discussion of the issue of "race" in the context of Aragonese majority-minority relations in David Nirenberg, *Communities of Violence: Persecution of Minorities in the Middle Ages* (Princeton, N.J., 1996), 149–150.

36. On dark-complexioned enemies of Christ, see Jordan, "Last Tormenter," 36.

37. Zafran, "Iconography of Antisemitism," 21.

38. It is, however, interesting to note that in spite of the fact that the hooked nose does not appear in *Bible moralisée* caricatures, it is frequently assumed to be there by modern scholars. For example, Michael Camille writes in his article "Visual Signs of the Sacred Page: Books in the *Bible moralisée,*" *Word and Image* 5 (1989): 118, that the medieval viewer "could hardly miss the hook-nosed Jews" in the *Bible moralisée.* Yet both the illustrations reproduced in Camille's article and the other examples I have studied depict Jews with quite straight noses. This demonstrates the flexible and dialogic nature of images: the modern viewer reads subsequent practices into medieval works informed by a very different tradition. The hooked nose does appear in works from the mid–thirteenth century. See the caricature in a King's Remembrancer Roll, dating to 1240, examined by Cecil Roth in *Essays and Portraits in Anglo-Jewish History* (Philadelphia, 1962), 23—although here the fact that the devil is bending the Jew's nose with his finger suggests that the outward appearance was held to reflect moral status rather than some biological or racial determination. The topos of the crooked nose does not seem to have become a commonplace until the fifteenth century (Zafran, "Iconography of Antisemitism," 20; and Mellinkoff, *Outcasts,* 127–129).

39. Zafran, "Iconography of Antisemitism," 7.

40. In general, representations of Jews are considerably harsher and more hostile in the French manuscript than in the Latin; this is a second major difference between the two manuscripts (after the differing formats). Although it is always possible that personal approaches of the individual artists involved may account for such differences, I have not been able to correlate the harsher images with any other detectable stylistic characteristics, much less with any of the hands identified by Branner. I think it more likely that the divergence arises from the differences between the nature and audiences of Latin and vernacular commentaries; a parallel contrast in levels of "nastiness" in anti-Jewish discourse appears in Latin and vernacular literature (the term and the observation are those of Miri Rubin, offered in comments during the Medieval Studies conference "The Body of Christ," Rice University, Houston, Texas, November 1995), suggesting the subtle yet powerful

ways in which artistic conventions are affected by and reflect the ethos of the corresponding texts. I discuss this point at greater length in the conclusion.

41. Suzanne Lewis, "*Tractatus Adversus Judaeos* in the Gulbenkian Apocalypse," *Art Bulletin* 68 (1986): 552 n. 48.

42. Zafran, "Iconography of Antisemitism," 21. Zafran's suggestion that the profile convention might have been developed for Jews to emphasize the hooked Semitic nose is undercut by the presence of the former but not the latter characteristic in the *Bible moralisée.* The noses in profile occasionally seem rather long, but they are not hooked.

43. As was maintained by Reiner Haussherr in "Sensus litteralis und sensus spiritualis in der Bible moralisée," *Frühmittelalterliche Studien* 6 (1972): 356–380.

44. Vienna ÖNB cod. 1179, fol. 16B and b: "Hic uxor Putiphar pulcritudinem perpendens Ioseph super illicito amore eum convenit." "Per mulierem istam carnalis designatur molestia, que etiam perfectos peccare compellit, unde nemo sine crimine vivit. Illa quidem minis et blandimentis ihm agressa nichil suum quod viciosus est in eo invenit, quia peccatum non fecit, nec in ore eius inventum est mendatium."

45. See, for example, Vienna ÖNB cod. 1179, fol. 121b; and Vienna ÖNB cod. 2554, fol. 53vd.

46. Vienna ÖNB cod. 1179, fol. 16C and c: "Hic dimisso pallio in manibus tenentis a mulieris malicia Ioseph mundus evasit." "Hic iustus noster serpentis divertans astutiam mundane vanitatis in manu provocantis reliquit amictum eligens abiectus esse in domo domini magis quam habitare in tabernaculis peccatorum."

47. Vienna ÖNB cod. 1179, fol. 16D and d: "Hic mulier vestibus cissis e vulsis crinibus e missis lacrimis coram marito falsam de Ioseph facit querelam." "Hic Signagoga [*sic*] varias se mentita per iesum passam iniurias coram pontifice sue ceterisque legis doctoribus falsis criminibus xm. accusat unde in eum insurrexerunt testes iniqui et mentita est iniquitas sibi."

48. In Vienna ÖNB cod. 1179, Jews are explicitly mentioned in 11.5 percent of the commentary texts. There are similar statistics for Vienna ÖNB cod. 2554: 15.7 percent of the commentary texts. By contrast, Jews are depicted in 304 (39 percent) of the commentary roundels in Vienna ÖNB cod. 1179 and 210 (39.7 percent) of the commentary roundels in Vienna ÖNB cod. 2554. Such figures are an interesting but unnecessary indication of the phenomenon in question, since any cursory examination of the manuscripts reveals that the images are far more anti-Jewish than the text. In this, the text of the *Bible moralisée* parallels contemporary Scholastic writings: Gilbert Dahan points out in the conclusion to his exhaustive study *Les intellectuels chrétiens et les juifs au moyen âge* (Paris, 1990), 583, that Christian intellectuals of the twelfth and thirteenth centuries paid quantitatively little attention to the "Jewish Question."

49. Albert Blaise, *Lexicon Latinitatis Medii Aevi,* CCCM (Turnhout, Belgium, 1975), 486.

50. Vienna ÖNB cod. 1179, fol. 3c: "Hoc quod Deus quievit die vii. significat christum qui requiescet in die iudicii et amplexabitur amicos suos et conculcabit inimicos suos in inferno sub pedibus eius."

51. These latter two groups are discussed in chapter 4.

52. Vienna ÖNB cod. 1179, fol. 87b: "Dagon qui prostratus ad terram cecidit et pedes et manus amisit significat sanctam ecclesiam que diabolem abstulit et eum detrudit et confundit."

53. Vienna ÖNB cod. 1179, fol. 10a: "Hic omnipotens quod [?] figurative abrahe imposuit verasciter misericordia mediante in proprio filio exposuit offerens laudis sacrificium in salute credentium."

54. The quote is from Isa. 53:7: "Sicut ovis ad occisionem ducetur" (Like a sheep he is led to the slaughter).

55. For a survey of the philosophical literature on the "Other," see M. Theunissen, *The Other: Studies in the Social Ontology of Husserl, Heidegger, Sartre, and Buber* (Cambridge, Mass., 1986). Although consideration of the "Other" seems to dominate literary and cultural studies at the moment, medieval art historiography is still in its infancy in respect to this question. Michael Camille is a pioneer in this area: see his preface to *The Gothic Idol* as well as his *Image on the Edge.* An unusually lucid if somewhat oversimplified summary of the subject may be found in Sander Gilman, *Difference and Pathology: Stereotypes of Sexuality, Race, and Madness* (Ithaca, N.Y., and London, 1985), 15–35.

56. On this, see the remarks of Grayzel in *The Church and the Jews,* 59.

57. This is, for example, the thrust of the article by Gavin Langmuir comparing the stances toward Jews of Bernard of Clairvaux, Peter the Venerable, and Peter Abelard: "The Faith of Christians and Hostility Towards Jews," *Studies in Church History* 29 (1992): 77–92.

58. See chapter 4.

59. In this, the images of the *Bible moralisée* are similar to discursive trends in colonial texts, which, according to the critic Homi Bhabha, displayed a consistent fear that the subaltern would metamorphize into the occupier, and the colonizer into the "native" (Homi Bhabha, "The Other Question: Stereotype, Discrimination and the Discourse of Colonialism," in *The Location of Culture* [London and New York, 1994], 70). I should add that in spite of this correspondence, I have serious reservations regarding the degree to which the modern colonial experience (and thus postcolonial theory) can be applied to medieval culture in general, and to medieval Jewish-Christian relations in particular, which were not predicated upon a mercantilist economy and in most respects do not conform to the modern colonizer-colonized model.

Chapter 2. The Root of All Evil

1. Bonaventure, quoted in C. Spicq, *Esquisse d'une histoire de l'exégèse latine au moyen âge* (Paris, 1944), 269: "Tota Scriptura est quasi una cithara, et inferior chorda per se non facit harmoniam sed cum aliis."

2. PL 144:234, 424; quoting I Tim. 6:10; for the shift in approaches to the vices, see Lester Little, "Pride Goes before Avarice: Social Change and the Vices in Latin Christendom," AHR 76 (1971): 16–49.

3. The most influential canonical definition of usury is that of Gratian, *Decretum,* C. 14, q. 3.

4. On medieval economic teaching, see especially T. P. McLaughlin, "The Teaching of the Canonists on Usury (XII, XIII, XIV Centuries),"

Mediaeval Studies 1 (1939): 81–147; 2 (1940): 1–22; John T. Noonan, *The Scholastic Analysis of Usury* (Cambridge, Mass., 1957); John W. Baldwin, *The Medieval Theories of the Just Price: Romanists, Canonists, and Theologians in the Twelfth and Thirteenth Centuries,* Transactions of the American Philosophical Society, n.s., 49, no. 4 (Philadelphia, 1959); J. Gilchrist, *The Church and Economic Activity in the Middle Ages* (London, 1969); and Benjamin Nelson, *The Idea of Usury: From Tribal Brotherhood to Universal Otherhood,* 2d ed. (Chicago, 1969).

5. This exception is based on Ambrose's reading of Deut. 23:20, which was incorporated into Gratian, *Decretum,* C. 14, q. 4, c. 12. See Nelson, *The Idea of Usury,* 15–16, for a discussion of twelfth- and thirteenth-century decretists who continued to accept this interpretation.

6. See the letter of Honorius III dated 1219 instructing Soissons prelates not to exceed their brief regarding Jewish usury, in RHGF 19:688. Papal condemnations of Jews' excessive interest rates (as in, for example, Canon 67 of the Fourth Lateran Council [Mansi 22:1054], which censures *graves immoderatasve usuras*) imply that the collection by Jews of moderate interest was tolerated; this is the argument of Kenneth R. Stow, "Papal and Royal Attitudes towards Jewish Lending in the Thirteenth Century," *AJS Review* 6 (1981): 161–184, here 162–165. See, too, the interesting letter of Innocent III (1208) ordering the prioress of Amesbury to repay money lent to the priory by a family of Roman merchants. Although the pope orders that only the principal be repaid, the fact remains that the loan was clearly a usurious one and that Innocent was intervening on behalf of known usurers: *Selected Letters of Pope Innocent III concerning England,* ed. C. R. Cheney, W. H. Semple, et al. (London, 1953), 100–101. I am indebted to Robert Stacey for this reference.

7. See, for example, the careful and restrained treatment of profit on lending by the Parisian canon Robert of Flamborough, *Liber Poenitentialis,* ed. J. J. Francis Firth (Toronto, 1971), 191–192; compare with the stricter approach of Robert de Courson, who apparently composed his treatise against usury in part to combat legists' efforts at accommodation: Robert de Courson, "Le traité *De Usura* de Robert de Courson," ed. Georges Lefèvre, *Travaux et mémoires de l'Université de Lille* 10:30 (1902), introduction, ix, 65–67. On Romanist approaches, see T. P. McLaughlin, "Canonists on Usury," *Mediaeval Studies* 1 (1939): 84–94; and Baldwin, *Medieval Theories of the Just Price,* 20–31.

8. See, for example, Robert de Courson, *De Usura,* 7; and Peter the Chanter, *Verbum Abbreviatum* in PL 205:158. On these and other conservative theologians, see Nelson, *The Idea of Usury,* 12–14; John W. Baldwin, *Masters, Princes, and Merchants: The Social Views of Peter the Chanter and His Circle,* 2 vols. (Princeton, N.J., 1970), chaps. 14, 15; Odd Langholm, *Economics in the Medieval Schools: Wealth, Exchange, Value, Money, and Usury according to the Paris Theological Tradition, 1200–1350* (Leiden, 1992), 45–52, 81–85.

9. On the intersection of religious and economic rhetoric, see Jacques le Goff, *La bourse et la vie: Économie et religion au moyen âge* (Paris, 1986); now translated as *Your Money or Your Life: Economy and Religion in the Middle Ages,* trans. Patricia Ranum (New York, 1988); and R. Po-Chia Hsia, "The Usurious Jew: Economic Structure and Religious Representations in an Anti-Semitic Discourse," in *In and Out of the Ghetto:*

Jewish-Gentile Relations in Late Medieval and Early Modern Germany, ed. R. Po-Chia Hsia and Hartmut Lehmann (Washington, D.C., and Cambridge, 1995), 161–176.

10. N. M. Haring, "Peter Cantor's View on Ecclesiastical Excommunication and Its Practical Consequences," *Mediaeval Studies* 11 (1949): 100.

11. See le Goff, *La Bourse et la Vie,* 35; Lester Little, *Religious Poverty and the Profit Economy in Medieval Europe* (Ithaca, N.Y., 1978), 36–37.

12. I should note here that the *Bible moralisée* illustrations clearly distinguish moneybags from alms purses. The former are invariably quite large and oval, whereas the latter are much smaller, are triangular, and dangle from their owners' belts. See, for example, Vienna ÖNB cod. 1179, fols. 28b and 146a. In Vienna ÖNB cod. 1179, fol. 143a, an image accompanying a text discussing almsgiving depicts a figure giving in kind, not in cash.

13. For examples, see again le Goff, *La Bourse et la Vie,* 35, and Little, *Religious Poverty,* 36–37. By contrast, artworks from the eleventh and early twelfth centuries do not represent usurers as Jews. See *Sculpture Romane de Haute-Auvergne* (Aurillac, 1966), 76–77; and Priscilla Baumann, "The Deadliest Sin: Warnings against Avarice and Usury on Romanesque Capitals in Auvergne," *Church History* 59 (1990): 7–18.

14. At least in France and England, although even there Jewish economic activity remained far more diversified than Christian polemics suggest. See Robert Stacey, "Jewish Lending and the Medieval English Economy," in *A Commercialising Economy: England 1086 to c. 1300,* ed. Richard Britnell and Bruce M. S. Campbell (Manchester and New York, 1995), 78–101. For other regions, see Alexander Gieysztor, "Les juifs et leurs activités économiques en europe orientale," *Gli Ebrei Nell'Alto Medioevo,* Settimane di Studio del Centro Italiano di Studi Sull'Alto Medioevo 26 (1980): 489–528.

15. These assumptions appear, for example, in works as disparate in depth and focus as Norman F. Cantor, *The Civilization of the Middle Ages* (New York, 1993), 365; Robert M. Seltzer, *Jewish People, Jewish Thought: The Jewish Experience in History* (New York, 1980), 356; and Little, *Religious Poverty,* 45–46. For more detailed discussions of Jewish moneylending activities, see Solomon Grayzel, ed., *The Church and the Jews in the XIIIth Century* (Philadelphia, 1933), 41–44; Stow, "Papal and Royal Attitudes"; Joseph Shatzmiller, *Shylock Reconsidered: Jews, Moneylending, and Medieval Society* (Berkeley and Los Angeles, 1990); Jordan, *The French Monarchy and the Jews: From Philip Augustus to the Last Capetians* (Philadelphia, 1989), 26ff.; and Robert Chazan, *Medieval Jewry in Northern France: A Political and Social History* (Baltimore, 1973), 15–17.

16. The article cited earlier by Robert Stacey ("Jewish Lending and the Medieval English Economy") is an extremely useful and important step in that direction, at least for the case of England.

17. Shatzmiller, *Shylock Reconsidered,* 47. On the degree to which usurers became stereotyped as Jews, see the discussions of Rabinowitz, *The Social Life of the Jews,* 24, 44; Joshua Trachtenberg, *The Devil and the Jews: The Medieval Conception of the Jew and Its Relation to Modern Antisemitism* (New Haven, Conn., 1943; reprint, with introduction by Marc Saperstein, Philadelphia, 1983), 188; Grayzel, *The Church and the Jews,* 41.

18. Robert de Courson, *De Usura,* 53: "Iudei . . . nihil habent nisi de usura . . ." The same assumption about Jewish involvement in moneylending underlies the following remark in his section on penance: "Et notandum quod si Iudaeus aliquis vel quicumque alius accesserit ad baptismum non valet ei effectus baptismi nisi pro posse suo omnia que per usuras vel alio modo illicite acquisivit restituat vel opere vel integro saltem affectu." Robert de Courson, *Summa* VIII.l., in V. L. Kennedy, "Robert Courson on Penance," *Mediaeval Studies* 7 (1945): 313.

19. Thomas of Chobham, *Summa Confessorum,* ed. F. Broomfield (Louvain, 1968), 510: Article 7, Distinctio 6, Quaestio XIa (De Usura), cap. IIII (de variis casibus).

20. I owe this observation to Dwayne E. Carpenter of Boston College.

21. The Latin text of Canon 67 of the Fourth Lateran Council appears in *Constitutiones Concilii quarti Lateranensis una cum commentariis glossatorum,* ed. Antonio Garcia y Garcia (Vatican City, 1981), 106–107. See, too, decrees issued by councils in Paris ca. 1200 (Mansi 22:681–685) and in 1213 (Mansi 22:850); these are partially reproduced and translated in Grayzel, *The Church and the Jews,* 300–301, 306–307. Statute 67 from the Parisian synod held under Eudes de Sully in 1200 ("nullus clericus fidejubeat Iudeo vel feneratori . . .") also appears in *Les statuts synodaux français du XIIIe siècle,* vol. 1, *Les statuts de Paris et le synodal de l'Ouest (XIIIe siècle),* ed. and trans. Odette Pontal, Collection de documents inédits sur l'histoire de France, vol. 9 (Paris, 1971), 76.

22. The vocabulary of both manuscripts similarly imposes the equating of Jews and usurers, for the word "Jew" is frequently partnered with the word for "usurer" in the texts. Indeed, the words are so closely identified that confusion easily arises: it is often impossible to determine whether references to "iudei feneratores" should be translated as "Jews and usurers" or "Jewish usurers," or perhaps simply as "usurers."

23. PL 182:567.

24. Mansi 22:852; Grayzel, *The Church and the Jews,* 306–307.

25. *Recueil des actes de Philippe Auguste,* IV, no. 1554; discussed in Jordan, *The French Monarchy and the Jews,* 82–85. Whether Philip was truly concerned for the poor or was exploiting the issue for propagandistic purposes does not affect the basic point that usurers were presented as preying upon the poor, and that the incorporation of this concern into an ordinance on the Jews serves to set an essentially secular act within the religious realm.

26. *Commentaria* on Rubric to X.v.19, cited in McLaughlin, "Canonists on Usury," 111. Innocent's argument supports the suggestion I made earlier—that the conditions allegedly pushing Jews into moneylending affected Christians as much as Jews, if not more.

27. Vienna ÖNB cod. 2554, fol. 1c: "La terre senefie sainte eglise. Li oisel senefient les diverses genz del monde qi accrochent sainte eglise. Li gros poisson senefie les gros usuriers qi mainivent les petiz ce sunt la pouvre gent."

28. Vienna ÖNB cod. 2554, fol. 1va: "Ce qe deu garnist la mer de diverses manieres de poissons senefie iesu crist qi garni le munde de diverses manieres de genz . . ." Vienna ÖNB cod. 1179, fol. 3a: ". . . diversis generibus hominum."

29. Vienna ÖNB cod. 2554, fol. 30a: "Li bocu senefie celui qi est bocu de mauves avoir si con d'usure et de couvoitise et de tricherie. Li tigneus senefie l'usurier qi est plains de tigne d'usure et de malaventure et Deu les maudist." [The hunchback signifies he who is deformed by bad riches, such as from usury and avarice and deceit. The scurvied man signifies the usurer who is full of the stain of usury and of misdeeds, and God curses them.] Robert de Courson cites this text as an authority for refusing to accept money from usurers, in *De Usura,* 29.

30. According to John E. Boswell, *The Kindness of Strangers: The Abandonment of Children in Western Europe from Late Antiquity to the Renaissance* (New York, 1988), 201, an Ostrogothic law code forbade the pawning of a child, indicating that the practice was not unknown in sixth-century Italy, at least. Boswell does not mention whether the practice continued into the High Middle Ages. The biblical story (IV Kings 4:1–7) of the poor widow who could not redeem her children from her creditor (called *creditor* in the Vulgate but *feneratores* in the *Bible moralisée* version) may have rendered the practice at least theoretically familiar to medieval Christians.

31. As, for example, Courson, *De Usura.*

32. Mary Douglas, *Purity and Danger: An Analysis of the Concepts of Pollution and Taboo* (London and New York, 1966), 42–58.

33. For Paul's "spirit" and "letter" contrast, see especially Galatians 3. For a fairly typical medieval approach to this dichotomy, see Peter of Blois, *Contra perfidiam Judaeorum,* PL 207:825–870 (especially col. 855, where Peter mocks Levitical dietary precepts).

34. "Manifesta transgressio littere legis que propria Iudeis sicut in sacrificiis et purgationibus et in huisusmodi est enim in communis gentibus de adulterio, rapina, avaricia et similibus." *Biblia Latina cum Glossa Ordinaria: Facsimile Reprint of the Editio Princeps Adolph Rusch of Strassburg 1480/81,* 4 vols., intro. Karlfried Froehlich and Margaret T. Gibson (Turnhout, Belgium, 1992), I.240 (marginal gloss).

35. Peter of Poitiers, *Summa de Confessione,* ed. Jean Longère CCCM 60 (Turnhout, Belgium, 1980), 8. Early penitentials proscribed the eating of dead flesh (John T. McNeill and Helena M. Gamer, *Medieval Handbooks of Penance* [New York, 1965], 112), of scabs, lice, or excreta (ibid., 113), and of a variety of forbidden meats and drinks (ibid., 120–121, 131–134, 157–159, 191, 313), as well as any carelessness with or dirtying of the host (ibid., 114–117, 195, 230, 278, 308–310). Prohibitions on women entering churches or receiving communion during menses (ibid., 197: "the time of impurity") and requirements that men who have slept with their wives wash before entering church (ibid., 211) likewise conflate physical and spiritual cleanliness.

36. "O quam mundas debetis habere manus, qui manibus vestris tractatis corpus Jesu Christi." Cited in R. W. Hunt, *The Schools and the Cloister: The Life and Writings of Alexander Nequam (1157–1217),* ed. and rev. by Margaret Gibson (Oxford, 1984), 90.

37. PL 217:773–916.

38. See, for example, the synodal statute from 1216 in *Les status synodaux français du XIIIe siècle,* ed. Pontal, 142. The subject is discussed at length in Miri Rubin, *Corpus Christi: The Eucharist in Late Medieval Culture* (Cambridge, 1991), 43–49.

39. See, for example, I Tim. 3:8 ("turpe lucrum"), Titus 1:11 ("turpis lucri"), and I Pet. 5:2 ("turpis lucri"); and Augustine, *Confessions,* Book V.xii ("filthy cash which soils the hand that holds it"), trans. F. J. Sheed, rev. ed. (Indianapolis, 1993), 81.

40. I do not have space here to do justice to so vast a topic, but a few examples can be provided. An exemplum told by Stephen Langton (based on the biblical text Deut. 14:12: "immundas ne commedatis") recounts that the body of a monk found to have hoarded money was thrown on a dung heap (Beryl Smalley, "Exempla in the Commentaries of Stephen Langton," *Bulletin of the John Rylands Library* 17 [1933]: 126); and on the facade of an *hôtel* in Goslar, a usurer is depicted defecating a coin (le Goff, *La Bourse et la Vie,* 36). Jacques de Vitry told an exemplum of an ape that could smell the stench of unjustly acquired coins (*Die Exempla aus den Sermones feriales et communes des Jakob von Vitry,* ed. Joseph Greven [Heidelberg, 1914], 60–61). Robert Grosseteste, bishop of Lincoln, wrote: "Lords who benefit from Jewish usury drink the blood of victims they ought to protect; their hands and garments are steeped in blood, and they themselves become fuel for the eternal fire"; quoted in Nicholas C. Vincent, "Jews, Poitevins, and the Bishop of Winchester, 1231–1234," *Studies in Church History* 29 (1992): 131. On money, filth, and excrement, see Sigmund Freud, *The Interpretation of Dreams,* trans. James Strachey (London, 1954), 200, 403; le Goff, *La Bourse et la Vie,* 51; and Little, *Religious Poverty,* 34.

41. For accusations of ritual murder against the Jews in medieval France, see Jordan, *The French Monarchy and the Jews,* 17–19. On ritual murder in general, see Hermann L. Strack, *The Jew and Human Sacrifice,* trans. from the 8th edition by the author (London, 1909; repr., New York, 1971); R. Po-Chia Hsia, *The Myth of Ritual Murder: Jews and Magic in Reformation Germany* (New Haven, Conn., 1988), 2–4; and the collected articles in *The Blood Libel Legend,* ed. Alan Dundes (Madison, Wis., 1991). For a discussion of artistic representations of the accusation, see Zafran, "Iconography of Antisemitism," chap. 2. It should be noted that there is no other hint of the charge of ritual murder or child murder in either *Bible moralisée* manuscript.

42. This is also connected in the manuscripts to the Jews' exegetical "carnality" and ritual "bloodiness": see chapter 3.

43. Note that in many murder libels, the Jews are alleged to throw the bodies of their victims into latrines.

44. The story is recounted in Miri Rubin, "Imagining the Jew: The Late Medieval Eucharistic Discourse," in *In and Out of the Ghetto: Jewish-Gentile Relations in Late Medieval and Early Modern Germany,* ed. R. Po-Chia Hsia and Hartmut Lehmann (Washington, D.C., and Cambridge, 1995), 177–208. Innocent's letter appears in PL 216:886, excerpted in Grayzel, *The Church and the Jews,* 137–140. It is also worthy of note that the Jewish usurer's route to the Host is in most instances a female client or servant, disqualified by virtue of her own body from consecrating the Body of Christ. The sermon of Nequam cited earlier continues: "Vobis [sacerdotibus] datum est quod non est datum alicui angelorum, nulli nisi mari, nulli nisi sacerdoti datum est conficere corpus domini." ["To you is given what is not given to any of the angels, nor to anyone except a male, and except a priest, is it given to effect the body of the lord."] Hunt, *The Schools and the Cloister,* 90.

45. Rubin ("Imagining the Jew," 206) discusses a fifteenth-century accusation that "strongly stress[ed] the polluting effect of usury, the scatological associations with Jews, in a whole gamut of fiendish names and characterizations." Rubin also stresses the emphasis on purging the Jew from the Christian body in later desecration accusations, in "Desecration of the Host: The Birth of an Accusation," *Studies in Church History* 29 (1992): 169–185.

46. Vienna ÖNB cod. 1179, fol. 77d: "Uxor . . . significat carnem quae facit animam obdormire per cupiditatem per gulam et aufert ab ea vii virtutes et sic gratiam domini derelinquit."

47. See, for example, statute 67 from the Parisian synod already cited in note 21; the decree of the Council of Trier (1227) in Mansi 23:32, excerpted in Grayzel, *The Church and the Jews,* 318–319; and the regulations of the bishop of Worcester in Mansi 23:121 and Grayzel, *The Church and the Jews,* 320–321.

48. *Recueil des actes de Philippe Auguste,* II, no. 955, and IV, no. 1554; discussed in Jordan, *The French Monarchy and the Jews,* 62, 83.

49. Letter of Innocent III to Philip Augustus, PL 215:502; excerpted in Grayzel, *The Church and the Jews,* 104–109.

50. Robert Chazan, *Medieval Stereotypes and Modern Antisemitism* (Berkeley, 1997), notes how frequently standard anti-Jewish topoi were given hostile modifications in the twelfth century.

51. Peter the Venerable, *The Letters of Peter the Venerable,* ed. Giles Constable (Cambridge, Mass., 1967), 1:329 (Letter 130).

52. Rigord, *Gesta Philippi Augusti,* in Henri Delaborde, ed., *Oeuvres de Rigord et de Guillaume le Breton,* 2 vols. (Paris, 1882–85), 25. But note that the "defiling" amounts to using the chalices to feed their children cakes dipped in wine: blasphemy from the Christian point of view, perhaps, but not necessarily intentional gestures of contempt on the Jews' part. See also RHGF 12:215.

53. John Chrysostom, *Discourses against Judaizing Christians,* trans. Paul W. Harkins (Washington, D.C., 1979), Discourse I, 10 ("the synagogue is a den of robbers"), 15 ("a lodging place for robbers and cheats"), 25 ("shall I tell you of their plundering, their covetousness, their abandonment of the poor, their thefts, their cheating in trade?"), etc. On Chrysostom's anti-Judaism, see Wayne A. Meeks and Robert L. Wilken, *Jews and Christians in Antioch in the First Four Centuries of the Common Era* (Missoula, Mont., 1978); and Robert Wilken, *John Chrysostom and the Jews: Rhetoric and Reality in the Late Fourth Century* (Berkeley, 1983).

54. "Non est numerus tuae avaritiae, nec finis tuae malitiae. Cumulus enim arenae maris non potest adaequari cupiditati tuae." *Disputatio Ecclesiae et Synagogae,* in *Thesaurus Novus Anecdotorum,* vol. 5, ed. Edmund Martène and Ursinus Durand (Paris, 1717), col. 1504. A partial English translation may be found in A. Lukyn Williams, ed., *Adversus Judaeos: A Bird's-Eye View of Christian Apologiae until the Renaissance* (Cambridge, 1935), 382.

55. In *De Contemptu Mundi,* Innocent III cites Judas's betrayal and subsequent suicide as an "exemplum contra cupiditatem"; PL 217:720. See, too, Little, "Pride Goes before Avarice," 53.

56. Thomas Aquinas, *Summa Theologica*, trans. English Dominican Fathers, 2d ed. (London, 1916–38), vol. 10, 331–332. See John Y. B. Hood, *Aquinas and the Jews* (Philadelphia, 1995).

57. Vienna ÖNB cod. 2554, fol. 2vb: "Ce qe Caym offre la mauvese gerbe senefie les gieus, qi font offrande de fraimture et de couvoitise et dex les refuse . . ." Identification of Cain with Jews is standard, but various Christian authorities presented differing interpretations of his offering and the reasons for its rejection. See Ruth Mellinkoff, "Cain and the Jews," *Journal of Jewish Art* 6 (1979): 16–38.

58. Note again the links forged among filth, money, and the Jews.

59. For a lucid discussion of the distinct functions of metaphor, synecdoche, and metonymy, see Janet Martin Soskice, *Metaphor and Religious Language* (Oxford, 1985), 57. On metaphor in Scholastic sermons, see N. Bériou and D. L. d'Avray, "The Image of the Ideal Husband in Thirteenth-Century France," in *Modern Questions about Medieval Sermons: Essays on Marriage, Death, History, and Sanctity*, ed. N. Bériou and D. L. d'Avray (Spoleto, 1994).

60. Vienna ÖNB cod. 1179, fol. 74c: "Filia qui comparuit coram patrem cum tympanis et cymbalis ut congaudet suo patri significat synagogam quae comparuit coram christo et in rebus mundanis scilicet ceremonalibus denariis et carnibus suo christo congaudebat."

61. This idea is echoed in a statement made by William of Auvergne, who considered the tendency toward avarice to be a primary component of Jewish nature ("Sciebat namque legislator eam esse Judaeorum malitiam . . . et eam esse eorundem cupditatem et avaritiam, ut nec fratribus, hos est Judeis, ab usuris parcerent, nisi alienis ad usuram dare permittenter . . ." William of Auvergne, *Opera Omnia* [Paris, 1674; repr., Frankfurt, 1963], I:24D) and a primary cause of their most fundamental error: their failure to recognize the abrogation of the Old Law. William's attitude is analyzed in Beryl Smalley, "William of Auvergne, John de la Rochelle, and St. Thomas Aquinas on the Old Law," in *Studies in Medieval Thought and Learning from Abelard to Wycliff* (London, 1981), 121–181. See also Lesley Smith, "William of Auvergne and the Jews," *Studies in Church History* 29 (1992): 107–117.

62. Vienna ÖNB cod. 1179, fol. 105B: "Scripsit David epistolam ad Joab misitque ad eum per manum Urie, scribans in epistola: ponite Uriam ex adverso belli ubi fortissimus praelium et derelinquite eum ut percussus intereat."

63. Vienna ÖNB cod. 1179, fol. 105b: "Hoc significat ihm xpm qui tradidit judeis veteram legem quam non intellexerunt per quam non intellectam occasionaliter perpetuam damnabuntur."

64. For a creative and nuanced interpretation of representations of Jews worshiping idols (accompanied, however, by several errors concerning Jewish status in medieval Europe), see Michael Camille, *The Gothic Idol: Ideology and Image-Making in Medieval Art* (Cambridge, 1989), chap. 4.

65. For example, I Pet. 4:3 and I Thess. 1:9. See the discussion in Rosemary Ruether, *Faith and Fratricide: The Theological Roots of Anti-Semitism* (New York, 1974), 76–77.

66. PL 35:2113; discussed in Bernhard Blumenkranz, "Augustin et les juifs, Augustin et le judaïsme," in *Recherches augustiniennes* 1 (1958): 230;

reprinted in B. Blumenkranz, *Juifs et Chrétiens Patristique et Moyen Âge* (London, 1977).

67. Book 2, Part 2, Tractate 8, Section I, Qu. I, tit. II. M.I. c. 2: "Utrum ritus Iudaeorum sit quasi idololatria." Solutio: "Ad quod dicendum est quod non est aequale peccatum ipsis Iudaeis observare ritum legalium et idololatrare." Alexander of Hales, *Summa Theologica,* ed. Bonaventure Marrani, vol. 3 (Florence, 1930), 730.

68. *Discourses,* 22–23.

69. For example, in the *Disputatio Judei cum Christiano* of Gilbert Crispin (PL 159:1034, now superseded by *The Works of Gilbert Crispin, Abbot of Westminster,* ed. Anna Sapir Abulafia and G. R. Evans [London, 1986]), the Christian is forced to argue that the Old Testament does not ban all figural imagery. On this polemical treatise, see Bernhard Blumenkranz, "'La Disputatio Judei cum Christiano' de Gilbert Crispin, abbé de Westminster," *Revue du moyen âge latin* 4 (1948): 237–252; reprinted in Blumenkranz, *Juifs et Chrétiens.*

70. Alan of Lille, *The Art of Preaching,* trans. Gillian R. Evans (Kalamazoo, Mich., 1981), 38.

71. *Verbum Abbreviatum:* "Sicut enim idololatra latriam et servitutem, quae Deo debetur, exhibet idolo; ita avarus, serviens potius pecuniae quam Deo, cultum Deo debitum exhibet pecuniae et nummo." PL 205:75.

72. *De Contemptu Mundi:* "Sicut enim idololatra servit simulacro, sic et avarus thesauro. Ille spem ponit in idolatria, et iste spem constituit in pecunia." PL 217:721.

73. Vienna ÖNB cod. 1179, fol. 68a: "Filii Israel qui dominum dimiserunt diabolem adoraverunt significant illos qui desperant de domino et adorant cupiditatem et luxuriam et dominum vilipendunt."

74. That the man is to be taken to be a Jew is confirmed by the following commentary text, which calls for the abandonment of cupidity and infidelity.

75. Compare also the condensation in the commentary image of the more elaborate text interpreting the episode concerning Jephtah's daughter, discussed earlier in this chapter.

76. See also Vienna ÖNB cod. 2554, fols. 34b and 58d; and Vienna ÖNB cod. 1179, fol. 64b.

77. Vienna ÖNB cod. 1179, fol. 69d: "Nemus significat iudeos feneratores et infideles quos deus destruet in die iudicii in pena infernali."

78. Vienna ÖNB cod. 1179, fol. 71d: "Illi qui constituerunt Abimalech natum de choitu fornicario in regem significant iudeos et pravos infantes [*sic*] qui facient de antichristo natum a diabolo regem. Illi qui exspoliaverunt deos suos propter ornamentum Abimalech significant pravos et infideles qui adorabunt antichristum et de cupiditate et fenore honorabunt." In the years just after the making of the *Bible moralisée,* it became common for Christian works of art to imply an association of Jews with the Antichrist. See, for example, the illustration at the top of an English receipt roll from the 1230s reproduced in Vivian Lipman, *The Jews of Medieval Norwich* (London, 1967) (I am indebted to Robert Stacey for this reference), and the English Apocalypses discussed in Suzanne Lewis's stimulating article, "*Tractatus Adversus Judaeos* in the Gulbenkian Apocalypse," *Art Bulletin* 68 (1986): 543–566.

79. Vienna ÖNB cod. 2554, fol. 25va: "Ce qe li peuples moyses aora le torel qe il auoit formei senefie les mescreanz et les populicanz qi forment contre le commandement deu le deiable et croient en boc et laorent."

80. Smalley, "William of Auvergne," 150.

81. The goat was commonly considered to be the favorite animal of or a disguise for the devil in the Middle Ages. See Trachtenberg, *The Devil and the Jews,* 47. The *Bible moralisée* image discussed earlier suggests that disgust for Old Testament sacrifices may have contributed to the negative connotations of goats in Christian literature.

82. The topos of Jewish involvement with the devil was, of course, already of great antiquity by the thirteenth century. This issue is far too extensive to discuss here, but see the comments of Joshua Trachtenberg, who pointed out that the term "Synagogue of Satan" appeared in the New Testament (Apoc. 2:9 and 3:9) and that the diabolical connections of the Jews were subjects of sermons, mystery plays, and popular tales throughout the Middle Ages.

83. Betraying a similar train of thought, Thomas of Chobham called the devil the greatest usurer of them all: "diabolus fenerator est pessimus, quia nichil dat nobis de pecunia sua nisi ad usuram gravissimam"; Thomas of Chobham, *Sermones,* CCCM 82A, ed. Franco Morenzoni (Turnhout, Belgium, 1993), 65 (Sermo 6, line 57).

84. On artistic representations of the obscene rites alleged to have been performed by heretics, see chapter 4, as well as my article "Jews, Heretics and the Sign of the Cat in the *Bible moralisée,*" *Word and Image* 8 (1992): 362–377.

85. Vienna ÖNB cod. 1179, fol. 74d: "Puella qui petiit sibi vitam per quadraginta dies elongari significat sinagogam qui voluit suam vitam et petiit elongari quia voluit iterum in lucris temporalibus commorari."

86. Quoted in Baldwin, *Medieval Theories of the Just Price,* 48.

87. ". . . conquirunt *corvos,* id est alios foeneratores similes sibi ut similes contractus exerceant . . ." Robert de Courson, *De Usura,* xi.

88. PL 14:391.

89. PL 9:874.

90. *Biblia Latina cum Glossa Ordinaria,* I.39.

91. Thomas of Chobham, *Sermones,* 243 (Sermo 23, line 363).

92. *The Bestiary of Guillaume le Clerc, originally written in 1210–11,* trans. George Claridge Druce (Ashford, Kent, 1936), lines 615, 653–654. See also *Bestiary: Being an English Version of Bodleian Library Oxford MS Bodley 764,* trans. Richard Barber (Woodbridge, 1993), 159.

93. Léopold Hervieux, *Les fabulistes latins,* vol. 4, *Eudes de Chériton et ses dérivés* (Paris, 1896), 204.

94. It does, however, appear in the twelfth-century English *Bestiary,* trans. Barber, 116: "Frogs signify heretics and their demons who linger at the banquet of the decadent senses . . ."

95. Vienna ÖNB cod. 2554, fol. 29b: "Li fruez senefie l'usurier qi est enflez d'usure et de couvoitise."

96. Caesarius of Heisterbach, *Dialogus Miraculorum,* 2 vols., ed. Joseph Strange (Cologne, 1851), dist. 10, cap. 69 (vol. 2, p. 263). A toad is associated with usury in dist. 2, cap. 32 (vol. 1, p. 206). There are also references to toads in dist. 4, cap. 86 (vol. 1, p. 252) and dist. 10, caps. 67 and

68 (vol. 2, pp. 261–263). See, too, the story told by Otto of St. Blaise concerning Fulk de Neuilly and a usurer in MGH Script. 20.330.

97. Trachtenberg, *The Devil and the Jews,* 115–116.

98. Ibid., 205–206.

99. For more toad imagery, see Janetta Rebold Benton, *The Medieval Menagerie: Animals in the Art of the Middle Ages* (New York, London, and Paris, 1992); and Mary E. Robbins, "The Truculent Toad in the Middle Ages," in *Animals in the Middle Ages: A Book of Essays,* ed. Nona C. Flores (New York and London, 1996), 25–47. Debra Hassig, *Medieval Bestiaries: Text, Image, Ideology* (Cambridge, 1995), does not, unfortunately, discuss either toads or ravens, in spite of her interest in anti-Jewish imagery.

100. A commentary text to Lev. 22:19 in Vienna ÖNB cod. 1179, fol. 52a, and Vienna ÖNB cod. 2554, fol. 30c, stipulates that offerings tainted by usury, greed, and simony must be rejected—a directive that would be applicable only in the case of Christian usurers. This commentary closely parallels a text in the *Summa* of Robert de Courson (IX.p) citing the same Levitical verse as authority for restoring the proceeds of "raptore, feneratore, symoniaco" to their rightful owners. Robert de Courson, "Robert Courson on Penance," ed. V. L. Kennedy, *Mediaeval Studies* 7 (1945): 318.

101. This is naturally a huge topic. Select evidence for clerical moneylending from the period of the making of the *Bible moralisée* includes Robert of Flamborough, *Liber Poenitentialis,* 251: "Si quis clericus detectus fuit usuras accipere placuit degredari et abstinere," and a canon from a council at Montpellier (1214): "Ut clerici usuras non exerceant" (Mansi 22:941). On Christian moneylending, see the works cited in note 4, as well as Baldwin, *Masters, Princes, and Merchants,* esp. 1:297–311; Shatzmiller, *Shylock Reconsidered,* 73; and Grayzel, *The Church and the Jews,* 44–45. Bernard of Clairvaux asserts that some Christian moneylenders acted "worse than any Jew" (*The Letters of St. Bernard of Clairvaux,* trans. Bruno James [London, 1953], no. 391)—a rhetorical trope that nevertheless testifies to the perceived severity of the problem.

102. The Vulgate text refers to "Benjaminites"; the *Bible moralisée* presumably calls them Sodomites because of their desire to rape the male sojourner in Bethlehem.

103. Vienna ÖNB cod. 1179, fol. 82d: "Sodomite . . . significant infideles qui deum relinquerunt et sunt spersi per mundum et inter christianos locis habitant in diversis."

104. Until Louis VIII's *stabilimentum* on the Jews ended governmental involvement in Jewish usury in 1223, Christian clerks recorded the bonds of Jewish usurers. See Jordan, *The French Monarchy and the Jews,* 62–65, 77.

105. Letter of Innocent III to Philip Augustus (1205), PL 215:502; excerpted in Grayzel, *The Church and the Jews,* 104–109.

106. *Recueil des actes de Philippe Auguste,* II, no. 955.

107. Mansi 22:1087; *Recueil des actes de Philippe Auguste,* IV, no. 1554; on monastic indebtedness to Jews, see Jordan, *The French Monarchy and the Jews,* 67, 83–84.

108. Vienna ÖNB cod. 1179, fol. 152a: "Saxum id est mens iusti fertur de loco id est de iusticia ad culpam . . ."

109. Vienna ÖNB cod. 1179, fol. 65c: "Illi mendaces quibus credidit Josue quos salvavit significant mendaces iudeos feneratores qui dicunt principibus et prelatis quod meliores sunt quam sint ut sic vita eorum incolumis conservetur." The folio that presumably carried the parallel commentary is missing from the French manuscript.

110. According to Colette Beaune, the fleur-de-lis first became an important symbol of the Capetians early in the reign of Louis VIII: *The Birth of an Ideology: Myths and Symbols of Nation in Late Medieval France,* trans. Susan Ross Huston, ed. Fredric L. Cheyette (Berkeley, Los Angeles, and Oxford, 1991), 208.

111. For attitudes toward Jewish lenders in the south of France, see R. W. Emery, "Le prêt d'argent juif en Languedoc et Roussillon," in *Juifs et judaïsme de Languedoc,* Cahiers de Fanjeaux 12 (Toulouse, 1977), 85–96, now buttressed by Shatzmiller, *Shylock Reconsidered.*

112. In thus discrediting moneylending by associating it with Jewish infidelity, the text stands a contemporary strategy on its head. Peter the Chanter asserts (PL 205:158) that princes claimed that Christian as well as Jewish moneylenders were "our Jews" so that they could avoid prosecution for lending at interest.

113. See note 6 above.

114. See especially Gavin Langmuir, "*Tamquam servi:* The Change in Jewish Status in French Law about 1200," in *Les juifs dans l'histoire de France,* ed. M. Yardeni (Leiden, 1980); and Jordan, *The French Monarchy and the Jews,* 56–72.

115. *Verbum Abbreviatum,* PL 205:158.

116. Paris, BN lat. 17509, fols. 102–103.

117. Thomas of Chobham, *Summa Confessorum,* 510 (Art. 7, Dist. 6, Quaestio XIa, cap. iiii).

118. See the letter of Innocent III to Philip Augustus dated 1214, PL 217:229, excerpted in Grayzel, *The Church and the Jews,* 138–141. The Parisian moralists' campaign against usury is the subject of chapter 15 of Baldwin, *Masters, Princes, and Merchants.*

119. For references to the expulsion and readmission, see note 28 in the introduction.

120. *Recueil des actes de Philippe Auguste,* II, no. 955, and IV, no. 1555.

121. *Veterum scriptorum et monumentorum historicum, dogmaticorum, moralium: Amplissima collectio,* 9 vols., ed. Edmund Martène and Ursinus Durand (Paris, 1724–33), I.1181–1182. On Philip's Jewish policy, see Jordan, *The French Monarchy and the Jews,* 23–90. See Robert Chazan, ed., *Church, State, and Jew in the Middle Ages* (New York, 1980), 208–210, for an English translation of the text of Philip's 1219 decree, which is, however, criticized by Jordan, *The French Monarchy and the Jews,* 281 n. 3.

122. *Layettes,* II, no. 1610. See Jordan, *The French Monarchy and the Jews,* 93–104, for the most recent discussion of the *Stabilimentum.*

123. Jordan, *The French Monarchy and the Jews,* 128–154.

124. Stow, "Papal and Royal Attitudes."

125. See especially folios 58d, 100b, and 117a of Vienna ÖNB cod. 1179.

126. The question was recently and forcefully posed by Robert Stacey in his review of Jordan's *French Monarchy and the Jews* in *Speculum* 66

(1991): 648–650; see also Jordan, *The French Monarchy and the Jews,* 89; Gavin Langmuir, "Judei nostri and Capetian Legislation," *Traditio* 16 (1960): 209–239; and Chazan, *Medieval Jewry in Northern France,* 105–106.

127. Vienna ÖNB cod. 1179, fol. 83a: "Ruth [*sic:* the Vulgate text reads Naomi] habens duas filias inter se sibi contrarias significat sanctam ecclesiam quae habet duas manerias hominum. Quidam hominum eam secuntur alii eam dimittunt et relinqunt."

128. Robert de Courson, *De Usura,* 81; discussed in Baldwin, *Masters, Princes, and Merchants,* 1:302.

129. *Contra Amaurianos,* ed. Clemens Baeumker, Beitrage zur Geschichte der Philosophie des Mittelalters 24 (Munich, 1926), 1; Stephen of Bourbon, *Anecdotes Historiques: Legendes et apologues tirés du recueil inédit d'Étienne de Bourbon,* ed. Lecoy de la Marche (Paris, 1877), 307.

130. Pierre des Vaux-de-Cernay, *Histoire Albigeoise,* trans. Pascal Guébin and Henri Maisonneuve (Paris, 1951), 7; Latin text in RHGF 19:6. On the White League, see Guillaume de Puy-Laurent, *Historia Albigensium,* in RHGF 19:203A.

131. Mansi 25:411, excerpted in Solomon Grayzel, *The Church and the Jews in the XIIIth Century,* vol. 2, *1254–1314,* ed. Kenneth R. Stow (New York, 1989), 227–228.

132. For an isolated attempt to apply the Vienne decree to Jews, see Grayzel, *The Church and the Jews,* 2:229 n. 5. Usury is by no means the only issue linking Jews and heretics in the iconography of the *Bible moralisée:* see chapter 4.

133. R. I. Moore, *The Formation of a Persecuting Society: Power and Deviance in Western Europe* (Oxford, 1987).

134. The bibliography on the development of preaching in the early thirteenth century is extensive. See especially Jean Longère, *La prédication médiévale* (Paris, 1983); Richard H. Rouse and Mary A. Rouse, *Preachers, Florilegia, and Sermons: Studies on the Manipulus Florum of Thomas of Ireland* (Toronto, 1979); Louis-Jacques Bataillon, *La prédication au XIIIe siècle en France et Italie* (London, 1993); and D. L. d'Avray, *The Preaching of the Friars: Sermons Diffused from Paris before 1300* (Oxford, 1985).

135. On exempla, see *Les exempla médiévaux: introduction à la recherche,* ed. Jacques Berlioz and Marie Anne Polo de Beaulieu (Carcassonne, 1992); Louis-Jacques Bataillon, "*Similitudines* et *Exempla* dans les sermons du XIIIe siècle," in *The Bible in the Medieval World: Essays in Memory of Beryl Smalley,* ed. Katherine Walsh and Diane Wood (Oxford, 1985), 191–205; Claude Bremond, Jacques le Goff, and J.-C. Schmitt, *L'Exemplum,* Typologie des sources du moyen âge occidental 40 (Turnhout, Belgium, 1982); J.-Th. Welter, *L'Exemplum dans la littérature religieuse et didactique du Moyen Âge* (Geneva, 1973).

136. R. I. Moore, *The Origins of European Dissent* (London, 1977), 249.

Chapter 3. The People of the Book

1. Vienna ÖNB cod. 1179, fol. 202B and b: "Caput nichanoris et dextram quam superbe extenderant contra ierusalem suspenderunt." "Hoc

significat quod in ecclesia ante chorum erigitur figura crucifixi in signum victorie ipsius. Et inter christianos permissi cum judei habitare in testimonium fidei, propter libros legis quod deferunt in captivitate in qua sunt propter peccata sua."

2. What follows is intended to provide essential background, not to be a comprehensive discussion of the topic, which is far too vast even to begin to cover here.

3. For the church fathers' defense against Marcion, who rejected the Old Testament as well as the Incarnation, see *The Cambridge History of the Bible,* vol. 2, *The West from the Fathers to the Reformation,* ed. G. W. H. Lampe (Cambridge, 1969), 170–171.

4. The phrase is taken from the *De Altercatione Ecclesiae et Synagogae Dialogus* of Pseudo-Augustine, PL 42:1134; partial English translation in A. Lukyn Williams, ed., *Adversus Judaeos: A Bird's-Eye View of Christian Apologiae until the Renaissance* (Cambridge, 1935), 326–338.

5. In his magisterial survey *Les intellectuels chrétiens et les juifs au moyen âge* (Paris, 1990), 584–585.

6. I do not mean to suggest that without this justification the Jews would not have been allowed to remain in Europe, as has sometimes been asserted (see my later discussion of Jeremy Cohen). Although this is obviously too complex an issue to address in this note, I feel compelled to point out that such an assumption would presuppose that both an a priori intolerance and an ability to conceive of, if not effect, massive repression were intrinsic to medieval Christianity. As will become clear, I have yet to be convinced that this was the case. Intolerance and repression did, of course, become increasingly common in the later Middle Ages (although even then they were not omnipresent), but it does not follow that they were therefore always latent and waiting to emerge.

7. Augustine of Hippo, *De Civitate Dei,* 18:46, in *Corpus Christianorum Series Latina* 48 (Turnhout, 1955), 643–645; English translation in *A Select Library of the Nicene and Post-Nicene Fathers of the Christian Church,* trans. Marcus Dods, ed. Philip Schaff, vol. 2 (repr., Grand Rapids, Mich., 1983), 389.

8. On early Christian attitudes toward Jews and Judaism, see John Gager, *The Origins of Anti-semitism: Attitudes toward Judaism in Pagan and Christian Antiquity* (New York and Oxford, 1983); and Rosemary Ruether, *Faith and Fratricide: The Theological Roots of Anti-Semitism* (New York, 1974).

9. *Letters of Bernard of Clairvaux,* trans. Bruno James (London, 1953), 460–462.

10. Text in Gilbert Dahan, "L'Article *Iudei* de la *Summa Abel* de Pierre Chantre," *Revue des études augustiniennes* 27 (1981): 105–126, here 106.

11. PL 214:864–865; partial translation in Solomon Grayzel, ed., *The Church and the Jews in the XIIIth Century* (Philadelphia, 1933), 92–95.

12. PL 207:825, partial translation in Williams, *Adversus Judaeos,* 401.

13. *Summa confessorum,* 434.

14. Alexander of Hales, *Summa Theologica,* vol. 3, ed. Bonaventure Marrani (Florence, 1930), 729–730 (Inq. III Tract. VIII. Sect. I. Quaest. I Tit. II—740).

15. The heterogeneity of Christian attitudes, if not theology, toward

Jews is the subject of the Gavin Langmuir article "The Faith of Christians and Hostility towards Jews," *Studies in Church History* 29 (1992): 77–92, which compares the stances toward Jews of Bernard of Clairvaux, Peter the Venerable, and Peter Abelard.

16. Stephen Langton, for example, wrote: "Unde Iudei fugiunt a facie Domini et certe plures sunt qui agunt contra conscientiam et bene sciunt fidem nostram esse meliorem sua, et bene sciunt quod Dominus fuit incarnatus et passus, et tamen volunt sequi patres suos . . ."; quoted in Gilbert Dahan, "Exégèse et polémique dans les commentaires de la Genèse d'Étienne Langton," in *Les juifs au regard de l'histoire: Mélanges en l'honneur de Bernhard Blumenkranz,* ed. Gilbert Dahan (Paris, 1985), 146.

17. Similarly, legal restrictions on Jews could have neutral, mild, or hostile inflections; see John A. Watt, "Jews and Christians in the Gregorian Decretals," *Studies in Church History* 29 (1992): 93–105.

18. See, for example, Hom. I,2 in Origen, *Homélies sur le Lévitique,* Sources chrétiennes 286, ed. and trans. Marcel Borret (Paris, 1981), 70–73.

19. Ralph of Flaix, *In Leviticum,* ed. M. de la Bigne, *Maxima Bibliotheca Patrum,* vol. 17 (Lyon, 1677). See Dahan, *Les intellectuels chrétiens,* 388; and Beryl Smalley, "William of Auvergne, John de la Rochelle, and St. Thomas Aquinas on the Old Law," in Beryl Smalley, *Studies in Medieval Thought and Learning from Abelard to Wycliff* (London, 1981), 121–181.

20. See, for example, Dahan, "Exégèse," 147: "les juifs sont intemporels; des contemporains de Jésus aux Juifs parisiens ou anglais qu'Étienne Langton a pu côtoyer, il y a parfaite continuité, parfaite identité."

21. For a full discussion of the pointed hat, see chapter 1.

22. For references to this canon, see chapter 1, note 12.

23. Emile Mâle, *The Gothic Image: Religious Art in France of the Thirteenth Century,* trans. Dora Nussey (New York, 1972), 161–162.

24. For interesting examples of manuscripts utilizing the scroll to represent the Old Testament, see Herrad of Hohenbourg, *Hortus Deliciarum,* 2 vols., ed. Rosalie Green, Michael Evans, Christine Bischoff, and Michael Curschmann (London, 1979); and Erlangen, Universitatsbibliothek MS 186: *Miscellany,* fol. 57v. For a fascinating discussion of the scroll, see Michael Camille, "Visual Signs of the Sacred Page: Books in the Bible moralisée," *Word and Image* 5 (1989): 111.

25. For example, in the hands of the supposed "donor" figures on monastic portals, such as that from Moutiers-St.-Jean (Burgundy) at the Cloisters, Metropolitan Museum of Art, New York City. The more recent (and more likely) suggestion that the figures are intended to represent Old Testament kings does not invalidate the possibility that the appearance of the scroll is intended to refer to the antiquity of the monastic foundation.

26. For example, Mâle, *The Gothic Image,* 174.

27. Jeremy Cohen, *The Friars and the Jews: The Evolution of Medieval Anti-Judaism* (Ithaca, N.Y., and London, 1982). Cohen's is the highest-profile and most forceful presentation of this thesis, but it was not the first. See Benzion Dinur, *Israel in the Diaspora,* 2d ed. (Tel Aviv, 1958–72) [Hebrew].

28. Most notably by Robert Chazan in *Daggers of Faith: Thirteenth-Century Christian Missionizing and Jewish Response* (Berkeley, 1988). See also the reviews by Joseph Shatzmiller in *Jewish Social Studies* 46 (1984): 331–333; and by Robert I. Burns in *Catholic Historical Review* 70 (1984): 90–93.

29. The influence that Cohen's book continues to exert on the field, in spite of the many criticisms to which it has been subjected, is evidenced in the fact that no fewer than nine papers were dedicated to its reassessment at the Twenty-ninth International Congress on Medieval Studies at Western Michigan University, Kalamazoo, Michigan, May 5–8, 1994.

30. The *Bible moraliseé* is of particular relevance to the questions raised in Cohen's work because of the close relation of its commentary to subsequent mendicant exegetical tradition. Although the two earliest exemplars both date to the early to mid-1220s, and thus antedate most of the texts discussed in Cohen's study by several decades, the later two exemplars, which date to perhaps 1235 and 1240, have actually been attributed, albeit not conclusively, to the Dominican studium of St.-Jacques in Paris. (See the introduction at "The Question of Sources.") Images of friars certainly feature prominently in the illustrations of the later two manuscripts, and it is clear that the exegetical tradition informing both versions of the *Bible moralisée* was a major influence on the early Parisian Dominicans. As I pointed out in the introduction, there are no figures that can be positively identified as mendicants in the images of the two earliest *Bible moralisée* exemplars.

31. Vienna ÖNB cod. 2554, fol. 26va: "Ce qe Dex bailla a Moyses les ii. rais de clartei senefie iesu crist qi bailla les ii lois a ses prelaz por parleir a son peuple." Note that in this verse the *karnaim* of the Hebrew Bible are translated as rays of light, following twelfth-century Parisian scholarship, rather than as horns, as is found in the Vulgate ("cornuta esset facies sua"). The Latin *Bible moralisée* manuscript (fol. 39c), however, reads: "Hoc quod deus dedit Moysi duo clara cornua [two shining horns] significat ihm xpm qui prelatis suis tradidit duas leges," and the accompanying image depicts Moses with horn-shaped rays emerging from his temples; this seems to be a conflation of the older and the newer interpretations. Ruth Mellinkoff, *The Horned Moses in Medieval Art and Thought* (Berkeley and Los Angeles, 1970), 69, called the parallel scene in the three-volume version of the *Bible moralisée* one of the earliest examples of the penetration of theologians' rationalizations of the horns as rays of light into a work of art. Since both Vienna ÖNB cod. 1179 and the French exemplar are earlier still, these manuscripts may well be the earliest expressions of such influence—reinforcing the conclusion that the iconographer was closely tied to the University of Paris, where the reinterpretation was introduced.

32. Vienna ÖNB cod. 1179, fol. 62c: "Moyses qui mortuus est in monte et incineratus significat mortem veteris legis quam christiani incinerant cum honore." Versions of this interpretation appear in the interlinear *Biblia Latina cum Glossa Ordinaria: Facsimile Reprint of the Editio Princeps Adolph Rusch of Strassburg 1480/81,* 4 vols., intro. Karlfried Froehlich and Margaret T. Gibson (Turnhout, Belgium, 1992), (I.427): "Quia dispensatione domini lex est finita, succedente gratia . . ." and in Richard of St. Victor; neither, however, stresses the honor to be

accorded the Old Law. Augustine refers to the honorable interment of the Law in Letter 82, 2, 16 (*Epistolae,* ed. Alois Goldbacher, CSEL 34 [Vienna, 1985], 367). Although Du Cange (4:325) defines *incinerare* as *in cineres redigere,* the commentary medallion depicts a burial. There is some precedent for this usage: the inscription on Peter Comestor's tomb, once in St.-Victor, clearly uses *incineratum* to mean buried: "Petrus eram quem petra tegit, dictusque Comestor/Nunc comedor, vivus docui, nec cesso docere / Mortuus, ut dicat qui me videt incineratum: / Quod sumus iste fuit; erimus quandoque quod hic est" (PL 198: 1048).

33. The relatively positive tone adopted here in regard to the Old Law (in spite of the fact that the text stresses the Law's obsolescence) stands out when contrasted with the parallel moralization in the later, three-volume version of the *Bible moralisée* (Oxford Bod. 270b, fol. 93vc): "On a mountain [Moses] died; in a valley he was buried. Because the Law was glorious in its time, but compared to the Gospel it seems abstruse and humble." ["Quia lex tempore suo gloriosa fuit. Sed respectu evangelium abscondita videtur et humilis."] The contrast persists in the commentary image, which portrays a blinded Synagoga falling off to the right as her crown slips off her head; Holy Church stands commandingly in the center, this time displaying no pity or tenderness, and two Dominicans look on approvingly from the left. In general, there are interesting and significant changes from the commentary of the earlier pair to that of the later pair of thirteenth-century *Bibles moralisées*; I plan to investigate these differences more fully in the future.

34. Vienna ÖNB cod. 2554, fol. 6vc: "Ce qe jacob guerpist la vielle et prent la iuene senefie iesu crist qi bote la vielle loi arriers ensus de lui et se prent a sainte eglise qi est iuene et bele."

35. This interpretation was common in the works of the early church fathers (Rosemary Ruether, *Faith and Fratricide,* 135) and was a favorite image of Bernard of Clairvaux (see, for example, Bernard of Clairvaux's *De Diligendo Deo* in PL 182:973–980; translated in Bernard of Clairvaux, *Selected Works,* trans. G. R. Evans [New York and Mahwah, N.J., 1987], 179–184).

36. Vienna ÖNB cod. 1179, fol. 12d: "Hic synagoga cum filiabis suis in oculo uno habens maculam incredulitatis, in alio invidie . . ."

37. Vienna ÖNB cod. 1179, fol. 56b: "Senex . . . significat iudeos qui deferebant mandata iesu christi et tamen sua significatia ignorabant." This text is a paraphrase of the marginal gloss (*Biblia Latina cum Glossa Ordinaria* I.306).

38. *Biblia Latina cum Glossa Ordinaria* I.306.

39. The bulk of these texts will be discussed in chapter 5.

40. Vienna ÖNB cod. 1179, fol. 246c: "Hic sunt excommunicati et maledicti iudei qui negant veritatem et veram expositionem sacre scripture. Et heretici qui in eas suas falsitates admittent. Et falsi decretiste qui sacram scripturam inducunt ut per eam litigent de terrenis."

41. Vienna ÖNB cod. 1179, fol. 187c: "Hoc significat quod iudei iniqui per legem quam ab ipso domino susceperant volebant evangelium destruere et credentes in iesum."

42. Vienna ÖNB cod. 1179, fol. 37c: "Moyses qui destruxit tabulas significat legem veterem. Populus qui petiit veniam et tunc moyses repa-

ravit tabulas novas significat ihm xpm qui reformat sanctam ecclesiam ut suam faciat voluntatem."

43. "Hic sinagoga frangitur a dei filio."

44. For example, in ca. 1204 Jews swore on a *rotulum* in the presence of the king not to leave his domains: Jordan, *The French Monarchy and the Jews,* 57.

45. Mansi 22:356; PL 215:502 and 1291. See, too, the decree of the 1213 council in Mansi 22:850.

46. On Philip Augustus's policy of recording previously unwritten customs and agreements of all kinds, see John W. Baldwin, *The Government of Philip Augustus: Foundations of French Royal Power in the Middle Ages* (Berkeley, Los Angeles, and London, 1986), 355. On market procedures, see R. D. Face, "Techniques of Business in the Trade between the Fairs of Champagne and the South of Europe in the Twelfth and Thirteenth Centuries," *Economic History Review,* 2d ser., 10 (1958): 427–438. Note that the word *rotulum* was applied both to Torah scrolls and to financial accounts and legal documents. I have recently become aware of the fascinating work of Brigitte Bedos-Rezak on the subject of Christian attitudes toward Jewish textuality. See her articles "Les juifs et l'écrit dans la mentalité eschatologique," *Annales HSS* 5 (1994): 1049–1063, and "The Confrontation of Orality and Textuality: Jewish and Christian Literacy in Eleventh- and Twelfth-Century Northern France," in *Rashi 1040–1990: Hommage à Ephraim E. Urbach,* ed. Gabrielle Sed-Rajna (Paris, 1993), 541–558.

47. PL 215:502.

48. Mansi 22:850; partial translation in Grayzel, *The Church and the Jews,* 307. It is important to note that the decree seems to deal with Christian, not Jewish, moneylenders, but that the employment of the word "synagogue" implicitly relates Christian economic transgressions to Jewish infidelity.

49. See the discussion of the Theophilus legend in chapter 4. In this legend the sinner's contract with the devil is patently modeled on economic transactions, and possession of the written instrument itself becomes the central issue in the contest between good and evil. The illustration of this pact in the Ingeborg Psalter portrays Theophilus kneeling and performing homage to a bestial devil prominently flourishing the written contract, which has the form of a *rotulum.*

50. On mocking gestures in Passion imagery, see Gertrude Schiller, *Iconography of Christian Art,* vol. 2, *The Passion of Jesus Christ,* trans. Janet Seligman (Greenwich, Conn., 1972); and William Chester Jordan, "The Last Tormenter."

51. For the accusation that Jews mock Christians on Good Friday, see the same letter of Innocent III to Philip Augustus, dated 1205, in PL 215: 501–503; partial translation in Grayzel, *The Church and the Jews,* 108–109. For legislation prohibiting Jews from appearing in public on Good Friday, see Canon 68 of the Fourth Lateran Council (*Constitutiones Concilii quarti Lateranensis,* ed. Antonio Garcia y Garcia [Vatican City, 1981]; partial translation in Grayzel, *The Church and the Jews,* 308–309), and law 7.24.2 of the *Siete Partidas* (see Dwayne E. Carpenter, *Alfonso X and the Jews: An Edition of and Commentary on Siete Partidas 7.24 "De los*

Judios," University of California Publications on Modern Philology, vol. 115 [Berkeley and Los Angeles, 1986], 29, 65–66).

52. See also Vienna ÖNB cod. 1179, fol. 44b, on which Synagoga is depicted mocking Jesus while holding a scroll of the Law and being observed by two Jews. On folio 54c, Synagoga holds a scroll while cursing Jesus; on folio 176b, a Jew holding a scroll points at Jesus in accusation. For an original and stimulating rereading of Holy Week violence, see David Nirenberg, *Communities of Violence: Persecution of Minorities in the Middle Ages* (Princeton, N.J., 1996), 200–230.

53. Vienna ÖNB cod. 1179, fol. 108d: "Hoc significat iudeos qui post resurrectionem iesu christi quasi suspensi nec in caelo nec in terra in mundo remanserunt."

54. In this it closely approximates the comment of Raban Maur incorporated into the *Glossa ordinaria* (II.76), which equated Absalom with the Jews, pierced by the devil with the spears of avarice, luxury, and pride.

55. An image on folio 14b of Vienna ÖNB cod. 1179 also combines these same signs and personages: the Jews who pay Judas to hand over Jesus carry both a scroll and a moneybag.

56. Vienna ÖNB cod. 2554, fol. 40va: "Ce qe Samuel moru . . . et li phylistini enfistrent ioie senefie le boen prelat ou le boen cloistrier qi muert . . . et li mescreant et li mauves en ont ioie et molt en sunt lie."

57. Statutes for the University of Paris issued by Robert de Courson dictated behavior at the funerals of students and masters, suggesting that these ceremonies may not always have been decorous. Henri Denifle, *Chartularium Universitatis Parisiensis,* 4 vols. (Paris, 1891–99; repr., Brussels, 1964), 1:78ff.

58. Vienna ÖNB cod. 2554, fol. 66c: "et Dex lor dist alez et morez por moi."

59. On the medieval legend of St. Denis, see Charles J. Liebman Jr., *Étude sur la vie en prose de Saint Denis* (Geneva, N.Y., 1942). The Life of Dionysius the Areopagite, with whom St. Denis was identified, appears in AASS Oct. II (Oct. 3) (Brussels, 1970), 8–130.

60. Baldwin, *The Government of Philip Augustus,* 377–378, 391–392.

61. Vienna ÖNB cod. 2554, fol. 18a: "Ce qe Moyses ieta ius la verge et ele devint colueure senefie qe iesu criz mist ius et abati la viez loi par la novele. La colueure qi est venimeuse et poignanz senefie les gieus et les mescreanz qi mentienent la viez loi et il sunt point et envelimei [*sic*] de colueure."

62. Bernhard Blumenkranz, "La représentation de Synagoga dans les *Bibles moralisées* françaises du XIIIe au XVe siècle," *Proceedings of the Israel Academy of Science and Humanities* 5 (1971–76): 77.

63. Augustine, *Tractatus Adversus Judaeos* in PL 42:51ff.

64. Peter the Venerable, *Adversus Judaeorum Inveteratam Duritiam,* ed. Yvonne Friedman, CCCM 58 (Turnhout, Belgium, 1985), 100.

65. Vienna ÖNB cod. 1179, fol. 194a: "Hoc significat quod dominus legem moysi quam neminem ad perfectionem duxit spiritualiter exposuit et sic debere adimpleri. Docuit paulus dicens omnia in figura contingebant illi et cotidie per legem propria conviscebat iudeos."

66. Vienna ÖNB cod. 1179, fol. 186a: "Hoc significat quod Synagoga

invitata ad fidem propter legalia sua sacramenta predicationem fidei contempsit."

67. See, for example, Vatican, Biblioteca Apostolica cod. Rossian 555, fol. 127bis verso, reproduced in Thérèse Metzger and Mendel Metzger, *Jewish Life in the Middle Ages: Illuminated Hebrew Manuscripts of the Thirteenth to Sixteenth Centuries* (Fribourg, 1982), 180. In Hebrew manuscript illustrations of Temple sacrifices, the sacrificial animal is slaughtered on the altar: see fol. 1 of the *Mishneh Torah* manuscript, formerly in the Frankfurt Municipal Library (MS Ausst. 6), now in a private collection in New York, reproduced in Bezalel Narkiss, *Hebrew Illuminated Manuscripts* (Jerusalem, 1969), pl. 60.

68. Examples include the lower register of the Ezechiel window at Chartres, the inner ambulatory Sulpicius I window at Bourges, and the illustrations of the month of December in the nearly contemporary calendars of the Ingeborg Psalter (fol. 9r) and the Philadelphia Free Library Lewis MS 185 (fol. 31v).

69. An array of sources testifies to clerical attempts to isolate the products of kosher slaughtering. In a letter to the count of Nevers, Innocent III complained that Jews offered meat leavings to Christians, even though they would not touch meat slaughtered by Christians (PL 215: 1291; partial translation in Grayzel, *The Church and the Jews,* 126–127). A Parisian synod of 1200 (Mansi 22:681–683) instructed Christian butchers not to let Jews slaughter meat for them, and a statute of the Paris synod meeting of ca. 1213 prohibited butchers from allowing Jews to touch meat destined for Christian tables (*Les statuts synodaux français du XIIIe siècle,* vol. 1, *Les statuts de Paris et le synodal de l'Ouest (XIIIe siècle),* ed. and trans. Odette Pontal, Collection de documents inédits sur l'histoire de France, vol. 9 [Paris, 1971], 90). Councils in Béziers (1246) and Albi (1254) prohibited Jews from selling meat on fast days or in Christian markets, and ordered Christians not to use Jews' food or drink (Mansi 23:701, 850).

70. See the discussion of interreligious conflict attending the meat markets of the fourteenth-century Crown of Aragon, in Nirenberg, *Communities of Violence,* 169–172.

71. Vienna ÖNB cod. 1179, fol. 125b: "Hoc significat iudeos et pravos philosophos qui sunt nutantes in fide et infirmi in sua lege et consulunt maiorem suorum magistrorum qui nesciens de re e consilium ab eis suo nomine bitzebuch vocabatur."

72. Vienna ÖNB cod. 1179, fol. 26a: "Magi qui mutaverunt aquam in sanguinem sed non sicut Moyses significant malos homines qui in quantum possunt avertuntur a vero sensu verbum domini commutare." The closest parallel to this commentary that I have found in contemporary exegesis is in the *Commentary on Exodus* by Nicholas of Tournai (according to P. Glorieux, *Répertoire des Maîtres en Théologie de Paris au XIIIe siècle,* 2 vols. [Paris, 1933–34], a master of theology in Paris ca. 1226): "malefici pharaonis sunt qui scripturam sacram adulterant felle miscendo et superfluis honerant"; the polemic here is (interestingly) against heretics, decretists, and advocates rather than Jews (BN MS lat. 17268, fol. 78vb).

73. The language of this text echoes patristic polemics against the early second-century Aquila translation that accuse Jews of "altering the

Scriptures" (see Ruether, *Faith and Fratricide,* 122). The sense of the text, however, would not be restricted to the meaning intended by the church fathers; rather, the text would have been chosen for its contemporary resonance.

74. The *Bible moralisée* thus helps set the scene for that event. There is still little consensus in the considerable literature on the trial of the Talmud regarding why Gregory IX and the French court would have accorded so much attention to the accusations of Nicholas Donin, when for many centuries it had been Church policy not to interfere in internal Jewish religious matters. Some scholars have proposed that the uniquely intense personal piety of Louis IX (or, alternatively, of Blanche) was the decisive factor in inspiring the Parisian trial. In an article published in 1992 ("Marian Devotion and the Talmud Trial of 1240," in *Religionsgespräche im Mittelalter,* ed. Bernard Lewis and Friedrich Niewöhner [Wiesbaden, 1992], 61–76), William Chester Jordan suggested that the centrality of the cult of the Virgin in France at this time made the charge that the Talmud insulted Mary particularly shocking. Both suggestions are plausible, but the texts and images of the *Bible moralisée* suggest that an additional factor came into play. If the clerics at Louis IX's court had been educated in a tradition already highly suspicious of, even questioning the legitimacy of, Jewish exegesis and practice, Donin's accusations would have fallen on receptive ears. Intellectual and exegetical developments in Paris during the preceding decades thus helped pave the way for the trial.

75. Vienna ÖNB cod. 2554, fol. 22a: "Ce qe li fil isrl se plainstrent a moyses qe il ne pooent boivre de l'eue qi trop iert amere senefie les clers et les prelaz et les boens crestiens qi vindrent devant iesu crist et se plainstrent et distrent qe il poeent boivre de l'eue amere ce fu de la doctrine de la viez loi."

76. Vienna ÖNB cod. 1179, fol. 32a: "Filii israel non valentes potare aquas amaras significant clericos scolares imbuti scientia seculari quibus nititur esse amara scientia spiritalis."

77. See Michael A. Signer, "Peshat, Sensus Litteralis, and Sequential Narrative: Jewish Exegesis and the School of St. Victor in the Twelfth Century," in *The Frank Talmage Memorial,* vol. 1, ed. Barry Walfish (Haifa, 1993), 203–216; Dahan, *Les intellectuels chrétiens;* Beryl Smalley, *The Study of the Bible in the Middle Ages,* 3d ed. (Oxford, 1984); and Aryeh Grabois, "The Hebraica Veritas and Jewish-Christian Intellectual Relations in the Twelfth Century," *Speculum* 50 (1975): 613–634. Also still useful on this topic are Herman Hailperin, *Rashi and the Christian Scholars* (Pittsburgh, 1963); Raphael Loewe, "The Medieval Christian Hebraists of England: The *Superscriptio Lincolniensis,*" *Hebrew Union College Annual* 28 (1957): 205–252; and Charles Singer, "Hebrew Scholarship in the Middle Ages among Latin Christians," in *The Legacy of Israel,* ed. Edwyn R. Bevan and Charles Singer (Oxford, 1928), 283–314.

78. Grabois, "Hebraica Veritas," 618.

79. Ibid., 628–630.

80. Smalley, *The Study of the Bible in the Middle Ages,* 103–104.

81. Ibid., 151–156; Jean Chatillon, "Le mouvement théologique dans la France de Philippe Auguste," in *La France de Philippe Auguste: Le temps des mutations* (Actes du Colloque International organisé par le CNRS, Paris, 1980), ed. Robert-Henri Bautier (Paris, 1982), 881–902, here 893.

82. Signer, "Peshat." See, too, the interesting article by Sarah Kamin, "Affinities between Jewish and Christian Exegesis in Twelfth-Century Northern France," *Proceedings of the World Congress of Jewish Studies* 9 (1985): 141–155.

83. Grabois, "Hebraica Veritas," 625. On the popularity of Comestor's *Historia,* see James H. Morey, "Peter Comestor, Biblical Paraphrase, and the Medieval Popular Bible," *Speculum* 68 (1993): 6–35.

84. See especially the remarks of Peter the Venerable in *Adversus Judaeorum,* chap. 5.

85. Smalley, *The Study of the Bible in the Middle Ages,* 110.

86. Cited in C. Spicq, *Esquisse d'une histoire de l'exégèse latine au moyen âge,* Bibliothèque Thomiste 26 (Paris, 1944), 92. Grabois, "Hebraica Veritas," 626, points out that decretists would have been especially concerned about the influence of Jewish exegesis, since all Catholic legislation was based on authorities that could be traced back to Scripture.

87. Grabois, "Hebraica Veritas," 629.

88. Langton, for example, wrote: "Qui vero solam historiam sequebantur scilicet antiqui veteris synagogae sola terrena expectabant." ("Those who followed only the [literal] history, that is, the ancients of the old synagogue, awaited only earthly things.") Paris, BN lat. 14414, fol. 115a, published in George Lacombe and Beryl Smalley, "Studies on the Commentaries of Cardinal Stephen Langton," *Archives d'histoire doctrinale et littéraire du moyen âge* 5 (1930): 43.

89. See Hugh of St. Victor, *The Didascalicon,* trans. Jerome Taylor (New York and London, 1961), 92 (Book Three, Chapter 8). In the *Verbum Abbreviatum,* Peter the Chanter criticizes excessive and unnecessary allegorical interpretation, significantly citing in support of his position a certain "Judaeus litteratus" who challenged the allegorical exegesis of a master at Reims. PL 205:553, discussed in John W. Baldwin, *Masters, Princes, and Merchants: The Social Views of Peter the Chanter and His Circle* (Princeton, N.J., 1970), 1:94. For further discussion of literal exegesis in the thirteenth century, see Spicq, *Esquisse d'une histoire de l'exégèse latine,* 267–285.

90. The phrase is that of John Baldwin, offered in a private telephone conversation. I am extremely grateful for his illuminating remarks on this subject.

91. The phrase is from Freud, *Civilization and Its Discontents.* I am indebted to Ronald Schechter for directing me to this text and for many helpful discussions relating to "Franco-Jewry."

92. Moses Maimonides, *The Guide of the Perplexed,* ed. Shlomo Pines (Chicago and London, 1962), 2:535–538. His was not the first, but the "most comprehensive and ambitious" medieval Jewish attempt to rationalize the commandments. The assessment is that of Isadore Twersky, *Introduction to the Code of Maimonides (Mishneh Torah)* (New Haven, Conn., and London, 1980), 373; see pages 374–459 of Twersky's book for a discussion of Maimonides' approach.

93. *De legibus* in William of Auvergne, *Opera Omnia,* 2 vols. (Paris, 1674; repr., Frankfurt, 1963), 1:19. Note, however, that adoption of Maimonidean theory by no means amounted to philo-Judaism. In the same discussion (p. 25), William remarks, "Sciebat namque legislator eam esse Judaeorum malitiam, ut uxores odiosas, quae ab eis non nisi per mor-

tem separari possent, occiderent; sciebat et eam esse eorundem cupiditatem et avaritiam, ut nec fratribus, hos est Judaeis, ab usuris parcerent, nisi alienis ad usuram dare permitterentur. . . . Fecit igitur legislator per huiusmodi permissiones, quod in tali populo fieri potuit videlicet eos per minorum malorum permissionem a majoribus averti."

94. For a summary of the issues and events, see Charles Touati, "Les deux conflits autour de Maimonide et des études philosophiques," *Cahiers de Fanjeaux* 12 (1977): 173–184; and idem, *Prophètes, Talmudistes, Philosophes* (Paris, 1990), especially 201–217. See chapter 4 below for further discussion of Maimonidean controversies, Jewish and Christian.

95. Vienna ÖNB cod. 1179, fol. 202b: "Hoc significat quod in ecclesia ante chorum erigitur figura crucifixi in signum victorie ipsius. Et inter christianos permissi cum judei habitare in testimonium fidei, propter libros legis quod deferunt in captivitate in qua sunt propter peccata sua."

96. Otto von Simpson, *The Gothic Cathedral: Origins of Gothic Architecture and the Medieval Conception of Order* (Princeton, N.J., 1984), 134.

97. Alain Erlande-Brandenburg, *The Cathedral: The Social and Architectural Dynamics of Construction,* trans. Martin Thom (Cambridge, 1994), 127–128.

98. On the early thirteenth-century choir screen at Notre-Dame de Paris, see Marcel Aubert, "Les Trois Jubés de Notre-Dame de Paris," *Revue de l'art ancien et moderne* 43 (1923): 105–118.

99. Note that the choir barrier of the commentary roundel parallels a representation of the Temple in the biblical roundel directly above it. On the baldachin as symbol of the Temple in the *Bible moralisée,* see Reiner Haussherr, "Templum Salamonis und Ecclesia Christi: zu einem Bildvergleich der Bible moralisée," *Zeitschrift für Kunstgeschichte* 31 (1968): 101–121.

100. Quoted in Craig Wright, *Music and Ceremony at Notre Dame of Paris, 500–1550* (Cambridge, 1989), 14. On Prévostin, see George Lacombe, *La vie et les oeuvres de Prévostin,* Bibliothèque Thomiste XI (Paris and Le Saulchoir, 1927).

101. Vienna ÖNB cod. 1179, fols. 39d and 40a: "Hoc significat bonos prelatos qui volunt verba sancte ecclesie loqui cum plebe et populi dicunt quod audire subtilitatem nequeunt ihu xpi." "Moyses . . . significat bonum theologum qui loquitur populo grosse et subtilitatem scriptur loco et tempore nititur retinere." Vienna ÖNB cod. 2554, fol. 26vb and c: "Ce qe Moyses volt parleir a son pueple et li pueples ne pot soffrir sa grant clartei ains le refusa senefie les prelaz qi vulent parleir a pueple et li pueples les refusent et dient qe il ne puent entendre la subtilitei de la devinitei iesucrist." "Ce qe Moyses prist le voil et le mist devant lui et retint sa clartei en soi senefie le boen devin qi retient sa subtilitei a soi et parole au pueple grossement selonc ce qe il sunt." This commentary sequence was examined by James Michael Heinlen, whose dissertation stressed the relationship of the overall *Bible moralisée* commentary to the contemporary reform program. Heinlein linked this specific commentary sequence to the exegesis of Stephen Langton. James Michael Heinlein, "The Ideology of Reform in the French Moralized Bible" (Ph.D. diss., Northwestern University, 1991), 153–157.

102. See, for example, Alain de Lille's *Summa de arte praedicatoria,* PL 210:685–1012 (in English, Alan of Lille, *The Art of Preaching,* trans.

Gillian R. Evans [Kalamazoo, Mich., 1981]); and the prologue to Jacques de Vitry's *Sermones ad Status* (in *Prêcher d'Exemples: Récits de prédicateurs du moyen âge,* ed. Jean-Claude Schmitt [Paris, 1985], 47–48). See, too, the comments of the anonymous Franciscan preacher (1230–31) complaining about masters who use "verba subtilia et clamosa" in their sermons and thus obscure the meaning of the text "like a rabbi"; cited in Marie-Madeleine Davy, *Les sermons universitaires parisiens de 1230–31* (Paris, 1931), 113 n. 2.

103. C. A. Robson, "Vernacular Scriptures in France," in *The Cambridge History of the Bible,* vol. 2, *The West from the Fathers to the Reformation,* ed. G. W. H. Lampe (Cambridge, 1969), 441. See, too, Guy de Poenck, *La Bible et l'activité traductrice dans les pays romans avant 1300* (Heidelberg, 1969–70); and Serge Lusignan, *Parler vulgairement: Les intellectuels et la langue française au XIIIe et XIVe siècles* (Paris, 1988).

104. Leonard E. Boyle, "Innocent III and Vernacular Versions of Scripture," in *The Bible in the Medieval World: Essays in Memory of Beryl Smalley,* ed. Katherine Walsh and Diane Wood (Oxford, 1985), 97–107.

105. The question of heresy may also be implicit in the reference to the crucifix as a sign for Christ's victory. In one sense, this text testifies eloquently to the Jews' conceptual centrality within Christian doctrine: for Christ to be "victorious" there must be a vanquished party; in this text, as in so many Christian works, the Jews fulfill this function. However, Jews were not the only figures whose conquest could signify Christ's victory. A chronicle written very shortly before or at the same time as the *Bible moralisée* casts a different type of person in this role: during the Albigensian Crusade, the cross of Christ was set at the top of a tower "as a sign of victory" over the Albigensian heretics (Pierre des Vaux-de-Cernay, *Historia Albigensium,* RHGF 19:32; and idem, *Histoire Albigeoise,* trans. Pascal Guébin and Henri Maisonneuve [Paris, 1951]). There is no guarantee that either the redactor or the reader of the *Bible moralisée* was familiar with this episode, but it seems worth noting that Albigensian heretics are mentioned on the very next folio of the Latin manuscript (Vienna ÖNB cod. 1179, fol. 203b).

106. See, too, my reading of the different page layouts adopted in the two exemplars in the introduction.

107. Vienna ÖNB cod. 2554, fol. 21d: "Ce qe li fil israel vindrent as dous montaignes et a la mer et il se plenstrent a moyses senefie les apostles qi furent entre dous mons li uns des mons senefie le deiable et li autre males genz et la mers ce est li mundes . . ."

108. See chapter 2.

109. Vienna ÖNB cod. 1179, fol. 91a: "Saul . . . significat iudeos qui faciebant contra voluntatem domini et propter hoc facti sunt areptici et diabolus intravit in corda eorum quo facto simul corpus et animam destruxerunt."

Chapter 4. The Sign of the Cat

1. Vienna ÖNB cod. 1179, fol. 63d. Note that there is no mention of a "wall" in the Vulgate, which describes waters as swelling up "in the likeness of a mountain" (*ad instar montis*). The reference to a wall may have been chosen because it more closely approximates the spirit of the com-

mentary, and/or it may have been inspired by Exod. 14:22, which describes the waters of the Red Sea as *quasi murus.* The parallel biblical text is missing from the French manuscript; the later three-volume version (Oxford Bodl. MS 270b, fol. 95vD and d) retains the comparison of the waters of the Jordan to a mountain, and its moralization closely follows the *Biblia Latina cum Glossa Ordinaria: Facsimile Reprint of the Editio Princeps Adolph Rusch of Strassburg 1480/81,* 4 vols., intro. Karlfried Froehlich and Margaret T. Gibson (Turnhout, Belgium, 1992).

2. There is no doubt that the word *publicani* is used here to refer to some kind of heretic. According to Du Cange (vol. 6), the word *populicani* (or *poblicani* or *publicani*) was used in the eleventh century to refer to Manichaean heretics, and was later used as an appellation for Waldensians. Canon 27 of the Third Lateran Council includes *publicani* among the groups of heretics condemned by name. Parisian texts employing the term include a decree of the Council of Paris in 1212 (Mansi 22:850–851) and a sermon delivered by Stephen of Tournai when he was a theology master (Paris, BN lat. 14,935, fol. 8vb: "Quibus novus hereticorum cecus qui populicani vocantur . . ."). Stephen is clearly referring to Cathars: he goes on to describe the heretics' ritual of *consolamentum.* Stephen of Bourbon said that *popelicani* was the French word for Manichaeans (see Stephen of Bourbon, *Anecdotes Historiques: Legendes et apologues tirés du recueil inédit d'Étienne de Bourbon,* ed. A. Lecoy de la Marche [Paris, 1877], 300). See also the discussion of the "sect" known as *publicani* in R. I. Moore, *The Origins of European Dissent* (London, 1977), 183–185. Arno Borst, *Die Katharer* (Stuttgart, 1953), 247, supplements Du Cange with a list of twelfth- and thirteenth-century sources mentioning *popelicani.* Let me state here that I shall make no attempt to specifically identify the *populicani* referred to in the *Bible moralisée. Albigensi* are explicitly mentioned twice in the Latin manuscript (fols. 96c and 203b) and once in the French manuscript (fol. 40vd), but no precise heretical doctrines are addressed or refuted, and, as I argue below, the commentary is not a polemic directed against any particular heretics but against a nexus of ideas and activities labeled "heretical." For further discussion of the term and its connection to New Testament publicans, see the final section of this chapter.

3. On patristic anti-Jewish polemics, see especially Rosemary Radford-Ruether, "The *Adversus Judaeos* Tradition in the Church Fathers: The Exegesis of Christian Anti-Judaism," in *Aspects of Jewish Culture in the Middle Ages,* ed. P. E. Szarmach (Albany, N.Y., 1979), 27–50; and B. Blumenkranz, "Vie et survie de la polémique anti-juive," *Studia Patristica* 1 (1957): 460–476.

4. Jean Longère, *Les Oeuvres oratoires des maîtres parisiens au XIIe siècle,* 2 vols. (Paris, 1975), 411. See 318 n. 49 and 410–433 for more examples. Jews and heretics are also mentioned together in two sermons recorded in a study of Romance preaching in the thirteenth century: Michel Zink, *La prédication en langue romane avant 1300* (Paris, 1976), 193.

5. Paris, BN lat. ms. 2514, fol. 19a.

6. Marie-Madeleine Davy, *Les sermons universitaires parisiennes de 1230–31* (Paris, 1931), 201, 182.

7. Alan of Lille, *Contra Hereticos Libri Quatuor,* in PL 210:305–430. See also the heresiological tract of Evrard of Béthune, cited in Jaroslav

Pelikan, *The Christian Tradition: A History of the Development of Doctrine,* vol. 3, *The Growth of Medieval Theology (600–1300)* (Chicago, 1978), 246. The *Liber Antihaeresis,* a Waldensian work of ca. 1190 directed against the Cathars, claims to maintain the faith of God and the sacraments of the Church ". . . not only against [Cathars], but against Jews and Gentiles and all sects that calumniate them . . ." Christiane Thouzellier, *Catharisme et Valdéisme en Languedoc à la fin du XIIe et au début du XIIIe siècle* (Paris, 1966), 78. See, too, Raoul Manselli, "La polémique contre les juifs dans la polémique antihérétique," *Cahiers de Fanjeaux* 12 (1977): 251–268.

8. Canon 26 deals with Jews and Saracens; Canon 27 with heretics.

9. I am indebted to Dwayne E. Carpenter for this observation. See his work on the legislation of Alfonso the Wise: *Alfonso X and the Jews: An Edition of and Commentary on Siete Partidas 7.24 "De los Judios,"* University of California Publications on Modern Philology, vol. 115 (Berkeley and Los Angeles, 1986). Carpenter points out (p. 84) that the *Siete Partidas* prescribed the same penalties for Christians turning to Judaism as for those who lapsed into heresy.

10. Guillaume le Breton, *Philippidos,* I.429–431, in Henri Delaborde, ed., *Oeuvres de Rigord et de Guillaume le Breton,* 2 vols. (Paris, 1882–85), 2:24. Note again the identification of Jews with filth.

11. Vienna ÖNB cod. 2554, fol. 50a: "Ce qe Salomons conut la verae mere par la pitie qe il vit en li et li rendi son enfant senefie iesu crist qi par son grant sens conu sainte eglise a veraie mere et par la grant pitie qe il vit en li et il li bailla le vif enfant ce est les boens crestiens qi meinent en vives oevres. Et li mort remestrent a la synagogue ce furent gieu et mescreant et populican et tuit mauves."

12. In Vienna ÖNB cod. 1179, infidels and publicans are mentioned together on folios 52b and c; 76c; 80a; 79b, c, and d; 81a; 96b; 97b; 98c; 102a; 120a, b, and d; and 126a. In Vienna ÖNB cod. 2554, miscreants and publicans are mentioned together on folios 20vd; 23c; 25va; 26c and d; 29vc; 30d; 30va; 62vb; 65a, b, c, and d; 35vc and d; 41c; 42a; 43vd; 50a; 53c and d; and 53va and b.

13. Vienna ÖNB cod. 1179, fol. 204A and a: "Et qui in sinistro cornu erant viderunt quod contritum esset dextrum cornu secuti sunt post Judam et suos a tergo. Et in gravatum est prelium. Et occiderunt multi ex hiis et illius et Judas cecidit." "Hoc significat quod post persecutionem martricidarum in ecclesia insurrexerunt heretici et impugnabant fidem iesu christi, trahentes ad societas eorum quos poterant . . ."

14. Engelbert Kirschbaum, *Lexikon der Christlichen Ikonographie* (Rome, 1970), vol. 2, col. 216.

15. Jeanne Courcelle and Pierre Courcelle, "Quelques illustrations du 'Contra Faustum' de Saint Augustin," in *Oikoumene, Studi Paleochristiani pubblicati in onore de Concilio Ecumenico Vaticano II* (Catania, 1964), 6. In a recent article, Elizabeth Pastan argued that the figures wearing Jewish caps in the half medallion below the Marriage of Cana lancet from the cathedral at Troyes should be understood as heretics (Elizabeth Carson Pastan, "*Tam haereticos quam Judeos:* Shifting Symbols in the Glazing of Troyes Cathedral," *Word and Image* 10 [1994]: 66–83). Pastan dates the Troyes lancet to ca. 1220.

16. Strassbourg, Bibliotheque de la Ville, fol. 65r, reproduced in Her-

rad of Hohenbourg, *Hortus Deliciarum,* ed. Rosalie Green, Michael Evans, Christine Bischoff, and Michael Curschmann (London, 1979).

17. See, for example, David Berger, "Christian Heresy and Jewish Polemic in the Twelfth and Thirteenth Centuries," *Harvard Theological Review* 68 (1975): 287–303.

18. Henry Kraus, *The Living Theatre of Medieval Art* (Bloomington, Ind., and London, 1967), 131. In *"Tam haereticos quam Judeos,"* Elizabeth Pastan provides a more thorough and thoughtful analysis of the same image, well grounded in the social and historical context.

19. B. Blumenkranz, *Le juif médiéval au miroir de l'art chrétien* (Paris, 1966), 135.

20. Alexander of Hales, *Summa Theologica,* vol. 3, ed. Bonaventure Marrani (Florence, 1930), 737: "recessus a fide ecclesiastica quam prius tenuit."

21. Such activities were not only the basis of pedagogy and scholarship; they also were essential to pastoral duties, as the penitentials eloquently testify. Accordingly, contemporary Parisian theological practice, concerned as it was with practical morality, inclined toward the creation of ever-finer distinctions. In the following discussion of visual polemics, my aim is not to ignore or deny the Scholastics' ability and desire to discriminate between disparate groups but to highlight the tension between the lucidity and rigidity of theological distinctions and the comparative disorderliness of contemporary society.

22. This, essentially, is the argument forwarded by Elizabeth Pastan in *"Tam haereticos quam Judeos."*

23. Fols. 79d, 80a, 81a, 98c, 117d, and 229d. I have found only one such figure in the French manuscript (on fol. 23c). I have not been able to detect any pattern in the use of this pictorial device; it is employed by at least three different artists (as identified by Branner) and in four different biblical books.

24. RHGF 12:547–551. Note that the (orthodox) eremitical preacher and monastic reformer Robert d'Arbrissel is described in very similar terms: PL 171:1483–1485.

25. Walter Map, *De Nugis Curialium,* ed. Montague Rhodes James, Anecdota Oxoniensa 14 (Oxford, 1914), 62.

26. This iconographic symbol is established primarily in fourteen different roundels in Vienna ÖNB cod. 1179 and in nine in Vienna ÖNB cod. 2554. See the appendix of my dissertation for a list of these roundels.

27. Guillaume le Clerc, *The Bestiary of Guillaume le Clerc, originally written in 1210–11,* trans. George Claridge Druce (Ashford, Kent, 1936).

28. See, for example, *Bestiary: Being an English Version of Bodleian Library Oxford MS Bodley 764,* trans. Richard Barber (Woodbridge, 1993), 109; T. H. White, ed., *The Book of Beasts, Being a Translation from a Latin Bestiary of the Twelfth Century* (New York, 1984), 90; and the entries in the following bestiaries: Aberdeen University Library MS 24, fol. 23v; Cambridge, Corpus Christi College Library MS 53, f197v; Douai Bibliotheque municipale MS 711, fol. 23r; London BM Add. MS 11283, fol. 15r; and Oxford Bodleian Ashmole 1511, fol. 35v.

29. Two exceptions to this rule are Janetta Benton, *The Medieval Menagerie: Animals in the Art of the Middle Ages* (New York, London, and

Paris, 1992); and Herbert Friedman, *A Bestiary for St. Jerome: Animal Symbolism in European Religious Art* (Washington, D.C., 1980).

30. I am not arguing that the cat appears as a symbol for heresy for the very first time in the *Bible moralisée;* far too small a sample of medieval art survives for any such assertion. There are, moreover, one or two possible precedents: Janetta Benton (*Medieval Menagerie,* p. 93) noted that a cat-headed human carved in the cloister in Le Puy might symbolize heresy; and Michael Camille convincingly connected a depiction of a cat-idol in the Maccabees frontispiece to the late twelfth-century Winchester Bible to contemporary misperceptions of heretics as cat worshipers (*The Gothic Idol: Ideology and Image-Making in Medieval Art* [Cambridge, 1989], 66–67). But I do not think that any previous existing work of art used the sign of the cat as systematically and extensively as does the *Bible moralisée.*

31. Vienna ÖNB cod. 1179, fol. 83a: ". . . [hoc] significat sancta ecclesia qui habet duas manerias hominum. Quidam hominum eam secuntur, alii eam dimittunt et relinqunt [*sic*]."

32. Alexander Nequam identified precisely the same grouping (Jews, tyrants, heretics, and false brothers) as agents of Satan: cited in P. Buc, *L'Ambiguïté du Livre: Prince, Pouvoir, et Peuple dans les commentaires de la Bible au moyen âge* (Paris, 1994), 217 (no reference provided).

33. Vienna ÖNB cod. 1179, fol. 203b: "Hoc significat quod qui sunt cum Jesu sunt in fide trinitatis sed ingruente tempore temptationis in ecclesia ut de Albigensibus incredulis et de terra Ierosolimitana recedunt et relinquunt Dominum suum et secuntur seculi delicias. Sed qui electi sunt ad octavam aetatem et ad vitam aeternam propter Dominum suum et cum domino suo constanter persecutionem paciuntur." ("This signifies that those who are with Jesus are in the faith of the Trinity. But in the time of temptation that is coming into the Church, they will give up the Land of Jerusalem and the [fight against] the Albigensian heretics and will abandon their Lord and follow earthly delights. But those who are elected to the Eighth Age and to eternal life will resolutely suffer persecution on behalf of their Lord and with their Lord.")

34. *De Nugis Curialium,* Dist. I, cap. xxx. The English translation is from Walter Map, *De Nugis Curialium (Courtiers' Trifles),* trans. Marbury Bladen Ogle and Frederick Tupper (London, 1924), 72–73. Although I have not located precedents for these images, they had a long and rich afterlife. Several fifteenth-century tractates against the Waldensians depict these sectarians kissing the anus of a goat, including a roundel in the margin of the frontispiece to Paris BN MS fr. 961 (reproduced in Jeffrey B. Russell, *A History of Witchcraft: Sorcerers, Heretics, and Pagans* [London, 1980], fig. 74); a full-page illumination in an anti-Waldensian tract now in the Brussels Bibliothèque Royale (reproduced on the cover of Pierre-François Fournier, *Magie et sorcellerie: essai historique* [Moulins, 1979]); and a nineteenth-century engraving after a fifteenth-century manuscript (reproduced in *Magie et Sorcellerie en Europe du Moyen Âge à nos jours,* ed. Robert Muchembled and Bengt Ankarloo [Paris, 1994]). By the seventeenth century at least, this had evolved into the "obscene kiss" of the devil's anus, which became a stock allegation during the early modern witchcraft hysteria; illustrations of this are far too numerous to list here. I hope to investigate the iconog-

raphy of witchcraft and its connections to antiheretical iconography in the future.

35. "Catari . . . [nominantur] a cato quia osculantur posteriora cati in cuius specie, ut dicunt, apparet eis Lucifer . . ." *Contra Hereticos,* PL 210: 366A. The etymological link between heresy and cats is of course still perpetuated in the German word *ketzer.* Berthold of Regensburg's discussion of the word, however, emphasizes metaphoric rather than ritual associations: "God called [the heretic] a Ketzer, because he can creep secretly where no man sees him, like the cat [*Katze*] . . ." See Berthold of Regensburg, *Vollständige Ausgabe seiner Predigten,* 2 vols., ed. Franz Pfeiffer (1862–80; repr., Berlin, 1965).

36. Cited in Joshua Trachtenberg, *The Devil and the Jews: The Medieval Conception of the Jew and Its Relation to Modern Antisemitism* (New Haven, Conn., 1943; reprint with introduction by Marc Saperstein, Philadelphia, 1983), 205–206.

37. Stephen of Bourbon, *Anecdotes Historiques,* 35, 323.

38. The *Bible moralisée* calls this "vir Dei" Gad, even though the Vulgate does not name him. Gad is the name of a prophet who chastises David in II Kings 24:11–19; presumably the similarity of their objectives inspired the use of the name.

39. Vienna ÖNB cod. 2554, fol. 52b: "Ce qe la fause prophete decut gad par sa fause prophetie et cil le crei senefie le fas hom mescreant qi par losanges et par fauses promesses decoit le boen escolier et le trait a soi et le torne a la soe partie et le feit pechier et aleir en contre les commandemenz iesu crist." I will discuss the identity of the victim of the miscreant's deceit later.

40. See chapter 2.

41. Vienna ÖNB cod. 2554, fol. 50vd: "Ce qe Salomons fu deceuz par fame et renoia deu et adora les ydles senefie le mauves escolier cui deiables engigne et decoit et il renie son creator et devient hom au deiable et deu se corroce a lui."

42. See Marc Bloch, "Les formes de la rupture de l'hommage dans l'ancien droit féodale," in *Mélanges Historiques* (Paris, 1963), 1:189–209; and Jacques le Goff, "The Symbolic Ritual of Vassalage," in *Time, Work, and Culture in the Middle Ages,* trans. Arthur Goldhammer (Chicago, 1980), 237–287.

43. For the form and vocabulary of the ritual of vassalage, see le Goff, "The Symbolic Ritual of Vassalage."

44. Vienna ÖNB cod. 1179, fol. 4B, and Vienna ÖNB cod. 2554, fol. 2B. For an analysis of this latter image, see Camille, *The Gothic Idol,* 90–91.

45. *Historia Scholastica* I.21, PL 198:1072; cited in Camille, *The Gothic Idol,* 91.

46. The tale of Theophilus was first translated from the Greek by Paul the Deacon in the eighth century, was put into verse by Hroswitha of Gandersheim (d. ca. 1003), and appeared as an exemplum in several eleventh- and twelfth-century sermons, including those of Fulbert of Chartres (PL 149:323–324) and Honorius of Autun (PL 172:993).

47. The tale was included in a vernacular collection of Miracles of the Virgin dating to ca. 1218–24 (Gautier de Coinci, *Les miracles de Nostre Dame par Gautier de Coinci,* ed. V. Frederick Koenig [Geneva, 1970],

1:50–177) and was turned into one of the first French miracle plays by Rutebeuf ca. 1260 (Rutebeuf, *Le miracle de Théophile,* ed. and trans. Jean Dufournet [Paris, 1977]). See, too, the twelfth- or thirteenth-century text *Conflictus Salamonis et Marculfi,* which portrays Solomon led astray by lust and ending up the "instrument of the devil"; discussed in Jacques le Goff, "Royauté biblique et idéal monarchique médiéval: Saint Louis et Josias," in *Les juifs au regard de l'histoire: Mélanges en l'honneur de Bernhard Blumenkranz,* ed. Gilbert Dahan (Paris, 1985), 157–167. The popularity of the Theophilus legend in the first half of the thirteenth century is also indicated by its frequent appearances in art. See A. Fryer, "Theophilus the Penitent as Represented in Art," *Archaeological Journal* 92 (1935): 287–333; and Michael W. Cothren, "The Iconography of Theophilus Windows in the First Half of the Thirteenth Century," *Speculum* 59 (1984): 308–341. Cothren asserts (p. 324) that the evocation of contemporary rituals and settings in the thirteenth-century glass programs (many elements of which, he points out, are paralleled in the *Bible moralisée*) heightened the sense of immediacy and thus the moral efficacy of the story.

48. For some examples (only a very small selection of a huge tradition), see J. B. Schneyer, *Die Sittenkritik in den Predigten Philipps des Kanzlers,* Beitrage zur Geschichte der Philosophie und Theologie des Mittelalters 39/4, (Münster, 1963), 8; C. Langlois, *La vie en France au moyen âge, d'après les moralistes du temps* (Paris, 1926); Davy, *Les sermons universitaires,* 90–94; Ch.-V. Langlois, "Sermons parisiens de la première moitié du XIIIe siècle," *Journal des Savants,* n.s. 14 (1916): 550–551.

49. See Davy, *Les sermons universitaires,* 86; and John W. Baldwin, *Masters, Princes, and Merchants: The Social Views of Peter the Chanter and His Circle,* 2 vols. (Princeton, N.J., 1970), 1:151.

50. Stephen C. Ferruolo, *The Origins of the University: The Schools of Paris and Their Critics, 1100–1215* (Stanford, Calif., 1985), 233.

51. Caesarius of Heisterbach, I.32.

52. Stephen of Bourbon, *Anecdotes Historiques,* 308. The *Bible moralisée* also comments that heretics are "too wise" (Vienna ONB cod. 2554, fol. 29vc).

53. Stephen of Bourbon, *Anecdotes Historiques,* 223.

54. An exception to this is the article by Gilbert Dahan, "Salatin, du miracle de Théophile," *Moyen Âge* 83 (1977): 445–468, which concentrates on the connotations of the name and character in Rutebeuf.

55. So, for example, Jacques de Vitry remarks in a sermon section against impious curiosity, "Quanti sunt hodie iudeis similes, qui relicto scripturarum consilio, observant somnis et fantasticas visiones et magis confidunt in somnis et signis quam in divinis scripturis." Paris BN MS lat. nouv. acq. 1537, fol. 229.

56. BN MS nouv. acq. lat. 338, fol. 197: "Nec magistri ad utilitatem audiunt, legunt, nec disputant, sed ut vocantur Rabbi," cited in Charles H. Haskins, "The University of Paris in the Sermons of the Thirteenth Century," AHR 10 (1904): 16; this reading makes considerably more sense than the transcription offered in Davy, *Les sermons universitaires,* 113 n. 2.

57. PL 155:1692.

58. Rutebeuf, *Le miracle de Théophile,* ll. 9–10.

59. Gautier de Coinci, *Les miracles de Nostre Dame par Gautier de Coinci,* vv. 417–418.

60. A high percentage of surviving letters from students to their parents are requests for money—for convenient English translations, see Charles H. Haskins, *Studies in Medieval Culture* (Oxford, 1929), 15–16. The "colleges," in fact, were originally houses of refuge for poor students. See Achille Luchaire, *L'Université de Paris sous Philippe-Auguste* (Paris, 1899), 28–29.

61. Stephen of Bourbon (*Anecdotes historiques,* 317) tells an exemplum about a student whose law books were stolen while he was at Vespers. The student consults a magician, who falsely accuses an innocent relative of the student. Finally, through divine intervention, the real thief confesses and gives the student the address of the Jew with whom he had pawned the books. Of course, it is the thief rather than the student who had recourse to a Jewish pawnbroker, but the exemplum nevertheless conveys the impression of fairly regular overlapping among the worlds of students, Jews, thieves, and pawnbrokers.

62. On the topography of Paris in the early thirteenth century, see Adrien Friedmann, *Paris, ses rues, ses paroisses du moyen âge à la Révolution* (Paris, 1959).

63. Cited in Aryeh Grabois, "The Hebraica Veritas and Jewish-Christian Intellectual Relations in the Twelfth Century," *Speculum* 50 (1975): 631 and n. 90. Interesting, too, is the letter of Innocent III to Philip Augustus complaining about the behavior of French Jews (PL 215: 503). Directly following criticism of Jewish pawnbroking, Innocent remarks that "it has recently been reported that a certain poor scholar had been found murdered in [the Jews'] latrine." The existence of such a rumor suggests that some type of encounter and/or physical proximity between a "poor scholar" and a Jew would not be uncommon.

64. Vienna ÖNB cod. 2554, fol. 52b: "Ce qe la fause prophete decut gad par sa fause prophetie et cil le crei senefie le fas hom mescreant qi par losanges et par fauses promesses decoit le boen escolier et le trait a soi et le torne a la soe partie et le feit pechier et aleir en contre les commandemenz iesu crist."

65. The Latin manuscript also interprets this scene as representing the peril posed by heresy to students, although its commentary is more succinct: "This signifies bad men and infidels who through their false promises try to entice good scholars from the way of virtue." (Vienna ÖNB cod. 1179, fol. 117d: "Hoc significat pravos homines et infideles qui per suas falsas promissiones conantur bonos scolares a via virtute removere.") In the commentary roundel, however, the "infidels" are not depicted as Jews but as ragged and unkempt ascetic figures. One holds a striped cat, while the other reaches out toward two tonsured students.

66. Vienna ÖNB cod. 2554, fol. 35va: "Ce qe les fames vindrent el temple por fere offrande et li prestre les traistrent a els et les decevrent senefie unes simples genz qi vienent devant uns mauves philosofes qi sunt mescreant et cilles enveliment et les decoivent par lor mauveise doctrine."

67. Folio 86a of the Latin manuscript: "Mulieres quae traverunt ad offerendum in templum et decepte fuerunt significant quosdam simplices

qui venerunt coram pravis philosophis et eos per eorum pravum decipiunt documentum."

68. Vienna ÖNB cod. 1179, fol. 108a: "Hoc significat iudeos et publicanos et pravos philosophos qui decipiunt populem per eorum ammonitionem munitas gentes trahunt ad suam fidem per diaboli suggestionem."

69. The conjunction of Jews, heretics, and philosophers also appears on folios 54c, 60b, 79d, 108a, 121b, 125b, 126c, 183b, and 190a of Vienna ÖNB cod. 1179; and folios 10a, 31d, 64vc, 47b, and 56 of Vienna ÖNB cod. 2554. In addition, philosophers are depicted as Jews even when Jews are not explicitly mentioned. See roundels 55vab and 56vc of Vienna ÖNB cod. 2554 and roundel 126c of Vienna ÖNB cod. 1179.

70. Vienna ÖNB cod. 2554, fol. 10a: "La fame qi se clama a son segnor et se plainst de ioseph senefie la synagoge qi se clama as phylosofes et se plainst de iesu crist et le mostre au doi."

71. A very similar commentary text appears on folio 31d of the same manuscript and folio 54c of the Latin manuscript, in which Miriam's reviling of her brother Moses (Num. 12:2) is compared to Synagoga, "who came before the philosophers and cursed Jesus Christ to them." [Vienna ÖNB cod. 2554, fol. 31d: "Ce qe marie mesdist a aron de moyses son frere senefie la synagogue qi vint devant les philosophes et mesdist a els de iesu crist"; Vienna ÖNB cod. 1179, fol. 54c: "Maria que conviciavit fratrem suum coram aaron significat synagogam que coram philosophis dextro filio domini maledixit."] In both commentary roundels, the philosophers are bearded and wear short round caps. (Interestingly, the phrase "to the right of the son of the Lord" describes the philosophers' positions in the corresponding roundel—it may even have been mistakenly [?] copied from the instructions written for or read to the artist.) A still more ambiguous reference to Synagoga's philosophers occurs in the commentary to the Third Book of Kings (19:3). When Jezebel threatens to kill Elijah for having destroyed her priests, the commentary text asserts, "[This] signifies Synagoga who said to Jesus Christ, 'since you have killed and destroyed my philosophers and have taken my [messengers? property?] I will make you die' and the humanity of Christ had fear of death and fled." [Vienna ÖNB cod., fol. 53vc: "Ce qe Gethzabel meneca Helye . . . senefie la Synagogue qui dist a iesu crist por ce qe tu as tue et destruit mes filosofes et les mes a tolu ie te ferai morir et l'umanitei de iesu crist si ot paor de mort et si s'enfui."] The perplexing text—does it refer to events in the past or in the future?—is not clarified by the commentary roundel. Jesus stands beside a rock beneath which lie three dead philosophers. Two are bearded; none wear hats. On the left stands perhaps the strangest representation of Synagoga in all medieval art. A large figure with a blank face and long, loose hair, she wears a Roman-style toga. Around her forehead is tied a snake, which may be a way of associating Synagoga's blindness with the devil. Walter Cahn of Yale University has communicated in private correspondence that he is aware of another thirteenth-century depiction of Synagoga with a serpent tied around her forehead, in the doorway of the church of Saint-Maurice at Épinal. See, too, W. S. Seiferth, *Synagogue and Church in the Middle Ages: Two Symbols in Art and Literature* (New York, 1970). It is possible that the toga may have been inspired by associations of philosophers with pagan culture. The image is not repeated in the comparable roundel in the Latin manuscript, which depicts a more standard Syna-

goga: seated, crowned, and bearing tablets of the Law. I discuss these and other images of Synagoga in a forthcoming article entitled "The Temple is My Body: Gender, Carnality and Synagoga in the *Bible moralisée.*"

72. Paris, BN MS lat. 11994.

73. Thouzellier, *Catharisme et Valdéisme en Languedoc,* 115.

74. Alan of Lille, *Contra Hereticos,* in PL 210:307, 332.

75. Baldwin, *Masters, Princes, and Merchants,* 1:89.

76. On Alan of Lille, see Ferruolo, *Origins of the University,* 244; on Stephen and Absolom, see Luchaire, *L'Université de Paris,* 22–23. René Delègue, *L'Université de Paris, 1224–44* (Paris, 1902), 8, also discusses Parisian masters who were opposed to philosophy; Baldwin (*Masters, Princes, and Merchants,* 1:102–107) lucidly discusses the question of the relationship between theology and philosophy. See also Marie-Thérèse d'Alverny, "Les nouveaux apports dans les domaines de la science et de la pensée au temps de Philippe-Augustue: La Philosophie," in Robert-Henri Bautier, *La France de Philippe Auguste: Le temps des mutations* (Actes du Colloque International organisé par le CNRS, Paris, 1980), 864–880. For further discussion of medieval allegations that philosophy led to heresy, see Gerard Verbeke, "Philosophy and Heresy: Some Conflicts between Reason and Faith," in *The Concept of Heresy in the Middle Ages,* ed. W. Lourdeaux and D. Verhelst, Medievalia Lovaniensia Series I, Studia IV (The Hague, 1976), 172–197.

77. For the text of the decree ordering the burning of the Amaurician heretics and an account of their beliefs, see Henri Denifle, *Chartularium Universitatis Parisiensis,* 4 vols. (Paris, 1891–99; repr., Brussels, 1964), 1:70, nos. 11 and 12. The legal grounds for the trial have recently been reexamined by J. M. M. H. Thijssen, "Master Amalric and the Amalricians: Inquisitorial Procedure and the Suppression of Heresy at the University of Paris," *Speculum* 71 (1996): 43–65.

78. For additional medieval accounts of the condemnations, see Guillaume le Breton, *Gesta Philippi,* in Delaborde, ed., *Oeuvres de Rigord et de Guillaume le Breton,* 2:230–233; Caesarius of Heisterbach, *Dialogus Miraculorum,* 1:304–307; and *Contra Amaurianos.* Luchaire discusses the events in *L'Université de Paris,* 38–40. Other modern analyses of the episode include Marie-Thérese d'Alverny, "Une fragment du procès des Amauriciens," *Archives d'histoire doctrinale et littéraire du moyen âge* 25/26 (1950–51): 325–336; Baldwin, *Masters, Princes, and Merchants,* 1:20; G. C. Capelle, *Autour du Décret de 1210: Amaury de Bène,* Bibliotheque Thomiste 16 (Paris, 1932); Moore, *Origins of European Descent,* 227; and G. Théry, *Autour du décret de 1210: David de Dinant,* Bibliotheque Thomiste 6 (Le Saulchoir, Kain, Belgium, 1925–26).

79. Guillaume le Breton, *Gesta Philippi,* 2:233.

80. For the text of Courson's ban, see Denifle, *Chartularium,* 1:78–79, no. 20.

81. d'Alverny, "Une fragment," 327.

82. For example, Delègue, *L'Université de Paris, 1224–44,* 13; and Fernand van Steenberghen, *Aristotle in the West: The Origins of Latin Aristotelianism,* trans. Leonard Johnston (Louvain, 1955), 73.

83. References to Aristotle in the works of Parisian theologians are collected in D. A. Callus, "Introduction of Aristotelian Learning to Oxford," *Proceedings of the British Academy* 29 (1943): 231.

84. Ferruolo, *Origins of the University,* 183.

85. Jacques de Vitry, *Die Exempla aus den Sermones feriales et communes des Jakob von Vitry,* ed. Joseph Greven (Heidelberg, 1914), 22, no. 28.

86. Cited in Ferruolo, *Origins of the University,* 240.

87. See A. Lecoy de la Marche, *La Chaire française au moyen âge, specialement au XIIIe siècle* (Paris, 1886), 459, 469; and Davy, *Les sermons universitaires,* 235, 253.

88. Noël Valois, *Guillaume d'Auvergne, Éveque de Paris (1228–49): Sa vie et ses ouvrages* (Paris, 1880), 232. On William, see also Jacob Guttmann, *Die Scholastik des Dreizehnten Jahrhunderts in ihren Beziehungen zum Judenthum und zur Jüdischen Literatur* (Breslau, 1902), 9–10, 13–30.

89. For episodes of royal intervention in university affairs, see Luchaire, *L'Université de Paris,* 34–35; Delègue, *L'Université de Paris, 1224–44,* 15–17, 22, 36–46.

90. Charles Petit-Dutaillis, *Étude sur la vie et le règne de Louis VIII (1187–1226)* (Paris, 1894), 4–5.

91. See the remarks of the canonist Henry of Susa that the Fourth Lateran Council had to be circumspect in its condemnation of Amaury because he had powerful supporters; quoted in Robert Lerner, "The Uses of Heterodoxy: The French Monarchy and Unbelief in the Thirteenth Century," *French Historical Studies* 4 (1965): 192.

92. This is speculative, but I base this assumption on the fact that many of the translations were instigated by a very prominent churchman—Archbishop Raymond of Toledo (Guttmann, *Die Scholastik,* 8).

93. Valois, *Guillaume d'Auvergne,* 205–206; Guttmann, *Die Scholastik,* 13–30; Davy, *Les sermons universitaires,* 123. William admired Avicebron so much that he thought he must be Christian (Guttmann, *Die Scholastik,* 12; see, too, Charles Singer, "The Jewish Factor in Medieval Thought," in *The Legacy of Israel,* 259).

94. Guttmann, *Die Scholastik,* 32–46.

95. Beryl Smalley, "William of Auvergne, John de la Rochelle, and St. Thomas Aquinas on the Old Law," in Beryl Smalley, *Studies in Medieval Thought and Learning from Abelard to Wycliff,* 139.

96. *Contra Amaurianos,* 17: "Si iudeus habet cognitionem veritatis, quam habemus, not oportet ut baptizetur."

97. See Jacques Verger, "L'exégèse de l'université," in *Le Moyen Âge et la Bible,* ed. Guy Lobrichon and Pierre Riché (Paris, 1984), 215; Beryl Smalley, *The Study of the Bible in the Middle Ages,* 3d ed. (Oxford, 1984), 255; and the discussion of Jewish-Christian intellectual contacts in chapter 3.

98. Zink, *La prédication en langue romane,* 280.

99. Smalley, *The Study of the Bible in the Middle Ages,* 234.

100. PL 213:749–808, cited in Gilbert Dahan, *La polémique chrétienne contre le judaïsme au Moyen Âge* (Paris, 1991), 100.

101. Davy, *Les sermons universitaires,* 113 n. 2. See, too, the anonymous twelfth- and thirteenth-century glosses on the Bible from the Abbey of St. Victor (Paris, BN MS lat. 14,793, fol. 83v), in which evil biblical figures are interpreted as "heretics, Jews, and philosophers."

102. *De legibus,* cap. 1, in *Opera Omnia,* 2 vols. (Paris, 1964; repr., Frankfurt, 1963).

103. See Aryeh Grabois, "L'exégèse rabbinique," in *Le Moyen Âge et la Bible,* ed. Guy Lobrichon and Pierre Riché (Paris, 1984), 237, 239–241, for an account of the influence of philosophy on twelfth-century Jewish exegetes.

104. For a survey of patristic and early Christian approaches to pagan philosophy, see Pelikan, *Growth of Medieval Theology,* 95–105. Of course, the polemical technique is no means a Christian monopoly: Christian condemnations of philosophy as "Jewish" and therefore unspiritual echo Jewish censure of *hochma yevanit,* "Greek wisdom" voiced, for example, in the Babylonian Talmud.

105. Nicholas M. Haring, "The Liberal Arts in the Sermons of Garnier de Rochefort," *Mediaeval Studies* 30 (1968): 47–77, here p. 51.

106. Vienna ÖNB cod. 1179, fol. 7d: "Quod pagani turrum edificant contra deum ad celum significat quod astrologi et dialetici ceterique philosophi falsa documenta docentes excecati sunt et confusi." In the sermon of Garnier de Rochefort cited earlier, astronomers (synonymous with astrologers in thirteenth-century Scholastic writings) were considered philosophers.

107. The same disciplines are condemned in various terms in many texts and roundels. The "bad children" of Judah whom God destroys (Genesis 38) are held in the French manuscript (Vienna ÖNB cod. 2554, fol. 8b) to signify "astronomers and dialecticians who err against God and nature." They appear in the adjoining roundel as tonsured clerics, one of whom carries a globe or an astrolabe. The comparable Latin commentary text calls these figures "those whose appetite is in glory and confusion"; they are also described as "impious" and "prideful" (Vienna ÖNB cod. 1179, fol. 15b: "Hoc significat quod illos quorum venter est et gloria in confusione. Deus destruit perdit impios et superbos resistit"). There are specific historical in addition to the broader polemical reasons why the vogue for astronomy and dialectic was often presented as a "judaification" of Christian studies. The science of astronomy/astrology was far more advanced in the Islamic world than in the Christian West, and the basic astronomical textbooks were written by Jews and by Muslims. See the collected essays of Bernard R. Goldstein, *Theory and Observation in Ancient and Medieval Astronomy* (London, 1985). Moreover, astrology was closely allied in Scholastic writings to magic and sorcery, with which Jews, in turn, were intimately associated (at least in myth and polemic, as the Theophilus legend demonstrates): see especially R. Po-Chia Hsia, *The Myth of Ritual Murder: Jews and Magic in Reformation Germany* (New Haven, Conn., 1988).

108. Vienna ÖNB cod. 1179, fol. 53d: "Filii israel qui nauseunt manna et petunt carnes significant pravos scolares qui nauseant theologiam et ut fiant divites addiscunt sciencias seculares."

109. In the remark quoted in chapter 2, Peter the Chanter wrote that the money sucked up by usurers was then "vomited" into princes' coffers: PL 205:158. There are images of Jews eating or sucking in coins on Vienna ÖNB cod. 2554, fol. 37d, and Vienna ÖNB cod. 1179, fol. 192c.

110. Vienna ÖNB cod. 1179, fol. 143c: "Quod iudei acceperunt mulieres paganas et cetera significat quod clerici qui non habent in ecclesia sanctum et bonum introitum non intelligunt sanctam evangelium propter legem mundanam quam sciverunt, qui non habent praeter de temporalibus intellectam."

111. The literature on theologians and "secular studies" in Paris is large and expanding rapidly. See Baldwin, *Masters, Princes, and Merchants,* 1:77–87; Haring, "The Liberal Arts"; d'Alverny, "Les nouveaux apports"; Jean Chatillon, "Le mouvement théologique dans la France de Philippe-Auguste," in *La France de Philippe Auguste: Le temps des mutations* (Actes du Colloque International organisé par le CNRS, Paris, 1980), ed. Robert-Henri Bautier (Paris, 1982); Schneyer, *Die Sittenkritik;* Langlois, "Sermons parisiens"; and Haskins, "University of Paris." Some interesting contemporary texts include Stephen Langton, *Commentary on the Book of Chronicles,* ed. Avrom Saltman (Ramat Gan, 1978), 171, attacking "decretists and pseudo-legists"; and the sermon literature collected in Jacques de Vitry, *Die Exempla aus den Sermones feriales et communes des Jakob von Vitry,* ed. Joseph Greven (Heidelberg, 1914), 19, no. 20; Davy, *Les sermons universitaires,* 253; and Lecoy de la Marche, *La Chaire,* 485. Diatribes against secular studies appear throughout the sermons in Paris, BN MS lat. 17509.

112. Vienna ÖNB cod. 1179, fol. 89b: "Filii israel . . . significant pravos scolares qui relinquiunt evangelium et theologiam et intrant Boloniam ut possint leges et decreta discere quibus ipsismet confundantur."

113. Vienna ÖNB cod. 2554, fol. 37b: "Ce qe li fil isrl alerent en paenie por armes avoir et li sarrazin lor fistrent et lor baillerent senefie les mauves escoliers qi leissent les evvangiles et la devinitei et vont a Bologne por aprendre lois et decrez et cil lor baillent et lor ensegnent tel chose qi les confont et destruit." The relation of this text to Honorius III's bull *Super Speculum,* which prohibited the study of civil law in Paris, is discussed by Reiner Haussherr, "Eine Warnung vor dem Studium von ziuilem und kanonischen recht in der *Bible moralisée,*" *Frühmittelalterforschung der Universität Munster* 9 (1975): 400–403; see, too, Michael Camille, "Visual Signs of the Sacred Page: Books in the *Bible moralisée,*" *Word and Image* 5 (1989): 111–130; and James Michael Heinlen, "The Ideology of Reform in the French Moralized Bible" (Ph.D. diss., Northwestern University, 1991), 181.

114. This aspect of heretical thought does not help identify the specific sect of heretics referred to. Denial of the sacraments was one of the most common of all heretical beliefs, shared by many different sects. Because in the wake of Gregorian reforms the Church laid ever greater emphasis on the role of the priesthood, all heresies necessarily had to confront the issue of the sacraments. Many twelfth-century heterodox sects either modified or entirely rejected the Catholic sacraments, particularly infant baptism and the Eucharist. For a Catholic description of Cathar rejection of the sacraments, see Alan of Lille, *Contra Hereticos,* in PL 210: 345–369. A Waldensian work against Cathars claimed to be defending the sacraments against all who calumniate them (Thouzellier, *Catharisme et Valdéisme en Languedoc,* 78). According to the *Contra Amaurianos,* 17–18, and Capelle, *Autour du Décret,* 35, the Amauricians claimed to have no need for the sacraments.

115. Vienna ÖNB cod. 1179, fol. 96b: "Servientes petentes nabal ipsi david ad comedendum et nabal ignorat ipsum et dehonestat et nuncios iesu cristi significant prelatos qui comparent coram infidelibus et publicanis et dicunt quod iesus cristus mandat eisque dabit eis ad comedendum et ridentque eum ignorant nec volunt ipsem esse suum dominum sed blasphemant."

116. See chapter 3.

117. Vienna ÖNB cod. 2554, fol. 30d: "Ce qe cil se gaba de deu et li fist la moe et dist mal de lui senefie les mescreanz et les populicanz qi se gabent de deu et de son sacrement et dient qe ce n'est riens . . ."

118. The story is recounted in eight text/roundel pairs that appear on folios 79 and 80 of the Latin manuscript and folios 64v, 65r, and 65v of the French manuscript.

119. Several discrepancies with the Vulgate version of this episode may be noted. The events are set in Bethlehem rather than in the Benjaminite city of Gaba. The men who come to abuse the deacon are called Sodomites, implying that they wished to sexually molest him, whereas the Vulgate text calls them "filii Belial (Absque iugo)," indicating that they were workingmen of low extraction.

120. This personification thus exemplifies once more the relative prominence of gender/femaleness in the vernacular manuscript.

121. Vienna ÖNB cod. 1179, fol. 79a: "Diaconus . . . significat bonos philosophos qui fuerunt inops in mundo de fide ihu xpi. Ille bonus homo qui eum hospitatus est significat ihm xpm qui philosophie in sua ecclesia dedit locum." Vienna ÖNB cod. 2554, fol. 64vd: "Ce qe li Dyakenes fu esgarez d'ostel en Bethlehem et li prudom le herberia senefie philosophie qi fu esgaree par le mi le monde de la creance et ihu crist la prist et la voia en sainte eglise."

122. Vienna ÖNB cod. 1179, fol. 79b: "Sodomite . . . significant infideles et publicanos qui veniunt ad sanctam ecclesiam ut eam destruant cum suis sacramentis, sed eam deus custodit et defendit." Vienna ÖNB cod. 2554, fol. 65a: "Ce qe li Sodomite vienent a l'ostel au proudome por prendre le Dyakene et li prudome le defent senefie les populicanz et les mescreanz qi vulent depecier et abatre le sacrement de sainte eglise et Dex la defent et garde."

123. Vienna ÖNB cod. 1179, fol. 79c and d: "Sodomite . . . significant infideles et publicanos qui abstulerunt philosophiam paganorum a Jeronimo et ab Augustino et illi grave sustinentes et mina inferentes super hoc doluerunt." "Sodomite . . . significant publicanos qui accipiunt philosophiam et ad nichilam et eam sub suis pedibus ponunt et conculcant." Vienna ÖNB cod. 2554, fol. 65b and c: "Ce qe li sodomite pristrent la fame . . . senefie les populicans et les mescreanz qi tolirent la filosophie des paiens a ierome et a augustine et cil le suffrirent et dolant en furent et dient q'ancore le comparront." "Ce qe li sodomite pristrent la fame et iurent a li a force et la tuerent senefie les populicans et les mescreanz qi prenent phylosophie et tuent et escachent et martirent et li tolent sa vertu."

124. Vienna ÖNB cod. 1179, fol. 80a: "Sodomite . . . significat publicanos et infideles qui eiciunt philosophiam et doctrinam paganorum et Jeroniumus et Augustinus eam recipientes super hoc graviter doluerunt." Vienna ÖNB cod. 2554, fol. 65d: "Ce qe li sodomite mistrent fors de lor ostel la fame . . . senefie les populicans et les mescreanz qi botent en sus dels phylosophie et la doctrine des paiens et ieromes et augustins la recoivent dolant."

125. Vienna ÖNB cod. 1179, fol. 80b and c: "Diaconus . . . significat ieronimum et augustinum qui philosophiam accipientes extra duram doctrinam paganorum posuerunt." "Diaconum . . . significat Jeroni-

mum et Augustinum qui tradiderunt xii patriarchis xii volumina ut ea ad apostolos duodecim aportarent." Vienna ÖNB cod. 2554, fol. 65va and b: "Ce qe li dyakenes trussa sa fame . . . senefie ierome et augustin qi pristrent filosophie et la mistrent ius de l'asne ce fu la dure doctrine des paiens." "Ce qe li Dyakenes depieca sa fame . . . ce senefie Jereume et augustin qi baillerent a xii patriarches les xii volumes por porter les as xii apostles." The twelve patriarchs are the subject of a treatise by Richard of St. Victor, translated and introduced by Grover A. Zinn: Richard of St. Victor, *The Twelve Patriarchs, The Mystical Ark, Book Three of the Trinity* (New York, Ramsay, and Toronto, 1979); they also figure prominently in Joachim of Fiore's tripartite scheme of history. On the twelve volumes, an otherwise curious phrase, see the comment of Chanter cited in Buc, *L'Ambiguïté du Livre,* 165 n. 97. The *Testament of the Twelve Patriarchs* was an early apocryphal work.

126. A black cloak over a white robe is usually identified as a Dominican habit. In fact, Dominic adopted a modified version of the rule for Augustinian canons, and the Dominican habit is identical to the Augustinian habit (see *Liber Ordinis Sancti Victoris Parisiensis,* ed. Lucas Jocque and Louis Milis [Turnhout, Belgium, 1984]). Since there are otherwise no traces of mendicants in this manuscript, since the figure represents Augustine, and since this commentary sequence is redolent with the intellectual legacy of the Augustinian Abbey of St.-Victor de Paris, I am reading this figure as an Augustinian canon.

127. As I suggested earlier, in its reverence of Jerome and Augustine, its construction of Philosophy as the handmaiden of theology, its echoing of *The Twelve Patriarchs* of Richard of St. Victor, its preoccupation with student morality, and its interest in but also concern regarding literal exegesis, this sequence and much of the Heptateuch commentary very closely echoes themes central to the Victorine spiritual and exegetical tradition. It will be remembered that Branner proposed the Abbey of St.-Victor as the site of redaction. There is, of course, no way to verify this, and in itself closeness to the Victorine exegetical tradition means little. The Victorines were the official confessors to the university student body; many were also university teachers, and anyone with a university education or a connection to a Parisian diocese would have had access to Victorine thought. It is, however, interesting that both Philip Augustus and Louis VIII seemed to have felt particularly close to the Victorine order: Philip directed that the abbey to be founded in honor of his victory at Bouvines be Victorine, and the Victorines benefited from the most generous bequests in Louis's will.

128. See Miri Rubin, *Corpus Christi: The Eucharist in Late Medieval Culture* (Cambridge, 1991), 17–19, 52–54.

129. On Host desecration accusations, see Miri Rubin, "Desecration of the Host: The Birth of an Accusation," *Studies in Church History* 29 (1992): 169–185.

130. This comment, which accords with my own observations, was offered by Miri Rubin at the conference "The Body of Christ" at Rice University, Houston, Texas, in November 1995.

131. Pseudo-Praepositinus of Cremona, *The Summa Contra Hereticos Ascribed to Praepositinus of Cremona,* ed. James A. Corbett and Joseph N. Garvin (Notre Dame, Ind., 1958).

132. The bibliography on the Albigensians, also called the Cathars, is extensive. See, most recently, Malcolm Lambert, *The Cathars* (London, 1998). For Cathar exegesis, see Shulamith Shahar, "The Relationship between Kabbalism and Catharism in the South of France," in *Les juifs dans l'histoire de France,* ed. Myriam Yardeni (Leiden, 1980), 56–58.

133. Malcolm Lambert, *Medieval Heresy: Popular Movements from the Gregorian Reform to the Reformation,* 2d ed. (Oxford, 1992), 72–74, 118–121.

134. On Catholic-heretical scriptural polemic, see the introduction to the *Summa Contra Hereticos* and the accompanying bibliography.

135. Vienna ÖNB cod. 2554, fol. 65vd: "Ce qe li peuples israel [vienent] devant Bethleem por prendre veniance del mesfet et cil ne les priserent gaires senefie les apostles qi sasemblerent et la vertu de lor paroles coru par tot le munde et li populicant priserent molt petit et els et lors paroles."

136. An accessible contemporary definition of heresy appears in the 1231 decretal of Gregory IX translated in Edward Peters, ed., *Heresy and Authority in Medieval Europe: Documents in Translation* (Philadelphia, 1985), 196–197; see the discussions and further references in Yves Dossat, *Église et hérésie en France au XIIIe siècle* (London, 1982), 48–50; and Lambert, *Medieval Heresy,* 5.

137. As mentioned in note 2, doctrinal issues are strikingly absent from the texts and images dealing with heresy (if one excludes from the rubric of antiheretical polemic the ubiquitous affirmations of basic Catholic doctrine. On this, see the remarks of Walter Cahn in his article "Heresy and the Interpretation of Romanesque Art," in *Romanesque and Gothic: Essays for George Zarnecki,* ed. Neil Stratford [Woodbridge, Suffolk, and Wolfeboro, N.H., 1987], 27–33).

138. Vienna ÖNB cod. 1179, fol. 225a: "Per Jezebel significantur magistri hereticorum qui vivunt in voluptate carnali et docent contra evangelium. Tales christiani non debent inter eos sustinere . . ."

139. For example, a twelfth-century bestiary connects demons from the Book of the Apocalypse to frogs, which "symbolize heretics and their demons who linger at the banquet of the decadent senses . . ." *Bestiary,* trans. Barber, 116.

140. See Cothren, "Iconography of Theophilus Windows," 308–341.

141. The episode of the golden calf has already been cited in chapter 3 as providing a forum in the Latin manuscript for accusing Jews of devil worship; in the French manuscript the charge encompasses heretics as well: "That the people of Moses adored the Calf they had created signifies the *miscreants* and the *populicanz* who form the Devil against the command of God, and believe in the he-goat and adore it." (Vienna ÖNB cod. 2554, fol. 25va: "Ce qe li peuples Moyses aora le torel qe il avoit formei senefie les mescreanz et les populicanz qi forment contre le commandement deu le deiable et croient en boc et laorent.") Unlike the commentary image in the Latin manuscript, the roundel in the French manuscript does not emphasize the Jewishness of the devil worshipers but depicts them with short, round caps or bareheaded.

142. Vienna ÖNB cod. 1179, fol. 165c: "Hoc significat quod heretici pervertunt sacram scripturam et exponunt ad libitum suum et magis eos significat qui bona sancte ecclesie mali et in malis expendunt."

143. Vienna ÖNB cod. 1179, fol. 236d: "Hoc significat dampnationem illorum qui scripturas corrumpunt et mutaverunt dulcedinem scripture in fetorem sensus carnalis ut fecerunt heretici maledicti." Compare with this quote from the *Liber contra Haereticos* of Evrard de Béthune: "Holy Scripture is sweet to those who live spiritually, but bitter to carnal people," cited in Manselli, "La polémique," 258.

144. Thouzellier, *Catharisme et Valdéisme en Languedoc,* 55. Such accusations against the Waldensians were extremely common, provoked by the fact that they translated the Scriptures into the vernacular and used them to preach without authority. Stephen of Bourbon records that Waldo himself was known to have commissioned a Romance translation of Scripture because he was unable to read Latin (Stephen of Bourbon, *Anecdotes Historiques,* 291). See Leonard E. Boyle, "Innocent III and Vernacular Versions of Scripture," in *The Bible in the Medieval World: Essays in Memory of Beryl Smalley,* ed. Katherine Walsh and Diane Woods (Oxford, 1985), 97–107.

145. PL 214:71.

146. Quoted in Thouzellier, *Catharisme et Valdéisme en Languedoc,* 117 n. 44: "utuntur tamen auctoritatibus scripturarum immo non utuntur sed abutuntur, quia nequeunt ratione demonstrare quod dicunt . . . adulterantes ea (scripturas) per pravum littere intellectum possint ea trahere ad perfidiam suam."

147. Stephen of Bourbon, *Anecdotes Historiques,* 309.

148. See the discussion in Thouzellier, *Catharisme et Valdéisme en Languedoc,* 222–223. I am presently preparing an article on sexual rhetoric in the polemics of the Albigensian Crusade.

149. Quoted in Manselli, "La polémique," 257.

150. Manichaeans were also known as Paulicians; it has been suggested (Du Cange, vol. 6) that *publicani* is a corruption of this word. Milan Loos (*Dualist Heresy in the Middle Ages* [Prague, 1974], 118 and 126 n. 109) speculates that the name, which was used in the *Gesta Francorum* to refer to members of the army of the "infidels," may have been derived from the town Philippopolis.

151. See Douglas R. A. Hare, "The Rejection of the Jews in the Synoptic Gospels and *Acts,*" in *Antisemitism and the Foundations of Christianity,* ed. Alan T. Davies (New York, 1979), 27–47.

152. See, for example, Matt. 18:17, where Jesus teaches that one who doesn't "listen to the church" should be regarded an *ethicus et publicanus.*

Chapter 5. In an Eternal Fire

1. For a particularly hysterical articulation of this position, see Norman Cohn, *The Pursuit of the Millennium,* rev. ed. (New York, 1970), which suggests (p. 79) that Jews were (repeatedly? occasionally?) attacked by "turbulent masses swept by eschatological hopes and fears." Andrew Colin Gow, *The Red Jews: Antisemitism in an Apocalyptic Age, 1200–1600* (Leiden, New York, and Cologne, 1995), argues that crescendoing eschatological expectation was largely responsible for later medieval anti-Judaism; Gow cites interesting sources, but his main thesis, in my view, is overstated. More measured statements of the same thesis include Je-

remy Cohen, *The Friars and the Jews: The Evolution of Medieval Antisemitism* (Ithaca, N.Y., 1982), 246–247; Allan Cutler, "Innocent III and the Distinctive Clothing of Jews and Muslims," *Studies in Medieval Culture* 3 (1970): 92–116; and Hyam Maccoby, *Judaism on Trial: Jewish-Christian Disputations in the Middle Ages* (London and Washington, D.C., 1993), 5–6.

2. Note, however, that in Rom. 11:26 Paul holds that eventually all Israel will be saved.

3. Although in the early Christian tradition Apocalypse was often read as an allegory about the present age rather than the end of time, as early as the Carolingian period and certainly by the twelfth century it came to be understood primarily as an eschatological text. Yves Christe, "The Apocalypse in the Monumental Art of the Eleventh through Thirteenth Centuries," in *The Apocalypse in the Middle Ages,* ed. Richard K. Emmerson and Bernard McGinn (Ithaca, N.Y., and London, 1992), 237.

4. For a recent bibliography of medieval commentaries on Apocalypse, see Richard K. Emmerson and Ronald B. Herzman, *The Apocalyptic Imagination in Medieval Literature* (Philadelphia, 1992), 223–227. The best study is probably Guy Lobrichon, *L'Apocalypse des théologiens au XIIe siècle* (Paris, 1979). Useful compilations of medieval eschatological texts include *La fin des temps: Terreurs et prophéties au Moyen Âge,* trans. Claude Carozzi and Huguette Taviani-Carozzi (Paris, 1982); and *Apocalyptic Spirituality: Treatises and Letters of Lactantius, Adso of Montier-ender, Joachim of Fiore, the Franciscan Spirituals, Savonarola,* trans. Bernard McGinn (New York, 1979).

5. The section "On the End of the World" in Hugh of St. Victor's *On the Sacraments of the Christian Faith (De Sacramentis),* trans. Roy J. Deferrari (Cambridge, Mass., 1951), for example, is derived entirely from Augustine.

6. Serm. Caillau et Saint-Yves II, 11, *Miscel. Agostin,* I.255–264; discussed in Bernhard Blumenkranz, "Augustine et les juifs, Augustin et le judaïsme," reprinted in Blumenkranz, *Juifs et Chrétiens Patristique et Moyen Âge* (London, 1977), 235.

7. Blumenkranz ("Augustine et les juifs") certainly reads Augustine in this way, calling his vision an "entrée massive des juifs dans l'église."

8. Augustine of Hippo, *De civitate Dei* 20.30, *Corpus Christianorum Series Latina* 48 (Turnhout, Belgium, 1955), 755–758.

9. There is as yet no comprehensive study of Jews in medieval Christian eschatological thought (Robert E. Lerner is reportedly preparing a study of Jews in Joachite eschatology); what follows will therefore be but a very preliminary and general sketch of a vast and complex topic. For an analysis of the subject in the works of one later thirteenth-century thinker, see Robert E. Lerner, "Millénarisme littérale et vocation des juifs chez Jean de Roquetaillade," *Mélanges de l'École Française de Rome: Moyen Âge* 102 (1990): 311–315.

10. Hugh of St. Victor, *On the Sacraments of the Christian Faith (De Sacramentis),* 453.

11. Quoted in Gilbert Dahan, "Exégèse et polémique dans les commentaires de la Genèse d'Étienne Langton," in *Les juifs au regard de l'histoire: Mélanges en l'honneur de Bernhard Blumenkranz,* ed. Gilbert Dahan (Paris, 1985), 148.

12. Avranches, Bibliothèque de la Ville, MS 16, fols. 64ff., quoted in Adolf Katzenellenbogen, *The Sculptural Programs of Chartres Cathedral* (New York and London, 1964), 135 n. 129 (my translation).

13. Inq. III Tract. VIII. Sect. I. Quaest. I Tit. II—740 (Alexander of Hales, *Summa Theologica,* vol. 3, ed. Bonaventure Marrani [Florence, 1930], 729–730). On this titulus, see chapter 3.

14. On Joachim and the conversion of the infidels, see Benjamin Z. Kedar, *Crusade and Mission: Europeans Approaches toward the Muslims* (Princeton, N.J., 1984), 112–116. On Joachite eschatology in general, see Marjorie Reeves, *Joachim of Fiore and the Prophetic Future* (New York, 1977); Emmerson and Herzman, *Apocalyptic Imagination,* 1–35; E. Randolph Daniel, "Joachim of Fiore: Patterns of History in the Apocalypse," in *Apocalypse in the Middle Ages,* ed. Richard K. Emmerson and Bernard McGinn (Ithaca, N.Y., and London, 1992), 72–88.

15. PL 207:863.

16. Peter the Venerable, *Adversus Judaeorum Inveteratam Duritiam,* ed. Yvonne Friedman (Turnhout, Belgium, 1985), xxii.

17. Bernard McGinn, *Antichrist: Two Thousand Years of the Human Fascination with Evil* (San Francisco, 1994), 127.

18. See R. Emmerson, *Antichrist in the Middle Ages: A Study of Medieval Apocalypticism, Art, and Literature* (Seattle, 1981), 79–83; Suzanne Lewis, "*Tractatus Adversus Judaeos* in the Gulbenkian Apocalypse," *Art Bulletin* 68 (1986): 555–556. Joshua Trachtenberg, *The Devil and the Jews: The Medieval Conception of the Jew and Its Relation to Modern Antisemitism* (New Haven, Conn., 1943; reprint with introduction by Marc Saperstein, Philadelphia, 1983), devotes an entire chapter to "Antichrist" (pp. 32–43), but note that in spite of the book's subtitle most of his sources are postmedieval. Gow, *The Red Jews,* cites numerous examples of increasingly sinister descriptions of Jews' place in apocalyptic thought, although, as noted earlier, I find his main thesis generally unpersuasive.

19. For this reason I do not concentrate primarily on the illustrations of the Apocalypse of John in Vienna ÖNB cod. 1179. On this cycle, see Yves Christe, "La cité de la Sagesse," *Cahiers de Civilisation Médiévale* 31 (1988): 29–35.

20. PL 91:923–934. Bede's commentary is the main source for the *Glossa ordinaria* commentary to Tobias; in the *Glossa,* however, Bede's commentary appears in a considerably more abridged form than is found in the *Bible moralisée.* The cycle of Tobit and Tobias appears in the archivolt of the North Transept at Chartres, which is roughly contemporary to the *Bible moralisée* (ca. 1210–25); Katzenellenbogen (*Sculptural Programs of Chartres Cathedral,* 72–73) explicates its appearance there with reference to Bede's commentary.

21. Vienna ÖNB cod. 1179, fol. 181b: "Fel piscis malitiam significat diaboli quam priusquam iudaicus populus cognoverit operantem in antichristo, postquam dominus eum de medio subtraxerit in fine mundi fide christi omnes illuminabuntur." My translation of this passage is somewhat tentative—the temporal progression differs slightly from that in Bede. See PL 91:934 for the parallel commentary in Bede, but note that Bede makes no mention of the Antichrist. The line is not incorporated at all into the *Glossa ordinaria,* at least in the Strassburg edition of 1480/81 (*Biblia Latina cum Glossa Ordinaria: Facsimile Reprint of the Editio Prin-*

ceps Adolph Rusch of Strassburg 1480/81, 4 vols., intro. Karlfried Froehlich and Margaret T. Gibson [Turnhout, Belgium, 1992], 2:339–340).

22. For another positive representation of the Jews' conversion, see Vienna ÖNB cod. 1179, fol. 225c, which illustrates the commentary text to Apoc. 3:7–12: "Hoc quod promittit iudeos adorare ad pedes eorum et quod eos a magna temptatione conservabit significat quod in adventu antichristi convertentur ad fidem iudei et deum in sancta ecclesia adorabunt . . ." ("That he promised the Jews [that he will make them] adore at their feet and that he will preserve them from great temptation signifies that at the coming of the Antichrist Jews will be converted to the faith and will adore God in the Holy Church . . .")

23. Vienna ÖNB cod. 1179, fol. 118c: "Hoc significat quod iesus christus comparuit coram iudeis et infidelibus et dixit eis quod spiritus sanctus non descendet in eis donec precipiat, scilicet, in die iudicii, quando omnino penitentes de peccatis et complendo mandata domini ad fidem recipientur christianam."

24. Vienna ÖNB cod. 2554, fol. 52va: "Ce q'elye vint a acab et li dist qi il ne ploueroit mes en sa terre devant ce qe il commandast senefie iesu crist qi vint devant les gieus et devant toz cels qe deiauble ont enbaillie et lors dist li sainz esperiz ne descendera sor vos devant ce qe ie le commanderai ce iert au ior del juise qe vos vos repenterez et guerpirez vostre fole creance." Note the similarity of the wording of this text to the *Adversus Judaeorum* of Peter the Venerable, who refers (p. 74) to the *insania erroris* of the Jewish religion. He also, like this image, stressed the Jews' link to the devil.

25. Vienna ÖNB cod. 2554, fol. 48vb: "Ce qe David ne polt eschaufeu par la couverture senefie iesu crist qi ne polt eschaifeir de l'amor as gieus. Ce qe David s'eschaufa de la pucele sens engendreir rien de li senefie iesu crist qi au ior del iuise s'eschaufera de la synagogue sens engendreir rien de li."

26. Vienna ÖNB cod. 1179, fol. 111a: "Hoc significat iesum christum qui non potuit calefieri morte [*sic*] iudeorum. David . . . significat iesum christum qui in die iudicii incipiet calefieri per synagogam sine ipsius sinagoge generatione."

27. This association is stressed, moreover, in a text appearing a few folios earlier, which in explicating II Kings 6:20–23 comments, "[That David told Michol that she would die together with her children because she mocked him] signifies Jesus Christ cursing Synagoga who mocked him and she was dying in a most horrible death together with her children." (Vienna ÖNB cod. 1179, fol. 103a: "Hoc significat ihm xpm maledicentem synagogam que ei illusit et ipsa cum parvulis morte pessima moriebatur.") Note that the *Bible moralisée* alters the biblical narrative to considerably increase the severity of Michol's (and thus of Synagoga's) offense and punishment. Note, too, that the "mistake" in the III Kings 1:1 commentary, if it is such, is replicated in Oxford Bodleian MS 270b, fol. 161a.

28. This question is, of course, indirectly answered in the many images labeling Jews *filii diaboli.*

29. Vienna ÖNB cod. 2554, fol. 6d: "Ce q'Esau vint apres por demandeir sa beneicon et li peres li dist qe iacob l'emportoit senefie le gieus et les mescreans qi vendrunt au ior del iugement devant ihesu crist por sa

beneicon et il lo dira trop avez tardie li crestien l'emportent." On interpretations of Cain and Abel, of which this is a typical example, see Gilbert Dahan, "L'exégèse de l'histoire de Caïn et Abel du XIIe au XIVe s. en Occident," RTAM 49 (1982): 46–48; and Ruth Mellinkoff, *The Mark of Cain* (Berkeley and Los Angeles, 1981).

30. The comparable image in the Latin manuscript (Vienna ÖNB cod. 1179, fol. 12a) also depicts Jews with moneybags.

31. See Emile Mâle, *The Gothic Image: Religious Art in France of the Thirteenth Century,* trans. Dora Nussey (New York, 1982), 356–383.

32. This image thus implies what is stated explicitly in other commentary texts: Vienna ÖNB cod. 1179, fol. 237d, for example, runs, "This signifies the damnation of the worldly and the rich of this world, who through temporal goods are made waste, far from all spiritual good." ("Hoc significat dampnationem terrenorum et mundi divitum, qui per bona temporalia ab omni bono spirituali silvestres efficiuntur.") On the association of Jews with greed, and the use of "Jewish greed" to define Christian deviants, see chapters 2 and 4.

33. The commentary glosses Exod. 12:29, in which the angel of death is sent to kill the firstborn of Egypt. Here, the imagery resembles traditional Last Judgment scenes, but it gains novel impact when juxtaposed with anti-Jewish texts.

34. Vienna ÖNB cod. 2554, fol. 20vd: "Ce qe li angles trespassa les seignies et tua les non seignies senefie qe li angles trespassera les boens au ior del iugement et detrechera les mescreanz et les populicanz et les trabuchera en enfer."

35. Vienna ÖNB cod. 1179, fol. 126a: "Hoc significat infideles et publicanos superbe consulentes ihesum christum de sua pessima fide quos ad voluntatem ihesu christi in corpore et anima ignis gehenne devoravit."

36. Vienna ÖNB cod. 2554, fol. 56va: "Ce qe li message vindrent a Helye demandeir conseil et il furent ars furent ars [*sic*] par lor orgoel senefie mescreanz et populicans qi venent devant iesu crist et demandent conseil de lor maladie ce est de lor fole creance par rapoines et li feus descendi par la priere de iesu crist qi toz les destruist." This text is part of an extended and apparently somewhat garbled commentary sequence (due perhaps to the loss of an intermediary Latin text); at one point (Vienna ÖNB cod. 2554, fol. 56b), the Jews are said to ask their own lord Bitzebuch for help.

37. Vienna ÖNB cod. 2554, fol. 56vc: "Elija . . . senefie iesu crist qi vint devant les mauves phylosofes et devant les granz meistres de la loi et lor dist qe il morroent et seroent dampnei et cors et ame et trabuchie en enfer."

38. The number of commentaries touching upon hell and damnation that do *not* refer to Jews in the texts and/or images is negligible.

39. Vienna ÖNB cod. 1179, fol. 181a: "Hoc significat fideles in fine mundi qui cum nimio gaudio current ad fidem iesu christi."

40. See discussion in chapter 1. Very similar compositions appear on folios 178d and 213b of the same manuscript.

41. Vienna ÖNB cod. 2554, fol. 43va: "Ce qe li autre sa corderent a hysbozet et le tindrent por lor signeor senefie qe li gieu et li populican et tuit li mauves sa corderont a antecrist et le tendront por lor signeor et diront qe il ne doit estre autre rois."

42. The bribing of the powerful by Jews (and anyone else who could afford it) for protection or for special privileges was both a frequent actual event and a recurrent literary topos. See, among too many texts to mention, Rigord's remark that on the eve of their expulsion from the Île-de-France the Jews attempted to win the support of counts, barons, archbishops, and bishops "donis et promissionibus magnis" (*Oeuvres de Rigord et de Guillaume le Breton,* ed. H. Delaborde [Paris, 1882], 1:28), and his description of a countess who protected Jews as "magnis muneribus Judeorum corrupta" (1:118–119).

43. Vienna ÖNB cod. 1179, fol. 101b: "Judeos et publicanos et omnes malignos qui eligent antichrist in regem et eum pro domino habebunt et pro deo adorabunt."

44. Another visual model for the position of Antichrist's arms is the blessing of Ephraim and Menasseh by Jacob (Gen. 48:14). This scene is interpreted in the French *Bible moralisée* (Vienna ÖNB cod. 2554, fol. 14va) as a figure for Jesus' Crucifixion; in turn, the significance of the Crucifixion (according to the commentary text and image) is the election of Christians and the rejection of the Jews: "Ce qe iacob croisa ses mains et mist sa destre main sor celui qi d'arrierement fu nez senefie le pere del ciel qi fist la croiz de son fil et dona sa beneicon as d'arrierement nez enfanz ce fu as cretiens." In the image, the crucified Jesus is flanked by, on his right, a young crowned and praying Holy Church and, on his left, Synagoga and three Jews bending down and away.

45. See Emmerson, *Antichrist;* and Bernard McGinn, "Portraying Antichrist in the Middle Ages," in *The Use and Abuse of Eschatology in the Middle Ages,* ed. Werner Verbeke, Daniel Verhelst, and Andries Welkenhuysen (Louvain, 1988), 1–48.

46. See Janet Martin Soskice, *Metaphor and Religious Language* (Oxford, 1985), 57–58: "A strong metaphor compels new possibilities of vision."

47. Vienna ÖNB cod. 1179, fol. 55b: "Maria qui lacrimata est et penitur significat iudeos et omnes peccatores qui penitant de peccatis. Moyses et Aaron orantes pro ea significant Petrum et Paulum qui orant pro peccatoribus quos deus orando recipit."

48. Vienna ÖNB cod. 2554, fol. 31vc: "Ce qe Marie se repenti de sa folie et Moyses et Aaron prirent a deu por li senefie les gieus et les mescreanz et toz autres pecheors qi ferunt repentant de lor forfes *devant* le ior del juise et Sanz Pere et Sainz Pol prerunt a deu por els" (my emphasis).

49. This revision to the Bible text was noted by James Michael Heinlen, "The Ideology of Reform in the French Moralized Bible" (Ph.D. diss., Northwestern University, 1991), 60 n. 62. Similar adjustments of the biblical text (usually to magnify the trespasses of evildoers) are evident in the treatment of Exod. 8:15 (Vienna ÖNB cod. 1179, fol. 26d, and Vienna ÖNB cod. 2554, fol. 19d) and as discussed elsewhere.

50. Neither the contemporary popes nor Peter the Chanter nor any of his followers explicitly stated or even hinted that the conversion of Jews had to be effected immediately. Peter the Chanter's traditionalism vis-à-vis the Jews is highlighted in Gilbert Dahan, "L'Article *Iudei* de la *Summa Abel* de Pierre Chantre," *Revue des études augustiniennes* 27 (1981): 105–126. A letter of Innocent III to Philip Augustus concerning the Jews (1205) displays no impatience concerning their conversion:

"Though it does not displease God, but is even acceptable to Him, that the Jewish Dispersion should live and serve under Catholic kings and Christian princes until such time as their remnant shall be saved . . ." PL 215:502; text and partial translation in Solomon Grayzel, ed., *The Church and the Jews in the XIIIth Century* (Philadelphia, 1933), 104–105.

51. See note 1.

52. *On the Sacraments of the Christian Faith (De Sacramentis),* 467.

53. Vienna ÖNB cod. 2554, fol. 26c: "Ce qe Moyses apela toz les amis deu et lor comanda tuer cels qi avoient meserre senefie l'apostoile qi apele tres toz les boens prelaz et lors dist prenez livre et chandoile et si escomeniez toz les usuriers et les populicans et toz les mescreanz." Fol. 26d: "Ce qe li fill israel tuerent cels qi avoient aorei l'eveel et boterent fors del tabernacle senefie les boens prelaz qi vienent a tot lors chandoiles et a tot lors livres et si escomenient toz les usuriers et toz les pupulicanz et les mescreanz et botent fors de sainte eglise."

54. Vienna ÖNB cod. 1179, fol. 38b: "Hoc significat apostolos qui precipiunt prelatis ut feneratores pupplicanos et iudeos excommunicent et eorum auctoritate ab ecclesia expellantur."

55. Vienna ÖNB cod. 1179, fol. 38c: "Hoc significat bonos prelatos qui per evangelica verba pravos feneratores extra ecclesia expellant et excommunicent."

56. The vindictiveness conveyed by this expression is particularly striking in view of the fact that Stephen Langton used this same biblical text as the springboard for an exemplum whose moral states that "the sentence of excommunication should not be done with rancor or hatred . . ." ("Sententia enim ecclesiastica fieri debet non ex rancore vel odio sed ex amore, ut occasione sententie alii convertantur ad gremium eccelsiae.") Beryl Smalley, "Exempla in the Commentaries of Stephen Langton," *Bulletin of the John Rylands Library* 17 (1933): 125.

57. Vienna ÖNB cod. 1179, fols. 48a (Jesus orders that all Jews and usurers be expelled outside the consortium of the holy), 55a (the pope expels infidels), and 246c (Jews, heretics, and false decretists are excommunicated); and Vienna ÖNB cod. 2554, fols. 29c (Jesus commands prelates to push usurers and miscreants out of the Church), 31vb (the pope pushes Jews and miscreants outside of Holy Church), and 9vc (good prelates excommunicate and curse Jews, usurers, and all miscreants). In addition, Adam rejecting his son Cain (an embroidery on Gen. 4:1–2) is compared to "Jesus Christ, who elected Christians and expelled Jews from Holy Church" (Vienna ÖNB cod. 1179, fol. 5a, and cod. 2554, fol. 2va).

58. Canon 71: "Iudeos vero ad remittendas usuras per secularem compelli precipimus potestatem et, donec illas remiserint, ab universis christifidelibus per excommunicationis sententiam eis omnino communio denegetur." *Constitutiones Concilii quarti Lateranensis una cum commentariis glossatorum,* ed. Antonio Garcia y Garcia (Vatican City, 1981), 114. Grayzel's edition of this canon is incomplete, and his translation is overly influenced by his own interpretation (*The Church and the Jews,* 312–313).

59. Grayzel, *The Church and the Jews,* 50.

60. Joseph Shatzmiller, "Jews Separated from the Communion of the Faithful in Christ in the Middle Ages," in *Studies in Medieval Jewish*

History and Literature, vol. 1, ed. Isadore Twersky (Cambridge, Mass., 1979), 307–314.

61. William C. Jordan, "Christian Excommunication of Jews in the Middle Ages: A Restatement of the Issues," *Jewish History* 1 (1986): 31–38.

62. R. I. Moore, *The Origins of European Dissent* (London, 1977), 252. See, for example, Canon 27 of the Third Lateran Council (Raymonde Foreville, *Latran I, II, III et Latran IV,* Histoire des conciles oecuméniques 6 [Paris, 1965], 222–223), and Canon 3 of the Fourth Lateran Council (*Constitutiones Concilii quarti Lateranensis una cum commentariis glossatorum,* ed. Garcia y Garcia, 47–51).

63. *Contra Amaurianos,* 1; and Stephen of Bourbon, *Anecdotes Historiques: Legendes et apologues tirés du recueil inédit d'Étienne de Bourbon,* ed. A. Lecoy de la Marche (Paris, 1877), 307.

64. Select more or less contemporary examples include canons from the council of Avignon in 1209 (Mansi 22:786), the council of Paris in 1212 (Mansi 22:825, 850–851), and the provincial council of Narbonne in 1227 (Mansi 23:23); on Parisian theological approaches to punishing usury, see John W. Baldwin, *Masters, Princes, and Merchants: The Social Views of Peter the Chanter and His Circle* (Princeton, N.J., 1970), 1:296–315, esp. 301.

65. Mansi 22:850–851; discussed in Baldwin, *Masters, Princes, and Merchants,* 1:302.

66. Guillaume de Puy-Laurent, *Historia Albigensium,* in RHGF 19: 203A; see, too, Odette Pontal, "De la défense à la pastorale de la foi: les épiscopats de Foulque, Raymond du Fauga et Bertrand de L'Isle Jourdain à Toulouse," *Cahiers de Fanjeaux* 20 (1991): 175–197.

67. In this the *Bible moralisée* anticipates the famous declaration of Pope Innocent IV that "the pope, who is vicar of Jesus Christ, has authority not only over Christians, but also over all infidels." Quoted in Cohen, *The Friars and the Jews,* 97. In his conclusion (pp. 248–264), Cohen focuses on this newly comprehensive conception of Christendom as the primary cause of "this new attitude toward the Jews"; as my later discussion will make clear, I do not embrace Cohen's privileging of theology.

68. Vienna ÖNB cod. 1179, fol. 38A: "Moyses precepit quod acciperent pulverem vituli et prohicient in aquam. Et dixit vos bibetis dominum vestrem et exibit per anum."

69. Vienna ÖNB cod. 1179, fol. 38a: "Hoc significat bonos christianos qui bibunt aquam baptismi ut per eam diabolus ab homine expellatur."

70. Heinlen noted this in his discussion of the parallel French commentary ("The Ideology of Reform in the French Moralized Bible," 46–47) and pointed out that passing gas was often called "expelling the devil."

71. Infant baptism was standard throughout the Middle Ages; in the twelfth and thirteenth centuries it took on even greater significance in the face of Catharist rejection of the practice.

72. Interesting, too, is the fact that the text specifies that the baptized Christians "drink" the baptismal water. This idea, not a standard part of the baptismal rite, obviously arises out of the related biblical text but also rather inevitably recalls another substance that was part of the post-

baptismal ceremony of the Mass: the eucharistic wine. This association is strengthened by the wording of the texts in question. Among the myriad reverberations that the phrase "expelling one's God through the anus" may have provoked in medieval culture, the most striking parallel is the contemporary debate over the nature and destination of the eucharistic bread: heretics and good Catholics alike (and Jewish polemicists as well) expended considerable energy arguing about the biological processes endured by the Body of Christ after ingestion. See Miri Rubin, *Corpus Christi: The Eucharist in Late Medieval Culture* (Cambridge, 1991), 37–38, and Daniel Lasker, *Jewish Philosophical Polemics against Christianity in the Middle Ages* (New York, 1977), for Jewish criticisms of eucharistic doctrine. This debate, then, and the entire subject of the Eucharist and communion, underlies and fleshes out the *Bible moralisée* exorcism image and perhaps the excommunicating images that follow. For the increasing emphasis on the purity of the participants in communion, see Rubin, *Corpus Christi,* 148–149.

73. See Mary C. Mansfield, *The Humiliation of Sinners: Public Penance in Thirteenth-Century France* (Ithaca, N.Y., and London, 1995), 186 n. 82.

74. Reform is, moreover, explicitly mentioned on the preceding folio: Vienna ÖNB cod. 1179, fol. 37c, runs, ". . . Moyses reparuit tablas novas significat ihm xpm qui reformat sanctam ecclesiam ut suam faciat voluntatem." The reform in question is illustrated with an image of Jesus casting Jews' scrolls to the ground.

75. Vienna ÖNB cod. 1179, fol. 38d: "Hos significat quod dominus papa bonos prelatos cum gaudio recipit et de beneficiis suis gracias reddit et dat eis suam benedictionem."

76. Vienna ÖNB cod. 1179, fol. 221a: "Hoc significat quod secreto plorandum est qui sunt infideles heretici qui alias pervertunt ad fidem per predicationem sunt revocandi." It is particularly difficult to account for the fact that "alias" is in the feminine; I am tempted to associate the gender of this word with the imagery of seduction, but this is of course purely speculative. It is possible that "alias" simply ought to be emended to "alios." The grammar of this text is in any case uncertain at best, and scribal errors abound throughout the manuscripts. I am grateful to J. Ward Jones for his "consult" on this translation.

77. Vienna ÖNB cod. 1179, fol. 221b: "Hoc significat quod qui vero perversi sunt excommunicati et laice potestati tradendi et igne comburendi."

78. On the links between confession and communion, and their relationship to teaching and preaching, see Rubin, *Corpus Christi,* 84–85.

79. Vienna ÖNB cod. 1179, fol 221c: "Hoc significat quod boni prelati diligenter investigant peccata subdiciorum suorum et frequenter invenirent in confessionibus sub operibus speciosis exterius pravam latuisse intencionem."

80. Baldwin, *Masters, Princes, and Merchants,* 1:322.

81. Bernard of Clairvaux, Alan of Lille, and Robert de Courson all supported the burning of heretics. For Robert's approach, see Baldwin, *Masters, Princes, and Merchants,* 1:322; for Robert's actual participation in the burning of heretics, see Pierre des Vaux-de-Cernay, *Historia Albigeoise,* trans. Pascal Guébin and Henri Maisonneuve (Paris, 1951), 197; for Alan, see PL 210:396; Bernard's approach is discussed in Christiane

Thouzellier, *Catharisme et Valdéisme en Languedoc à la fin du XIIe et au début du XIIIe siècle* (Paris, 1966), 102–104.

82. Thouzellier, *Catharisme et Valdéisme en Languedoc,* 151.

83. Henri Denifle, *Chartularium Universitatis Parisiensis,* 4 vols. (Paris, 1891–99; repr., Brussels, 1964), 1:70, nos. 11, 12. See Julien Havet, "L'hérésie et le bras seculier au moyen âge jusqu'au XIIIe siècle," *Bibliotheque de l'école des chartes* 41 (1880): 488–517, 570–670, for discussion and more examples.

84. Charles Petit-Dutaillis, *Étude sur la vie et le règne de Louis VIII (1187–1226)* (Paris, 1894), 316.

85. Pierre des Vaux-de-Cernay, *Histoire Albigeoise,* 66–67; Latin text in RHGF 19:32D.

86. Guillaume de Puy-Laurent, *Historia Albigensium,* in RHGF 19: 204A; Pierre des Vaux-de-Cernay refers to the burning at Lavaur of "an infinity of heretics" in *Histoire Albigeoise,* 94, and RHGF 19:46.

87. RHGF 19:204B.

88. Petit-Dutaillis, *Étude sur la vie et le règne de Louis VIII,* 317 and Catalogue no. 362. The act is dated "anno 1226, mense aprili" (in the old style 1226 went from 19 April 1226 to 11 April 1227). Petit-Dutaillis notes that he can find no evidence that any heretics were burned during Louis's sojourn in Languedoc. However, the lieutenant he left behind, Humbert de Beaujeu, apparently did order the execution of a Cathar bishop.

89. Havet ("L'hérésie et le bras seculier," 501–502) suggests that burning was chosen in preference to hanging as the form of execution for heresy because women were never hanged, but he admits that this does not fully account for the preference for burning over other forms of execution.

90. Further attempts to harness the cleansing properties of fire include the practice reported during the Black Death of burning the victims' bodies to prevent the spread of the disease.

91. Vienna ÖNB cod. 1179, fol. 52c: "Deus qui precipit quod lapidaretur significat iesum christum qui precipit regibus et comitibus quod interficiunt omnes infideles et puplicanos."

92. Innocent III concludes a letter to Philip Augustus dated January 1205 that consists primarily of complaints about the behavior of French Jews by admonishing the king to remove heretics from France. (PL 215:502 and Grayzel, *The Church and the Jews,* 105–109, no. 14.)

93. Another text in the Latin manuscript (Vienna ÖNB cod. 1179, fol. 96c) commends "good princes taking the cross [who] promise to kill all the albigenses with all their posterity." Simon de Montfort, called "Count Simon" in the chronicles, was leader of the Albigensian Crusade from 1209 until his death in 1218; Prince Louis assumed the cross in 1213 and campaigned in Languedoc in 1215, in 1219, and again (as king) in 1226. See Petit-Dutaillis, *Étude sur la vie et le règne de Louis VIII,* 184–202, 279–328. The Albigensian Crusade is also explicitly mentioned in fol. 203b; see chapter 4.

94. Vienna ÖNB cod. 1179, fol. 52b: ". . . infideles et puplicanos qui intelligere verbum domini nolunt nec umquam voluerunt."

95. Vienna ÖNB cod. 2554, fol. 30d: "Ce qe c'il se gaba de deu et li fist la moe et dist mal de lui senefie les mescreanz et les populicanz qi se gabent de deu et de son sacrement et dient qe ce n'est riens, et deu comande qe il soient ars et destruit et il si sunt."

96. See, for example, folio 57vb of Vienna ÖNB cod. 2554.

97. On the *Constitutio pro Judeis,* first issued in 1120 and reissued many times through the thirteenth century, see Grayzel, *The Church and the Jews,* 76–83, 92–95.

98. Edward Peters, ed., *The First Crusade: The Chronicle of Fulcher of Chartres and Other Source Materials* (Philadelphia, 1971), 102.

99. Bernard of Clairvaux, *Letters of Bernard of Clairvaux,* trans. Bruno James (London, 1953), 460–462, 465–466.

100. Dahan, "L'Article *Iudei.*"

101. Although see my summary of the Cohen thesis in chapter 3.

102. Rigord, in Delaborde, *Oeuvres de Rigord,* 118–119; English translations of Rigord and the Hebrew report by Ephraim of Bonn are given in Robert Chazan, ed., *Church, State and Jew in the Middle Ages* (New York, 1980), 304–306. Chazan discussed the case in "The Bray Incident of 1192: *Realpolitik* and Folk Slander," *Proceedings of the American Academy for Jewish Research* 37 (1969): 1–18. In response to William Chester Jordan, *The French Monarchy and the Jews: From Philip Augustus to the Last Capetians* (Philadelphia, 1989), 35–37, Chazan modified his view in "Ephraim ben Jacob's Compilation of Twelfth-Century Persecutions," *Jewish Quarterly Review* 84 (1994): 397–416, here 402 n. 22.

Conclusion

1. Vienna ÖNB cod. 1179, fol. 246c: commentary text to Apoc. 22: 18–21.

2. Most influentially by Gavin Langmuir, who in *Toward a Definition of Anti-Semitism* (Berkeley and Los Angeles, 1990) defined "anti-Semitism" as "irrational beliefs" such as ritual murder charges, etc., in contradistinction to "anti-Judaism," an intellectual response to "real" religious and exegetical differences. See also Robert Seltzer's review of Jeremy Cohen's *Friars and the Jews* in *Journal of Religion* 65 (1985): 114–115; Seltzer defines "popular Judeophobia" as the blood libel, the Host desecration charge, and well-poisoning accusations, the first two of which are at least alluded to in the images of the *Bible moralisée.*

3. I am, of course, far from the first or only historian to make these observations or draw this conclusion about elite/popular boundaries. See, for example, the remarks of Miri Rubin in *Corpus Christi: The Eucharist in Late Medieval Culture* (Cambridge, 1991), 115–116.

4. Tracy Ann Chapman, "The Female Audience for the *Bible moralisée:* Blanche of Castille and the Example of Vienna 2554" (master's thesis, University of Texas at Austin, 1995); and my forthcoming article "The Body Is My Temple."

5. See a similar assertion in David Nirenberg, *Communities of Violence: Persecution of Minorities in the Middle Ages* (Princeton, N.J., 1996), 6.

6. See chapter 3.

7. Vienna ÖNB cod. 1179, fol. 25c: "Hoc significat bonos prelatos qui exponendo verba evangelii falsa verba devorant iudeorum." Vienna ÖNB cod. 2554, fol. 18vc: "Ce qe Moyses et Aaron geterent ius la verge et ele mua en colueure et devora celes as enchanteors senefie les boens prelaz qi gietent et espartcent la parole de l'evangile et ele devore et abat la fause parole des gieus et des mescreanz."

BIBLIOGRAPHY

Manuscripts

Paris, Bibliothèque Nationale lat. 384: Stephen Langton, *Gloss on Leviticus*
Paris, BN lat. 2514: Jean Halgrin d'Abbeville, *Homilies*
Paris, BN lat. 3258: Robert de Courson, *Summa*
Paris, BN lat. 6191: Gilles de Paris, *Karolinus.*
Paris, BN lat. 11993: Bishop Brunus, *Commentary on the Pentateuch*
Paris, BN lat. 14414: Stephen Langton, *Commentaries*
Paris, BN lat. 14525: Abbots Absolon and John of St. Victor, *Sermons*
Paris, BN lat. 14859: Prévostin, Peter Cantor, Stephen Langton, Alan of Lille, *Sermons*
Paris, BN lat. 14935: Stephen of St. Geneviève, *Sermons*
Paris, BN lat. 17268: Nicholas of Tournai, *Commentary on Exodus*
Paris, BN lat. 17509: Jacques de Vitry, *Sermones vulgares*
Paris, BN nouv. acq. lat. 1537: Jacques de Vitry, *Sermones dominicales et festivales*
Vienna, Österreichische Nationalbibliothek cod. 1179: *Bible moralisée* (Latin)
Vienna, ÖNB cod. 2554: *Bible moralisée* (French)

Primary Sources

Alan of Lille. *The Art of Preaching.* Translated by Gillian R. Evans. Kalamazoo, Mich., 1981.
———. *Contra Hereticos Libri Quatuor.* In *Patrologiae cursus completus, series Latina.* Vol. 210:305–430. Edited by J. P. Migne. Paris, 1844–55.
Alexander of Hales. *Summa Theologica.* Vol. 3. Edited by Bonaventure Marrani. Florence, 1930.
Annals of St.-Bertin. Ninth-Century Histories. Vol. 1. Translated by Janet L. Nelson. Manchester and New York, 1991.
Apocalyptic Spirituality: Treatises and Letters of Lactantius, Adso of Montier-en-der, Joachim of Fiore, the Franciscan Spirituals, Savonarola. Translated by Bernard McGinn. New York, 1979.
Augustine of Hippo. *City of God.* Translated by Marcus Dods. In *A Select Library of the Nicene and Post-Nicene Fathers of the Christian Church.* Vol. 2. Edited by Philip Schaff. Reprinted, Grand Rapids, Mich.,1983.
———. *De Civitate Dei.* In *Corpus Christianorum Series Latina* 48. Turnhout, Belgium, 1955.
———. *Confessions.* Rev. ed. Translated by F. J. Sheed. Indianapolis, 1993.

———. *Epistolae.* In CSEL 34.
———. *Letters.* Translated by J. G. Cunningham. In *A Select Library of the Nicene and Post-Nicene Fathers of the Christian Church.* Vol. 1. Edited by Philip Schaff. Reprinted, Grand Rapids, Mich., 1983.
Berger, David, ed. *The Jewish-Christian Debate in the High Middle Ages: A Critical Edition of the Nizzhon Vetus.* Philadelphia, 1979.
Bernard of Clairvaux. *Letters of Bernard of Clairvaux.* Translated by Bruno James. London, 1953.
———. *San Bernardo Opere.* Edited by Ferruccio Gastadelli. Milan, 1987.
———. *Selected Works.* Translated by G. R. Evans. New York and Mahwah, N.J., 1987.
Berthold of Regensburg. *Vollständige Ausgabe seiner Predigten.* 2 vols. Edited by Franz Pfeiffer. 1862–80. Reprinted, Berlin, 1965.
Bestiary: Being an English Version of Bodleian Library Oxford MS Bodley 764. Translated by Richard Barber. Woodbridge, 1993.
La Bible moralisée illustrée conservée à Oxford, Paris, et Londres. 4 vols. Edited by A. de Laborde. Paris, 1911–27.
Bible moralisée. Codex Vindobonensis 2554 Vienna, Österreichische Nationalbibliothek. Commentary and translation of biblical texts by Gerald B. Guest. London, 1995.
Bible moralisée, Faksimile-Ausgabe im Originalformat des Codex Vindobonensis 2554 der Österreichischen Nationalbibliothek. 2 vols. Edited by Reiner Haussherr. Graz and Paris, 1973.
Biblia Latina cum Glossa Ordinaria: Facsimile Reprint of the Editio Princeps Adolph Rusch of Strassburg 1480/81. 4 vols. Introduction by Karlfried Froehlich and Margaret T. Gibson. Turnhout, Belgium, 1992.
Biblia sacra cum glossa ordinaria. Strassbourg, ca. 1480.
Breder, Günter. *Die Lateinische Vorlage des Altfranzösischen Apokalypsenkommentars des 13. Jahrhunderts (Paris, B.N., MS. Fr. 403).* Münster, 1960.
Caesarius of Heisterbach. *Dialogus Miraculorum.* 2 vols. Edited by Joseph Strange. Cologne, 1851.
Chazan, Robert, ed. *Church, State, and Jew in the Middle Ages.* New York, 1980.
Constitutiones Concilii quarti Lateranensis una cum commentariis glossatorum. Edited by Antonio Garcia y Garcia. Vatican City, 1981.
Contra Amaurianos. Edited by Clemens Baeumker. Beitrage zur Geschichte der Philosophie des Mittelalters 24. Münster, 1926.
The Correspondence of Pope Gregory VII. Translated by Ephraim Emerton. New York and London, 1960.
Delaborde, Henri, ed. *Oeuvres de Rigord et de Guillaume le Breton.* 2 vols. Paris, 1882–85.
Denifle, Henri, ed. *Chartularium Universitatis Parisiensis.* 4 vols. Paris, 1891–99. Reprinted, Brussels, 1964.
Deuchler, Florens, ed. *Der Ingeborg Psalter—Le Psautier d'Ingeburge de Danemark (Vollständige Faksimile-Ausgabe im originalformat der Handschrift Ms. 9 olim 1695 aus dem Besitz des Musée Condé-Chantilly).* Graz, 1967.
Disputatio Ecclesiae et Synagogae. In *Thesaurus Novus Anecdotorum.* Vol. 5. Edited by Edmund Martène and Ursinus Durand. Paris, 1717.

La fin des temps: terreurs et prophéties au Moyen Âge. Translated by Claude Carozzi and Huguette Taviani-Carozzi. Paris, 1982.
Gautier de Coinci. *Les miracles de Nostre Dame par Gautier de Coinci.* Edited by V. Frederick Koenig. Geneva, 1970.
Gilbert Crispin. *The Works of Gilbert Crispin, Abbot of Westminster.* Edited by Anna Sapir Abulafia and G. R. Evans. London, 1986.
de Grandrue, Claude. *Le Catalogue de la bibliothèque de l'abbaye de Saint-Victor de Paris de Claude de Grandrue (1514).* Paris, 1983.
Grayzel, Solomon, ed. *The Church and the Jews in the XIIIth Century.* Philadelphia, 1933.
———. *The Church and the Jews in the XIIIth Century.* Vol. 2, *1254–1314.* Edited by Kenneth R. Stow. New York, 1989.
Guillaume le Clerc. *The Bestiary of Guillaume le Clerc, originally written in 1210–11.* Translated by George Claridge Druce. Ashford, Kent, 1936.
Guillaume de Puylaurens. *Historia Albigensium.* RHGF 19.
Hefele, Charles Joseph. *Histoire des Conciles.* 11 vols. Paris, 1907–31.
Herrad of Hohenbourg. *Hortus Deliciarum.* 2 vols. Edited by Rosalie Green, Michael Evans, Christine Bischoff, and Michael Curschmann. London, 1979.
Hervieux, Léopold, ed. *Les fabulistes latins.* Vol. 4, *Eudes de Chériton et ses dérivés.* Paris, 1896.
Hugh of St. Victor. *The Didascalicon.* Translated by Jerome Taylor. New York and London, 1961.
———. *On the Sacraments of the Christian Faith (De Sacramentis).* Translated by Roy J. Deferrari. Cambridge, Mass., 1951.
Innocent III. *Opera Omnia.* In PL 214–217.
———. *Selected Letters of Pope Innocent III concerning England.* Edited by C. R. Cheney and W. H. Semple, et al. London, 1953.
Jacques de Vitry. *Die Exempla aus den Sermones feriales et communes des Jakob von Vitry.* Edited by Joseph Greven. Heidelberg, 1914.
———. *Die Exempla des Jakob von Vitry.* Edited by Goswin Frenken. Munich, 1941.
———. *The Exempla or Illustrative Stories from the Sermons of Jacques de Vitry.* Edited by Thomas Frederick Crane. London, 1890.
———. *Lettres de Jacques de Vitry (1160/70–1240).* Edited by R. B. C. Huygens. Leiden, 1960.
———. *Sermones ad Status.* In *Prêcher d'Exemples: Récits de prédicateurs du moyen âge.* Edited by Jean-Claude Schmitt. Paris, 1985.
John Chrysostom. *Discourses against Judaizing Christians.* Translated by Paul W. Harkins. Washington, D.C., 1979.
Layettes du Trésor des chartes. Edited by A. Teulet et al. 5 vols. Paris, 1863–1909.
Lecoy de la Marche, A., ed. *L'Esprit de nos Aïeux: Anecdotes et bons mots tirés des manuscrits du XIIIe siècle.* Paris, 1888.
Liber Ordinis Sancti Victoris Parisiensis. Edited by Lucas Jocque and Louis Milis. Turnhout, Belgium, 1984.
Magie et Sorcellerie en Europe du Moyen Âge à nos jours. Edited by Robert Muchembled and Bengt Ankarloo. Paris, 1994.
Mansi, Johannes Dominicus. *Sacrorum Conciliorum Nova et Amplissima Collectio.* 54 vols. Graz, 1960–61.
Map, Walter. *De Nugis Curialium.* Edited by Montague Rhodes James. Anecdota Oxoniensia 14. Oxford, 1914.

———. *De Nugis Curialium (Courtier's Trifles).* Translated by Marbury Bladen Ogle and Frederick Tupper. London, 1924.
Marcus, Jacob R., ed. *The Jew in the Medieval World: A Source Book, 315–1791.* New York, 1983.
McNeill, John T., and Helena M. Gamer. *Medieval Handbooks of Penance.* New York, 1965.
Moses Maimonides. *The Guide of the Perplexed.* Vol. 2. Edited by Shlomo Pines. Chicago and London, 1962.
Odo of Cheriton. *The Fables of Odo of Cheriton.* Edited and translated by John C. Jacobs. Syracuse, N.Y., 1985.
Origen. *Homélies sur le Lévitique.* Sources chrétiennes 286. Edited and translated by Marcel Borret. Paris, 1981.
Peter of Blois. *Contra perfidiam Judaeorum.* In PL 207:825–870.
Peter the Chanter. *Verbum Abbreviatum.* In PL 205:1–554.
Peter of Poitiers. *Summa de Confessione.* Edited by Jean Longère. CCCM 60. Turnhout, Belgium, 1980.
Peter the Venerable. *Adversus Judaeorum Inveteratam Duritiam.* Edited by Yvonne Friedman. CCCM 58. Turnhout, Belgium, 1985.
———. *The Letters of Peter the Venerable.* Edited by Giles Constable. Cambridge, Mass., 1967.
Peters, Edward, ed. *Heresy and Authority in Medieval Europe: Documents in Translation.* Philadelphia, 1985.
Pierre des Vaux-de-Cernay. *Historia Albigensium.* In RHGF 19.
———. *Histoire Albigeoise.* Translated by Pascal Guébin and Henri Maisonneuve. Paris, 1951.
Potthast, Augustus, ed. *Regesta pontificum romanorum.* 2 vols. Berlin, 1874–75.
Pseudo-Praepositinus of Cremona. *The Summa Contra Hereticos Ascribed to Praepositinus of Cremona.* Edited by James A. Corbett and Joseph N. Garvin. Notre Dame, Ind., 1958.
Ralph of Flaix. *In Leviticum.* Edited by M. de la Bigne. *Maxima Bibliotheca Patrum.* Vol. 17. Lyon, 1677.
Recueil des actes de Philippe Auguste. Edited by H.-F. Delaborde et al. 4 vols. Paris, 1916–79.
Les Registres de Philippe Auguste. Vol. 1, *Texte.* Edited by John W. Baldwin. Paris, 1992.
Richard of St. Victor. *Liber Exceptionum.* Edited by Jean Chatillon. Paris, 1958.
———. *The Twelve Patriarchs, The Mystical Ark, Book Three of the Trinity.* Translated and introduced by Grover A. Zinn. New York, Ramsay, and Toronto, 1979.
Rigord. *De Gestis Philippi Augusti, Francorum Regis.* In RHGF 17. Edited by M. J. J. Brial. Paris, 1878.
Robert de Courson. "Le traité *De Usura* de Robert de Courson." Edited by Georges Lefèvre. *Travaux et mémoires de l'Université de Lille* 10:30 (1902).
———. "Robert Courson on Penance." Edited by V. L. Kennedy. *Mediaeval Studies* 7 (1945): 291–336.
Robert of Flamborough. *Liber Poenitentialis.* Edited by J. J. Francis Firth. Toronto, 1971.
Rutebeuf. *Le miracle de Théophile.* Edited and translated by Jean Dufournet. Paris, 1977.

Les statuts synodaux français du XIIIe siècle. Vol. 1, *Les statuts de Paris et le synodal de l'Ouest (XIIIe siècle).* Edited and translated by Odette Pontal. Collection de documents inédits sur l'histoire de France, vol. 9. Paris, 1971.

Stephen of Bourbon. *Anecdotes historiques: Légendes et apologues tirés du recueil inédit d'Étienne de Bourbon.* Edited by A. Lecoy de la Marche. Paris, 1877.

Stephen Langton. *Commentary on the Book of Chronicles.* Edited by Avrom Saltman. Ramat Gan, 1978.

———. *Selected Sermons of Stephen Langton.* Edited by Phyllis B. Roberts. Toronto, 1980.

Stephen of Tournai. *Sermones.* In PL 211.

Thomas Aquinas. *Summa Theologica.* Translated by English Dominican Fathers. 22 vols. 2d ed. London, 1916–38.

Thomas of Chobham. *Sermones.* Edited by Franco Morenzoni. CCCM 82A. Turnhout, Belgium, 1993.

———. *Summa Confessorum.* Edited by F. Broomfield. Louvain, 1968.

Veterum scriptorum et monumentorum historicum, dogmaticorum, moralium: Amplissima collectio. 9 vols. Edited by Edmund Martène and Ursinus Durand. Paris, 1724–33.

William of Auvergne. *Opera Omnia.* 2 vols. Paris, 1674. Reprint, Frankfurt, 1963.

Williams, A. Lukyn, ed. *Adversus Judaeos: A Bird's-Eye View of Christian Apologiae until the Renaissance.* Cambridge, 1935.

Secondary Sources

Alexander, Jonathan J. G. *Medieval Illuminators and Their Methods of Work.* New Haven, Conn., 1992.

d'Alverny, Marie-Thérèse. "Les nouveaux apports dans les domaines de la science et de la pensée au temps de Philippe-Auguste: la philosophie." In Bautier, *La France de Philippe Auguste,* 864–880.

———. "Une fragment du procès des Amauriciens." AHDLMA 25/26 (1950–51): 325–336.

Aubert, Marcel. *La Sculpture française au moyen âge.* Paris, 1946.

———. "Les Trois Jubés de Notre-Dame de Paris." *Revue de l'art ancien et moderne* 43 (1923): 105–118.

d'Avray, D. L. *The Preaching of the Friars: Sermons Diffused from Paris before 1300.* Oxford, 1985.

Ayres, Larry M. "Parisian Bibles in the Berlin Staatsbibliothek." *Pantheon* 40 (1982): 5–13.

Baldwin, John W. "L'Entourage de Philippe-Auguste et la famille royale." In Bautier, *La France de Philippe Auguste,* 59–73.

———. *The Government of Philip Augustus: Foundations of French Royal Power in the Middle Ages.* Berkeley, Los Angeles, and London, 1986.

———. "Masters at Paris, 1179–1215." In *Renaissance and Renewal in the Twelfth Century,* edited by Robert L. Benson and Giles Constable, 154–158. Cambridge, Mass., 1982.

———. *Masters, Princes, and Merchants: The Social Views of Peter the Chanter and His Circle.* 2 vols. Princeton, N.J., 1970.

———. *The Medieval Theories of the Just Price: Romanists, Canonists, and Theologians in the Twelfth and Thirteenth Centuries.* Transactions of the American Philosophical Society, n.s., 49, no. 4. Philadelphia, 1959.

———. "*Persona et Gesta:* The Image and Deeds of the Thirteenth-Century Capetians. The Case of Philip Augustus." *Viator* 19 (1988): 195–207.

———. *The Scholastic Culture of the Middle Ages, 1000–1300.* Prospect Heights, Ill., 1971.

———. "Studium et Regnum: The Penetration of University Personnel into French and English Administration at the Turn of the Twelfth and Thirteenth Centuries." *Revue des études Islamiques* 44 (1976): 199–215.

Barthes, Roland. *Mythologies.* Translated by Annette Lavers. New York, 1972.

Bartlett, Robert. *Gerald of Wales, 1146–1223.* Oxford, 1982.

———. *The Making of Europe: Conquest, Colonization, and Cultural Change 950–1350.* Princeton, N.J., 1993.

———. "Symbolic Meanings of Hair in the Middle Ages." *Transactions of the Royal Historical Society,* 6th ser., 4 (1994): 43–60.

Bataillon, Louis-Jacques. "De la *lectio* à la *praedicatio:* commentaires bibliques et sermons au XIIIe siècle." *Revue des sciences philosophiques et théologiques* 70 (1986): 559–575.

———. *La prédication au XIIIe siècle en France et Italie.* London, 1993.

———. "*Similitudines* et *Exempla* dans les sermons du XIIIe siècle." In Walsh and Wood, *The Bible in the Medieval World,* 199–217.

Baumann, Priscilla. "The Deadliest Sin: Warnings against Avarice and Usury on Romanesque Capitals in Auvergne." *Church History* 59 (1990): 7–18.

Bautier, Robert-Henri. "La personalité du roi." In Bautier, *La France de Philippe Auguste,* 33–57.

———. "La place du règne de Philippe Auguste dans l'histoire de la France médiévale." In Bautier, *La France de Philippe Auguste,* 11–27.

———, ed. *La France de Philippe Auguste: Le temps des mutations.* Actes du Colloque International organisé par le CNRS, Paris, 1980. Paris, 1982.

Beaune, Colette. *The Birth of an Ideology: Myths and Symbols of Nation in Late Medieval France.* Edited by Fredric L. Cheyette and translated by Susan Ross Huston. Berkeley, Los Angeles, and Oxford, 1991.

Bedos-Rezak, Brigitte. "The Confrontation of Orality and Textuality: Jewish and Christian Literacy in Eleventh- and Twelfth-Century Northern France." In *Rashi 1040–1990: Hommage à Ephraim E. Urbach,* edited by Gabrielle Sed-Rajna, 541–558. Paris, 1993.

———. "Les juifs et l'écrit dans la mentalité eschatologique." *Annales HSS* 5 (1994): 1049–1063.

Beer, Rudolf. "Les principaux manuscrits à peinture de la Bibliothèque Impériale de Vienne." *Bulletin de la société française de reproductions de manuscrits à peintures* 2 (1912): 11–13.

Benton, Janetta Rebold. *The Medieval Menagerie: Animals in the Art of the Middle Ages.* New York, London, and Paris, 1992.

Berger, David. "Christian Heresy and Jewish Polemic in the Twelfth and Thirteenth Centuries." *Harvard Theological Review:* 68 (1975): 287–303.

———. "Mission to the Jews and Jewish-Christian Contacts in the Polemical Literature of the High Middle Ages." *American History Review* 91 (1986): 576–591.

———, ed. *History and Hate: The Dimensions of Anti-Semitism.* Philadelphia, 1986.

Berger, Samuel. *La Bible française au moyen âge.* Paris, 1884.

———. *Quam notitiam linguae hebraicae habuerunt christiani medii aevi temporibus in Gallia.* Nancy, 1883.

Bériou, N., and D. L. d'Avray. "The Image of the Ideal Husband in Thirteenth-Century France." In *Modern Questions about Medieval Sermons: Essays on Marriage, Death, History, and Sanctity,* edited by N. Bériou and D. L. d'Avray. Spoleto, 1994.

Berlioz, Jacques, and Marie Anne Polo de Beaulieu, eds. *Les exempla médiévaux: introduction à la recherche.* Carcassonne, 1992.

Bhabha, Homi. "The Other Question: Stereotype, Discrimination, and the Discourse of Colonialism." In *The Location of Culture,* 66–84. London and New York, 1994.

Blaise, Albert. *Lexicon Latinitatis Medii Aevi.* CCCM. Turnhout, Belgium, 1975.

Bloch, Marc. "Les formes de la rupture de l'hommage dans l'ancien droit féodale." In *Mélanges Historiques,* vol. 1, 189–209. Paris, 1963.

The Blood Libel Legend. Edited by Alan Dundes. Madison, Wis., 1991.

Blumenkranz, Bernhard. "Augustin et les juifs, Augustin et le judaïsme." *Recherches augustiniennes* 1 (1958): 225–241. Reprinted in B. Blumenkranz, *Juifs et Chrétiens Patristique et Moyen Âge.* London, 1977.

———. "Badge." In *Jewish Encyclopedia,* 4:62–74. Philadelphia, 1971.

———. "'La Disputatio Judei cum Christiano' de Gilbert Crispin, abbé de Westminster." *Revue du moyen âge latin* 4 (1948): 237–252. Reprinted in Blumenkranz, *Juifs et Chrétiens.*

———. *Le juif médiéval au miroir de l'art chrétien.* Paris, 1966.

———. "La polémique antijuive dans l'art chrétien du moyen âge." *Bulletino d'Instituto storico italiano per il medio evo* 77 (1965): 21–43.

———. "La représentation de Synagoga dans les *Bibles moralisées* françaises du XIIIe au XVe siècle." *Proceedings of the Israel Academy of Science and Humanities* 5 (1971–76): 70–91.

———. "Vie et survie de la polémique anti-juive." *Studia Patristica* 1 (1957): 460–476.

Bonnard, Fourier. *L'Histoire de l'Abbaye royale et de l'Ordre des chanoines réguliers de St.-Victor de Paris.* Vol. 1, *Première période (1113–1500).* Paris, 1904.

Borst, Arno. *Die Katharer.* Stuttgart, 1953.

Boswell, John E. *The Kindness of Strangers: The Abandonment of Children in Western Europe from Late Antiquity to the Renaissance.* New York, 1988.

Boyle, Leonard E. "Innocent III and Vernacular Versions of Scripture." In Walsh and Wood, *The Bible in the Medieval World,* 97–107.

Branner, Robert. *Manuscript Painting in Paris during the Reign of St. Louis.* Berkeley and Los Angeles, 1977.

———. "Le premier évangélaire de la Ste.-Chapelle." *Revue de l'art* 3 (1969): 37–48.

———. *St. Louis and the Court Style in Gothic Architecture.* London, 1965.

Bremond, Claude, Jacques le Goff, and J.-C. Schmitt. *L'Exemplum.* Ty-

pologie des sources du moyen âge occidental 40. Turnhout, Belgium, 1982.
Brown, Elizabeth A. R. "La notion de la légitimité et la prophétie à la cour de Philippe Auguste." In Bautier, *La France de Philippe Auguste,* 77–110.
———. "Vincent de Beauvais and the *Reditus regni francorum ad stirpem Caroli imperatoris.*" In *Vincent de Beauvais: Intentions et Réceptions d'une oeuvre encyclopédique au moyen âge,* 167–196. Paris, 1990.
Brown, Harold O. J. *Heresies.* Garden City, N.Y., 1984.
Brown, Peter. *Augustine of Hippo.* Berkeley and Los Angeles, 1969.
Buc, Philippe. *L'Ambiguïté du livre: Prince, pouvoir, et peuple dans les commentaires de la Bible au moyen âge.* Paris, 1994.
———. "Pouvoir royal et commentaires de la Bible (1150–1350)." *Annales ESC* 44 (1989): 691–713.
———. "*Vox Clamantis in Deserto?* Pierre le Chantre et la prédication laïque," *Revue Mabillon,* n.s., 65 (1993): 5–47.
Bulard, Marcel. *Le Scorpion: Symbol du peuple juif dans l'art réligieux des XIVe, XVe, XVIe siècles.* Paris, 1935.
Burr, David. "Poverty as a Constituent Element in Olivi's Thought." In *Poverty in the Middle Ages,* edited by D. Flood, 71–78. Werl / Westf., 1975.
Büttner, Philippe. "Bilder zum Betreten der Zeit: Bible moralisée und Kapetingisches Königtum." Ph.D. diss., Basel University, 1996.
Cahn, Walter. "A Defense of the Trinity in the Citeaux Bible." *Marsyas* 11:58 (1962–64): 58–62.
———. "Heresy and the Interpretation of Romanesque Art." In *Romanesque and Gothic. Essays for George Zarnecki,* edited by Neil Stratford, 27–33. Woodbridge, Suffolk, and Wolfeboro, N.H., 1987.
Callus, D. A. "Introduction of Aristotelian Learning to Oxford." *Proceedings of the British Academy* 29 (1943): 229–281.
The Cambridge History of the Bible. Vol. 2, *The West from the Fathers to the Reformation.* Edited by G. W. H. Lampe. Cambridge, 1969.
Camille, Michael. *The Gothic Idol: Ideology and Image-Making in Medieval Art.* Cambridge, 1989.
———. *Image on the Edge: The Margins of Medieval Art.* Cambridge, Mass., 1992.
———. "Visual Signs of the Sacred Page: Books in the Bible moralisée." *Word and Image* 5 (1989): 111–130.
Cantor, Norman F. *The Civilization of the Middle Ages.* New York, 1993.
Capelle, G. C. *Autour du Décret de 1210: Amaury de Bène.* Bibliothèque Thomiste 16. Paris, 1932.
Carpenter, Dwayne E. *Alfonso X and the Jews: An Edition of and Commentary on Siete Partidas 7.24 "De los Judios."* University of California Publications on Modern Philology, vol. 115. Berkeley and Los Angeles, 1986.
Chapman, Tracy Ann. "The Female Audience for the Bible moralisée: Blanche of Castille and the Example of Vienna 2554." Master's thesis, University of Texas at Austin, 1995.
Chatillon, Jean. "La Bible dans les écoles du XIIe siècle." In Lobrichon and Riché, *Le Moyen Âge et la Bible,* 163–197.
———. "Introduction." In Richard of St. Victor, *Liber Exceptionum,* edited by Jean Chatillon. Paris, 1958.

———. “Le mouvement théologique dans la France de Philippe Auguste.” In Bautier, *La France de Philippe Auguste,* 881–902.
Chazan, Robert. “The Blois Incident of 1171.” *Proceedings of the American Academy for Jewish Research* 36 (1968): 13–31.
———. “The Bray Incident of 1192: *Realpolitik* and Folk Slander.” *Proceedings of the American Academy for Jewish Research* 37 (1969): 1–18.
———. *Daggers of Faith: Thirteenth-Century Christian Missionizing and Jewish Response.* Berkeley, 1988.
———. “Ephraim ben Jacob’s Compilation of Twelfth-Century Persecutions.” *Jewish Quarterly Review* 84 (1994): 397–416.
———. “Medieval Anti-Semitism.” In *History and Hate: The Dimensions of Anti-Semitism,* edited by David Berger, 49–65. Philadelphia, 1986.
———. *Medieval Jewry in Northern France: A Political and Social History.* Baltimore, 1973.
———. *Medieval Stereotypes and Modern Antisemitism.* Berkeley, 1997.
Choffel, Jacques. *Louis VIII le Lion.* Paris, 1983.
Christe, Yves. “The Apocalypse in the Monumental Art of the Eleventh through Thirteenth Centuries.” In *The Apocalypse in the Middle Ages,* edited by Richard K. Emmerson and Bernard McGinn, 234–258. Ithaca, N.Y., and London, 1992.
———. “La cité de la Sagesse.” *Cahiers de Civilisation Médiévale* 31 (1988): 29–35.
Cohen, Jeremy. *The Friars and the Jews: The Evolution of Medieval Anti-Judaism.* Ithaca, N.Y., and London, 1982.
———. “Mendicants, the Medieval Church, and the Jews: Dominican and Franciscan Attitudes towards the Jews in the Thirteenth and Fourteenth Centuries.” Ph.D. diss., Cornell University, 1978.
———. “Scholarship and Intolerance in the Medieval Academy: The Study and Evaluation of Judaism in European Christendom.” AHR 91 (1986): 592–613.
Cohn, Norman. *The Pursuit of the Millennium.* Rev. ed. New York, 1970.
Copleston, F. C. *A History of Medieval Philosophy in the West.* New York, 1974.
Cothren, Michael W. “The Iconography of Theophilus Windows in the First Half of the Thirteenth Century.” *Speculum* 59 (1984): 308–341.
Courcelle, J., and P. Courcelle. “Quelques illustrations du ‘Contra Faustum’ de Saint Augustin.” In *Oikoumene, Studi Paleochristiani pubblicati in onore de Concilio Ecumenico Vaticano II,* 1–9. Catania, 1964.
Cutler, Allan. “Innocent III and the Distinctive Clothing of Jews and Muslims.” *Studies in Medieval Culture* 3 (1970): 92–116.
Cutler, Allan, and Helen Cutler. *The Jew as the Ally of the Muslims: Medieval Roots of Anti-Semitism.* Notre Dame, Ind., 1986.
Dahan, Gilbert. “L’Article *Iudei* de la *Summa Abel* de Pierre Chantre.” *Revue des études augustiniennes* 27 (1981): 105–126.
———. “L’exégèse de l’histoire de Caïn et Abel du XIIe au XIVe s. en Occident.” RTAM 49 (1982): 46–48.
———. “Exégèse et polémique dans les commentaires de la Genèse d’Étienne Langton.” In *Les juifs au regard de l’histoire: Mélanges en l’honneur de Bernhard Blumenkranz,* edited by Gilbert Dahan, 129–148. Paris, 1985.

———. *Les intellectuels chrétiens et les juifs au moyen âge.* Paris, 1990.

———. "Les interpretations juives dans les commentaires du Pentateuch de Pierre le Chantre." In Walsh and Wood, *The Bible in the Medieval World,* 131–155.

———. *La polémique chrétienne contre le judaïsme au Moyen Âge.* Paris, 1991.

———. "Salatin, du miracle de Théophile." *Moyen Âge* 83 (1977): 445–468.

Daniel, E. Randolph. "Joachim of Fiore: Patterns of History in the Apocalypse." In *The Apocalypse in the Middle Ages,* edited by Richard K. Emmerson and Bernard McGinn, 72–88. Ithaca, N.Y., and London, 1992.

Davy, Marie-Madeleine. *Les sermons universitaires parisiens de 1230–31.* Paris, 1931.

Deanesly, Margaret. *The Lollard Bible and Other Medieval Biblical Versions.* Cambridge, 1920.

Delègue, René. *L'Université de Paris, 1224–44.* Paris, 1902.

Delisle, Léopold. "Livres d'images destinés à l'instruction religieuse et aux exercices de pieté des laïques." *Histoire littéraire de la France* 31 (1893): 213–285.

Delisle, Léopold, and P. Meyer. *L'Apocalypse français au XIIIe siècle.* Paris, 1901.

Dinur, Benzion. *Israel in the Diaspora.* 2d ed. 2 vols. Tel Aviv, 1958–72. [Hebrew]

Dossat, Yves. *Église et hérésie en France au XIIIe siècle.* London, 1982.

Douglas, Mary. *Purity and Danger: An Analysis of the Concepts of Pollution and Taboo.* London and New York, 1966.

Duby, Georges. *France in the Middle Ages.* Translated by Juliet Vale. Oxford and Cambridge, Mass., 1991.

Dufeil, M.-M. *Guillaume de St.-Amour et la Polémique Universitaire Parisienne, 1250–59.* Paris, 1972.

Dunbabin, Jean. *France in the Making, 843–1180.* Oxford, 1985.

Emery, R. W. "Le prêt d'argent juif en Languedoc et Roussillon." *Cahiers de Fanjeaux* 12 (1977): 85–96.

Emmerson, Richard Kenneth. *Antichrist in the Middle Ages: A Study of Medieval Apocalypticism, Art, and Literature.* Seattle, 1981.

Emmerson, Richard Kenneth, and Ronald B. Herzman. *The Apocalyptic Imagination in Medieval Literature.* Philadelphia, 1992.

Erlande-Brandenburg, Alain. *The Cathedral: The Social and Architectural Dynamics of Construction.* Translated by Martin Thom. Cambridge, 1994.

Face, R. D. "Techniques of Business in the Trade between the Fairs of Champagne and the South of Europe in the Twelfth and Thirteenth Centuries." *Economic History Review,* 2d ser., 10 (1958): 427–438.

Fawtier, Robert. *The Capetian Kings of France: Monarchy and Nation (987–1328).* Translated by Lionel Butler and R. J. Adam. New York, 1960.

Ferruolo, Stephen C. *The Origins of the University: The Schools of Paris and Their Critics, 1100–1215.* Stanford, Calif., 1985.

Finkelstein, Louis. *Jewish Self-Government in the Middle Ages.* New York, 1924.

Flam, Conrad. "Lautlehre des französischen Textes in Codex Vindobonensis 2554." Ph.D. diss., Halle, 1909.

Foreville, Raymonde. "L'Image de Philippe-Auguste dans les sources contemporaines." In Bautier, *La France de Philippe Auguste,* 115–130.

———. *Latran I, II, III et Latran IV.* Histoire des conciles oecuméniques 6. Paris, 1965.

Fournier, Pierre François. *Magie et sorcellerie: essai historique.* Moulins, 1979.

Freud, Sigmund. *The Interpretation of Dreams.* Translated by James Strachey. London, 1954.

Friedman, Herbert. *A Bestiary for St. Jerome: Animal Symbolism in European Religious Art.* Washington, D.C., 1980.

Friedmann, Adrien. *Paris, ses rues, ses paroisses du moyen âge à la Révolution.* Paris, 1959.

Fryer, A. "Theophilus the Penitent as Represented in Art." *Archaeological Journal* 92 (1935): 287–333.

Funkenstein, Amos. "Anti-Jewish Propaganda: Pagan, Christian, and Modern." *Jerusalem Quarterly* 19 (1981): 56–72.

———. "Changes in the Patterns of Christian Anti-Jewish Polemic in the Twelfth Century [Hebrew]." *Zion,* n.s., 33 (1968): 125–144.

Gager, John. *The Origins of Anti-semitism: Attitudes toward Judaism in Pagan and Christian Antiquity.* New York and Oxford, 1983.

Garnier, Francois. "L'Imagerie biblique médiévale." In Lobrichon and Riché, *Le Moyen Âge et la Bible,* 401–428.

Gieysztor, Alexander. "Les juifs et leurs activités économiques en europe orientale." *Gli Ebrei Nell'Alto Medioevo,* Settimane di Studio del Centro Italiano di Studi Sull'Alto Medioevo 26 (1980): 489–528.

Gilchrist, J. *The Church and Economic Activity in the Middle Ages.* London, 1969.

Gilman, Sander. *Difference and Pathology: Stereotypes of Sexuality, Race, and Madness.* Ithaca, N.Y., and London, 1985.

Glorieux, P. *Répertoire des Maîtres en Théologie de Paris au XIIIe siècle.* 2 vols. Paris, 1933–34.

Golb, Norman. *Les juifs de Rouen au Moyen Âge: Portrait d'une culture oubliée.* Rouen, 1985.

Goldstein, Bernard R. *Theory and Observation in Ancient and Medieval Astronomy.* London, 1985.

Gow, Andrew Colin. *The Red Jews: Antisemitism in an Apocalyptic Age, 1200–1600.* Leiden, New York, and Cologne, 1995.

Grabois, Aryeh. "L'exégèse rabbinique." In Lobrichon and Riché, *Le Moyen Âge et la Bible,* 233–260.

———. "The Hebraica Veritas and Jewish-Christian Intellectual Relations in the Twelfth Century." *Speculum* 50 (1975): 613–634.

Grayzel, Solomon. "Jewish-Christian Relations in the First Millennium." In Pinson, *Essays on Anti-semitism,* 83–92.

Guttmann, Jacob. *Die Scholastik des Dreizehnten Jahrhunderts in ihren Beziehungen zum Judenthum und zur Jüdischen Literatur.* Breslau, 1902.

Hailperin, Herman. *Rashi and the Christian Scholars.* Pittsburgh, 1963.

Hallam, Elizabeth M. *Capetian France, 987–1328.* London and New York, 1980.

de Hamel, Christopher. *Glossed Books of the Bible and the Origins of the Paris Booktrade.* Totowa, N.J., 1984.

Hare, Douglas R. A. "The Rejection of the Jews in the Synoptic Gospels and *Acts.*" In *Antisemitism and the Foundations of Christianity,* edited by Alan T. Davies, 27–47. New York, 1979.

Haring, Nicholas M. "The Liberal Arts in the Sermons of Garnier de Rochefort." *Mediaeval Studies* 30 (1968): 47–77.

———. "Peter Cantor's View on Ecclesiastical Excommunication and Its Practical Consequences." *Mediaeval Studies* 11 (1949): 100–112.

Haseloff, Arthur. "La miniature en France de Philippe-Auguste à la mort de St. Louis." In *Histoire de l'art,* vol. 2, pt. 1, edited by André Michel, 329–341. Paris, 1906.

Haskins, Charles H. *Studies in Medieval Culture.* Oxford, 1929.

———. "The University of Paris in the Sermons of the Thirteenth Century." AHR 10 (1904): 1–27.

Hassig, Debra. *Medieval Bestiaries: Text, Image, Ideology.* Cambridge, 1995.

Haussherr, Reiner. "Beobachtungen an den Illustrationen zum Buche Genesis in der Bible moralisée." *Kunstchronik* 19 (1966): 313–314.

———. "Eine Warnung vor dem Studium von ziuilem und kanonischen Recht in der *Bible moralisée.*" *Frühmittelalterforschung der Universität Munster* 9 (1975): 390–404.

———. "Petrus Cantor, Stephan Langton, Hugo von St. Cher und der Isaias-Prolog der *Bible moralisée.*" In *Verbum et Signum. Festschrift Friedrich Ohly,* edited by H. Fromm, W. Harms, and V. Ruberg, 347–364. Munich, 1975.

———. "Sensus litteralis und sensus spiritualis in der Bible moralisée." *Frühmittelalterliche Studien* 6 (1972): 356–380.

———. "Templum Salamonis und Ecclesia Christi: zu einem Bildvergleich der Bible moralisée." *Zeitschrift für Kunstgeschichte* 31 (1968): 101–121.

———. "Uber die Auswahl des Bibeltextes in der Bible moralisée." *Zeitschrift für Kunstgeschichte* 51 (1988): 126–146.

———. "Zur Darstellung Zeitgenössischer Wirklichkeit und Geschichte in der *Bible moralisée* und in illustrationen von Geschichtsschreibung im 13. Jahrhundert." In *Il Medio Oriente e l'Occidente nell'arte de XIII secolo,* edited by Hans Belting, 211–220. International Congress of the History of Art, Bologna, 1979. Bologna, 1982.

Havet, Julien. "L'hérésie et le bras seculier au moyen âge jusqu'au XIIIe siècle." *Bibliotheque de l'école des chartes* 41 (1880): 488–517, 570–670.

Hedeman, Anne D. *The Royal Image: Illustrations of the "Grandes Chroniques de France," 1274–1422.* Berkeley and Los Angeles, 1991.

Heider, Gustav. "Beitrage zur christlichen Typologies aus Bilderhandschriften des Mittelalters." *Jahrbuch der KK. Central-commission* 5 (1861): 34.

Heimann, Adelheid. "Jeremiah and His Girdle." *Journal of the Warburg and Courtauld Institutes* 25 (1962): 1–8.

Heinlen, James Michael. "The Ideology of Reform in the French Moralized Bible." Ph.D. diss., Northwestern University, 1991.

Hermann, Julius. *Die Westeuropäischen Handschriften und Inkunabeln der Gotik und der Renaissance.* Vol. 1, *Englische und Französische Handschriften des XIII. Jahrhunderts.* Leipzig, 1935.

Hertz, Neil. "Medusa's Head: Male Hysteria under Political Pressure." In *The End of the Line: Essays on Psychoanalysis and the Sublime,* 161–191. New York, 1985.

Hood, John Y. B. *Aquinas and the Jews.* Philadelphia, 1995.

Hsia, R. Po-Chia. *The Myth of Ritual Murder: Jews and Magic in Reformation Germany.* New Haven, Conn., 1988.

———. "The Usurious Jew: Economic Structure and Religious Representations in an Anti-Semitic Discourse." In *In and Out of the Ghetto: Jewish-Gentile Relations in Late Medieval and Early Modern Germany,* edited by R. Po-Chia Hsia and Hartmut Lehmann, 161–176. Washington, D.C., and Cambridge, 1995.

Hughes, Diane. "Distinguishing Signs: Ear-rings, Jews, and Franciscan Rhetoric in the Italian Renaissance City." *Past and Present* 112 (1986): 3–59.

Hunt, R. W. *The Schools and the Cloister: The Life and Writings of Alexander Nequam (1157–1217).* Edited and revised by Margaret Gibson. Oxford, 1984.

Jacobs, E. F. "Innocent III." In *Cambridge Medieval History,* vol. 6, edited by Z. N. Brooke, C. W. Prévité-Orton, and J. R. Tanner, chap. 1. Cambridge, 1929.

Jordan, William Chester. "Christian Excommunication of Jews in the Middle Ages: A Restatement of the Issues." *Jewish History* 1 (1986): 31–38.

———. *The French Monarchy and the Jews: From Philip Augustus to the Last Capetians.* Philadelphia, 1989.

———. "The Last Tormenter of Christ: An Image of the Jew in Ancient and Medieval Exegesis, Art, and Drama." *Jewish Quarterly Review* 78 (1987): 21–47.

———. "Marian Devotion and the Talmud Trial of 1240." In *Religionsgespräche im Mittlealter,* edited by Bernard Lewis and Friedrich Niewöhner, 61–76. Wiesbaden, 1992.

———. "Problems of the Meat Market of Béziers, 1240–1247: A Question of Anti-Semitism." *Revue des études juives* 135 (1976): 31–49.

Kamin, Sarah. "Affinities between Jewish and Christian Exegesis in Twelfth-Century Northern France." *Proceedings of the World Congress of Jewish Studies* 9 (1985): 141–155.

Katzenellenbogen, Adolf. *Allegories of the Virtues and Vices in Mediaeval Art.* London, 1939.

———. *The Sculptural Programs of Chartres Cathedral.* Baltimore, 1959.

Kedar, Benjamin Z. *Crusade and Mission: Europeans Approaches toward the Muslims.* Princeton, N.J., 1984.

Kennedy, V. L. "The Content of Courson's *Summa.*" *Mediaeval Studies* 9 (1947): 81–107.

———. "Robert Courson on Penance." *Mediaeval Studies* 7 (1945): 291–336.

Kessler, Herbert L. "Reading Ancient and Medieval Art." *Word and Image* 5 (1988): 1.

Kirschbaum, Engelbert. *Lexikon der Christlichen Ikonographie.* 4 vols. Rome, 1970.

Kisch, Guido. "The Jew in Medieval Law." In Pinson, *Essays on Antisemitism,* 103–111.

———. "The Yellow Badge in History." *Historia Judaica* 19 (1957): 89–146.

Kovarik, Robert J. "The Albigensian Crusade: A New View." *Studies in Medieval Culture* 3 (1970): 81–91.
Kraus, Henry. *The Living Theatre of Medieval Art.* Bloomington, Ind., and London, 1967.
Laborde, Alexandre de. *Étude sur la Bible moralisée illustrée.* Paris, 1927.
Lacombe, George. *La vie et les oeuvres de Prévostin.* Bibliothèque Thomiste XI. Paris and Le Saulchoir, 1927.
Lacombe, George, and Beryl Smalley. "Studies on the Commentaries of Cardinal Stephen Langton." AHDLMA 5 (1930): 5–182.
Ladner, Gerhart B. "Medieval and Modern Understanding of Symbolism: A Comparison." In *Images and Ideas in the Middle Ages,* 239–282. Rome, 1983.
Lambert, Malcolm. *The Cathars.* London, 1998.
———. *Medieval Heresy: Popular Movements from the Gregorian Reform to the Reformation.* 2d ed. Oxford, 1992.
Langholm, Odd. *Economics in the Medieval Schools: Wealth, Exchange, Value, Money and Usury according to the Paris Theological Tradition, 1200–1350.* Leiden, 1992.
Langlois, Charles. "Sermons parisiens de la première moitié du XIIIe siècle." *Journal des savants,* n.s., 14 (1916): 488–494, 548–559.
———. *La vie en France au moyen âge, d'après les moralistes du temps.* Paris, 1926.
Langmuir, Gavin. "The Faith of Christians and Hostility towards Jews." *Studies in Church History* 29 (1992): 77–92.
———. "Judei nostri and Capetian Legislation." *Traditio* 16 (1960): 203–239.
———. "*Tamquam servi:* The Change in Jewish Status in French Law about 1200." In *Les juifs dans l'histoire de France,* edited by M. Yardeni, 24–54. Leiden, 1980.
———. *Toward a Definition of Anti-Semitism.* Berkeley and Los Angeles, 1990.
Lasker, Daniel J. *Jewish Philosophical Polemics against Christianity in the Middle Ages.* New York, 1977.
Lecoy de la Marche, A. *La Chaire française au moyen âge, specialement au XIIIe siècle.* 2d ed. Paris, 1886.
Leff, Gordon. *Heresy in the Later Middle Ages.* Manchester, 1967.
———. *Medieval Thought.* Chicago, 1958.
Le Goff, Jacques. *La Bourse et la vie: Économie et religion au moyen âge.* Paris, 1986. English translation, *Your Money or Your Life: Economy and Religion in the Middle Ages.* Translated by Patricia Ranum. New York, 1988.
———. *The Dawn of Modern Banking.* New Haven, Conn., and London, 1979.
———. "Royauté biblique et idéal monarchique médiéval: Saint Louis et Josias." In *Les juifs au regard de l'histoire: Mélanges en l'honneur de Bernhard Blumenkranz,* edited by Gilbert Dahan, 157–167. Paris, 1985.
———. "The Symbolic Ritual of Vassalage." In *Time, Work, and Culture in the Middle Ages,* translated by Arthur Goldhammer, 237–287. Chicago, 1980.
Lerner, Robert E. *The Heresy of the Free Spirit in the Later Middle Ages.* Berkeley and Los Angeles, 1972.

———. "Millénarisme littérale et vocation des juifs chez Jean de Roquetaillade." *Mélanges de l'École Française de Rome: Moyen Âge* 102 (1990): 311–315.

———. "Poverty, Preaching, and Eschatology in the Revelation Commentaries of 'Hugh of St. Cher.'" In Walsh and Wood, *The Bible in the Medieval World,* 157–189.

———. "The Uses of Heterodoxy: The French Monarchy and Unbelief in the Thirteenth Century." *French Historical Studies* 4 (1965): 189–203.

Lewis, Andrew W. *Royal Succession in Capetian France: Studies on Familial Order and the State.* Cambridge, 1981.

Lewis, Suzanne. "*Tractatus Adversus Judaeos* in the Gulbenkian Apocalypse." *Art Bulletin* 68 (1986): 543–566.

Liebman, Charles J., Jr. *Étude sur la vie en prose de Saint Denis.* Geneva, N.Y., 1942.

Lipman, Vivian. *The Jews of Medieval Norwich.* London, 1967.

Lipton, Sara. "Jews, Heretics and the Sign of the Cat in the *Bible moralisée.*" *Word and Image* 8 (1992): 362–377.

———. "Jews in the Commentary Texts and Illustrations of the Early Thirteenth-Century *Bibles moralisées.*" Ph.D. diss., Yale University, 1991.

———. "The Root of All Evil: Jews, Money, and Metaphor in the *Bible moralisée.*" *Medieval Encounters* 1 (1995): 301–322.

Little, Lester. "Evangelical Poverty, the New Money Economy, and Violence." In *Poverty in the Middle Ages,* edited by D. Flood, 11–26. Werl / Westf., 1975.

———. "Pride Goes before Avarice: Social Change and the Vices in Latin Christendom." AHR 76 (1971): 16–49.

———. *Religious Poverty and the Profit Economy in Medieval Europe.* Ithaca, N.Y., 1978.

Lobrichon, Guy. *L'Apocalypse des théologiens au XIIe siècle.* Paris, 1979.

———. "Une nouveauté: Les gloses de la Bible." In Lobrichon and Riché, *Le Moyen Âge et la Bible,* 95–114.

Lobrichon, Guy, and Pierre Riché, eds. *Le Moyen Âge et la Bible.* Paris, 1984.

Loewe, Raphael. "The Medieval Christian Hebraists of England: The *Superscriptio Lincolniensis.*" *Hebrew Union College Annual* 28 (1957): 205–252.

———. "The Medieval History of the Latin Vulgate." In *The Cambridge History of the Bible,* 2:101–154.

Longère, Jean. *Les Oeuvres oratoires des maîtres parisiens au XIIe siècle.* 2 vols. Paris, 1975.

———. *La prédication médiévale.* Paris, 1983.

———, ed. *L'Abbaye Parisienne de Saint-Victor au moyen âge.* Paris and Turnhout, Belgium, 1991.

Loos, Milan. *Dualist Heresy in the Middle Ages.* Prague, 1974.

Lucas, Léopold. "Innocent III et les juifs." *Revue des études juives* 35 (1897): 247–255.

Luchaire, Achille. *Social France at the Time of Philip Augustus.* Translated by Edward Benjamin Krehbiel. New York, 1912.

———. *L'Université de Paris sous Philippe-Auguste.* Paris, 1899.

Luscombe, David. "Peter Comestor." In Walsh and Wood, *The Bible in the Medieval World,* 109–129.

Lusignan, Serge. *Parler vulgairement: Les intellectuels et la langue française au XIIIe et XIVe siècles.* Paris, 1988.

Maccoby, Hyam. *Judaism on Trial: Jewish-Christian Disputations in the Middle Ages.* London and Washington, D.C., 1993.

Mairinger, Franz. "Physikalische methoden zur sichtbarmachung verblasster oder getilgter Tinter." *Restoration of Book Paintings and Ink: Restaurator* 5 (1981/82): 45–56.

Mâle, Emile. *The Gothic Image: Religious Art in France of the Thirteenth Century.* Translated by Dora Nussey. New York, 1972.

Manselli, Raoul. "La polémique contre les juifs dans la polémique antihérétique." *Cahiers de Fanjeaux* 12 (1977): 251–268.

Mansfield, Mary C. *The Humiliation of Sinners: Public Penance in Thirteenth-Century France.* Ithaca, N.Y., and London, 1995.

Marrow, James H. *Passion Iconography in Northern European Art of the Late Middle Ages and Early Renaissance.* Kortrijk, Belgium, 1979.

McGinn, Bernard. *Antichrist: Two Thousand Years of the Human Fascination with Evil.* San Francisco, 1994.

———. "Portraying Antichrist in the Middle Ages." In *The Use and Abuse of Eschatology in the Middle Ages,* edited by Werner Verbeke, Daniel Verhelst, and Andries Welkenhuysen, 1–48. Louvain, 1988.

McLaughlin, T. P. "The Teaching of the Canonists on Usury (XII, XIII, XIV Centuries)." *Mediaeval Studies* 1 (1939): 81–147; 2 (1940): 1–22.

Meeks, Wayne A., and Robert L. Wilken. *Jews and Christians in Antioch in the First Four Centuries of the Common Era.* Missoula, Mont., 1978.

Mellinkoff, Ruth. "Cain and the Jews." *Journal of Jewish Art* 6 (1979): 16–38.

———. *The Horned Moses in Medieval Art and Thought.* Berkeley and Los Angeles, 1970.

———. *The Mark of Cain.* Berkeley and Los Angeles, 1981.

———. *Outcasts: Signs of Otherness in Northern European Art of the Later Middle Ages.* 2 vols. Berkeley and Los Angeles, 1993.

———. "The Round, Cap-Shaped Hats Depicted on Jews in BM Cotton Claudius B.iv." *Anglo-Saxon England* 2 (1973): 155–165.

Merrill, Alison Ann. "A Study of the Ingeborg Psalter Atelier." Ph.D. diss., Columbia University, 1994.

Metzger, Thérèse, and Mendel Metzger. *Jewish Life in the Middle Ages: Illuminated Hebrew Manuscripts of the Thirteenth to Sixteenth Centuries.* Fribourg, 1982.

Monod, Bernard. "Juifs, sorciers, et hérétiques au moyen âge." REJ 46 (1903): 237–245.

Moore, R. I. *The Formation of a Persecuting Society: Power and Deviance in Western Europe.* Oxford, 1987.

———. *The Origins of European Dissent.* London, 1977.

Morey, James H. "Peter Comestor, Biblical Paraphrase, and the Medieval Popular Bible." *Speculum* 68 (1993): 6–35.

Mundy, John H. *Liberty and Political Power in Toulouse, 1050–1230.* New York, 1954.

Narkiss, Bezalel. *Hebrew Illuminated Manuscripts.* Jerusalem, 1969.

Nebbai-Dalla Guarda, Donatella. *La Bibliothèque de l'Abbaye de Saint-Denis en France du IXe au XVIIIe siècle.* Paris, 1985.

Nelson, Benjamin. *The Idea of Usury: From Tribal Brotherhood to Universal Otherhood.* 2d ed. Chicago, 1969.

Newman, Louis Israel. *Jewish Influence on Christian Reform Movements.* New York, 1925.
Nirenberg, David. *Communities of Violence: Persecution of Minorities in the Middle Ages.* Princeton, N.J., 1996.
Noonan, John T. *The Scholastic Analysis of Usury.* Cambridge, Mass., 1957.
Parkes, James. *The Conflict of Church and Synagogue: A Study in the Origins of Antisemitism.* London, 1934. Reprint, New York, 1977.
Pastan, Elizabeth Carson. "*Tam haereticos quam Judeos:* Shifting Symbols in the Glazing of Troyes Cathedral." *Word and Image* 10 (1994): 66–83.
Pelikan, Jaroslav. *The Christian Tradition: A History of the Development of Doctrine.* Vol. 3, *The Growth of Medieval Theology (600–1300).* Chicago, 1978.
Pétavel, Emmanuel. *La Bible en France ou les traductions françaises des saintes écritures.* Paris, 1864.
Peters, Edward, ed. *The First Crusade: The Chronicle of Fulcher of Chartres and Other Source Materials.* Philadelphia, 1971.
Petit-Dutaillis, Charles. *Étude sur la vie et le règne de Louis VIII (1187–1226).* Paris, 1894.
Pinson, Koppel, ed. *Essays on Anti-semitism.* 2d ed., revised and enlarged. New York, 1946.
de Poenck, Guy. *La Bible et l'activité traductrice dans les pays romans avant 1300.* Heidelberg, 1969–70.
Pontal, Odette. "De la défense à la pastorale de la foi: Les épiscopats de Foulque, Raymond du Fauga et Bertrand de L'Isle Jourdain à Toulouse." *Cahiers de Fanjeaux* 20 (1991): 175–197.
Porcher, Jean. *Medieval French Miniatures.* Translated by J. Brown. New York, 1960.
Rabinowitz, Louis. *The Social Life of the Jews of Northern France as Reflected in the Rabbinic Literature of the Period (12th to 14th centuries).* London, 1938.
Radford-Ruether, Rosemary. "The *Adversus Judaeos* Tradition in the Church Fathers: The Exegesis of Christian Anti-Judaism." In *Aspects of Jewish Culture in the Middle Ages,* edited by P. E. Szarmach, 27–50. Albany, N.Y., 1979.
Reeves, Marjorie. *Joachim of Fiore and the Prophetic Future.* New York, 1977.
Reider, Joseph. "Jews in Medieval Art." In Pinson, *Essays on Anti-semitism,* 93–102.
Robbins, Mary E. "The Truculent Toad in the Middle Ages." In *Animals in the Middle Ages: A Book of Essays,* edited by Nona C. Flores, 25–47. New York and London, 1996.
Robert, Ulysse. *Les signes d'infamie au moyen âge.* Paris, 1891.
Robson, C. A. "Vernacular Scriptures in France." In *The Cambridge History of the Bible,* 2:436–452.
Roth, Cecil. *Essays and Portraits in Anglo-Jewish History.* Philadelphia, 1962.
Rouse, Richard H., and Mary A. Rouse. "Biblical Distinctions in the Thirteenth Century." AHDLMA 41 (1974): 27–37.
———. *Preachers, Florilegia, and Sermons: Studies on the Manipulus Florum of Thomas of Ireland.* Toronto, 1979.
Rubens, Alfred. *A History of Jewish Costume.* London, 1967.

Rubin, Miri. *Corpus Christi: The Eucharist in Late Medieval Culture.* Cambridge, 1991.

———. "Desecration of the Host: The Birth of an Accusation." *Studies in Church History* 29 (1992): 169–185.

———. "Imagining the Jew: The Late Medieval Eucharistic Discourse." In *In and Out of the Ghetto: Jewish-Gentile Relations in Late Medieval and Early Modern Germany,* edited by R. Po-Chia Hsia and Hartmut Lehmann, 177–208. Washington, D.C., and Cambridge, 1995.

Ruether, Rosemary. *Faith and Fratricide: The Theological Roots of Anti-Semitism.* New York, 1974.

Runciman, Steven. *The Medieval Manichee.* Cambridge, 1947.

Russell, Jeffrey B. *A History of Witchcraft: Sorcerers, Heretics, and Pagans.* London, 1980.

Santirocco, Matthew. *Unity and Design in Horace's Odes.* Chapel Hill, N.C., and London, 1986.

Schiller, Gertrude. *Iconography of Christian Art.* Vol. 2, *The Passion of Jesus Christ.* Translated by Janet Seligman. Greenwich, Conn., 1972.

Schlauch, Margaret. "The Allegory of Church and Synagogue." *Speculum* 14 (1938): 448–464.

Schmitt, Jean-Claude. *Prêcher d'Exemples: Récits de prédicateurs du moyen âge.* Paris, 1985.

Schneyer, J. B. *Die Sittenkritik in den Predigten Philipps des Kanzlers.* Beitrage zur Geschichte der Philosophie und Theologie des Mittelalters 39/4. Münster, 1963.

Sculpture Romane de Haute-Auvergne. Aurillac, 1966.

Seiferth, W. S. *Synagogue and Church in the Middle Ages: Two Symbols in Art and Literature.* New York, 1970.

Seltzer, Robert M. *Jewish People, Jewish Thought: The Jewish Experience in History.* New York, 1980.

Shachar, I. *The Judensau: A Medieval Anti-Jewish Motif and Its History.* London, 1974.

Shahar, Shulamith. "The Relationship between Kabbalism and Catharism in the South of France." In *Les juifs dans l'histoire de France,* edited by Myriam Yardeni, 55–62. Leiden, 1980.

Shatzmiller, Joseph. "Jews Separated from the Communion of the Faithful in Christ in the Middle Ages." In *Studies in Medieval Jewish History and Literature,* vol. 1, edited by Isadore Twersky, 307–314. Cambridge, Mass., 1979.

———. *Shylock Reconsidered: Jews, Moneylending, and Medieval Society.* Berkeley and Los Angeles, 1990.

Signer, Michael A. "Peshat, Sensus Litteralis, and Sequential Narrative: Jewish Exegesis and the School of St. Victor in the Twelfth Century." In *The Frank Talmage Memorial,* vol. 1, edited by Barry Walfish, 203–216. Haifa, 1993.

Singer, Charles. "Hebrew Scholarship in the Middle Ages among Latin Christians." In *The Legacy of Israel,* edited by Edwyn R. Bevan and Charles Singer, 283–314. Oxford, 1928.

———. "The Jewish Factor in Medieval Thought." In *The Legacy of Israel,* edited by Edwyn R. Bevan and Charles Singer, 173–282. Oxford, 1928.

Smalley, Beryl. "The Bible in the Medieval Schools." In *The Cambridge History of the Bible,* 2:197–220.

———. "Exempla in the Commentaries of Stephen Langton." *Bulletin of the John Rylands Library* 17 (1933): 121–129.
———. "Ralph of Flaix on *Leviticus.*" RTAM 36 (1968): 35–82.
———. *The Study of the Bible in the Middle Ages.* 3d ed. Oxford, 1983.
———. "William of Auvergne, John de la Rochelle, and St. Thomas Aquinas on the Old Law." In *Studies in Medieval Thought and Learning from Abelard to Wycliff,* 121–181. London, 1981.
Smith, Lesley. "William of Auvergne and the Jews." *Studies in Church History* 29 (1992): 107–117.
Soskice, Janet Martin. *Metaphor and Religious Language.* Oxford, 1985.
Southern, R. W. "Beryl Smalley and the Place of the Bible in Medieval Studies." In Walsh and Wood, *The Bible in the Medieval World,* 1–16.
Spicq, C. *Esquisse d'une histoire de l'exégèse latine au moyen âge.* Bibliothèque Thomiste 26. Paris, 1944.
Spiegel, Gabrielle M. "The *Reditus Regni ad Stirpem Karoli Magni:* A New Look." *French Historical Studies* 7 (1971): 145–174.
Stacey, Robert. "Jewish Lending and the Medieval English Economy." In *A Commercialising Economy: England, 1086 to c. 1300,* edited by Richard Britnell and Bruce M. S. Campbell, 78–101. Manchester and New York, 1995.
Steenberghen, Fernand van. *Aristotle in the West: The Origins of Latin Aristotelianism.* Translated by Leonard Johnston. Louvain, 1955.
Stork, Hans-Walter. *Die Wiener französische Bible moralisée Codex 2554 der Österreichischen Nationalbibliothek.* St. Ingbert, 1992.
Stow, Kenneth R. *Alienated Minority: The Jews of Medieval Latin Europe.* Cambridge, Mass., and London, 1992.
———. "The Good of the Church, the Good of the State: The Popes and Jewish Money." *Studies in Church History* 29 (1992): 237–252.
———. "Papal and Royal Attitudes toward Jewish Lending in the Thirteenth Century." *AJS Review* 6 (1981): 161–184.
Strack, Hermann L. *The Jew and Human Sacrifice.* 8th ed. Translated by H. L. Strack. London, 1909. Reprint, New York, 1971.
Strayer, Joseph R. *The Albigensian Crusades.* New York, 1971.
———. "France: The Holy Land, the Chosen People, and the Most Christian King." In *Action and Conviction in Early Modern Europe: Essays in Memory of E. Harbison,* edited by Theodore Rabb and J. Siegel, 3–16. Princeton, N.J., 1969.
Théry, Gabriel. *Autour du décret de 1210: David de Dinant.* Bibliothèque Thomiste 6. Le Saulchoir, Kain, Belgium, 1925–26.
Theunissen, M. *The Other: Studies in the Social Ontology of Husserl, Heidegger, Sartre, and Buber.* Cambridge, Mass., 1986.
Thijssen, J. M. M. H. "Master Amalric and the Amalricians: Inquisitorial Procedure and the Suppression of Heresy at the University of Paris." *Speculum* 71 (1996): 43–65.
Thouzellier, Christiane. *Catharisme et Valdéisme en Languedoc à la fin du XIIe et au début du XIIIe siècle.* Paris, 1966.
Touati, Charles. "Les deux conflits autour de Maimonide et des études philosophiques." *Cahiers de Fanjeaux* 12 (1977): 173–184.
———. *Prophètes, Talmudistes, Philosophes.* Paris, 1990.
Trachtenberg, Joshua. *The Devil and the Jews: The Medieval Conception of the Jew and Its Relation to Modern Antisemitism.* New Haven,

Conn., 1943. Reprint with introduction by Marc Saperstein, Philadelphia, 1983.
Turberville, A. S. "Heresies and Inquisition in the Middle Ages, 1000–1305." In *Cambridge Medieval History,* vol. 6, edited by Z. N. Brooke, C. W. Prévité-Orton, and J. R. Tanner, chap. 20. Cambridge, 1929.
Turcheck, Jacqueline. "Twelfth-Century Illuminated Manuscripts from the Abbey of St.-Victor de Paris." Ph.D. diss., University of Virginia, 1988.
Twersky, Isadore. *Introduction to the Code of Maimonides (Mishneh Torah).* New Haven, Conn., and London, 1980.
Unterkircher, Franz. *Abendländische Buchmalerei.* Vienna, 1952.
Valois, Noël. *Guillaume d'Auvergne, Éveque de Paris (1228–49): Sa vie et ses ouvrages.* Paris, 1880.
Verbeke, Gerard. "Philosophy and Heresy: Some Conflicts between Reason and Faith." In *The Concept of Heresy in the Middle Ages,* edited by W. Lourdeaux and D. Verhelst. Medievalia Lovaniensia Series I, Studia IV. The Hague, 1976.
Verger, Jacques. "Des écoles à l'université: la mutation institutionelle." In Bautier, *La France de Philippe Auguste,* 817–846.
———. "L'exégèse de l'université." In Lobrichon and Riché, *Le Moyen Âge et la Bible,* 199–232.
Vincent, Nicholas C. "Jews, Poitevins, and the Bishop of Winchester, 1231–1234." *Studies in Church History* 29 (1992): 119–131.
Vitzthum, Georg. *Die Pariser Miniaturmalerei von der Zeit des hl. Ludwig bis zu Philipp von Valois und ihr Verhältnis zur Malerei in Westeuropa.* Leipzig, 1907.
von Simpson, Otto. *The Gothic Cathedral: Origins of Gothic Architecture and the Medieval Conception of Order.* Princeton, N.J., 1984.
Walsh, Katherine, and Diane Wood, eds. *The Bible in the Medieval World: Essays in Memory of Beryl Smalley.* Oxford, 1985.
Watt, John A. "Jews and Christians in the Gregorian Decretals." *Studies in Church History* 29 (1992): 93–105.
Welter, J.-Th. *L'Exemplum dans la littérature religieuse et didactique du Moyen Âge.* Geneva, 1973.
Werner, Karl Ferdinand. "Die legitimät der Kapetinger und die Entstehung des 'Reditus regni Francorum ad stirpem Karoli.'" *Welt als Geschichte* 3 (1952): 203–225.
White, T. H., ed. *The Book of Beasts, Being a Translation from a Latin Bestiary of the Twelfth Century.* New York, 1984.
Wilken, Robert. *John Chrysostom and the Jews: Rhetoric and Reality in the Late Fourth Century.* Berkeley, 1983.
Wilmart, André. "Une lettre sur les Cathares du Nivernais (v. 1221)." *Revue Bénédictine* 47 (1935): 72–74.
Wright, Craig. *Music and Ceremony at Notre Dame of Paris, 500–1550.* Cambridge, 1989.
Zafran, Eric. "The Iconography of Antisemitism: A Study of the Representation of the Jews in the Visual Arts of Europe, 1400–1600." Ph.D. diss., New York University Institute of Fine Arts, 1973.
Zink, Michel. *La prédication en langue romane avant 1300.* Paris, 1976.

INDEX

Designer: Steve Renick

Compositor: G&S Typesetters, Inc.

Text: 10.5/12 Garamond

Display: Garamond

Printer: Thomson-Shore, Inc.